THE FAIRCHILD DIRECTORY OF

INTERIOR
DESIGN
SCHOOLS

2011

INTERIOR
THE FAIRCHILD DIRECTORY OF
DESIGN
SCHOOLS

Vice President & General Manager, Fairchild Education & Conference Division: **Elizabeth Tighe**
Executive Editor: **Olga T. Kontzias**
Senior Associate Acquiring Editor: **Jaclyn Bergeron**
Assistant Acquisitions Editor: **Amanda Breccia**
Editorial Development Director: **Jennifer Crane**
Creative Director: **Carolyn Eckert**
Production Director: **Ginger Hillman**
Production Editor: **Andrew Fargnoli**
Assistant Art Director: **Sarah Silberg**
Editorial Assistant: **Lauren Vlassenko**
Editorial Research: **Suzette Lam**
Cover and Text Design: **Carolyn Eckert**
Page Composition: **Mike Suh, Vanessa Han**
Art and Layout Assistants: **Andrea Lau, Carly Grafstein**

Library of Congress Catalog Card Number: 2010 941 931

ISBN: 978-1-60901-189-5

GST R 133004424

Printed in the United States of America

TP 09

PHOTO CREDITS
Front Cover: © Ralf Schultheiss/Corbis; *Back Cover* (top to bottom): © Jeff Greenberg / Alamy; Thomas Barwick/Getty Images; Dimitri Vervitsiotis/Getty Images; *Title Page:* © Tim Pannell/ Corbis; *Page 7:* © Green Stock/Alamy; *Page 8–9:* © Spectral-Design/iStockphoto; *Page 10:* © Vadym Andrushchenko/iStockphoto; *Page 12:* © Alex Segre/Alamy; *Page 14:* © Beaux Arts/Alamy; *Page 17:* © Molotovcoketail/iStockphoto; *Page 18:* © Vegafx1318/Fotolia; *Page 21:* © alchena/Fotolia; *Page 22:* © ShutterWorx/iStockphoto; *Page 26:* Courtesy of WWD; *Page 55:* © Victor Zastol`skiy/iStockphoto; *Page 56:* © Vladimir/iStockphoto; *Page 380:* Courtesy of WWD

CONTENTS

INTRODUCTION:
About This Directory

Are you interested in an Interior Design education, but unsure of what school you should apply to? *The Fairchild Directory of Interior Design Schools* was created especially for you.

While most college guides offer information about the overall size, setting, and cost of a school, very few provide additional details about specific majors or departments. And among the more specialized directories available, not one focuses exclusively on the study of Interior Design—until now.

The Fairchild Directory of Interior Design Schools comprises information about more than 400 schools in the United States and Canada that offer undergraduate and graduate programs in Interior Design, Interior Architecture, and related areas. Each listing includes the school's name and location, the Interior Design majors and degrees available, and the school's Web site address. A school's Web site is a great place to learn more about its Interior Design program, read about the courses and facilities available to students, and even view examples of student work. We encourage readers to visit the Web sites of schools they find interesting to learn more about what each program has to offer.

Since location plays such an important role in the college selection process, the school listings are arranged alphabetically by state. Additional indexes allow readers to select schools by degree level, major specialization, or alphabetically by name.

Following the state-by-state listing of schools, extended profiles of more than 150 programs provide a detailed picture of what an Interior Design student at each school is likely to experience. In addition to general school data on enrollment, tuition, and campus setting, each extended profile features in-depth information about the following:

- Degrees, admission requirements, and graduation rates
- Student demographics including male/female, full-time/part-time, and international/minority
- Faculty demographics including full-time/part-time, certification, and affiliations with professional and/or academic associations
- Scholarships and financial aid
- Program description and philosophy
- Facilities
- Availability of online/distance learning
- Courses of instruction
- Internship requirements and typical placement
- Study abroad opportunities
- Job placement rates
- Notable alumni
- Student activities and organizations
- Faculty specializations and research

The information contained in the extended profiles was collected from questionnaires that Fairchild Books sent to schools offering majors, concentrations, or areas of emphasis in Interior Design, Interior Architecture, or related areas. Schools that returned completed questionnaires received extended profiles in the directory; inclusion of an extended profile in no way indicates endorsement of the school by Fairchild Books.

With the exception of standard editorial revision for length and style, the content of the extended profiles remains exactly as it was submitted by the school officials (usually program directors, department heads, or media personnel) at the institutions themselves. Portions of the questionnaires that were left blank are indicated as "not reported" within the extended profile. All of the data submitted by the schools reflects conditions as of Spring 2010 and Fairchild Books has every reason to believe that the information contained within the extended profiles is accurate. Readers should check with a specific college or university to verify information that may have changed since the publication of this directory, particularly tuition, enrollment statistics, and graduation rates.

As a leading publisher of textbooks for Interior Design, Fairchild Books has a unique understanding of Interior Design education and the needs of Interior Design students. The next few pages of this directory contain readings to orient prospective students to the Interior Design profession and help them navigate their Interior Design education. From the importance of the portfolio and choosing the right internship to understanding the differences between design schools and liberal arts programs, these readings provide invaluable insight that will set any Interior Design student on the path to success.

It was our goal in creating this directory to provide prospective Interior Design students with one complete resource that will help them identify schools they may wish to apply to. We hope this directory serves as a good first step towards finding the Interior Design program that is right for you.

About Fairchild Books

Fairchild Books is a leading publisher of textbooks and educational resources for students of interior design, fashion, merchandising, and retailing. As part of the Fairchild Fashion Group—publishers of *Women's Wear Daily*—Fairchild Books has a unique, insider access to all aspects of the fashion and design worlds. Our Interior Design authors come from the top of the academic and professional communities and our books have received many awards and accolades, including the Joel Polsky prize from the American Society of Interior Designers and inclusion on the NCIDQ recommended reading list. Learn more about Fairchild Books at www.fairchildbooks.com.

Following the state-by-state listing of schools, extended profiles of more than 150 programs provide a detailed picture of what an Interior Design student at each school is likely to experience.

YOUR INTERIOR DESIGN EDUCATION:
An Important First Step

So you have a good eye, innate sense of style, and the ability to sketch a drapery treatment? Not enough. Have a flair for furnishings, love to shop for antiques, and can even rewire a lamp? Still not enough. While these are all excellent traits, design today must start with the proper education.

Interior design is a serious business, one that involves not only the knowledge of color, scale, and decoration, but construction, codes, and plumbing. It's a business where thousands of dollars can be spent on hotel carpeting or custom upholstery—mistakes and miscalculations can be costly. With so much money on the line, this is not a job for the novice. As new technology and products in the marketplace develop and increasingly complicated building codes and standards change, clients will expect more and designers will have to keep up.

The self-taught designer (or decorator as the case may be) will be a remnant of the past—they undermine the credibility of the field as a whole and muddy the waters between bona fide interior designers and the public. To become a design professional, your career should be built on five platforms—formal education (two- to four-year programs), work experience, passing the National Council for Interior Design Qualification (NCIDQ) exam, licensing approval, and joining professional organizations.

American Society of Interior Designers (ASID) reports that at least 50 percent of all practicing designers in the United States have completed two or more years of college or vocational training and 45 percent have completed a four-year college program. Of these numbers, 40 percent obtained an interior design degree and the remainder received degrees in fine arts, liberal arts, and architecture. There are presently more than 160 accredited interior design programs in the United States and Canada.

While residential design is certainly an area one can practice without a formal education, contract (also known as commercial or business) design and other specialty areas will always require and demand the proper schooling. In addition, education will definitely be a huge advantage

as many employers will consider the level of education in reviewing your qualifications. In general, it is always best to be educated and informed. Period.

UNIVERSITY PROGRAM OR DESIGN SCHOOL?

An interior design degree from an Interior Design school, program, or university will certainly be one of the most beneficial building blocks for a career in this field. Besides the obvious educational benefits, the Design degree is often vital as an entrée to an entry-level position with a design firm and will distinguish an individual as an interior designer over the term interior decorator.

Perhaps one of the most important decisions in a design career is the choice of school. There are as many types of programs and degrees as there are chair and sofa styles—two-year or four-year program, large university, private design, or art school? Or a combination thereof? The choice can be a daunting one.

If you are looking for the traditional college experience, the interior design program housed within a university is a good choice. Nancy Kwallek, Director of the Interior Design program at the University of Texas, notes that attending a

The successful design career begins with a combination of both education and experience, in and out of the classroom.

college of interior design within a university can give you the "guarantee of a liberal arts/general education program by having to satisfy forty or more hours of liberal arts outside of a design education." There is also the chance to have "more opportunities to interact with interdisciplinary majors across campus," she states.

Design schools offer a more tailored environment as the focus is primarily on design. Cheryl Gulley, Associate Professor of Interior Design at Watkins College of Art & Design feels these types of schools offer "a much more integrated approach with electives available in other disciplines that are somewhat allied." Class sizes might be smaller, your contemporaries would be primarily design majors (as opposed to those taking classes as an elective), and in some cases, more appropriate and/or additional facilities and equipment are available.

Before choosing a school, first consider the area within the field of design you would like to specialize in and where you would like to work (both in terms of industry and geographical location). For example, if your goal is to become a production designer or set decorator, selecting a reputable and accredited design school or college that specializes in or has a strong course emphasis in these areas is naturally a good idea. Since these jobs are primarily located in New York, Los Angeles, and Chicago, you could tailor your search to schools in those cities as well.

Also check to see if the school is accredited. The Council for Interior Design Accreditation (CIDA, formerly known as FIDER) is a non-profit agency that sets very specific standards for the education of interior designers. They address and evaluate curriculum, faculty, and facilities, and accredit college and university interior design programs accordingly. (A list of these schools can be found at www.accredit-id.org.)

Curriculum is also a very important consideration (see the following section) as well as costs, location, alumni, and career placement options within the school. Zane Curry, Associate Professor and Chair of Interior Design at Texas Tech University advises students to "seriously consider the industry success of alumni, background and design experience of faculty, and "fit" of curriculum (more pragmatic versus more theoretical), and area in which the student wishes to work."

Location of the school can be important as those in or near a big city offer a wealth of exposure to design centers,

museums, and all things design related. Look at the size of the school—how large are the classes and the student body? Talking with faculty members is another important item on the list. What are their interests, backgrounds, and design and teaching philosophies? Visit several schools and talk with students about their experiences. Investigate the career placement department and inquire about internship and "study abroad" opportunities. See if you are comfortable with the facilities and campus and if possible, sit in on a class.

Many schools offer an interior design internship program which helps both students and employers get the most out of their internships and thus provide a smooth transition from classroom to workplace. Also, inquire about the graduation and employment rate and extracurricular activities such as guest lecturers and field trips.

Both the bookstore and Internet offer a wide array of information on choosing an interior design school. The top fifteen interior design schools in the country are ranked by DesignIntelligence and the Design Features Council (in conjunction with the Almanac of Architecture and Design) and proves to be a valuable tool. Their yearly findings are published in the book *America's Best Architecture and Interior Design Schools* (Greenway Communications, 2008) that covers industrial design and landscape architecture as well as interior design and traditional architecture schools. They also profile schools that offer the best value for your money and/or have the most prestigious educators.

In the end, trust your intuition. It will guide you to the most appropriate career choice and school.

THE DESIGN DEGREE

Interior design programs can be found in a variety of academic schools and departments. While interior design disciplines may typically fall in the school of interior design, programs may also be located in home economics/human ecology, fine arts, architecture, environmental design, industrial design, and applied art/commercial design.

There are several different types of degrees available in interior design programs. Your selection will naturally depend on the chosen area of specialty. Industry experts and employers recommend a full interior design program (four-year bachelor's degree is the norm) to be the most beneficial for a design career.

While the types of degrees often vary in scope from school to school, the following are the most common degrees available:

Bachelor Degree: This is the most common path and is comprised of an intensive four-year course of study that includes both professional and educational courses as well as fundamentals and theory. Students can obtain this degree through Bachelor of Arts, Bachelor of Science, and Bachelor of Fine Arts. A student can meet the obligations for membership in national professional organizations by combining education requirements with internships and work experience. A Bachelor's also allows students to take the NCIDQ exam.

Associate Degree: Associate of Arts, Associate of Science, and Associate of Applied Science are the most common versions and this degree is generally obtained in a one- to two-year program. Students can also continue this program and apply their credits to a Bachelor's Degree.

Certificate: This is a one- to two-year course of study that covers the introductory aspects of interior design and in some cases includes advanced level courses in specialty areas. It is also one of the most popular choices for those who want to become residential interior designers or specialize in sales or other allied areas of the field such as kitchen and bath designers. (It is important to note that this will not meet the criteria needed for certification, however, it may meet the need for kitchen and bath designer certification.)

Graduates may also continue their education with a Master's Degree (generally two-year program of study) or more specialized certification in areas such as kitchen and bath design. This degree will focus on advanced studies consisting of research and special projects. Some interior design students move into the master of architecture program as well.

IN AND OUT OF THE CLASSROOM: COURSE CURRICULUM AND EXTRA CURRICULAR ACTIVITIES

The successful design career begins with a combination of both education and experience, in and out of the classroom. While there is no substitute for a thorough blend of classes and technical instruction tailored to a specific specialty, the practical hands-on extracurricular experience often provides the finishing touch.

When choosing a school "there is not a one size fits all solution," says Scott Ageloff, Vice President for Academic Affairs at the New York School of Interior Design. "A student should try and determine their goals and objectives and find the CIDA-accredited school whose curriculum in the best fit in term of its focus," he explains.

Curriculum naturally plays a major role in school selection and while introductory courses are necessary, more specialized classes tailored to a student's career goals will follow. The basic interior design curriculum should include a mixture of fundamental and educational courses and studio experience. Courses will focus on interior, color and design theory, drafting (both manual and CAD) and rendering, decorative arts, and architectural history. Further studies will incorporate textiles, kitchen and bath design, space planning, furniture design, environmental design, construction and building, mechanical systems, codes, lighting, global design, and other specialized areas of study in the curriculum.

The majority of interior design educators agree that business courses are a must. Accounting, marketing, business ethics, advertising, public relations, sales, and even Web site design would all be beneficial electives to take. In the future, look for schools to make these subjects a required part of the curriculum.

Students are also encouraged to take courses that will help them excel professionally.

"A good interior design program will require a professional practice course that will prepare students to understand the business of interior design as well as assist them in cover letter and resume writing, portfolio preparation, and job interviewing," explains Mary Beth Robinson, former Associate Professor of Interior Design at the University of Tennessee-Knoxville. The interior design degree should be well rounded and balanced with courses in liberal arts or humanities. Psychology is another important subject as so much of interior design has its roots in human interaction and society.

Learning must not stop with graduation or holiday recess. Sherri Donghia, former executive Vice President/Creative Director of the renowned fabric and furniture firm Donghia, is a lifelong traveler. She advises students to carry journals with them wherever they go, jotting down sketches, watercolors, ideas, and take photographs. Donghia also notes "Olympic class shopping is a great educator, especially when you are traveling," as many of her flea market treasures found in distant lands have led to the inspiration of many a textile design.

Donghia also urges students to "continue your education through books, newspapers, trade journals, and every sort of magazine—the more obscure the better." Visit museums, art galleries and go to the cinema. Study the decorative arts, as history has much to teach us and books are free at the local library. Attend workshops, lectures, designer showhouses, and keep your senses and mind open. Inspiration is everywhere.

And most importantly, give back. Gulley notes that students at Watkins are encouraged to "participate in community service projects such as Habitat for Humanity." Design students at Texas Tech University are involved in Lifeworks, a local charity organization that designs apartment interiors for foster children who are making a life on their own.

Excerpted from **Re-de-sign: New Directions for Your Interior Design Career** *by Cathy Whitlock. Fairchild Books © 2009*

PROFESSIONAL STANDARDS:
The Value of Accreditation

Colleges and universities must meet state and national requirements in order to be accredited learning institutions. Obtaining a diploma or degree involves a great deal of time and study. It requires dedication, persistence, and, in many cases, a great deal of money. Through the accreditation process and by complying with established standards, institutions assure, at least in part, that the students will have the opportunity to academically prepare for real careers in the real world.

The National Association of Schools of Art and Design is the national accrediting agency for art and design and art and design-related disciplines. Approximately 297 schools are currently accredited by NASAD, primarily at the collegiate level, but also including postsecondary non-degree-granting schools for the visual arts disciplines.

In addition to the school's accreditation, an optional requirement within the interior design profession for a college or university is CIDA (Council for Interior Design Accreditation) accreditation.

CIDA is an organization that monitors postsecondary interior design programs in the United States and Canada. This organization uses professional interior design standards that are recognized internationally. These standards are defined in their accreditation manual, which can be found on the CIDA Web site (www. accredit-id.org). The standards are very broad and comprehensive. Standard 2 states, for example, "Global context for design," and Standard 3, "Human behavior—the work of the interior designer is informed by knowledge of behavioral science and human factors." The CIDA standards highlight the breadth of an education in the field of interior design.

The CIDA Web site has a list of schools that are CIDA-accredited. This accreditation is prestigious. The most progressive interior design programs strive for this recognition. Even though CIDA is a nonprofit association, it is very expensive to have a program accredited and to continually update the accreditation. The expense and prestige of a CIDA program is due to the research, the lengthy review process, and the periodic assessment; all these ensure that an accredited program delivers the necessary educational value.

Each learning institution weighs the expenses related to CIDA against CIDA's relevance and importance to its interior design department. When potential interior design students are looking at colleges and universities, CIDA can be a definite draw. Increased enrollment means greater program growth, which amounts to more advantages for the student. All schools, CIDA-accredited or not, should aspire to those standards.

For a complete list of CIDA-accredited programs, please visit: www.accredit-id.org

Adapted from **Careers in Interior Design** *by Nancy Asay and Marciann Patton. Fairchild Books © 2010*

TODAY'S INTERIOR DESIGN PROFESSION:
There Are Many Options.
Which One Is Right for You?

The role of interior designers in today's society is more complex and comprehensive than that of their predecessors. An interior designer's education emphasizes assessing the function of a space, surveying a client's needs, and involving the client in the process.

Interior designers currently provide the following services:

- Help determine project goals and objectives
- Analyze a client's needs, goals, and life and safety requirements
- Formulate preliminary design concepts that are appropriate, functional, and aesthetic
- Allocate, organize, and arrange a space to suit its function
- Generate ideas for the functional and aesthetic possibilities of a space
- Develop documents and specifications relative to interior spaces in compliance with applicable building and safety codes
- Create illustrations and renderings
- Develop and present final design recommendations through appropriate presentation media
- Prepare working drawings and specifications for non–load-bearing11 interior construction, materials, finishes, space planning, furnishings, fixtures, and equipment
- Monitor and manage construction and installation of designs
- Collaborate with professional services of other licensed practitioners in the technical areas of mechanical, electrical, and load-bearing design as required for regulatory approval
- prepare and administer bids and contract documents as a client's agent
- review and evaluate design solutions during implementation
- select and specify fixtures, furnishings, products, lighting solutions, materials, and colors
- purchase products and fixtures
- design and manage fabrication of custom furnishings and interior details

In addition to the numerous services professional interior designers perform, the industries and fields in which they may concentrate are diverse. In the broadest sense, interior design projects may be divided into two main categories: **residential interior design** and **contract or commercial design**. Within each of these two categories are many subdivisions. The discussion that follows outlines the many opportunities that exist for interior designers.

RESIDENTIAL INTERIOR DESIGN

Residential design focuses on the planning and specifying of interior materials and products used in private residences. It implies that an interior designer is working within an environment in which an individual resides for a relatively fixed period of time. Most of the time, an individual person enters into a contract with a designer to design the interior of his or her family's home. An exception is the design of so-called model homes. In that instance, an interior designer creates a homelike environment but is providing services to a real estate developer or management office. Similarly, many corporations hire interior designers to create spaces for employees to live in while on temporary assignment. The area of assisted living, generally for senior citizens, is a bridge between residential and contract design. Although these quarters are designed to house residents in their own spaces, a managing agent contracts for the design.

Residential design includes the following subspecializations:
- Model apartments
- Retirement housing
- Assisted-living quarters
- Multi-dwelling complexes
- Apartments, condominiums, cooperatives
- Home entertainment design
- Bath design
- Kitchen design
- Home office design
- Recreational and therapeutic design (e.g., spa, sauna, pool, and workout areas)
- Storage design
- Children's rooms

CONTRACT OR COMMERCIAL DESIGN

The contract interior designer works within environments in which a company, rather than an individual, is contracting for the design services. The interior permanent or temporary space is where a variety of activities may be carried out for work and pleasure. Within this broad category are several sub-specializations, among them the following:

Corporate design, which includes design for staff and executive offices, conference rooms, teleconferencing centers, workstations, computer stations, training facilities, relocation, or corporate apartments.

Entertainment design, which includes interiors, lighting, sound, and other technologies for movies, television, videos, theater, clubs, concerts, and theme and amusement parks.

Facilities management, which includes the organizational management of generally large business operations. Specialists in this area address safety and health issues, lighting and acoustical needs, scheduling of maintenance, and coordinating of office expansions, downsizing, and relocations. This specialty relies on substantial communication among the interior designer, builders, engineers, and business decision makers.

Health-care design, which includes designs for hospitals, medical and dental offices, psychiatric facilities, clinics, ambulatory care centers, halfway houses, hospices, adult homes, rehabilitation centers, and nursing homes.

Hospitality and restaurant design, which includes designs for hotels, motels, restaurants, country clubs, golf courses, cruise ships, nightclubs, and recreational facilities.

Institutional and governmental design, which includes designs for schools, government buildings, prisons, community centers, airports, rail stations, houses of worship, shelters, museums, stadiums, arenas, and libraries.

Retail and store planning design, which includes designs for specialty and department stores, supermarkets, salons, shopping malls, showrooms, art galleries, trade shows, exhibitions, and displays.

Adapted from **Foundations of Interior Design** *by Susan J. Slotkis. Fairchild Books © 2006*

Is Interior Design Right for You? A Dozen Questions to Ask Yourself

1. How committed am I to the intensity and cost of this formal course of study?

2. How far do I intend to go in the field? Do I see this as a full-time professional career, a pastime, or a sideline to something else?

3. What specialties, if any, have I identified that I want to pursue?

4. Am I prepared to defer financial success for the first few years of my career?

5. Am I self-motivated and self-directed?

6. Do I enjoy working with and for people?

7. Can I manage my time and have the discipline necessary to meet deadlines and other requirements?

8. Can I manage the work performed by others?

9. Do I have the creative potential to carry out innovative design solutions?

10. Can I communicate my ideas visually, verbally, and in writing?

11. If necessary, will I be able to work outside a nine-to-five schedule?

12. Am I passionate about design?

INTERPRETING THE INITIALS:
A Breakdown of Professional & Academic Associations

American Academy of Healthcare Interior Designers (AAHID)—An organization offering certification for proficiency in health-care design (www.aahid.org).

American Lighting Association (ALA)—A trade association that offers several levels of certification in lighting design (www.americanlightingassoc.com).

American Society of Interior Designers (ASI D)—The leading national organization for interior designers in the United States (www.asid.org).

American Society of Furniture Designers (ASFD)—Professional organization dedicated to advancing, improving, and supporting the profession of furniture design (www.asfd.com).

Association of Registered Interior Designers of Ontario (ARIDO)—A self-regulatory professional organization for interior designers in Ontario, Canada (www.arido.ca).

Council for Interior Design Accreditation (CIDA)—Accreditation to interior design college or university programs that have met established criteria (www.accredit-id.org).

The Design Association (UK)—With members in 34 countries, this society holds a British Royal Charter for accrediting and representing professionals in many fields of design (www.design-association.org).

Environmental Design Research Association (EDRA)—An international, interdisciplinary organization that advances and disseminates behavior and design research toward improving understanding of the relationships between people and their environments (www.edra.org).

Green Building Certification Institute (GBCI)—Manages the Leadership in Energy and Environmental Design (LEED) accreditation for building professionals (www.gbci.org).

International Federation of Interior Architects/Designers/Architects (IFI)—Provides a forum for international discussion among design professionals; currently in 45 countries on every continent (www.ifiworld.org).

International Interior Design Association (IIDA)—An organization of interior designers from all over the world (www.iida.com).

Interior Design Educators Council (IDEC)—An organization of interior design educators (www.idec.org).

Interior Designers of Canada (IDC)—An official organization of Canadian interior designers (www.interiordesigncanada.org).

National Council for Interior Design Qualification (NCIDQ)—The organization that administers the NCIDQ exam, which grants an interior design certification earned after formal education and experience. Passing the NCIDQ exam is part of this process (www.ncidq.org).

National Kitchen and Bath Association (NKBA)—A trade organization that offers a certification program for kitchen and bath designers (www.nkba.org)

U.S. Green Building Council (USGBC)—Is responsible for developing and promoting the Leadership in Energy and Environmental Design (LEED) program, as green-building rating system (www.usgbc.org).

Adapted from **Careers in Interior Design** *by Nancy Asay and Marciann Patton. Fairchild Books © 2010*

Many schools offer student chapters of professional organizations like ASID and IIDA.

Students can benefit greatly and jump-start their career by joining a professional organization. Membership can provide both learning and access to professionals that results in networking and employment through access to a job bank, student mentoring programs, and portfolio and resume reviews. There is also a student newsletter, scholarship competition, chapter events, seminars, and workshops. And by joining as a student, they can obtain an Allied membership after graduation.

There is power, knowledge, and camaraderie in numbers. Both students and interior design professionals are encouraged to join forces with one or many of the professional resources and organizations at their disposal. A number of specialty organizations that support career activities such as the American Society of Furniture Designers, International Society of Lighting Designers, and American Academy of Healthcare Interior Designers are also available for membership.

Excerpted from **Re-de-sign: New Directions for Your Interior Design Career** *by Cathy Whitlock. Fairchild Books © 2009*

SHOWCASE YOUR TALENT:
The Interior Design Portfolio

Practitioners of architecture, interior design, and landscape architecture recognize portfolios as a part of the professional culture. Designers are unique and require special communication methods. We communicate visually and graphically, with most of our work described in two- and three-dimensional media. Every designer has created a portfolio. Every designer owns one. And every designer is continually updating one.

Portfolios are also used for assessment and evaluation in educational programs.

They are used for career advancement, and you will need to present your portfolio in job interviews when seeking an internship or full-time employment.

Institutions of higher education may require you to submit a portfolio as a criterion for admission into their design programs. Many of these programs have a limited enrollment, partly because the foundation of education is based on studio education.

In a program with limited enrollment in the junior and senior years, students compete for spots at the end of their sophomore year. An admission portfolio is a portfolio used in this process. This review process may also include an evaluation of your grade point average and some type of written requirement, such as an essay or design philosophy statement. This portfolio will consist of work from your previous classes.

Your portfolio provides documented evidence that you have learned skills necessary to succeed in the profession.

Your portfolio provides documented evidence that you have learned skills necessary to succeed in the profession. It is a qualitative assessment of work that shows a variety of work and skill.

It is a qualitative assessment of work that shows a variety of work and skill. The guidelines and requirements for an admission portfolio are likely to be dictated to you and vary from school to school. Check your school's guidelines for acceptable portfolio contents and formats.

Some schools allow you to be present at the review while others do not. You may be told what categories of work to show and in what type of portfolio case to present this work. Pay close attention to what is requested. Digital work may not be a submission medium, even though much of your work may be computer based. The admissions committee will have standards for reviewing your work, and a digital format may not currently fit their procedures. Ask for clarification on digital submissions if the school's guidelines are unclear.

Adapted from **Design Portfolios: Moving from Traditional to Digital** *by Diane M. Bender. Fairchild Books © 2008*

A portfolio is more than just a repository of past work; it is a unique object of work in itself. It is an organized collection of artifacts that demonstrates your skills and abilities as a designer. What you put in the portfolio and how it is presented will vary depending on its intent and audience.

There are several uses for a portfolio. Portfolios can be used for learning and self-evaluation; many designers use their portfolio as a means to review, critique, and reflect on their own work. A portfolio offers a way to identify your strengths and weaknesses, by allowing you to review your work in one consolidated format.

EXPERIENCE IS THE BEST TEACHER:
The Interior Design Internship

An internship is a supervised work experience within a profession (*Business Dictionary*, 2008). For an interior design internship, the work experience most often takes place in a design firm, design studio, showroom in a design center, retail establishment, or design-related firm.

It provides opportunities for interaction between the student, a firm, and the university. At most higher educational institutions, students are required to complete an internship for specific number of work hours or on-the-job training for credit hours.

Most importantly, an internship is designed to assist the student in the transition from theory or hypothetical scenarios to professional interior design practice. However, before you, the student, begin an internship, you must choose where you want to transition these theories and hypothetical scenarios—in short, all that you are learning in your academic programs—into your future professional life. To make this decision, you must consider your future goals—professional and personal.

COMMON INTERNSHIP QUESTIONS AND ANSWERS

When stepping into a new environment, somewhere you've never been before, or even when taking on a new responsibility in perfectly familiar territory, it's natural to feel some anxiety or to simply be unsure about practical concerns. The good news is that internships are far from uncharted territory. As the seasoned interior designer turns to precedent students before signing off on a new project, you can learn from those who have interned before you. The following questions, common among students heading into internships, and their subsequent answers, will help put any anxiety or uncertainty to rest:

What if I do not know what type of design I'd prefer?
Evaluate your skills. In what area is your best work—

residential or commercial; CAD; hand-drafting; selection of materials, and so on? What piques your interest as you read about or work on various types of design in studio—residential (materials, kitchens, space planning) or commercial (space planning, CAD, material selection for office or other commercial types, conducting code search, writing specifications)?

Where should I intern? What area of the country or city? Or should I go abroad?
Look at multiple possibilities. Where would you like to live for a short period of time or in the future? This may be the opportunity to see if you like the area or city. Do you have relatives or friends who would be willing to house you temporarily? If you need to stay closer to your university, consider all the firms within the city or surrounding area. If you are interested in an international internship, start examining and researching early. These may take a year to obtain.

How many resumes and cover letters should I send?
That will depend on the number of firms in the area or city. Do not limit yourself. The more you send, the greater the chance of obtaining an internship and obtaining it early.

What if they reject me?
Let's turn this around and ask, what can I learn from this rejection? Maybe your interview skills need work and the list of possible interview questions should be reviewed. It may be that some design skill(s) may have been missing. If so, determine ways to improve these skills. Maybe this firm

Evaluate your skills. In what area is your best work—residential or commercial; CAD; hand-drafting; selection of materials, and so on? What piques your interest . . . ?

is not the right firm and a different type of firm should be considered. An in-depth self-evaluation is important.

What if I don't have the right skills?
Examine your skills: what skills were lacking and can you hone these skills? Or are your skills more appropriate for another type of design firm?

I'm afraid. I've never worked before. What if they don't like me?
Practice mock interviews with professionals, other students, or in your career placement center at your institution. Consider the skills you have and review your projects and know the requirements. Research the firm; know all you can about them. Being well prepared will help boost your confidence level.

What are budget considerations? How much money will I need to support myself during the internship?
The amount of money needed will depend upon where you obtain an internship. At the same time as you are considering various locations, investigate the cost of living: cost of temporary rentals, food, and transportation. Then, you will be able to determine how much you will need during that time period.

What are my school's requirements for completing an internship?
Each program will be different. Therefore, you should begin by visiting your academic advisor to learn the process and requirements.

What are some networking options or contacts that have been made in the past?
Networking among professionals may seem intimidating, but interior design professionals are more than happy to meet, visit, and give advice. Some of these professionals may become your employer or a connection to other employment. So, make a list of contacts—those you have met at seminar, career days, or even visited in their showrooms or other locations. Continue to add to this list as you attend.

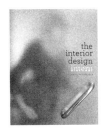

Adapted from **The Interior Design Intern** *by Linda Nussbaumer. Fairchild Books © 2011*

NEVER TOO EARLY TO PLAN:
Advice for the Student

If you are an undergraduate studying design, narrow your majors of interest and work with an academic adviser to develop a curriculum of study as soon as possible. Realize no decision is permanent and one area of expertise could easily lead you down the path of another. You might graduate in commercial interiors with a specialty towards restaurant design and eventually become a commercial product designer. Many students find a double major assists in their marketability as well. Try to target areas in the country where building and the economy are prosperous and match your specialization.

Design schools and colleges are filled with career information and assistance; be sure to utilize them. Talk to faculty members and professionals in the field. Network and join professional organizations as a student. Use the career resource library and check out extracurricular events. According to Thom Hauser, Interior Design-area Chair at the University of Georgia's Lamar Dodd School of Art, "Many schools will bring in diverse practitioners to make presentations in a number of courses and sit on project review panels. We visit a variety of firms during our annual fall field trips and rotate among New York City, San Francisco, and Chicago. About 50 percent of our students go each year and about 90 to 95 percent go on at least one of the three while they are in the program."

Also, take advantage of the schools' invaluable assistance with the preparation of resumes, cover letters, and portfolio preparation. As Hauser notes, "Students take a one-hour course on preparing resumes, letters of introduction, portfolios, and interview skills.

This is in preparation for internships for the spring or summer before their final year in the curriculum. All students submit personal design philosophy statements, resumes, and digital portfolios as part of their senior exit class."

Specialization starts early, as noted by Zane Curry, Associate Professor and Associate Chair of Interior Design at Texas Tech University, "Firms expect a higher entry level of knowledge and skill than in the past...and also seem to be more concerned with the knowledge of CAD skills, sustainability, and green design, and a high level of basic interior design skills in the areas of space planning and quick sketch."

Other valuable tips include:

- Join professional organization(s) as a student. This will allow you access to professionals and useful networking experience that could lead to a potential job.
- Begin to develop your resume, cover letters, and portfolio while in school. Fine tune these upon graduation and tailor all three to specific areas of your search. (See resume writing for further information.)
- Enter your work in competitions, magazines, professional conferences, and designer show houses when possible.
- Attend workshops, exhibitions, and conferences related to your major.
- Consider "shadowing" an interior design professional for a day. It's an excellent way to see and experience the actual job up close and personal.
- Try to land an internship.
- Mary Ellen Robinson, former interior design professor at the University of Tennessee–Knoxville advises to "research the firm before you interview. Even if a company does not have a position, a student can request a tour of the firm and be introduced to the company in their process of researching businesses."
- Network whenever possible and above all keep learning!

Excerpted from **Re-de-sign: New Directions for Your Interior Design Career** *by Cathy Whitlock. Fairchild Books*

Build Your Interior Design Library
with Fairchild Books

Foundations of Interior Design
Susan J. Slotkis

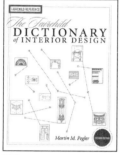

The Fairchild Dictionary of Interior Design
Martin M. Pegler

Hand Drawing for Designers
Douglas R. Seidler
Amy Korte

Design Portfolios: Moving from Traditional to Digital
Diane M. Bender

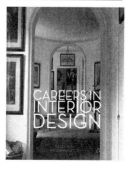

Careers in Interior Design
Nancy Asay & Marciann Patton

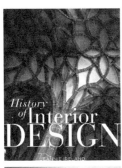

History of Interior Design
Jeannie Ireland

Writing for Interior Design
Patricia Eakins

coming soon

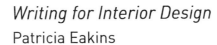

Drafting & Design: Basics for Interior Design
Travis Wilson

the interior design intern

The Interior Design Intern
Linda Nussbaumer

NEW *directions* FOR YOUR *interior*DESIGN *career*

re-de-sign

*Re-de-sign: New Directions for Your
Interior Design Career*
Cathy Whitlock

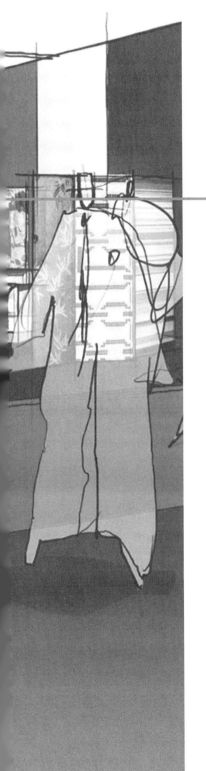

State-by-State Listing of Schools

ALABAMA

Auburn University
Auburn, AL
College of Human Sciences
Department of Consumer Affairs
Interior Design (B.S., M.S.)
www.humsci.auburn.edu/cahs/index.php
● EXTENDED PROFILE ON PAGE 58

Samford University
Birmingham, AL
School of Education & Professional Studies
Department of Interior Design
Interior Design (B.A.)
http://dlserver.samford.edu/intd/program.html

University of Alabama
Tuscaloosa, AL
College of Human Environmental Sciences
Department of Clothing, Textiles and Interior Design
Human Environmental Sciences: Interior Design (B.S.)
www.ches.ua.edu/departments/ctd/interior_design_
requirements.shtml

Virginia College, Birmingham
Birmingham, AL
Southern Institute School of Interior Design
Interior Design (B.F.A.)
www.vc.edu/bachelor-degrees/interior-design-
birmingham.cfm

ARIZONA

Arizona State University
Tempe, AZ
School of Architecture & Landscape Architecture
Interior Design (B.S.)
Master of Science in the Built Environment (MSBD)
Master of Science in Design (MSD)
Design, Environment & Arts (PhD)
http://design.asu.edu/
● EXTENDED PROFILE ON PAGE 60

Art Center Design College, The
Tucson, AZ
Interior Design Department
Interior Design (B.A.)
www.theartcenter.edu
● EXTENDED PROFILE ON PAGE 62

Art Institute of Phoenix, The
Phoenix, AZ
Interior Design Department
Interior Design (B.S.)
www.artinstitutes.edu/phoenix/
● EXTENDED PROFILE ON PAGE 64

Art Institute of Tucson, The
Tucson, AZ
Interior Design (B.A.)
www.artinstitutes.edu/tucson

Collins College
Phoenix, AZ
School of Visual Arts & Design
Interior Design (B.F.A.)
www.collinscollege.edu/programs/interior-design.asp
● EXTENDED PROFILE ON PAGE 66

Mesa Community College
Mesa, AZ
Interior Design (A.A.S., certificate)
www.mesacc.edu/academics/design/int/

Northern Arizona University
Flagstaff, AZ
College of Arts & Letters
School of Art
Interior Design (B.S.)
www.cal.nau.edu/art/id/default.asp

Phoenix College
Phoenix, AZ
Applied Technology, Family & Consumer Sciences
Interior Design (A.A.S.)
Kitchen & Bath Design (certificate)
www.pc.maricopa.edu/index.php?page=29&sublink=520

Pima Community College
Tucson, AZ
Arts, Humanities & Communication
Interior Design (A.A., A.A.S.)
http://www.pima.edu/program/interior-design/
● EXTENDED PROFILE ON PAGE 68

Scottsdale Community College
Scottsdale, AZ
Division of Applied Sciences
Interior Design (A.A.S.)
http://plone.scottsdalecc.edu/appsci/interior-design-
program

ARKANSAS

Harding University
Searcy, AR
Department of Art & Design
Interior Design (B.S.)
www.harding.edu/art/interior_design/index.html

University of Arkansas
Fayetteville, AR
Fay Jones School of Architecture
Interior Design (B.I.D.)
http://architecture.uark.edu/734.php

University of Central Arkansas
Conway, AR
Department of Family and Consumer Sciences
Interior Design (B.A., B.S.)
http://uca.edu/facs/programs/interiordesign.php

CALIFORNIA

Academy of Art University
San Francisco, CA
School of Interior Architecture & Design
Interior Architecture & Design (B.F.A., M.F.A.)
www.academyart.edu
• EXTENDED PROFILE ON PAGE 70

Allan Hancock College
Santa Maria, CA
Applied Social Sciences
Family & Consumer Sciences: Interior Merchandising
   (A.A.S., certificate)
www.hancockcollege.edu/Default.asp?Page=1360

American InterContinental University, Los Angeles
Los Angeles, CA
Interior Design Department
Interior Design (B.F.A.)
http://la.aiuniv.edu/degree-programs/interior-architecture-degree-program/

American River College
Sacramento, CA
Fine and Applied Arts Area
Interior Design (A.A., certificate)
Kitchen & Bath Design (certificate)
www.arc.losrios.edu/Programs_of_Study/FAA.htm
• EXTENDED PROFILE ON PAGE 72

Antelope Valley College
Lancaster, CA
Technical Education
Interior Design (A.A., certificate)
www.avc.edu/academics/teched/

Art Center Design College
Pasadena, CA
Environmental Design (B.S.)
www.artcenter.edu/accd/programs/undergraduate/environmental_design.jsp

Art Institute of California (The)–Hollywood
North Hollywood, CA
Interior Design (B.S.)
www.artinstitutes.edu/hollywood

Art Institute of California (The)–Inland Empire
San Bernardino, CA
Interior Design (B.S.)
www.artinstitutes.edu/inland-empire
• EXTENDED PROFILE ON PAGE 74

Art Institute of California (The)–Los Angeles
Santa Monica, CA
Interior Design (B.S.)
www.artinstitutes.edu/los-angeles

Art Institute of California (The)–Orange County
Santa Ana, CA
Interior Design (B.S.)
www.artinstitutes.edu/orangecounty/
• EXTENDED PROFILE ON PAGE 76

Art Institute of California (The)–San Diego
San Diego, CA
Interior Design (B.S.)
www.artinstitutes.edu/san-diego/
• EXTENDED PROFILE ON PAGE 78

Art Institute of California (The)–San Francisco
San Francisco, CA
Interior Design (B.S.)
www.artinstitutes.edu/sanfrancisco/
• EXTENDED PROFILE ON PAGE 80

Butte College
Oroville, CA
Digital Arts & Design Department
Interior Design (A.S., certificate)
www.butte.edu/curriculum/degrees_and_programs.html

California College of the Arts
San Francisco, CA
Interior Design Program
Interior Design (B.F.A.)
www.cca.edu/academics/interior-design

California State Polytechnic University
Pomona, CA
Department of Architecture
Interior Architecture (M.I.D.)
www.csupomona.edu/~arc/masterinterior.html

California State University, Chico
Chico, CA
Department of Art & Art History
Interior Design (B.F.A.)
www.csuchico.edu/art/programs/ID/InteriorDesign.shtml

California State University, Fresno
Fresno, CA
Department of Art & Design
Interior Design (B.A.)
www.csufresno.edu/artanddesign/

California State University, Long Beach
Long Beach, CA
College of the Arts
Interior Design (B.F.A.)
www.csulb.edu/depts/design/

California State University, Northridge
Northridge, CA
Department of Family & Consumer Sciences
Interior Design (B.S.)
http://fcs.csun.edu/

California State University, Sacramento
Sacramento, CA
College of Arts & Letters
Department of Design
Interior Architecture (B.S., certificate)
www.al.csus.edu/design/intd.html
- **EXTENDED PROFILE ON PAGE 82**

Cañada College
Redwood City, CA
Interior Design Department
Interior Design (A.A., certificate)
Kitchen & Bath Design (certificate)
http://canadacollege.edu/
- **EXTENDED PROFILE ON PAGE 84**

Chabot College
Hayward, CA
School of the Arts
Interior Design Department
Interior Design (A.A., certificate)
Kitchen & Bath Design (certificate)
www.chabotcollege.edu
- **EXTENDED PROFILE ON PAGE 86**

Chaffey College
Rancho Cucamonga, CA
Interior Design (A.S., certificate)
www.chaffey.edu/interior_design/index.shtml

City College of San Francisco
San Francisco, CA
Department of Architecture
Architectural Interiors (A.A.)
www.ccsf.edu/arch
- **EXTENDED PROFILE ON PAGE 88**

College of the Canyons
Santa Clarita, CA
Architecture & Interior Design Program
Interior Design (A.S., certificate)
www.canyons.edu/departments/intd/

Cuesta College
San Luis Obispo, CA
Interior Design (A.A., certificate)
www.cuesta.edu/deptinfo/humdev/intdes.htm

Design Institute of San Diego
School of Interior Design
Interior Design (B.F.A.)
www.disd.edu
- **EXTENDED PROFILE ON PAGE 90**

Fashion Institute of Design & Merchandising
Los Angeles, CA
Department of Interior Design
Interior Design (A.A.)
www.fidm.edu//majors/interior-design/
- **EXTENDED PROFILE ON PAGE 92**

Fullerton College
Fullerton, CA
Division of Technology & Engineering
Interior Design Assistant (A.S., certificate)
http://techneng.fullcoll.edu/ad.html

Interior Designers Institute
Newport Beach, CA
Interior Design (A.A., B.A., M.A.)
www.idi.edu
- **EXTENDED PROFILE ON PAGE 94**

International Academy of Design & Technology–Sacramento
Sacramento, CA
Interior Design (A.A.S., B.F.A.)
www.iadtsacramento.com/programs.asp

Long Beach City College
Long Beach, CA
Interior Design (A.A., certificate)
http://interiordesign.lbcc.edu/index.html

Los Angeles Mission College
Sylmar, CA
Interior Design (A.A., certificate)
www.lamission.edu/interiordesign/

Modesto Junior College
Modesto, CA
Allied Health Division
Family & Consumer Sciences Department
Interior Design (A.A., A.S., certificate)
www.mjc.edu/prospective/programs/fcs/interiordesign/

Monterey Peninsula College
Monterey, CA
Life Science Division
Department of Interior Design
Interior Design (A.A., certificate)
www.mpc/edu/academics/lifescience/interiordesign
• **EXTENDED PROFILE ON PAGE 96**

Moorpark College
Moorpark, CA
Department of Interior Design
Interior Design: Residential Design (A.S)
www.moorparkcollege.edu
• **EXTENDED PROFILE ON PAGE 98**

Mount San Antonio College
Walnut, CA
Consumer Science & Technologies Department
Interior Design (A.S.)
Kitchen & Bath Design (A.S.)
www.mtsac.edu/instruction/business/csdt/programs/id-career-program-main.html

Ohlone College
Newark, CA
Art Department
Interior Design (A.A., certificate)
www.ohlone.edu/instr/interiordesign/

Orange Coast College
Costa Mesa, CA
Consumer & Health Sciences
Interior Design (A.S., certificate)
www.orangecoastcollege.edu/academics/divisions/consumer_health/interior_design

Otis College of Art & Design
Los Angeles, CA
Department of Architecture/Landscape/Interiors
Architecture/Landscape/Interiors (B.F.A.)
www.otis.edu
• **EXTENDED PROFILE ON PAGE 100**

Palomar College
San Marcos, CA
Interior Design (A.A., certificate)
www.palomar.edu/interiordesign/

Saddleback College
Mission Viejo, CA
Advanced Technology & Applied Science Division
Consumer Services: Interior Design (A.A., A.S., certificate)
www.saddleback.edu/atas/Interior%5FDesign/

San Diego Mesa College
San Diego, CA
Interior Design (A.S., certificate)
www.sdmesa.edu/interior-design/

San Diego State University
San Diego, CA
College of Professional Studies & Fine Arts
School of Art, Design & Art History
Applied Arts & Sciences: Interior Design (B.A.)
Studio Arts: Interior Design (M.A., M.F.A.)
http://art.sdsu.edu/areas_of_study/

San Francisco State University
San Francisco, CA
Department of Consumer & Family Studies/Dietetics
Interior Design (B.S.)
http://cfsd.sfsu.edu/programs.aspx

San Joaquin Delta College
Stockton, CA
Arts & Communication Division
Interior Design (A.A., certificate)
www.deltacollege.edu/div/finearts/intdesign/intdes.html

San Jose State University
San Jose, CA
School of Art & Design
Interior Design (B.F.A.)
http://ad.sjsu.edu/programs/interior_design/

Santa Barbara City College
Santa Barbara, CA
Interior Design (A.A.)
www.sbcc.edu/interiordesign/

Santa Monica College
Santa Monica, CA
Interior Architectural Design (A.A., certificate)
http://academy.smc.edu/intarc/

Santa Rosa Junior College
Petaluma, CA
Consumer & Family Studies Department
Interior Design (A.A., certificate)
www.santarosa.edu/instruction/instructional_
departments

Solano Community College
Fine and Applied Arts & Behavioral Science Division
Interior Design (A.S. certificate)
Fairfield, CA
www.solano.edu/fine%5Farts/disciplines.html

University of California, Berkeley Extension
San Francisco, CA
Art & Design Program
Interior Design & Interior Architecture (certificate)
www.unex.berkeley.edu/art
• **EXTENDED PROFILE ON PAGE 104**

University of California, Los Angeles Extension
Los Angeles, CA
Joint Study Program in Interior Architecture
Interior Architecture (M.I.Arch.)
www.uclaextension.edu/arc_ID
• **EXTENDED PROFILE ON PAGE 102**

Ventura College
Ventura, CA
Interior Design (certificate)
www.venturacollege.edu/departments/academic/
interior_design.shtml

West Valley College
Saratoga, CA
Applied Arts & Sciences Division
Interior Design (A.S., certificate)
www.westvalley.edu/id/

Westwood College
Multiple Campuses, CA
School of Design
Interior Design (B.S.)
www.westwood.edu/programs/school-of-design/interior-design/

Woodbury University
Burbank, CA
Department of Interior Architecture
Interior Architecture (B.F.A.)
http://mcd.woodbury.edu/interiorarchitecture/
• **EXTENDED PROFILE ON PAGE 106**

COLORADO

Art Institute of Colorado, The
Denver, CO
Interior Design Department
Interior Design (B.A.)
Kitchen & Bath Design (A.A.S.)
www.artinstitutes.edu/denver
• **EXTENDED PROFILE ON PAGE 108**

Arapahoe Community College
Littleton, CO
Interior Design (A.A.S., certificate)
http://www.arapahoe.edu/departments-and-programs/a-z-programs/interior-design

Colorado State University
Fort Collins, CO
College of Applied Human Sciences
Department of Design & Merchandising
Interior Design (B.A., M.S.)
www.dm.cahs.colostate.edu
• **EXTENDED PROFILE ON PAGE 110**

Pikes Peak Community College
Colorado Springs, CO
Interior Design (A.A.S.)
www.ppcc.edu/career/interior-design/

Red Rocks Community College
Lakewood, CO
Interior Design (A.A.S., certificate)
www.rrcc.edu/interiordesign/index.htm

Rocky Mountain College of Art & Design
Denver, CO
Department of Interior Design
Interior Design (B.F.A.)
www.rmcad.edu/interior-design/overview
• **EXTENDED PROFILE ON PAGE 112**

CONNECTICUT

Paier College of Art
Hamden, CT
Department of Interior Design
Interior Design (B.F.A.)
www.paiercollegeofart.edu
• **EXTENDED PROFILE ON PAGE 114**

University of Bridgeport
Bridgeport, CT
Shintaro Akatsu School of Design
Interior Design (B.S.)
www1bpt.bridgeport.edu/art/interior/

University of New Haven
West Haven, CT
College of Arts & Sciences
Interior Design (A.S., B.A.)
www.newhaven.edu/4616/

DELAWARE

Delaware College of Art & Design
Wilmington, DE
Interior Design (A.F.A.)
www.dcad.edu/site/degree_programs/interior_design/overview

Delaware Community & Technical College
Dover, DE
Engineering Technology
Interior Design (A.A.S.)
www.dtcc.edu/terry/engr/pages/programs/interior.html

FLORIDA

American Intercontinental University, South Florida
Weston, FL
School of Design
Interior Design (A.A., B.F.A.)
www.aiuniv.edu/Degree-Programs/School-Of-Design

Art Institute of Fort Lauderdale, The
Fort Lauderdale, FL
Interior Design (A.S., B.S.)
www.artinstitutes.edu/fort-lauderdale/design-502.asp

Art Institute of Jacksonville, The
Jacksonville, FL
Interior Design (B.F.A.)
www.artinstitutes.edu/jacksonville/design-502.aspx

Art Institute of Tampa, The
Tampa, FL
Interior Design (B.F.A.)
www.artinstitutes.edu/tampa/design-502.aspx

Brevard Community College
Melbourne, FL
Interior Technology Program
Interior Design Technology (A.S.)
Kitchen & Bath Design (certificate)
www.brevardcc.edu/careertech
• **EXTENDED PROFILE ON PAGE 116**

Broward College
Ft. Lauderdale, FL
Interior Design (A.A., certificate)
www.broward.edu/programs/

Florida International University
Miami, FL
School of Architecture
Interior Design (B.I.D., M.I.D.)
www2.fiu.edu/~soa/

Florida State University
Tallahassee, FL
Department of Interior Design, College of Visual Arts, Theatre & Dance
Interior Design (B.S., M.S., M.F.A.)
http://interiordesign.fsu.edu
• **EXTENDED PROFILE ON PAGE 118**

Indian River State College
Fort Pierce, FL
Advanced Technology
Interior Design Technology (A.S.)
Kitchen & Bath Design (certificate)
http://faculty.irsc.edu/dept/advancedtechnology/id/index.htm

International Academy of Design & Technology—Orlando
Orlando, FL
Interior Design (B.F.A.)
www.iadt.edu/programs/interior_design.asp

International Academy of Design & Technology—Tampa
Tampa, FL
Interior Design (B.F.A., A.S.)
www.academy.edu
• **EXTENDED PROFILE ON PAGE 120**

Miami Dade College
Miami, FL
School of Architecture & Interior Design
Interior Design (A.A.)
Interior Design Technology (A.A.S.)
www.mdc.edu/main/architecture/

Miami International University of Art & Design
Miami, FL
Department of Interior Design
Interior Design (B.F.A., M.F.A.)
www.aii.edu/miami/
• EXTENDED PROFILE ON PAGE 122

Palm Beach State College
Lake Worth, FL
Interior Design (A.S.)
www.palmbeachstate.edu/x4227.xml

Ringling College of Art and Design
Sarasota, FL
Interior Design Department
Interior Design (B.F.A.)
www.ringling.edu/ID.32.0.html

Seminole State College
Sanford, FL
Interior Design (A.S., B.A.S.)
Kitchen & Bath Design (certificate)
www.seminolestate.edu/interiordesign/

Southwest Florida College
Tampa, FL
The Institute of Interior Design
Interior Design (A.S., B.S.)
Kitchen & Bath Design (diploma)
www.swfc.edu/interiordesign/index.php

University of Florida
Department of Interior Design, College of Design, Construction & Planning
Interior Design (B.D., M.I.D., PhD)
www.dcp.ufl.edu/interior
• EXTENDED PROFILE ON PAGE 124

GEORGIA

American InterContinental University, Atlanta
Atlanta, GA
School of Design
Interior Design (B.F.A., A.A.)
www.aiuniv.edu/Degree-Programs/Bachelor-Of-Fine-Arts-In-Interior-Design

Art Institute of Atlanta, The
Atlanta, GA
Interior Design (B.F.A.)
www.artinstitutes.edu/atlanta
• EXTENDED PROFILE ON PAGE 126

Bauder College
Atlanta, GA
Department of Interior Design
Interior Design (A.A.)
http://atlanta.bauder.edu
• EXTENDED PROFILE ON PAGE 128

Brenau University–Evening Weekend College
Gainesville, GA
Department of Interior Design
Interior Design (B.F.A., M.F.A.)
www.brenau.edu
• EXTENDED PROFILE ON PAGE 130

Brenau University–Women's College
Gainesville, GA
Department of Interior Design
Interior Design (B.F.A., M.F.A.)
www.brenau.edu
• EXTENDED PROFILE ON PAGE 132

Georgia Southern University
Statesboro, GA
Department of Hospitality, Tourism, & Family & Consumer Sciences
Interior Design (B.S.)
www.georgiasouthern.edu/majors
• EXTENDED PROFILE ON PAGE 134

Gwinnet Technical College
Lawrenceville, GA
Visual Arts, Fashion & Design
Interior Design (A.A.S., certificate)
www.gwinnetttech.edu

Lanier Technical College
Oakwood, GA
Interior Design (A.A.S., certificate)
www.laniertech.edu/

Savannah College of Art & Design
Atlanta, GA
Department of Interior Design, School of Building Arts
Interior Design (B.F.A., M.A., M.F.A.)
www.scad.edu/interior-design
• EXTENDED PROFILE ON PAGE 136

Savannah College of Art & Design
Savannah, GA
Department of Interior Design, School of Building Arts
Interior Design (B.F.A., M.A., M.F.A.)
www.scad.edu/interior-design
• **EXTENDED PROFILE ON PAGE 136**

University of Georgia
Athens, GA
Lamar Dodd School of Art
Interior Design (B.F.A., M.F.A.)
www.art.uga.edu/interiordesign
• **EXTENDED PROFILE ON PAGE 138**

Westwood College
Atlanta, GA
School of Design
Interior Design (B.S.)
www.westwood.edu
• **EXTENDED PROFILE ON PAGE 140**

Valdosta State University
Valdosta, GA
Interior Design (B.F.A.)
www.valdosta.edu/interiordesign/

HAWAII

Chaminade University
Honolulu, HI
Humanities & Fine Arts Division
Interior Design (A.A., B.F.A.)
www.chaminade.edu/ug/interior_design.php

IDAHO

Brigham Young University–Idaho
Rexburg, ID
College of Performing & Visual Arts
Interior Design Department
Interior Design (B.S.)
www.byui.edu/interiordesign/

University of Idaho
Moscow, ID
College of Art and Architecture
Department of Architecture & Interior Design
Interior Design (B.I.D)
www.uidaho.edu/caa/arch/interiordesign

ILLINOIS

College of DuPage
Glen Ellyn, IL
Interior Design Program
Interior Design (A.A.S.)
Kitchen & Bath Design (certificate)
www.cod.edu/interior_design/index.htm
• **EXTENDED PROFILE ON PAGE 144**

Columbia College Chicago
Chicago, IL
Department of Art & Design
Interior Architecture (B.F.A., M.F.A.)
www.colum.edu/Academics/Art_and_Design/
• **EXTENDED PROFILE ON PAGE 146**

Harper College
Palatine, IL
Department of Interior Design
Interior Design (A.A.S.)
www.harpercollege.edu/ind
• **EXTENDED PROFILE ON PAGE 148**

Harrington College of Design
Chicago, IL
Department of Interior Design
Interior Design (A.A.S., B.F.A., M.A., M.I.D.)
www.interiordesign.edu
• **EXTENDED PROFILE ON PAGE 150**

Illinois Central College
East Peoria, IL
Interior Design (A.A.S.)
www.icc.edu/catalog/cat_display.asp?id=157

Illinois Institute of Art–Chicago, The
Chicago, IL
Interior Design (B.F.A.)
www.artinstitutes.edu/chicago

Illinois Institute of Art–Schaumburg, The
Schaumburg, IL
Interior Design (B.F.A.)
www.artinstitutes.edu/schaumburg

Illinois State University
Normal, IL
Department of Family & Consumer Sciences
Family & Consumer Sciences: Interior & Environmental
    Design (B.A., B.S.)
http://fcs.illinoisstate.edu
• **EXTENDED PROFILE ON PAGE 152**

International Academy of Design & Technology–Chicago
Chicago, IL
Interior Design (B.F.A.)
www.iadtchicago.edu
- **EXTENDED PROFILE ON PAGE 154**

International Academy of Design & Technology–Schaumburg
Shaumburg, IL
Interior Design (B.F.A.)
www.iadtschaumburg.com
- **EXTENDED PROFILE ON PAGE 156**

Joliet Junior College
Joliet, IL
Arts & Sciences Division
Interior Design (A.A.S., certificate)
www.jjc.edu/academics/divisions/arts-sciences/fine-arts/interior-design

Robert Morris College
Chicago, IL
Institute of Technology & Media
Interior Design (A.A.S.)
www.robertmorris.edu/artanddesign/interior/courselist

School of the Art Institute of Chicago
Chicago, IL
Department of Architecture, Interior Architecture & Designed Objects
Interior Architecture (B.I.Arch.)
Master of Architecture: Interior Design Emphasis (MArch)
www.saic.edu/degrees_resources/ug_degrees/bia

Southern Illinois University Carbondale
Carbondale, IL
College of Applied Sciences & Arts
School of Architecture
Interior Design (B.S.)
www.architecture.siuc.edu/

Triton College
River Grove, IL
Division of Career Education
Interior Design (A.A.S., certificate)
Kitchen & Bath Design (A.A.S.)
www.triton.edu

INDIANA

Art Institute of Indianapolis, The
Indianapolis, IN
Interior Design (B.S.)
www.artinstitutes.edu/indianapolis

Ball State University
Muncie, IN
Department of Family & Consumer Sciences
Interior Design (B.A., B.S.)
www.bsu.edu/fcs
- **EXTENDED PROFILE ON PAGE 158**

Indiana State University
Terre Haute, IN
College Technology.
Department of Built Environment
Interior Design (B.S.)
www.indstate.edu/interior/

Indiana University, Bloomington
Bloomington, IN
Department of Apparel Merchandising & Interior Design
Interior Design (B.S.)
http://design.iub.edu/dsg/degree.shtml
- **EXTENDED PROFILE ON PAGE 160**

Indiana University–Purdue University Indianapolis
Indianapolis, IN
Purdue School of Engineering and Technology
Interior Design Technology (A.S., B.S.)
www.engr.iupui.edu/intr

Indiana Wesleyan University
Wesleyan, IN
School of Arts & Humanities
Interior Design (B.S.)
www.indwes.edu/Undergraduate/BS-Interior-Design/

Ivy Tech Community College of Indiana
Columbus, IN
Interior Design (A.A.S.)
Kitchen & Bath Design (A.A.S.)
www.ivytech.edu/columbus
- **EXTENDED PROFILE ON PAGE 162**

Ivy Tech Community College of Indiana
South Bend, IN
Interior Design (A.A.S.)
Kitchen & Bath Design (A.A.S.)
www.ivytech.edu/interiordesign/

Purdue University

West Lafayette, IN
Department of Interior Design
Interior Design (B.A.)
www.cla.purdue.edu/ad/interior/

Vincennes University

Vincennes, IN
Family & Consumer Sciences Department
Interior Design (A.A., A.A.S.)
www.vinu.edu/cms/opencms/academic_resources/
majors/factsheets/factsheet_0074.html

IOWA

Hawkeye Community College

Waterloo, IA
Arts Programs
Interior Design (A.A.A.)
www.hawkeyecollege.edu/academics/programs/arts/
interior-design/default.aspx

Iowa State University

Ames, IA
College of Design
Interior Design Program
Interior Design (B.F.A., M.F.A.)
www.design.iastate.edu/interiordesign/index.php
• **EXTENDED PROFILE ON PAGE 142**

Kirkwood Community College

Cedar Rapids, IA
Business & Information Technology Programs
Interior Design (A.A.S.)
www.kirkwood.edu/site/index.php?d=535

Scott Community College

Davenport, IA
Interior Design (A.A.S.)
www.eicc.edu/highschool/programs/career/design/
interior/index.html

University of Northern Iowa

Cedar Falls, IA
School of Applied Human Sciences
Interior Design (B.A.)
www.uni.edu/dtgfs/InteriorDesign/

Western Iowa Technical Community College

Sioux City, IA
Interior Design (A.A.S.)
www.witcc.edu/programs

KANSAS

Art Institute of Kansas City, The

Lenexa, KS
Interior Design (B.A.)
www.artinstitutes.edu/kansas-city

Fort Hays State University

Hays, KS
College of Arts & Sciences
Department of Art & Design
Interior Design (B.F.A.)
www.fhsu.edu/art-and-design/bfa-interior-design/

Johnson County Community College

Overland Park, KS
Department of Interior Design
Interior Design (A.A.S.)
Interior Entrepreneurship (A.A.S.)
Interior Merchandising (A.A.S.)
www.jccc.edu/home/depts
• **EXTENDED PROFILE ON PAGE 164**

Kansas State University

College of Architecture, Planning & Design
Department of Interior Architecture & Product Design
Interior Architecture & Product Design (B.I.Arch.,
    M.I.Arch.)
http://www.capd.ksu.edu/iapd/

Kansas State University

College of Human Ecology
Department of Apparel, Textiles & Interior Design
Interior Design (B.S.)
www.humec.k-state.edu/atid/
• **EXTENDED PROFILE ON PAGE 166**

Pittsburgh State University

Pittsburgh, KS
College of Arts & Sciences
Department of Family & Consumer Sciences
Interior Design (B.S.)
www.pittstate.edu/academics/program-detail
.dot?id=15628

University of Kansas

Lawrence, KS
School of Architecture, Design & Planning
Environmental/Interior Design (B.F.A.)
www.sadp.ku.edu/design/interior.index.shtml
• **EXTENDED PROFILE ON PAGE 168**

Wichita Area Technical College
Wichita, KS
Interior Design Program
Interior Design (A.A.S.)
Kitchen & Bath Design (certificate)
www.watc.edu
• **EXTENDED PROFILE ON PAGE 170**

KENTUCKY

Murray State University
Murray, KY
College of Science, Engineering & Technology
Interior Design (B.S.)
www.murraystate.edu/Academics/CollegesDepartments

Sullivan College of Technology & Design
Louisville, KY
Department of Interior Design
Interior Design (A.A.S., B.A., diploma)
www.sctd.edu
• **EXTENDED PROFILE ON PAGE 172**

University of Kentucky
Lexington, KY
School of Interior Design, College of Design
Interior Design (B.A., M.A.)
www.uky.edu/Design/interiordesign.html
• **EXTENDED PROFILE ON PAGE 174**

University of Louisville
Louisville, KY
College of Arts & Sciences
Department of Fine Art – Hite Art Institute
Interior Architecture (B.F.A.)
http://louisville.edu/art/

Western Kentucky University
Bowling Green, KY
Department of Family & Consumer Sciences
Design, Merchandising & Textiles: Interior Design (B.S.)
www.wku.edu/Dept/Academic/chhs/cfs/
• **EXTENDED PROFILE ON PAGE 176**

LOUISIANA

Delgado Community College
New Orleans, LA
Arts Department, Division of Arts & Humanities
Interior Design (A.A., diploma)
www.dcc.edu
• **EXTENDED PROFILE ON PAGE 178**

Louisiana State University
Baton Rouge, LA
Department of Interior Design
Interior Design (B.I.D.)
http://design.lsu.edu/Interior_Design
• **EXTENDED PROFILE ON PAGE 180**

Louisiana Tech University
Ruston, LA
School of Architecture
Interior Design (B.I.D)
www.latech.edu/tech/liberal-arts/architecture/

University of Louisiana, Lafayette
Lafayette, LA
School of Architecture & Design
College of the Arts
Interior Design (B.S.)
http://soad.louisiana.edu/programs-inter.html

MARYLAND

Anne Arundel Community College
Arnold, MD
Interior Design Department
Interior Design (A.A., certificate)
www.aacc.edu
• **EXTENDED PROFILE ON PAGE 190**

Community College of Baltimore County
Baltimore, MD
Interior Design (A.A.S.)
www.ccbcmd.edu/arts/interiordesign.html

Harford Community College
Bel Air, MD
Arts & Design Program
Interior Design (A.A.S)
www.harford.edu/vpaa/interior/faces.asp

Howard Community College
Columbia, MD
Arts & Humanities Division
Interior Design (A.A.)
www.howardcc.edu/academics

Montgomery College
Rockville, MD
Applied Technologies Department
Interior Design (A.A., A.A.S., certificate)
www.montgomerycollege.edu/curricula/descriptions/
cdintdesign.htm

MASSACHUSETTS

Bay Path College
Longmeadow, MA
Business: Interior Design (B.S.)
www.baypath.edu/UndergraduateExperience/Majors/
Business/InteriorDesign.aspx

Becker College
Worcester, MA
Interior Design (B.A.)
www.becker.edu/pages/245.asp

Boston Architectural College
Boston, MA
School of Interior Design
Interior Design (B.I.D., M.I.D.)
www.the-bac.edu
• **EXTENDED PROFILE ON PAGE 182**

Endicott College
Beverly, MA
School of Visual and Performing Arts
Interior Design (B.S., M.F.A.)
www.endicott.edu
• **EXTENDED PROFILE ON PAGE 184**

Mount Ida College
Newton, MA
Chamberlayne School of Design
Interior Design (B.S.)
Master of Science in Management: Interior Design (MSM)
www.mountida.edu/sp.cfm?pageid=320

Newbury College
Brookline, MA
School of Arts, Science & Design
Interior Design (B.S.)
www.newbury.edu/

New England Institute of Art
Brookline, MA
Interior Design (B.S.)
www.artinstitutes.edu/boston

New England School of Art & Design at Suffolk University
Boston, MA
Interior Design Department
Interior Design (B.F.A., M.A.)
www.suffolk.edu/nesad
• **EXTENDED PROFILE ON PAGE 186**

University of Massachusetts, Amherst
Amherst, MA
Department of Art, Architecture & Art History
Design (B.F.A.)
Interior Design (M.A.)
www.umass.edu/architecture/programs/ugrad/bfa_arch
.htm

Wentworth Institute of Technology
Boston, MA
Department of Design & Facilities
Interior Design (B.A.)
www.wit.edu/df/DF_Home_page.html
• **EXTENDED PROFILE ON PAGE 188**

MICHIGAN

Adrian College
Adrian, MI
Interior Design (B.S.)
www.adrian.edu/academics/ID/courses.php

Art Institute of Michigan, The
Novi, MI
Interior Design (A.A.S., B.F.A.)
www.artinstitutes.edu/detroit

Baker College Auburn Hills
Auburn Hills, MI
Engineering/Technology Division
Interior Design (B.I.D., A.A.S)
Kitchen & Bath Design (certificate)
www.baker.edu/programs/detail/interior-design-bid/
• **EXTENDED PROFILE ON PAGE 192**

Central Michigan University
Mt. Pleasant, MI
Department of Human Environmental Studies
Interior Design (B.A.A., B.A., B.S.)
www.ehs.cmich.edu/hev
• **EXTENDED PROFILE ON PAGE 194**

College for Creative Studies
Detroit, MI
Interior Design Department
Interior Design (B.F.A.)
www.collegeforcreativestudies.edu/current/academics/
interior

Delta College
University Center, MI
Interior Design (A.B.S)
www3.delta.edu/Artic/post/id.htm

Eastern Michigan University
Ypsilanti, MI
Interior Design Program, College of Technology
Interior Design (B.S., M.S., PhD)
www.emich.edu/cot/undergrad_intdes.htm
• **EXTENDED PROFILE ON PAGE 196**

Ferris State University
Grand Rapids, MI
Kendall College of Art & Design
Interior Design (B.A.)
www.kcad.edu/

Finlandia University
Hancock, MI
International School of Art & Design
Integrated Design: Interior Design (B.F.A.)
www.finlandia.edu/interior-design.html

Grand Rapids Community College
Grand Rapids, MI
Business Department
Interior Design (A.A.S.)
www.grcc.edu/interiordesign

Henry Ford Community College
Dearborn, MI
Fine Arts & Fitness Division
Interior Design (A.A.S.)
https://my.hfcc.edu/

International Academy of Design & Technology–Detroit
Troy, MI
Department of Interior Design
Interior Design (B.F.A.)
www.iadtdetroit.com
• **EXTENDED PROFILE ON PAGE 198**

Lawrence Technological University
Southfield, MI
College of Architecture & Design
Interior Architecture (B.S., MID)
http://ltu.edu/architecture_and_design/
• **EXTENDED PROFILE ON PAGE 200**

Lansing Community College
Lansing, MI
Environmental, Design & Building Technologies Department
Interior Design (A.A.S.)
www.lcc.edu/edbt/interior_des/

Michigan State University
East Lansing, MI
School of Planning, Design & Construction
College of Agriculture & Natural Resources/College of Social Science
Interior Design (B.A.)
Interior Design & Facilities Management (M.A.)
Environmental Design (M.A.)
http://spdc.msu.edu/

Oakland Community College
Farmington Hills, MI
Interior Design (A.A.S.)
www.oaklandcc.edu/InteriorDesign/courses.aspx

Wayne State University
Detroit, MI
College of Fine, Performing & Communication Arts
Department of Art & Art History
Art: Interior Design (B.F.A., M.A.)
http://art.wayne.edu/interior_design.php

Western Michigan University
Kalamazoo, MI
College of Education & Human Development
Family & Consumer Sciences Department
Interior Design (B.S.)
www.wmich.edu/consumer/itd/index.html

MINNESOTA

Alexandria Technical Institute
Alexandria, MN
Art, Design & Media
Interior Design (A.A.S.)
www.alextech.edu/en/Students/Programs/Design/InteriorDesign

Art Institutes International (The)–Minnesota
Minneapolis, MN
Interior Design Department
Interior Design (A.A.S., B.S.)
www.artinstitutes.edu/minneapolis
• **EXTENDED PROFILE ON PAGE 202**

Brown College
Mendota Heights, MN
School of Design
Interior Design (B.S.)
www.browncollege.edu/programs/interior_design.asp

Century College
White Bear Lake, MN
Applied Arts & Design Careers
Interior Design (A.A.S., certificate)
www.century.edu/futurestudents/programs

Dakota County Technical College
Rosemount, MN
Interior Design (A.A.S., diploma)
www.dctc.edu/future-students/programs/interior-design.
cfm

Dunwoody College of Technology
Minneapolis, MN
Building, Construction & Service Technology
Interior Design (B.S.)
www.dunwoody.edu/building/idsg.html

University of Minnesota
Saint Paul, MN
Department of Design, Housing, and Apparel,
    College of Design
Interior Design (B.S.)
Design: Interior Design (M.A.)
Science: Interior Design (PhD)
http://dha.design.umn.edu/
• **EXTENDED PROFILE ON PAGE 204**

MISSISSIPPI

Antonelli College
Jackson, MS
Interior Design (A.A.B.)
www.antonellicollege.edu/interior_design.html

Mississippi College
Clinton, MS
Art Department
Interior Design (B.A., B.S.)
http://mc.edu/campus/academics/ART/Degrees.html

Mississippi State University
Mississippi State, MS
College of Architecture, Art & Design: Interior Design
    Program
Interior Design (B.S.)
http://caad.msstate.edu
• **EXTENDED PROFILE ON PAGE 214**

Northeast Mississippi Community College
Booneville, MS
Interior Design (A.A.)
www.nemcc.edu/

University of Southern Mississippi
Hattiesburg, MS
School of Construction
Interior Design (B.S.)
http://construction.usm.edu/
• **EXTENDED PROFILE ON PAGE 216**

MISSOURI

Maryville University
St. Louis, MO
College of Arts and Sciences
Interior Design (B.F.A.)
www.maryvile.edu/
• **EXTENDED PROFILE ON PAGE 206**

Missouri State University
Springfield, MO
Department of Fashion and Interior Design
Interior Design (B.S.)
www.missouristate.edu/fid
• **EXTENDED PROFILE ON PAGE 208**

Park University
Parkville, MO
College of Liberal Arts & Sciences
School of Arts & Humanities
Interior Design (B.A.)
www.park.edu/art/interiordesign.html

St. Louis Community College
St. Louis, MO
Interior Design (A.A.S.)
Kitchen & Bath Design (certificate)
www.stlcc.edu/Programs/Interior_Design/

University of Central Missouri
Warrensburg, MO
Department of Art & Design
Interior Design (B.F.A)
www.ucmo.edu/art/
• **EXTENDED PROFILE ON PAGE 210**

University of Missouri
Columbia, MO
Department of Architectural Studies, College of Human
    Environmental Sciences
Human Environmental Sciences: Interior Design (B.S.)
Human Environmental Sciences: Architectural Studies
    (B.S.)
Architectural Studies (M.A.)
http://arch.missouri.edu
• **EXTENDED PROFILE ON PAGE 212**

MONTANA

Montana State University
Bozeman, MT
Gallatin College
Interior Design (A.A.S.)
www.montana.edu/gallatincollege/programs/intdesign
.html

NEBRASKA

Metropolitan Community College
Omaha, NE
Language & Visual Arts Department
Interior Design (A.A.S., certificate)
www.mccneb.edu/intd/

University of Nebraska–Kearney
Kearney, NE
Interior Design Program
Department of Family Studies and Interior Design
College of Business and Technology
Interior Design (B.S.)
http://aaunk.unk.edu/catalogs/current/dpt/dptfsid.asp

University of Nebraska, Lincoln
Lincoln, NE
Department of Interior Design
Design (B.S.)
Interior Design (M.S.)
http://archweb.unl.edu
• EXTENDED PROFILE ON PAGE 236

NEVADA

Art Institute of Las Vegas, The
Henderson, NV
Interior Design (B.A.)
www.artinstitutes.edu/las-vegas

International Academy of Design & Technology–Las Vegas
Henderson, NV
Department of Interior Design
Interior Design (B.F.A.)
www.iadtvegas.com
• EXTENDED PROFILE ON PAGE 242

University of Nevada, Las Vegas
Las Vegas, NV
School of Architecture
Interior Architecture & Design (B.S.)
http://architecture.unlv.edu/interiors.html

University of Nevada, Reno
Reno, NV
Interior Design Program
Interior Design (B.S.)
www.unr.edu
• EXTENDED PROFILE ON PAGE 244

NEW HAMPSHIRE

Hesser College
Manchester, NH
Interior Design (A.S.)
www.hesser.edu/Pages/Interior_Design_Associate_
Degree.aspx

Manchester Community College
Manchester, NH
Interior Design (A.A.S., certificate)
www.manchestercommunitycollege.edu/academics/
programs/interior-design

New Hampshire Institute of Art
Manchester, NH
Interior Design (certificate)
www.nhia.edu/interior-design-3/

NEW JERSEY

Berkeley College
Paramus, NJ
Interior Design (B.S., A.A.S.)
http://berkeleycollege.edu/bachelors/Interior_Design

Brookdale Community College
Lincroft, NY
Interior Design (A.A.S.)
www.brookdalecc.edu/pages/828.asp

Kean University
Union, NJ
College of Visual & Performing Arts
Robert Busch School of Design
Interior Design (B.F.A.)
www.kean.edu/design
• EXTENDED PROFILE ON PAGE 238

New Jersey Institute of Technology
Newark, NJ
College of Architecture & Design
School of Art & Design
Interior Design (B.A.)
http://design.njit.edu
• EXTENDED PROFILE ON PAGE 240

NEW MEXICO

Art Center Design College, The
Albuquerque, NM
Interior Design Department
Interior Design (B.A.)
www.theartcenter.edu
- EXTENDED PROFILE ON PAGE 62

Santa Fe Community College
Santa Fe, NM
School of Arts & Design
Interior Design (A.A.S., certificate)
www.sfcc.edu/school_of_arts_and_design/interior_design

NEW YORK

Alfred State College
Alfred, NY
Interior Design Department
Interior Design (A.A.S.)
www.alfredstate.edu/academics/programs/interior-design
- EXTENDED PROFILE ON PAGE 246

Art Institute of New York City, The
New York, NY
Interior Design (A.A.S.)
www.artinstitutes.edu/new-york

Buffalo State (SUNY)
Buffalo, NY
Interior Design Department
Interior Design (B.F.A.)
http://view.buffalostate.edu/

Cazenovia College
Cazenovia, NY
Interior Design (B.F.A.)
http://www.cazenovia.edu

Cornell University
Ithaca, NY
College of Human Ecology
Department of Design & Environmental Analysis
Interior Design (B.S.)
Design (M.A.)
www.human.cornell.edu/che/DeA/index.cfm
- EXTENDED PROFILE ON PAGE 248

Fashion Institute of Technology
New York, NY
Department of Interior Design
Interior Design (A.A.S., B.F.A.)
www.fitnyc.edu/interiordesign
- EXTENDED PROFILE ON PAGE 250

Institute of Design & Construction
Brooklyn, NY
Architectural Technology: Interior Design (A.O.S.)
http://www.idc.edu/academics/associate-degree-programs.php

Monroe Community College
Rochester, NY
Visual & Performing Arts Department
Interior Design (A.A.S., certificate)
www.monroecc.edu/depts/vapa/interior.htm

Nassau Community College
Garden City, NY
Marketing/Retailing/Fashion
Interior Design/Home Furnishings (A.A.S.)
www.ncc.edu/Academics/AcademicDepartments/MarketingRetailingFashion

New York Institute of Technology
Old Westbury, NY
School of Architecture & Design
Interior Design (B.F.A.)
www.nyit.edu/architecture
- EXTENDED PROFILE ON PAGE 252

New York School of Interior Design
New York, NY
Interior Design (certificate)
Interior Design (A.A.S., B.F.A., M.F.A.)
History of the Decorative Arts (B.A.)
www.nysid.edu/architecture
- EXTENDED PROFILE ON PAGE 254

Onondaga Community College
Syracuse, NY
Department of Architecture + Interior Design
Interior Design (A.A.S.)
www.sunyocc.edu/academics.aspx?id=7260

Parsons The New School for Design
New York, NY
School of Constructed Environments
Interior Design (A.A.S., B.F.A., B.S., M.F.A.)
Architectural Design (B.F.A.)
Product Design (B.F.A)
Lighting Design (M.F.A.)
www.newschoo.edu/parsons/sce

Pratt Institute
Brooklyn, NY
School Art & Design
Interior Design (B.F.A., M.S.)
www.pratt.edu/academics/art_design
• **EXTENDED PROFILE ON PAGE 256**

Rochester Institute of Technology
Rochester, NY
College of Imaging Arts & Sciences
School of Design
Interior Design (B.F.A.)
http://cias.rit.edu/design
• **EXTENDED PROFILE ON PAGE 258**

Sage College
Albany, NY
Department of Visual Arts
Interior Design (B.F.A.)
www.sage.edu/academics/visualarts/programs/interior_
design

School of Visual Arts
New York, NY
Interior Design Department
Interior Design (B.F.A.)
www.sva.edu
• **EXTENDED PROFILE ON PAGE 260**

Suffolk Community College
Riverhead, NY
Fashion/Interior Design (A.A.S.)
www.sunysuffolk.edu/Curricula/INDA-AAS.asp

Syracuse University
Syracuse, NY
College of Visual & Performing Arts
Department of Design
Interior Design (B.F.A.)
http://vpa.syr.edu/art-design/design/
• **EXTENDED PROFILE ON PAGE 262**

Villa Maria College
Buffalo, NY
Interior Design Program
Interior Design (A.A.S., B.S.)
www.villa.edu/interior_design.html
• **EXTENDED PROFILE ON PAGE 264**

NORTH CAROLINA

Appalachian State University
Boone, NC
Department of Technology
Interior Design (B.S.)
www.tec.appstate.edu
• **EXTENDED PROFILE ON PAGE 218**

Art Institute of Charlotte, The
Charlotte, NC
Interior Design (B.A., A.A.S.)
www.artinstitutes.edu/charlotte

Cape Fear Community College
Wilmington, NC
Interior Design (A.A.S.)
http://cfcc.edu/programs/i-design/

Carteret Community College
Morehead City, NC
Department of Interior Design
Interior Design (A.A.S.)
www.carteret.edu
• **EXTENDED PROFILE ON PAGE 220**

Central Piedmont Community College
Charlotte, NC
Department of Interior Design
Interior Design (A.A.S.)
Residential Decoration (diploma)
http://arts.cpcc.edu/academics/interior-design
• **EXTENDED PROFILE ON PAGE 222**

East Carolina University
Greenville, NC
Department of Interior Design & Merchandising
Interior Design (B.S.)
www.ecu.edu/che/idmr/
• **EXTENDED PROFILE ON PAGE 224**

Halifax Community College
Weldon, NC
School of Business
Interior Design (A.A.S., certificate)
www.halifaxcc.edu/studntre/IntDes

High Point University
High Point, NC
Department of Interior Design
Interior Design (B.S.)
http://homefurnishings.highpoint.edu/
• **EXTENDED PROFILE ON PAGE 226**

Meredith College
Raleigh, NC
Department of Human Environmental Sciences
Interior Design (B.S.)
www.meredith.edu/hes/interior-design
• EXTENDED PROFILE ON PAGE 228

Randolph Community College
Asheboro, NC
Commercial & Artistic Production Division
Interior Design (A.A.S.)
www.randolph.edu/interiordesign

Salem College
Winston-Salem, NC
Art Department
Interior Design (B.A.)
www.salem.edu/academics/undergrad/interior-design

University of North Carolina at Greensboro
Greensboro, NC
Department of Interior Architecture
Interior Architecture (B.S., M.S.)
www.uncg.edu/iar/
• EXTENDED PROFILE ON PAGE 230

Western Carolina University
Cullowhee, NC
School of Art & Design
Interior Design (B.S.)
www.wcu.edu
• EXTENDED PROFILE ON PAGE 232

NORTH DAKOTA

North Dakota State University
Fargo, ND
Department of Apparel, Design & Hospitality
    Management
Interior Design (B.S., B.A.)
www.ndsu.edu/adhm/
• EXTENDED PROFILE ON PAGE 234

OHIO

Art Institute of Ohio (The)–Cincinnati
Cincinnati, OH
Interior Design (B.F.A., A.A.S.)
www.artinstitutes.edu/cincinnati

Bowling Green State University
Bowling Green, OH
School of Family & Consumer Sciences
Interior Design (B.S.)
www.bgsu.edu/colleges/edhd/fcs/interior
• EXTENDED PROFILE ON PAGE 266

Cleveland Institute of Art
Cleveland, OH
Interior Design (B.F.A.)
www.cia.edu/Majors_Interior_Design.aspx

College of Mount St. Joseph
Cincinnati, OH
Department of Interior Architecture & Design
Interior Architecture & Design (B.F.A.)
www.msj.edu
• EXTENDED PROFILE ON PAGE 268

Columbus College of Art & Design
Columbus, OH
Interior Design (B.F.A.)
www.ccad.edu/programs-of-study/majors/interior-design

Davis College
Toledo, OH
Department of Design
Interior Design (A.A.B.)
www.daviscollege.edu/programs.html

Kent State University
Kent, OH
Interior Design Program
College of Architecture and Environmental Design
Interior Design (B.A)
www.kent.edu/CAED/interiordesign

Miami University
Oxford, OH
School of Fine Arts
Department of Architecture & Interior Design
Interior Design (B.F.A.)
www.muohio.edu/interiordesign
• EXTENDED PROFILE ON PAGE 270

Ohio University
Athens, OH
School of Art
Human & Consumer Sciences: Interior Architecture
(B.S.)
www.finearts.ohio.edu/art
• EXTENDED PROFILE ON PAGE 272

Ohio State University, The
Columbus, OH
College of the Arts
Department of Design
Interior Space Design (B.S.)
Design Development (M.F.A.)
http://design.osu.edu
• EXTENDED PROFILE ON PAGE 274

Owens Community College
Toledo, OH
Center for Fine & Performing Arts
Interior Design (certificate)
https://www.owens.edu/academic_dept/fine_arts/
programs.html

Sinclair Community College
Dayton, OH
Interior Design (A.A.S.)
www.sinclair.edu/explore/interior-design

University of Akron
Akron, OH
Department of Clothing, Textiles & Interior Design
Interior Design (B.A.)
Clothing, Textiles & Interiors (M.A.)
www.uakron.edu
• EXTENDED PROFILE ON PAGE 276

University of Cincinnati
Cincinnati, OH
School of Architecture & Interior Design
Interior Design (B.S.)
www.daap.uc.edu/said
• EXTENDED PROFILE ON PAGE 278

Ursuline College
Pepperpike, OH
School of Professional Studies
Interior Design (B.A., certificate)
www.ursuline.edu/Academics/Graduate_Professional/
Bachelors_Programs/Interior_Design

Virginia Marti College of Art & Design
Lakewood, OH
Interior Design (A.A.B.)
www.vmcasd.edu
• EXTENDED PROFILE ON PAGE 280

OKLAHOMA

Oklahoma Christian University
Oklahoma City, OK
Interior Design Program
Department of Art & Design
Interior Design (B.F.A.)
www.oc.edu/academics/arts_sciences/art_design/
degree_plan/bfa_interior_design.aspx

Oklahoma State University
Stillwater, OK
Department of Design, Housing & Merchandising
Interior Design (B.S.)
Design, Housing & Merchandising (M.S., PhD)
http://ches.okstate.edu/dhm/
• EXTENDED PROFILE ON PAGE 282

University of Central Oklahoma
Edmond, Ok
Department of Design, College of Fine Arts & Design
Interior Design (B.F.A.)
Desigm (M.F.A.)
www.uco.edu/cfad/academics/design
• EXTENDED PROFILE ON PAGE 284

University of Oklahoma
Norman, OK
College of Architecture
Department of Interior Design
Interior Design (B.I.D.)
http://id.coa.ou.edu/
• EXTENDED PROFILE ON PAGE 286

OREGON

Art Institute of Portland, The
Portland, OR
Interior Design (B.F.A.)
www.artinstitutes.edu/portland

Marylhurst University
Marylhurst, OR
Art & Interior Design Department
Interior Design (B.F.A.)
www.marylhurst.edu/art/bfa-interiordesign.php

Oregon State University
Corvallis, OR
College of Health & Human Sciences
Department of Design & Human Environment
Interior Design (B.S.)
Design & Human Environment (M.A., M.S., PhD)
www.hhs.oregonstate.edu/dhe/undergraduate-interior-design

Portland Community College
Portland, OR
Interior Design (A.A.S., certificate)
Kitchen & Bath (certificate)
www.pcc.edu/programs/interior-design/

University of Oregon
Eugene, OR
Department of Architecture
Interior Architecture (B.I.Arch., M.I.Arch.)
http://architecture.uoregon.edu/

PENNSYLVANIA

Arcadia University
Glenside, PA
College of Arts, Humanities & Social Sciences
Department of Art & Design
Art: Interior Design (B.F.A.)
www.arcadia.edu/academic/default.aspx?id=3724

Art Institute of Philadelphia, The
Philadelphia, PA
Interior Design (B.S.)
www.artinstitutes.edu/philadelphia

Art Institute of Pittsburgh, The
Pittsburgh, PA
Interior Design (B.S.)
Kitchen & Bath Design (A.S.)
www.artinstitutes.edu/pittsburgh

Art Institute of York Pennsylvania, The
York, PA
Interior Design Department
Interior Design (B.S.)
Kitchen & Bath Design (A.S.)
www.artinstitutes.edu/york
• **EXTENDED PROFILE ON PAGE 288**

Chatham University
Pittsburgh, PA
Interior Architecture Program, Art & Design Division
Interior Architecture (B.I.Arch., M.I.Arch., M.S.)
www.chatham.edu/departments/
• **EXTENDED PROFILE ON PAGE 290**

Drexel University
Philadelphia, PA
Department of Architecture & Interiors
Interior Design (B.S.)
Interior Architecture & Design (B.S., M.S.)
www.drexel.edu/westphal/
• **EXTENDED PROFILE ON PAGE 292**

Harcum College
Bryn Mawr, PA
Center for Business & Professional Studies
Interior Design (A.A., A.S.)
www.harcum.edu

Indiana University of Pennsylvania
Indiana, PA
College of Health & Human Services
Department of Human Development & Environmental
    Studies
Interior Design (B.S.)
www.iup.edu/page.aspx?id=11943

La Roche College
Pittsburgh, PA
Department of Interior Design
Interior Design (B.S.)
www.laroche.edu/majors/interior-design/interior-design
.htm
• **EXTENDED PROFILE ON PAGE 294**

Lehigh Carbon Community College
Schnecksville, PA
School of Computer Science & the Arts
Kitchen & Bath Design (A.A.S.)
www.lccc.edu/academics/school-technology/kitchen-
and-bath-design aas

Marywood University
Scranton, PA
School of Architecture
Interior Architecture/Design (B.F.A., M.A.)
www.marywood.edu/architecture/interior-architecture/

Mercyhurst College
Erie, PA
Department of Interior Design
Interior Design (B.A., certificate)
http://interiordesign.mercyhurst.edu/
• **EXTENDED PROFILE ON PAGE 296**

Moore College of Art & Design
Philadelphia, PA
Interior Design (B.F.A., M.F.A.)
www.moore.edu/site/bfa_programs/interior_design/
summary

Northampton Community College
Bethlehem, PA
Interior Design (A.A.S.)
http://catalog.northampton.edu/Programs-and-Majors/
Interior-Design.htm

Philadelphia University
Philadelphia, PA
School of Architecture
Interior Design (B.S.)
Interior Architecture (M.S.)
www.philau.edu/architecture/
• EXTENDED PROFILE ON PAGE 298

RHODE ISLAND

New England Institute of Technology
Warwick, RI
Interior Design (A.S., B.S.)
www.neit.edu/

Rhode Island School of Design
Providence, RI
Division of Architecture and Design
Interior Architecture (B.F.A., M.I.Arch.)
www.risd.edu/interiorarch.cfm

SOUTH CAROLINA

Anderson University
Anderson, SC
College of Visual & Performing Arts
School of Interior Design
Interior Design (B.A.)
www.andersonuniversity.edu/

Art Institute of Charleston, The
Charleston, SC
Interior Design (B.F.A.)
www.artinstitutes.edu/charleston

Bob Jones University
Greenville, SC
Interior Design (B.F.A.)
www.bju.edu/academics/majors/viewmajor.
php?id=10683&p=0

Converse College
Spartanburg, SC
School of the Arts
Department of Art & Interior Design
Interior Design (B.F.A)
www.converse.edu/academics/schools-departments

Winthrop University
Rock Hill, SC
College of Visual & Performing Arts
Department of Design
Interior Design (B.F.A.)
www.winthrop.edu/vpa/design
• EXTENDED PROFILE ON PAGE 300

SOUTH DAKOTA

South Dakota State University
Brookings, SD
Consumer Sciences Department
Education & Human Sciences: Interior Design (B.S.)
www.sdstate.edu/ehs/programs/
• EXTENDED PROFILE ON PAGE 302

TENNESSEE

Art Institute of Tennessee (The)–Nashville
Nashville, TN
Interior Design Department
Interior Design (B.F.A.)
www.artinstitutes.edu/nashville
• EXTENDED PROFILE ON PAGE 304

Carson Newman College
Jefferson City, TN
School of Family & Consumer Sciences
Interior Design (B.S.)
www.cn.edu/fcs/default.htm

East Tennessee State University
Johnson City, TN
Department of Engineering Technology, Surveying &
Digital Media
Interior Design (B.S.)
www.etsu.edu/scitech/entc/
• EXTENDED PROFILE ON PAGE 306

Freed-Hardeman University
Henderson, TN
College of Arts & Humanities
Art: Interior Design (B.A.)
www.fhu.edu/academics/colleges/ArtsAndHumanities/
FineArts/Art

International Academy of Design &
Technology–Nashville
Nashville, TN
Interior Design (A.A.S., B.A.S.)
www.iadtnashville.com/programs/interior-design/
degrees.asp

Lambuth University
Jackson, TN
School of Arts & Communications
Family & Consumer Sciences: Interior Design (B.A., B.S.)
www.lambuth.edu/courses-a-programs/majors/345-family-a-consumer-sciences

Middle Tennessee State University
Murfreesboro, TN
Human Science Department
Interior Design (B.S.)
www.mtsu.edu/humansciences/
● EXTENDED PROFILE ON PAGE 308

O'More College of Design
Franklin, TN
Department of Interior Design
Interior Design (B.F.A.)
www.omorecollege.edu/content/interioroverview.html
● EXTENDED PROFILE ON PAGE 310

Pelissippi State Technical Community College
Knoxville, TN
Career/Technical Program
Interior Design Technology (A.A.S.)
www.pstcc.edu/departments/InteriorDesign

University of Memphis
Memphis, TN
Department of Architecture
Interior Design (B.F.A.)
http://architecture.memphis.edu
● EXTENDED PROFILE ON PAGE 312

University of Tennessee at Chattanooga
Chattanooga, TN
Department of Interior Design
Interior Design (B.S.)
www.utc.edu/Academic/InteriorDesign/

University of Tennessee, Knoxville
Knoxville, TN
College of Architecture & Design
Interior Design (B.S.)
www.arch.utk.edu/undergrad-id/index.html

Watkins College of Art, Design, & Film
Nashville, TN
Department of Interior Design
Interior Design (B.F.A.)
www.watkins.edu/
● EXTENDED PROFILE ON PAGE 314

TEXAS

Abilene Christian University
Abilene, TX
College of Arts & Sciences
Art & Design Department
Interior Design (B.S.)
www.acu.edu/academics/cas/art
● EXTENDED PROFILE ON PAGE 316

Amarillo College
Amarillo, TX
Interior Design (A.A.S., certificate)
www.actx.edu/interior/index.php

Art Institute of Austin, The
Austin, TX
Interior Design (B.F.A.)
www.artinstitutes.edu/Austin

Art Institute of Dallas, The
Dallas, TX
Interior Design (B.F.A.)
Kitchen & Bath Design (A.A.S.)
www.artinstitutes.edu/dallas

Art Institute of Houston, The
Houston, TX
Interior Design (B.F.A.)
www.artinstitutes.edu/houston

Austin Community College
Austin, TX
Interior Design Institute
Interior Design (certificate)
www.austincc.edu/ce/cp/design/

Baylor University
Waco, TX
Department of Family & Consumer Sciences
Interior Design (B.A.)
Family & Consumer Sciences: Interior Design (B.S.)
www.baylor.edu/fcs
● EXTENDED PROFILE ON PAGE 318

Collin College
Frisco, TX
Interior & Architectural Design (A.A.S., certificate)
www.collin.edu/iad

El Centro College
Dallas, TX
Interior Design (A.A.S.)
www.elcentrocollege.edu

El Paso Community College
El Paso, TX
Interior Design Technology (A.A.S.)
www.epcc.edu

Houston Community College
Houston, TX
Career & Technical Education
Interior Design (A.A.S.)
www.hccs.edu/hccs/business-community/career-
technical-education-programs/interior-design

Lonestar College System
Multiple Cities, TX
Interior Design (A.A., A.S., A.A.S., B.A., B.S., certificate)
www.lonestar.edu/interior-design.htm

Lamar University
Beaumont, TX
Family & Consumer Sciences Department
Interior Design (B.S.)
http://dept.lamar.edu/fcs/interior_des/prog_descr.htm

Sam Houston State University
Huntsville, TX
Department of Family & Consumer Sciences
Interior Design (B.A., B.S.)
www.shsu.edu/~hec_www/
• EXTENDED PROFILE ON PAGE 320

San Jacinto College
Pasadena, TX
Interior Design (A.A.S., certificate)
www.sjcd.edu/areas-study#interior-design

St. Mary's University
San Antonio, TX
Continuing Studies
Interior Design (certificate)
Kitchen & Bath Design (certificate)
www.stmarytx.edu/continuingstudies

Stephen F. Austin State University
Nacogdoches, TX
School of Human Sciences
Interior Design (B.S.)
www.sfasu.edu/hms
• EXTENDED PROFILE ON PAGE 322

Texas Christian University
Forth Worth, TX
Department of Design, Merchandising & Textiles
Interior Design (B.S.)
www.demt.tcu.edu
• EXTENDED PROFILE ON PAGE 324

Texas State University
San Marcos, TX
Department of Family & Consumer Sciences
Family & Consumer Sciences: Interior Design (B.S.)
www.fcs.txstate.edu
• EXTENDED PROFILE ON PAGE 326

Texas Tech University
Lubbock, TX
Department of Design, College of Human Sciences
Interior Design (B.I.D.)
Environmental Design (M.S.)
Interior & Environmental Design (PhD)
www.depts.ttu.edu/hs/dod/
• EXTENDED PROFILE ON PAGE 328

University of Houston
Houston, TX
Gerald D. Hines College of Architecture
Interior Architecture (B.S.)
www.arch.uh.edu/index.php

University of North Texas
Denton, TX
College of Visual Arts & Design
Department of Design
Interior Design (B.F.A., M.F.A.)
www.art.unt.edu/design
• EXTENDED PROFILE ON PAGE 330

University of Texas at Arlington
Arlington, TX
Interior Design Program
School of Architecture
Interior Design (B.S.)
www.uta.edu/architecture/academic/academic_home

University of Texas at Austin
Austin, TX
School of Architecture
Interior Design (B.S., M.I.D)
http://soa.utexas.edu/interiordesign/
• EXTENDED PROFILE ON PAGE 332

University of Texas at San Antonio
San Antonio, TX
College of Architecture
Interior Design (B.S.)
www.utsa.edu/architecture
• EXTENDED PROFILE ON PAGE 334

University of the Incarnate Word
San Antonio, TX
School of Interactive Media & Design
Interior Environmental Design (B.A.)
www.uiw.edu/ied/index.htm

Wade College
Dallas, TX
Interior Design (A.A.)
www.wadecollege.edu/content/index.php?page=interior-design

UTAH

Art Institute of Salt Lake City, The
Draper, UT
Interior Design (B.A.)
www.artinstitutes.edu/salt-lake-city

LDS Business College
Salt Lake City, UT
Interior Design (A.A.S., certificate)
www.ldsbc.edu/

Salt Lake Community College
Salk Lake City, UT
School of Arts & Communication
Interior Design (A.A.S.)
www.slcc.edu/interior
• EXTENDED PROFILE ON PAGE 336

Utah State University
Caine College of the Arts
Interior Design (B.A., B.I.D., B.S., M.S.)
http://interiordesign.usu.edu

Weber State University
Ogden, UT
College of Applied Science & Technology
Interior Design (B.S.)
www.weber.edu/interiordesign
• EXTENDED PROFILE ON PAGE 338

VIRGINIA

Art Institute of Washington, The
Arlington, VA
Interior Design (B.F.A.)
www.artinstitutes.edu/arlington

James Madison University
Harrisonburg, VA
School of Art & Art History
Interior Design (B.F.A.)
www.jmu.edu/art
• EXTENDED PROFILE ON PAGE 340

Lord Fairfax Community College
Middletown, VA
Division of Business, Technology, Science & Health Professions
Interior Design (certificate)
www.lfcc.edu
• EXTENDED PROFILE ON PAGE 342

Marymount University
Arlington, VA
Interior Design Department
Interior Design (B.A., M.A.)
www.marymout.edu/academics/programs/interior
• EXTENDED PROFILE ON PAGE 344

Northern Virginia Community College
Loudoun, VA
Interior Design (A.A.S.)
www.nvcc.edu/loudoun/humdiv/interior_design

Radford University
Radford, VA
Department of Interior Design & Fashion
Interior Design (B.F.A.)
Design Culture (B.S.)
Design Management (B.S.)
http://id f.asp.radford.edu/
• EXTENDED PROFILE ON PAGE 346

Tidewater Community College
Norfolk, VA
Arts and Design Technology
Interior Design (A.A.S., certificate)
www.tcc.edu/academics/programs/ot/adt/intedesi.htm

Virginia Commonwealth University
Richmond, VA
School of the Arts
Department of Interior Design
Interior Design (B.F.A., M.F.A.)
www.vcu.edu/arts/interiordesign/dept

Virginia Polytechnic Institute and State University
Blacksburg, VA
School of Architecture & Design
Interior Design (B.S.)
http://archdesign.vt.edu/interior-design

WASHINGTON

Art Institute of Seattle, The
Seattle WA
Interior Design Department
Interior Design (A.A.A., B.S.)
Residential Design (Diploma)
www.artinstitutes.edu/Seattle
- **EXTENDED PROFILE ON PAGE 348**

Bellevue College
Bellevue, WA
Interior Design Department
Interior Design (B.A.A.)
Interior Studies (A.A.)
http://bellevuecollege.edu
- **EXTENDED PROFILE ON PAGE 350**

Cornish College of the Arts
Seattle, WA
Design Department
Interior Design (B.F.A.)
www.cornish.edu/design

International Academy of Design & Technology—Seattle
Seattle, WA
Interior Design (A.A.S., B.F.A.)
www.iadtseattle.com/programs/interior-design.asp

Seattle Pacific University
Seattle, WA
Family & Consumer Sciences Department
Interior Design (B.A.)
www.spu.edu/depts/fcs/interior_design/index.html

Spokane Community College
Spokane, WA
Applied Visual Arts
Interior Design (A.A.S.)
www.spokanefalls.edu/TechProf/InteriorDesign

Washington State University, Pullman
Pullman, WA
Department of Interior Design
Interior Design (B.A., M.A.)
http:/id.wsu.edu
- **EXTENDED PROFILE ON PAGE 352**

Washington State University, Spokane
Spokane, WA
Department of Interior Design
Interior Design (B.A., M.A.)
http://id.wsu.edu
- **EXTENDED PROFILE ON PAGE 354**

WASHINGTON, DC

Corcoran College of Arts + Design
Interior Design (B.F.A., M.A.)
www.corcoran.edu/undergraduate_degrees/BFA_interior_design.php

George Washington University
Washington, DC
Columbian College of Arts & Sciences
Interior Design: (B.F.A., M.F.A.)
www.intd.gwu.edu/

WEST VIRGINIA

University of Charleston
Charleston, WV
Interior Design (B.A.)
www.ucwv.edu/academics/majors/interior_design_programs.aspx

West Virginia University
Morgantown, WV
Division of Design & Merchandising
Interior Design (B.S.)
www.design.wvu.edu
- **EXTENDED PROFILE ON PAGE 364**

WISCONSIN

Fox Valley Technical College
Appleton, WI
Interior Design (A.A.S.)
Kitchen & Bath Design (A.A.S)
www.fvtc.edu/public/academics/degree.aspx?plan=10-304-1

Gateway Technical College
Kenosha, WI
Interior Design (A.A.S.)
www.gtc.edu/program.asp?pid=10-304-1

Madison Area Technical College
Madison, WI
Center for Business & Applied Arts
Interior Design (A.A.A.)
http://matcmadison.edu/program-info/interior-design

Milwaukee Area Technical College
West Allis, WI
Business Division
Interior Design (A.A.S.)
http://matc.edu/student/offerings/intdsgnaas.html

Mount Mary College
Milwaukee, WI
Interior Design Department, Art & Design Division
Interior Design (B.A.)
www.mtmary.edu/dept_interiordesign.htm
- **EXTENDED PROFILE ON PAGE 356**

University of Wisconsin, Madison
Madison, WI
Design Studies Department, School of Human Ecology
Interior Design (B.S.)
Interior Environment (M.F.A., M.S., PhD)
www.sohe.wisc.edu/ds
- **EXTENDED PROFILE ON PAGE 358**

University of Wisconsin, Stevens Point
Stevens Point, WI
College of Professional Studies
Interior Architecture (B.F.A.)
http://www.uwsp.edu/ia/

University of Wisconsin, Stout
Menomonie, WI
Department of Art & Design
Interior Design (B.F.A.)
www.uwstout.edu/cas/artdes/index.shtml
- **EXTENDED PROFILE ON PAGE 360**

Waukesha County Technical College
Pewaukee, WI
Education, Interior Design & Human Services
Interior Design (A.A.S.)
www.wctc.edu
- **EXTENDED PROFILE ON PAGE 362**

Western Technical College
La Crosse, WI
Architecture, Graphics & Design Program
Interior Design (A.A.S.)
www.westerntc.edu/programs

CANADA

Algonquin College
Ottawa, ON
Interior Design Program, School of Media & Design
Interior Design (B.A.A.)
Kitchen & Bath Design (certificate)
www.algonquincollege.com/
- **EXTENDED PROFILE ON PAGE 366**

Art Institute of Vancouver, The
Vancouver, BC
Interior Design Department
Interior Design (diploma)
www.artinstitutes.edu/vancouver/
- **EXTENDED PROFILE ON PAGE 368**

British Columbia Institute of Technology
School of Construction & the Environment
Interior Design (diploma, certificate)
www.bcit.ca/study/programs/6160fdiplt

Centre for Arts & Technology
Kelowna, BC
Interior Design (diploma)
www.digitalartschool.com/programs/interior_design

Dawson College
Montreal, QC
Interior Design (diploma)
www.dawsoncollege.qc.ca/programs/creative-applied-arts/interior-design

Fanshawe College
London, ON
School of Design
Interior Design (diploma)
www.fanshawec.ca/en/DIT3/

Humber College
Toronto, ON
Design Cluster School of Applied Technology
Interior Design (B.A.A.)
http://humber.ca/appliedtechnology/
- **EXTENDED PROFILE ON PAGE 370**

Kwantlen Polytechnic University
Richmond, BC
Interior Design Department
Interior Design (B.I.D.)
www.kwantlen.ca/design/interior_design
- **EXTENDED PROFILE ON PAGE 372**

Mount Royal University
Calgary, AB
Department of Interior Design and Art History
Bachelor of Applied Interior Design
www.mtroyal.ca/ProgramsCourses/
FacultiesSchoolsCentres/Arts/Programs

Northern Alberta Institute of Technology
Edmonton, AB
Engineering & Applied Sciences
Interior Design Technology (diploma)
www.nait.ca/program_home_15655.htm

RCC Institute of Technology
Concord, ON
Interior Design Department, Academy of Design
Interior Design (diploma)
www.rccit.ca/academy-of-design/interior-design/
• **EXTENDED PROFILE ON PAGE 374**

Ryerson University
Toronto, ON
School of Interior Design
Interior Design (B.I.D.)
www.ryerson.ca/interior/
• **EXTENDED PROFILE ON PAGE 376**

Sheridan Institute of Technology & Advanced Learning
Oakville, ON
School of Animation, Arts & Design
Interior Design (B.A.A.)
www.sheridaninstitute.ca

St. Claire College
Windsor, ON
Interior Design (diploma)
www.stclaircollege.ca/programs/postsec/interior

University of Manitoba
Winnipeg, MB
Department of Interior Design
Interior Design (M.I.D.)
http://umanitoba.ca/interiordesign
• **EXTENDED PROFILE ON PAGE 378**

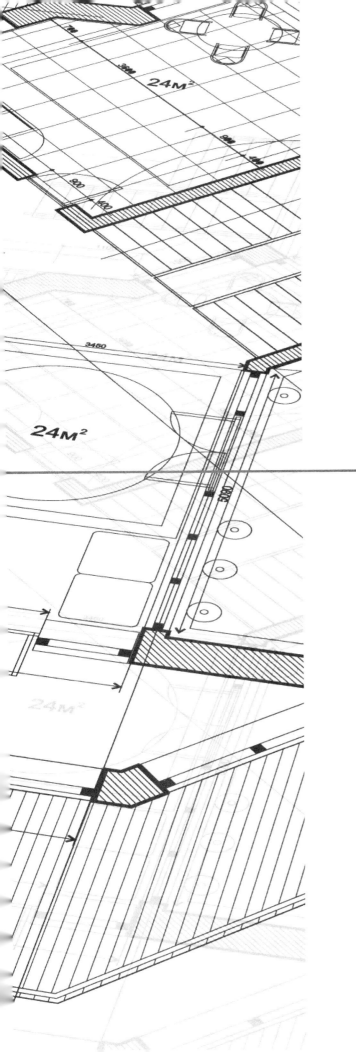

Extended Profiles

Auburn University

Department of Consumer Affairs, College of Human Sciences

308 Spidle Hall, Auburn University, AL 36849 | 334-844-4084 | www.humsci.auburn.edu/cahs/index.php

UNIVERSITY PROFILE
Public
Suburban
Residential
Semester Schedule
Co-ed

STUDENT DEMOGRAPHICS
Undergraduate: 30,913
Graduate: 3,689

Male: Not reported
Female: Not reported

Full-time: Not reported
Part-time: Not reported

EXPENSES
Tuition: $7900 (in-state)
$21,916 (out-of-state)

Room & Board: $9,630

ADMISSIONS
Quad Center
Auburn University, AL 36849
334-844-6425

DEGREE INFORMATION

Major / Degree / Concentration	Enrollment	Requirements for entry	Graduation rate
Interior Design Bachelor of Science	132	AU Freshman admission or 2.5 gpa for transfer; review of essay and portfolio upon entrance	Not reported
Consumer Affairs—Interiors Master of Science	3	3.0 gpa; 900 GRE	Not reported

TOTAL PROGRAM ENROLLMENT
Undergraduate: 132
Graduate: 97

Male: 3%
Female: 97%

Full-time: 100%
Part-time: 0%

International: Not reported
Minority: Not reported

Job Placement Rate: 80%

SCHOLARSHIPS / FINANCIAL AID
Most college and departmental scholarships are for students demonstrating need and/or academic achievement and promise. University scholarships for students with ACT of 30 or higher.

TOTAL FACULTY: 5
Full-time: 100%
Part-time: 0%
Online: Not reported

NCIDQ Certified: 1
Licensed Interior Designers: 1
LEED Certified: 1

INTERIOR DESIGN ADMINISTRATION
Dr. Carol L. Warfield, Head, Department of Consumer Affairs

PROFESSIONAL / ACADEMIC AFFILIATIONS
American Society of Interior Designers
International Interior Design Association
Interior Design Educators Council
Environmental Design Research Association

CIDA ACCREDITATION
Bachelor of Science in Interior Design (2008, 2014)

PROGRAM DESCRIPTION AND PHILOSOPHY

The philosophy of the Auburn University Design Program is based on the definition of Interior Design as endorsed by the Council for Interior Design Accreditation (CIDA), the National Council for Interior Design Qualification (NCIDQ), and major Interior Design associations of North America:

"Interior Design includes a scope of services performed by a professional design practitioner, qualified by means of EDUCATION, EXPERIENCE, and EXAMINATION, to protect and enhance the life, health, safety and welfare of the public." (Excerpted from the www.id-accredit.org Web site)

FACILITIES

Twenty-station computer lab w/ AutoCAD, Revit, SketchUp, and Adobe Photoshop and Dreamweaver. Beginning with the Freshman year, all students must also have their own laptops loaded with all of the software to be used in their studios. Additional facilities include the Jule Collins Smith Museum of Fine Art and the Digital Resources Center in AU Library.

ONLINE / DISTANCE LEARNING

Not available

COURSES OF INSTRUCTION

- Global Consumer Culture
- History of the Decorative Arts
- Materials and Components
- Business Practices
- Accounting
- Microeconomics
- Marketing
- Intro. to Interior Design
- Technical Design
- Visual Presentations I & II
- CAD for Interior Design
- Lighting Design/Environmental Systems
- Residential Interiors
- Non-Residential Interiors
- Interior Design-Commercial
- Interior Design-Institutional
- Internship

INTERNSHIPS

Required of majors

Placement: Architectural and Interior Design firms, business furnishings companies throughout the U.S. or abroad, eg., Gensler, Hirsch Bedner & Assoc., Perkins Eastman, Earl Swensson & Assoc., Workspace Solutions, IA (Interior Architects), U.S. Army Corps of Engineers, Hospitality Design & Procurement, Marc-Michael Interior Design, Inc., 2WR/Holmes Wilkins Architects, Innovative Office Solutions, Ethica Health & Retirement Communities

STUDY ABROAD

A 12-week immersion program, Joseph S. Bruno Auburn Abroad in Italy, is available to all students in the College. Students earn 16 semester hours of credit and an International Minor. Other study abroad opportunities are available as well.

NOTABLE ALUMNI

Not reported

STUDENT ACTIVITIES AND ORGANIZATIONS

American Society of Interior Designers, International Interior Design Association

FACULTY SPECIALIZATIONS AND RESEARCH

- Visual Presentations
- Commercial design/office systems
- Lighting design
- Painting
- Visual cultural history
- Community planning/economic development
- Sustainable design

Arizona State University

School of Architecture & Landscape Architecture

162 CDN, Tempe Campus, Tempe, AZ 85287-2105 | 480-965-3571 | http://design.asu.edu/

UNIVERSITY PROFILE
Public
Urban
Residential
Semester Schedule
Co-ed

STUDENT DEMOGRAPHICS
Undergraduate &
Graduate: 67,000

Male: 50%
Female: 50%

Full-time: 75%
Part-time: 25%

EXPENSES
Tuition: $13,000

ADMISSIONS
http://students.asu.edu/
admission

DEGREE INFORMATION

Major / Degree / Concentration	Enrollment	Requirements for entry	Graduation rate
Interior Design Bachelor of Science	180	Milestone review after Freshman year; accept highest ASU, Design gpa, best portfolio, and letter of intent scores	95

TOTAL PROGRAM ENROLLMENT
Undergraduate: 180
Graduate: 24

Male: 15%
Female: 85%

Full-time: 100%
Part-time: 0%

International: 20%
Minority: 80%

Job Placement Rate: 85%

SCHOLARSHIPS / FINANCIAL AID
Many forms of support are available.
Students should seek information on
ASU's Web site.

TOTAL FACULTY: 9
Full-time: 60%
Part-time: 40%

NCIDQ Certified: 2
Licensed Interior Designers: n/a
LEED Certified: 1

INTERIOR DESIGN ADMINISTRATION
Lauren McDermott, Interim School
Director

PROFESSIONAL / ACADEMIC AFFILIATIONS
American Society of Interior Designers
International Interior Design Association
Interior Design Educators Council

CIDA ACCREDITATION
Bachelor of Science in Design (2009, 2015)

PROGRAM DESCRIPTION AND PHILOSOPHY

The Arizona State University Interior Design program focuses on commercial Interior Design but also offers courses in residential design. Students are immersed in a learning experience that includes courses in design history; human behavior and the study of the interface of people and space as it is influenced by culture, history, and political and economic climates; design theories; and the rigor of design studio. Communication and the ability to translate the creative design process into a visual, verbal, and written language understood by others is also an important part of a student's training as a designer. A curriculum that emphasizes aesthetics, functionality, ambient influences, and technical expertise provide students with the tools to excel in the profession of Interior Design.

FACILITIES

All resources expected of a large research university are available to our students.

ONLINE / DISTANCE LEARNING

Not available

COURSES OF INSTRUCTION

- Interior Design Issues and Theories
- Introduction to Computer Modeling for Interior Design
- Design and Human Behavior
- Ambient Environment
- Interior Materials, Finishes, Specifications
- History of Interior Design
- Interior Design Codes
- Construction Methods in Interior Design

INTERNSHIPS

Required of majors at Junior level

STUDY ABROAD

Summer course; elective credit

NOTABLE ALUMNI

Not reported

STUDENT ACTIVITIES AND ORGANIZATIONS

Student chapter of International Interior Design Association

FACULTY SPECIALIZATIONS AND RESEARCH

- Sustainability
- Poetics of Materials
- Healthcare Design
- Arts and Crafts Movement
- Daylighting
- Building Information Modeling
- Digital Portfolio Design
- Latin American Architecture

The Art Center Design College

Interior Design Department

Tucson Campus: 2525 N. Country Club Rd., Tucson, AZ 85716 | 520-325-0123 | www.theartcenter.edu

Albuquerque Campus: 5000 Marble N.E., Albuquerque, NM 87110 | 520-254-7575 | www.theartcenter.edu

UNIVERSITY PROFILE

Public University
Suburban Setting
Residential Campus
Semester Academic Calendar
Co-ed

STUDENT DEMOGRAPHICS

Undergraduates: 36,386
Graduates: 15,885

Male: 47%
Female: 53%

Full-time: 92%
Part-time: 8%

EXPENSES

Tuition: $5,020 (in-state)

Room & Board:
$7,500 (in-state)
Tuition /Room & board:
$22,280 (out-of-state)

ADMISSIONS

201 Criser Hall
Gainesville, FL 32611
352-392-1365

DEGREE INFORMATION

Major / Degree / Concentration	Enrollment	Requirements for entry	Graduation rate
Interior Design Bachelor of Arts	132	ACT minimum score 20 or SAT minimum score 1,000; High School Diploma (minimum gpa 2.0) or GED; Essay and Personal Statement; Interview	82%
Landscape Architecture Bachelor of Arts	14	Not reported	Not reported

TOTAL PROGRAM ENROLLMENT

Undergraduate: 132
Graduate: n/a

Male: 14%
Female: 86%

Full-time: 56%
Part-time: 44%

International: 1%
Minority: 37%

JOB PLACEMENT RATE: 100%

SCHOLARSHIPS / FINANCIAL AID

The Art Center Design College offers a comprehensive need-based aid program for students who demonstrate financial need as determined by the Free Application for Federal Student Aid (FAFSA). The college also administers a number of scholarships for both entering and continuing Bachelor of Arts degree-seeking students.

Students Receiving Scholarships or Financial Aid: 62%

TOTAL FACULTY: 13

Full-time: 38%
Part-time: 62%
Online: n/a

NCIDQ Certified: 48%
Licensed Interior Designers: 48%
LEED Certified: 24%

INTERIOR DESIGN ADMINISTRATION

Marvin Woods, Chief Academic Officer
Madeleine Boos, AIA Interior Design Department Chair
Laura Snapp, Interior Design Curriculum Coordinator, Albuquerque

PROFESSIONAL / ACADEMIC AFFILIATIONS

American Society of Interior Designers
International Interior Design Association
Interior Design Educators Council

CIDA ACCREDITATION

Bachelor of Arts (2010, 2016) - Tucson
Bachelor of Arts in Interior Design (2008, 2014) - Albuquerque

PROGRAM DESCRIPTION AND PHILOSOPHY

The Art Center Design College has campuses in Tucson, AZ and Albuquerque, NM and provides an exemplary education in the field of Interior Design. Both colleges are regionally accredited by the Higher Learning Commission, and both Interior Design Programs are accredited by the Council of Interior Design Accreditation (CIDA).

The Interior Design Program motivates students to explore new ideas and accept challenges that are an integral part of higher education, and encourages students to seek innovative, responsible and responsive solutions. A strong emphasis is placed on balancing traditional design fundamentals with technology. Students develop the skills needed for success in the professional practice of Interior Design and NCIDQ certification. The program mission is to graduate creative, inquisitive, globally responsible and responsive professionals who are fully prepared to practice at the highest standards established by the Interior Design field.

The Art Center Design College encourages student interaction with working professionals. Each student is required to participate in a 150-hour internship with a design professional to support and supplement his or her school experience. Guest lecturers, workshops, fieldtrips, and pro-bono real life community projects are incorporated throughout the Interior Design program when possible.

FACILITIES

The Art Center Design College provides a student-focused environment committed to the highest standards of academic achievement, scholarly inquiry, creativity and citizenship in a diverse world community. Each campus is complete with its own individual facilities.

The Student Services Department is dedicated to the individual success of each student. Student Services provides assistance with academic advising, placement assistance, internships, information concerning housing, transportation, childcare options, student insurance, coping skills and relevant areas that directly affect student success.

Facilities that support student success include the following:
- 24/7 computer lab with machines that contain a wide array of software applications
- Campus library with student workspaces, computers, and a comprehensive range of informational resources (bound/ electronic) on site and from all over the country
- Campus bookstore with workspaces, resources and materials, and a variety of printing options and assistance
- Classrooms and Studios equipped with computers and work spaces
- Interior Design sample library which includes updated materials and product information for student use
- Tutoring and mentoring labs
- Student union

ONLINE / DISTANCE LEARNING
Not available

COURSES OF INSTRUCTION
Program coursework includes, but is not limited to, Design Drawing, Rendering, Space Planning I and II, Textiles and Surface Materials, Introduction to Lighting Design, CAD I and II, History of Architecture and Interior Design, Building Structures, Project Management, Advanced Presentation Skills, Residential Design and Commercial Design

INTERNSHIPS
Required of majors at Junior/Senior level

Interns are placed in a variety of opportunities within the Interior Design profession. This allows for a range of experiences in settings such as mid-size commercial design firms, small boutique firms specializing in upscale retail and hospitality, residential design firms, and facilities management within a university and/ or local government setting.

STUDY ABROAD
Not available

NOTABLE ALUMNI
The Art Center Design College has a high professional placement rate of graduates. Graduates' experiences vary from small 1- or 2- person design firms to large corporate environments both in the Southwest and throughout the USA.

STUDENT ACTIVITIES AND ORGANIZATIONS
IDSA (Interior Design Student Association) is the Interior Design student club, and it houses the student chapters of IIDA and ASID. IDSA raises money for pro-bono work and independent educational opportunities outside the classroom, including educational travel.

FACULTY SPECIALIZATIONS AND RESEARCH
Faculty is comprised of both working professionals and Interior Design educators. There is diversity within the instructional make-up. Faculty includes NCIDQ certified Interior Designers and registered architects with various specialties and areas of expertise, illustrators, artists, and historic preservationists to name a few of the different disciplines that contribute to the education of the Interior Design student.

Working professionals provide students with networking opportunities. Employing instructional staff with the appropriate education and experience also creates a forum for professional collaboration on project development and provides opportunities for industry-related seminars. Students receive up-to-date information, trends, and techniques in a variety of professional disciplines.

The Art Institute of Phoenix

Interior Design Department

2233 W. Dunlap Ave., Phoenix, AZ 85021-2859 | 602-331-7500 | www.artinstitutes.edu/phoenix/

UNIVERSITY PROFILE
Private
Suburban
Commuter
Quarter Schedule
Co-ed

STUDENT DEMOGRAPHICS
Undergraduate: 1,200
Graduate: n/a

Male: 50%
Female: 50%

Full-time: 90%
Part-time: 10%

EXPENSES
Tuition: $31,000

Room & Board:
$7,500 in-state;
tuition /room + board
$22,280 out-of-state

ADMISSIONS
2233 W Dunlap Ave.
Phoenix, AZ 85021-2859
1-800-474-2479

DEGREE INFORMATION

Major / Degree / Concentration	Enrollment	Requirements for entry	Graduation rate
Interior Design Bachelor of Science	100	2.0 gpa	60%

TOTAL PROGRAM ENROLLMENT
Undergraduate: 100
Graduate: n/a

Male: 5%
Female: 95%

Full-time: 90%
Part-time: 10%

International: Not reported
Minority: Not reported

Job Placement Rate: 80%

SCHOLARSHIPS / FINANCIAL AID
Not reported

TOTAL FACULTY: 10
Full-time: 50%
Part-time: 50%
Online: Not reported

NCIDQ Certified: 20%
Licensed Interior Designers: 20%
LEED Certified: 0%

INTERIOR DESIGN ADMINISTRATION
Not reported

PROFESSIONAL / ACADEMIC AFFILIATIONS
American Society of Interior Designers
International Interior Design Association
Interior Design Educators Council

CIDA ACCREDITATION
Bachelor of Arts (2006, 2012)

PROGRAM DESCRIPTION AND PHILOSOPHY

Students can pursue an Interior Design degree at The Art Institute of Phoenix. Our Interior Design degree program teaches students to take human elements into consideration when designing a space for living. The Interior Design degree program attracts creative individuals who want to improve quality of life through their designs. The Interior Design degree program emphasizes the design process with students developing concepts into functional designs. Interior Design degree students are taught in a hands-on environment with industry-related equipment and technology. The Interior Design degree program teaches traditional and computerized design skills. Course topics in the Interior Design degree program include space planning, textiles, and lighting. Interior Design degree students develop a portfolio to showcase their work to potential employers. Graduates of the Interior Design degree program are prepared to pursue entry-level jobs like Interior Designer, space planner, and draftsperson.

FACILITIES

We start with typical drawing and drafting their first quarter, then move into AutoCAD and REVIT in the first and second year.

ONLINE / DISTANCE LEARNING

There are some gen. ed. classes and ID classes that students can take online.

COURSES OF INSTRUCTION
- Drafting
- Human Factors and psychology of design
- Design Basics—3D
- Architectural Drafting
- Computer-Aided Design
- Design Process
- Introduction to Architecture
- Textiles and Finishes
- Visual Presentation
- Advanced Computer-Aided Design
- History of Furniture Design
- Design Development – Residential Design
- Computer 3D Architectural Modeling
- Codes—Barrier-Free Design
- Fundamentals of Working Drawings
- Design Development – Commercial Design
- Materials and Estimates
- Advanced Residential Design
- Computer Rendering
- History of Modern Architecture and Interior Design
- Corporate Design
- Building Systems and Materials
- Presentation Techniques
- Sustainable Design
- Hospitality Design
- Environmental Systems
- Advanced Construction Documents
- Lighting Design
- Interior and Architectural Detailing
- Health Care / Senior Design
- Graduate Project — Research and Programming
- Furniture Design
- Graduate Project — Design Development
- Graduate Project — Presentation and Defense
- Advanced Professional Development
- Portfolio Preparation

INTERNSHIPS
Required of majors at third year.

STUDY ABROAD
Over the summer quarter students can take classes abroad.

NOTABLE ALUMNI
Not reported

STUDENT ACTIVITIES AND ORGANIZATIONS
Not reported

FACULTY SPECIALIZATIONS/ RESEARCH
Not reported

Collins College

The School of Visual Arts and Design

4750 South 44th Pl., Phoenix AZ 85040 | 888-574-6777 | www.collinscollege.edu/programs/interior-design.asp

UNIVERSITY PROFILE
Private
Urban
Commuter
Quarter Schedule
Co-ed

STUDENT DEMOGRAPHICS
Undergraduate: 1,200
Graduate: 0

Male: 70%
Female: 30%

Full-time: 90%
Part-time: 10%

EXPENSES
Tuition: Not reported
Room & Board: n/a

ADMISSIONS
Collins College
Office of Admissions
4750 South 44th Pl., Phoenix
AZ 85040
888-574-6777

DEGREE INFORMATION

Major / Degree / Concentration	Enrollment	Requirements for entry	Graduation rate
Interior Design Bachelor of Fine Arts	60	Not reported	Not reported

TOTAL PROGRAM ENROLLMENT
Undergraduate: 60
Graduate: 0

Male: 15%
Female: 85%

Full-time: 100%
Part-time: 0%

International: Not reported
Minority: Not reported

Job Placement Rate: Not reported

SCHOLARSHIPS / FINANCIAL AID
Not reported

TOTAL FACULTY: 10
Full-time: 3
Part-time: 7
Online: Not reported

NCIDQ Certified: 3
Licensed Interior Designers: n/a
LEED Certified: 2

INTERIOR DESIGN ADMINISTRATION
Catherine Pliess, ASID, IIDA, IDEC
Department Chair

PROFESSIONAL / ACADEMIC AFFILIATIONS
American Society of Interior Designers
International Interior Design Association
Interior Design Educators Council

PROGRAM DESCRIPTION AND PHILOSOPHY

The Interior Design program at Collins College strives to provide a challenging educational experience committed to offering a supportive academic environment. The program provides opportunity for experiential learning and is guided by the ever-evolving body of knowledge of Interior Design.

Collins College is a creative and supportive community where individuals can immerse themselves in the hands-on development of their personal talent so that they can learn the skills and gain the confidence necessary to make an immediate and meaningful contribution to the creative workplace. The program provides an educational experience structured to prepare students for professional opportunities and career success in the field of Interior Design.

FACILITIES

The new facility Collins College moved into in January 2009 was designed to support instructional activities, program objectives and course goals. Equipment is available for this purpose. Classrooms are outfitted with projectors and computers as needed. A library is onsite with hours to accommodate working schedules. An online CECybrary is also available to all students. The CECybrary is a Web-enabled information center committed to facilitating the lifelong learning and achievement of the student.

For the Interior Design program, space was allocated for a Material Resource Room; this space is organized in the Construction Specification Institute numbering system and offers a fully stocked sample library. The library is maintained by a student assistant and is kept current with industry standard product information. This space also offers computers loaded with the lasted versions of AutoCAD and Adobe Creative Suite, and plotters and scanners needed to complete course assignments.

ONLINE / DISTANCE LEARNING

All our general education courses are offered online or on-ground, the student may select what is more convenient.

COURSES OF INSTRUCTION

Not reported

INTERNSHIPS

Required of majors after the successful completion of 144 credits. Interns are placed at various companies.

STUDY ABROAD

Available, for travel and/or internship

NOTABLE ALUMNI

Not reported

STUDENT ACTIVITIES AND ORGANIZATIONS

The Interior Design department at Collins College has an active student chapter of both the American Society of Interior Designers (ASID) and International Interior Design Association (IIDA). The school also has an active student council supporting several interesting student clubs.

FACULTY SPECIALIZATIONS AND RESEARCH

Not reported

Pima Community College

Interior Design Program

1255 N. Stone, Tucson, AZ 85709 | 520-206-7188 | www.pima.edu/program/interior-design/index.shtml

UNIVERSITY PROFILE
Public
Urban
Commuter
Semester Schedule
Co-ed

STUDENT DEMOGRAPHICS
Undergraduate: 178
Graduate: Not reported

Male: 10%
Female: 90%

Full-time: Not reported
Part-time: Not reported

EXPENSES
Tuition: $54 per credit
Room & Board: n/a

ADMISSIONS
Pima Community College
1255 N. Stone
Tucson, AZ 85709-3030
520-206-4500
gbrown@pima.edu

DEGREE INFORMATION

Major / Degree / Concentration	Enrollment	Requirements for entry	Graduation rate
Interior Design Associate of Applied Science	277	Open enrollment	33%
Interior Design Associate of Arts	277	Open enrollment	67%

TOTAL PROGRAM ENROLLMENT
Undergraduate: Not reported
Graduate: Not reported

Male: 10%
Female: 90%

Full-time: Not reported
Part-time: Not reported

International: 40%
Minority: Not reported

Job Placement Rate: Not reported

SCHOLARSHIPS / FINANCIAL AID
Pell Grants, Student Loans, Scholarships
of various sources

TOTAL FACULTY: 5
Full-time: 1
Part-time: 4
Online: 0

NCIDQ Certified: 4
Licensed Interior Designers: 5
LEED Certified: 1

INTERIOR DESIGN ADMINISTRATION
Gigi Brown, Department Head-Lead
Faculty

PROFESSIONAL / ACADEMIC AFFILIATIONS
American Society of Interior Designers
Interior Design Educators Council

PROGRAM DESCRIPTION AND PHILOSOPHY

We are a community college. The success of our students is our most important goal. Our program will continue to be a valued, innovative, and exciting career choice that will provide a much-needed and resourceful profession to the community.

FACILITIES

We have the latest software (Auto-CAD, Revit, Sketch-up, etc.) and 24 laptops in classrooms, along with many computer labs with all the latest editions of software.

ONLINE / DISTANCE LEARNING

Not available

COURSES OF INSTRUCTION

- Fundamental of Interior Design
- Visual Communications I &II
- Space planning I&II
- Color and Lighting
- History of Architecture &Interior Design I&II
- Matrials and Methods
- Business of Interior Design
- Enviornonmental Factors
- Textiles

INTERNSHIPS

Not required

STUDY ABROAD

EF tours and Go Ahead

NOTABLE ALUMNI

Not reported

STUDENT ACTIVITIES AND ORGANIZATIONS

American Society of Interior Designers, International Interior Design Association

FACULTY SPECIALIZATIONS AND RESEARCH

designing sacred spaces

COMMUNITY COLLEGE TRANSFERS

2+2 with Nothern Arizona University in Flagstaff, AZ

Academy of Art University

School of Interior Architecture & Design

79 New Montgomery, San Francisco, CA 94105 | 800-544-2787 | www.academyart.edu

UNIVERSITY PROFILE
Private
Urban
Residential & Commuter
Semester Schedule
Co-ed

STUDENT DEMOGRAPHICS
Undergraduate: 11,227
Graduate: 4,963

Male: 47%
Female: 53%

Full-time: 57%
Part-time: 43%

EXPENSES
Annual Tuition: $17,760
Room & Board: $13,500

ADMISSIONS
79 New Montgomery
San Francisco, CA 94105-3410
800-544-2787 or 415-274-2200
admissions@academyart.edu

DEGREE INFORMATION

Major / Degree / Concentration	Enrollment	Requirements for entry	Graduation rate
Interior Architecture & Design **Bachelor of Fine Arts**	910	Open enrollment policy*	Not reported
Interior Architecture & Design **Master of Fine Arts**	313	Open enrollment policy*	Not reported

* Academy of Art University requires all students in degree-seeking programs to have a high school diploma, a GED, or may be admitted by passing a Department of Education-`approved "ability to benefit" test if beyond the age of compulsory attendance.

TOTAL PROGRAM ENROLLMENT
Undergraduate: 910
Graduate: 313

Male: 22%
Female: 78%

Full-time: 53%
Part-time: 47%

International: 24%
Minority: 14%

Job Placement Rate: Not reported

SCHOLARSHIPS / FINANCIAL AID
Academy of Art University offers financial-aid packages consisting of grants, loans, and work-study to eligible students with a demonstrated need. Explore which aid packages are available to you to help make your dreams come true, options include: federal and state aid, Federal Work Study, Veterans Affairs/ Yellow Ribbon education benefits, private lenders' loans, scholarships, and tax credits. Low-interest loans are available to all eligible students, regardless of need.

Students Receiving Scholarships or Financial Aid: 56%

TOTAL FACULTY: 68
Full-time: 3%
Part-time: 97%
Online: 46%

NCIDQ Certified: Not reported
Licensed Interior Designers: Not reported
LEED Certified: Not reported

INTERIOR DESIGN ADMINISTRATION
Francesca Garcia-Marques, Director
Ken Frieders, Associate Director
Sharon Robertson, Associate Online Director
Ann Gaffney, Associate Directory Student Services/Academic Advisor
Laura Blumenfeld, Online Coordinator
Chris Becker, Lab Supervisor
Nancy Wong, Department Administrator

PROFESSIONAL / ACADEMIC AFFILIATIONS
American Society of Interior Designers
International Interior Design Association
Western Association of Schools and Colleges
National Association of Schools of Art and Design

CIDA ACCREDITATION
Bachelor of Fine Arts in Interior Architecture and Design (2008, 2014)

PROGRAM DESCRIPTION AND PHILOSOPHY

The program focus is to educate professional designers to go on to be certified designers. The department produces the very best Interior Designers to go on to design anything for anyone in the built environment: retail, residential, commercial, hospitality, etc. Our faculty is made up of working professionals who are NCICQ-certified and registered architects, as well as talented technicians in 3D design. Our CIDA-accredited program has been noted as "setting a new bar for the industry."

FACILITIES

A dedicated materials library, state-of-the-art computer studio, printing labs, wireless kiosk stations, open studio spaces, an exhibition space and presentation hall

ONLINE / DISTANCE LEARNING

The online School of Interior Architecture and Design currently offers Master of Fine Arts, Bachelor of Fine Arts, and Associate of Arts degree programs. The Interior Architecture & Design program integrates theory, design and technology in tandem with industry standards. Students thus develop the requisite intellectual, artistic, and ethical abilities necessary for professional practice.

Students are encouraged to achieve a balance between mastery of design skills and creativity, which will lead to innovative thinking about our inner and outer environment. Concern for spatial issues, design innovation, and attention to detail are emphasized under the direction of a faculty of professional experts. Final projects involve each student's personal interests and demonstrate an energetic and professional approach.

COURSES OF INSTRUCTION

- Conceptual Design
- Introduction to Construction Documents
- Perspective Drawing Techniques
- Materials
- Computer-Aided Drafting
- Senior Studio
- Interior Architecture & Design A & B
- Modelmaking
- Survey of Traditional/ Contemporary/Bay Area Architecture
- Building Construction
- 3D Modeling for IAD on the PC
- Advanced 3D Concepts
- Introduction to Lighting Design
- The Golden Section & Sacred Geometry
- Advanced Quick Sketch
- Portfolio Preparation
- Professional Practices
- Digital Imaging
- Spatial Design
- Sustainable Design
- Model Design Studio

INTERNSHIPS

Not Required. The University works with international brands and recruitment agencies on internships and job placement. Graduates have gone on to companies such as Anshen + Allen, Architecture International, Babey Moulton Jue & Booth, Backen Gillam Architects, Brayton Hughes Design Studios, Crate & Barrel, Ellerbe Becket, Inc., FME Architecture + Design, Hart Howerton, Hirsch Bedner Associates, Kishimoto Gordon Dalaya PC, Architecture Planning Interiors, KWID, Masco Contractor Services, LLC, MBH Architects, Paul Jones Architects Ltd., Saida + Sullivan Design Partners, Walter E. Smithe Custom Furniture, and Your Space Interiors.

STUDY ABROAD

Not available

NOTABLE ALUMNI

Gioi Tran, Barbara Barry, Honorary Doctorate Awarded to Orlando Diaz-Azcuy

STUDENT ACTIVITIES AND ORGANIZATIONS

International Interior Design Association, American Society of Itnerior Designers, American Institute of Architects

FACULTY SPECIALIZATIONS AND RESEARCH

Francesca Garcia-Marques, Director of Interior Architecture & Design, brings over 20 years of experience in the fields of interior architecture and Interior Design, exhibition curating and design, graphic design, and brand image design. Since 1995, Francesca has chaired the annual Masters of Architecture Lecture Series, presented by the American Institute of Architects in partnership with the Los Angeles County Museum of Art's Education Department. She has had over 60 articles on architecture, art and design published nationally and internationally in reviews such as *L'Arca, Casa Vogue, Domus* and *Progressive Architecture*.

American River College

Fine and Applied Arts Area

4700 College Oak Dr., Sacramento, CA 95841 | 916-484-8433 | www.arc.losrios.edu/Programs_of_Study/FAA.htm

UNIVERSITY PROFILE
Public
Suburban
Commuter
Semester Schedule
Co-ed

STUDENT DEMOGRAPHICS
Undergraduate: 41,627
Graduate: 0

Male: 48.68%
Female: 51.32%

Full-time: 37.25%
Part-time: 62.75%

EXPENSES
http://losrios.edu/lrc/lrc_
feepay.php

ADMISSIONS
4700 College Oak Dr.
Sacramento, CA 95841
916-484-8261
recadmis@arc.losrios.edu

DEGREE INFORMATION

Major / Degree / Concentration	Enrollment	Requirements for entry	Graduation rate
Interior Design Associate of Arts	Not reported	Not reported	Not reported
Para-Professional Interior Design Assistant Certificate	Not reported	Not reported	Not reported
Interior Retail Merchandising Certificate	Not reported	Not reported	Not reported
Kitchen and Bath Design Certificate* *NKBA accredited	Not reported	Not reported	Not reported

TOTAL PROGRAM ENROLLMENT
Undergraduate: 650
Graduate: 0

Male: 10%
Female: 90%

Full-time: 40%
Part-time: 60%

International: n/a
Minority: 25%

Job Placement Rate: Not reported

SCHOLARSHIPS / FINANCIAL AID
Scholarship information is available through our Financial Aid office: www.arc.losrios.edu/Support_Services/Financial_Aid.htm

TOTAL FACULTY: 7
Full-time: 28%
Part-time: 72%

NCIDQ Certified: 50%
Licensed Interior Designers: 50%
LEED Certified: 0%

INTERIOR DESIGN ADMINISTRATION
Dr. David Newnham, Dean
David Viar, President

PROFESSIONAL / ACADEMIC AFFILIATIONS
Not reported

PROGRAM DESCRIPTION AND PHILOSOPHY

Our program provides a foundation of education and skills for students in the expanding field of Interior Design. Topics include space planning, building and life-safety codes, and the Americans with Disabilities Act (ADA). Additionally, it covers reading construction documents, and architectural and furniture history.

FACILITIES

Design studio equipped with technology tools. Computer labs, learning resource center, library and extensive student support services: www.arc.losrios.edu/Support_Services/Academic_Support_Services.htm

ONLINE / DISTANCE LEARNING

Not reported

COURSES OF INSTRUCTION

- Design: Fundamentals
- Textiles
- Fundamentals of Interior Design
- History of Interior Architecture and Furnishings I
- History of Interior Architecture and Furnishings II
- Materials of Interior Design
- Interior Design Business Practices
- Interior Design Sales
- Beginning Interior Design Studio
- Interior Illustration and Rendering
- Interior Environment and Space Planning
- Beginning CADD for Interior Design
- Intermediate CADD for Interior Design
- Codes and Universal Access for Interior Design
- Codes and Universal Access Lab
- Reading Construction Documents

INTERNSHIPS

Required of majors

STUDY ABROAD

Not available

NOTABLE ALUMNI

Not reported

STUDENT ACTIVITIES AND ORGANIZATIONS

Information available at our Campus Life Web site: www.arc.losrios.edu/x2218.xml

FACULTY SPECIALIZATIONS AND RESEARCH

Not reported

COMMUNITY COLLEGE TRANSFERS

This information is available through our Transfer Services Web site: www.arc.losrios.edu/Support_Services/Transfer_Center.htm

The Art Institute of California–Inland Empire

Interior Design Department

674 E. Brier Dr., San Bernardino, CA 92408 | 909-915-2100 | www.artinstitutes.edu/inland-empire

UNIVERSITY PROFILE
Private
Suburban
Commuter
Quarter Schedule
Co-ed

STUDENT DEMOGRAPHICS
Undergraduate: 1,400
Graduate: Not reported

Male: 43%
Female: 57%

Full-time: Not reported
Part-time: Not reported

EXPENSES
Tuition: Not reported
Room & Board: Not reported

ADMISSIONS
674 E. Brier Dr.
San Bernardino, CA 92408
909-915-2100

DEGREE INFORMATION

Major / Degree / Concentration	Enrollment	Requirements for entry	Graduation rate
Interior Design Bachelor of Science	92	Not reported	Not reported

TOTAL PROGRAM ENROLLMENT
Undergraduate: 92
Graduate: n/a

Male: Not reported
Female: Not reported

Full-time: Not reported
Part-time: Not reported

International: Not reported
Minority: Not reported

Job Placement Rate: Not reported

SCHOLARSHIPS / FINANCIAL AID
Not reported

TOTAL FACULTY: 6
Full-time: 75%
Part-time: 25%
Online: n/a

NCIDQ Certified: Not reported
Licensed Interior Designers: 2
LEED Certified: 1

INTERIOR DESIGN ADMINISTRATION
Emam El Hout - President
Jonathan DeAscentis - Dean of Academic Affairs
Sara Sandoval - Academic Director - Interior Design

PROFESSIONAL / ACADEMIC AFFILIATIONS
American Society of Interior Designers
Interior Design Educators Council

PROGRAM DESCRIPTION AND PHILOSOPHY

Today's professional Interior Designers enhance the function and quality of interior environments. Their mission, significant in today's society, is to design spaces that improve the quality of life, protect the health, safety, and welfare of the public, and support increased productivity. The Interior Design Bachelor of Science degree program offers a well-rounded curriculum strengthened with numerous computer-based courses, preparing graduates to meet the current demands of the profession.

Other important topics explored include the areas of universal design, human factors, environmental and sustainable design, business aspects of the profession, and other issues related to the Interior Design field.

The Interior Design program begins with a foundation in art and design to increase artistic sensitivity. The program is designed to emphasize the areas of drafting, space planning, history of Interior Design, materials, lighting, and residential and contract/commercial design. Courses cover two-dimensional and three-dimensional computer-aided design, computer rendering, three-dimensional modeling, and architectural detailing/working drawing methods of presenting design ideas and communicating with related professional services. The analysis of client needs and desires to create design solutions that are aesthetically pleasing, functional, and in accordance with building codes and standards, is the essence of the Interior Design program.

GRADUATION REQUIREMENTS

To receive a Bachelor of Science degree in Interior Design, students must: receive a passing grade or credit for all required coursework; earn a minimum of 192 quarter credits; achieve a cumulative gpa of 2.0 or higher; meet portfolio or other requirements as outlined by the program; and satisfy all financial obligations to The Art Institute.

FACILITIES

Not reported

ONLINE / DISTANCE LEARNING

Not available

COURSES OF INSTRUCTION

- Fundamentals/Observational Drawing
- Fundamentals of Design
- Color Theory
- Computer Applications
- Drawing, Proportion, & Perspective
- Image Manipulation
- Career Development
- Portfolio II
- Basic Drafting
- Introduction to Interior Design
- Architectural Drafting
- Introduction to AutoCAD
- Programming & Space Planning I
- Design Basics 3D
- Architecture, Interiors & Furniture—Ancient to 1830
- Intermediate AutoCAD
- Programming & Space Planning II
- Perspective & Rendering
- Architecture, Interiors & Furniture—1830 to Present
- Architectural Detailing—AutoCAD
- Residential Design—Traditional
- Presentation Techniques
- Interior Design Sketch Techniques
- Human Factors
- Corporate Design
- Lighting Design
- Textiles
- Residential Design—Contemporary
- Construction Documents & Details I
- Materials & Specifications
- Interior Design Computer 3D Modeling
- Advanced Corporate Design
- Building Construction & Systems
- Building Codes & Regulations
- Interior Design Digital Camera & Lighting Techniques
- Institutional Design
- Commercial/Hospitality Design
- Construction Documents & Details II
- Senior Design—Studio (Healthcare, Retail, Hospitality)
- Thesis—Programming
- Business Management for Interior Designers
- Portfolio Preparation
- Thesis—Design
- Thesis—Presentation

INTERNSHIPS

Required after 9th Quarter

STUDY ABROAD

Available

NOTABLE ALUMNI

Not reported

STUDENT ACTIVITIES AND ORGANIZATIONS

Not reported

FACULTY SPECIALIZATIONS AND RESEARCH

Not reported

The Art Institute of California–Orange County

Interior Design Department

3601 W. Sunflower Ave., Santa Ana, CA 92704 | 714-830-0200 | www.artinstitutes.edu/orange-county/

UNIVERSITY PROFILE
Private
Suburban
Residential & Commuter
Quarter Schedule
Co-ed

STUDENT DEMOGRAPHICS
Undergraduate: 1,864
Graduate: 0

Male: Not reported
Female: Not reported

Full-time: Not reported
Part-time: Not reported

EXPENSES
Tuition: $30,000
Room & Board: $14,000

ADMISSIONS
3601 W. Sunflower Ave.
Santa Ana, CA 92704
714-830-0200
aicaocadm@aii.edu

DEGREE INFORMATION

Major / Degree / Concentration	Enrollment	Requirements for entry	Graduation rate
Interior Design Bachelor of Science	115	Application and interview	80%

TOTAL PROGRAM ENROLLMENT
Undergraduate: 115
Graduate: 0

Male: 11%
Female: 89%

Full-time: 56%
Part-time: 44%

International: 6%
Minority: 12%

Job Placement Rate: Not reported

SCHOLARSHIPS / FINANCIAL AID
The Art Institute of CA-Orange County has Student Financial Services to help students and their families develop a financial plan to ensure program completion. Specialists from this department help students complete applications for grants and loans applicable to students' circumstances. Once a student's eligibility is determined, the student and the specialist develop a plan for meeting educational expenses. Various loans are available to assist with educational costs as well as scholarships and grants.

Students Receiving Scholarships or Financial Aid: 80%

TOTAL FACULTY: 8
Full-time: 90%
Part-time: 10%
Online: 0%

NCIDQ Certified: 50%
Licensed Interior Designers: 20%
LEED Certified: 40%

INTERIOR DESIGN ADMINISTRATION
Ronni Whitman, IDEC, IIDA, ASID, NEWH-Academic Department Director, Interior Design

PROFESSIONAL / ACADEMIC AFFILIATIONS
American Society of Interior Designers
International Interior Design Association
Interior Design Educators Council

CIDA ACCREDITATION
Bachelor of Science in Interior Design (2009, 2015)

PROGRAM DESCRIPTION AND PHILOSOPHY

Our philosophy is based on the belief that the profession of Interior Design is a multifaceted discipline that combines art and design, science, technology, regulatory issues, ethics, historical references, psychology and sociology. These disciplines help students create interior spaces that enhance life, facilitate functional activity and support client objectives while protecting the health, safety, and welfare of the public. It is also our belief that it is the designer's responsibility to make every effort to advance the practice of environmental sustainabilty and advocate for socially responsible design and involvement. Learning-centered teaching methods focus on intellectual growth and the acquisition of career-specific competencies help students learn to create design solutions with multiple agendas: functional, aesthetic, economic, and regulatory.

Our mission is to prepare students for a variety of entry-level positions in the Interior Design field and to function as trained professionals able to conceive and develop viable, creative design solutions within the interior environment. Students focus on improving quality of life, increasing productivity, protecting the health, safety, and welfare of the public and meeting the challenges and demands of the Interior Design profession.

FACILITIES

Design Studios, computer labs, emerging technology, resource library, Getty Images, Industrial Design lab, and wireless Internet access in all campus buildings.

ONLINE / DISTANCE LEARNING

Courses are offered online through our sister school, The Art Institute On-Line.

COURSES OF INSTRUCTION

- Basic Drafting
- CAD
- Space Planning and Programming I and II
- Residential Design
- Corporate and Advanced Corporate Design
- Commercial and Hospitality Design
- Retail Design
- Institutional Design
- Codes and Regulations
- Building Construction and Systems
- Sustainable Design
- Business Practices
- Thesis Programming
- Thesis Design and Thesis Presentation

INTERNSHIPS

Required of majors at 10th quarter.

Placement:
- HKS
- H.Hendy and Assoc.
- Gettys Design
- Taylor
- Kelly Wearstler Interior Design
- Ziccardi Design Assoc.
- WestGroup
- Ware Malcolm
- Schlemmer Algarzie Assoc.
- Hatch Design
- Cadiz Design
- RS Studio

STUDY ABROAD

Quarter and shorter programs through Art Institute Consortium

NOTABLE ALUMNI

Not reported

STUDENT ACTIVITIES AND ORGANIZATIONS

Interior Design Club includes: ASID Student chapter, IIDA Student Center, Emerging Green Builders (EGB) chapter

FACULTY SPECIALIZATIONS AND RESEARCH

Institutional Design, Hospitality Design, Corporate Design, Residentail Design, LEED

The Art Institute of California–San Diego

Interior Design Department

7650 Mission Valley Rd., San Diego, CA 92108 | 858-598-1284 | www.artinstitutes.edu/sandiego

UNIVERSITY PROFILE
Private
Urban
Commuter
Quarter Schedule
Co-ed

STUDENT DEMOGRAPHICS
Undergraduate: Not reported
Graduate: Not reported

Male: Not reported
Female: Not reported

Full-time: Not reported
Part-time: Not reported

EXPENSES
Tuition: $30,000
Room & Board: n/a

ADMISSIONS
7650 Mission Valley Rd.
San Diego, CA 92108
858-598-1228
www.artinstitutes.edu/sandiego

DEGREE INFORMATION

Major / Degree / Concentration	Enrollment	Requirements for entry	Graduation rate
Interior Design Bachelor of Science	200	Application and interview	90%

TOTAL PROGRAM ENROLLMENT
Undergraduate: 200
Graduate: 0

Male: 20%
Female: 80%

Full-time: 80%
Part-time: 20%

International: 5%
Minority: 30%

Job Placement Rate: 85%

SCHOLARSHIPS / FINANCIAL AID
The Art Institute of CA - San Diego has Student Financial Services to help students and their families develop a financial plan to ensure program completion. Specialists from this department help students complete applications for grants and loans applicable to students' circumstances. Once a student's eligibility is determined, the student and the specialist develop a plan for meeting educational expenses. Various loans are available to assist with educational costs as well as scholarships and grants.

Students Receiving Scholarships or Financial Aid: 90%

TOTAL FACULTY: 10
Full-time: 7
Part-time: 5
Online: n/a

NCIDQ Certified: 75%
Licensed Interior Designers: 20%
LEED Certified: 10%

INTERIOR DESIGN ADMINISTRATION
Tricia Murray, M.Ed., ASID, IIDA, IDEC
Academic Director of Interior Design

PROFESSIONAL / ACADEMIC AFFILIATIONS
American Society of Interior Designers
International Interior Design Association
Interior Design Educators Council

PROGRAM DESCRIPTION AND PHILOSOPHY

Students can pursue an Interior Design degree at The Art Institute of California - San Diego. Our Interior Design degree program teaches students to take human elements into consideration when designing a space for living. The Interior Design degree program attracts creative individuals who want to improve quality of life through their designs. The Interior Design degree program emphasizes the design process with students developing concepts into functional designs. Interior Design degree students are taught in a hands-on environment with industry-related equipment and technology. The Interior Design degree program teaches traditional and computerized design skills. Course topics in the Interior Design degree program include space planning, textiles, and lighting. Interior Design degree students develop a portfolio to showcase their work to potential employers. Graduates of the Interior Design degree program are prepared to pursue entry-level jobs like Interior Designer, space planner, and draftsperson.

FACILITIES

- Computer Labs
- Drafting Lab
- Interior Design Resource Library-Materials Room
- Full Scale plotters, scanners, and printers on campus
- Wireless Internet Access throughout campus
- Student lounge with cafe

ONLINE / DISTANCE LEARNING

Not reported

COURSES OF INSTRUCTION

- Space Planning I & II
- Residential Design
- Corporate Design
- Institutional Design
- Commercial Design
- Hospitality Design
- Lighting Design
- Building Codes
- AutoCAD
- Construction Documents and Detailing

INTERNSHIPS

Available in 10th/11th quarter, but not required.

Interns are placed in both commercial and residential design firms; Carrier-Johnson, Gensler, Red Cashew, Hester Interiors, Young and Company, Aesthetics, Inc., Frazee Paints, etc.

STUDY ABROAD

Not available at this time, but planned for the future.

NOTABLE ALUMNI

Not reported

STUDENT ACTIVITIES AND ORGANIZATIONS

Weekly campus activities for all programs, American Society of Interior Designers Student Chapter

FACULTY SPECIALIZATIONS AND RESEARCH

Faculty possess a wide range of professional experience in various areas of commercial design, residential design, architecture, LEED projects-sustainable design, industrial arts design, etc.

The Art Institute of California–San Francisco

Interior Design Department

1170 Market St., San Francisco, CA 94102 | 1-888-493-3261 | www.artinstitutes.edu/sanfrancisco/

UNIVERSITY PROFILE
Private
Urban
Residential & Commuter
Quarter Schedule
Co-ed

STUDENT DEMOGRAPHICS
Undergraduate: Not reported
Graduate: Not reported

Male: Not reported
Female: Not reported

Full-time: Not reported
Part-time: Not reported

EXPENSES
Tuition: $30,000
Room & Board: $14,000

ADMISSIONS
1170 Market St.
San Francisco, CA 94102
415-865-0198
aicasfadm@aii.edu

DEGREE INFORMATION

Major / Degree / Concentration	Enrollment	Requirements for entry	Graduation rate
Interior Design Bachelor of Science	100	Application and interview	90%

TOTAL PROGRAM ENROLLMENT
Undergraduate: 100
Graduate: 0

Male: 40%
Female: 60%

Full-time: 80%
Part-time: 20%

International: 2%
Minority: 50%

Job Placement Rate: 90%

SCHOLARSHIPS / FINANCIAL AID
The Art Institute of CA - San Francisco
has Student Financial Services to help
students and their families develop
a financial plan to ensure program
completion. Specialists from this
department help students complete
applications for grants and loans
applicable to students' circumstances.
Once a student's eligibility is
determined, the student and the
specialist develop a plan for meeting
educational expenses. Various loans are
available to assist with educational costs
as well as scholarships and grants.

Students Receiving Scholarships or
Financial Aid: 90%

TOTAL FACULTY: 14
Full-time: 10%
Part-time: 90%
Online: n/a

NCIDQ Certified: 50%
Licensed Interior Designers: 80%
LEED Certified: 80%

INTERIOR DESIGN ADMINISTRATION
Jeff Nokkeo, Assoc. IIDA - Academic
Department Director - Interior Design

**PROFESSIONAL / ACADEMIC
AFFILIATIONS**
American Society of Interior Designers
International Interior Design Association
Interior Design Educators Council

PROGRAM DESCRIPTION AND PHILOSOPHY

Students can pursue an Interior Design degree at The Art Institute of California - San Francisco. Our Interior Design degree program teaches students to take human elements into consideration when designing a space for living. The Interior Design degree program attracts creative individuals who want to improve quality of life through their designs. The Interior Design degree program emphasizes the design process with students developing concepts into functional designs. Interior Design degree students are taught in a hands-on environment with industry-related equipment and technology. The Interior Design degree program teaches traditional and computerized design skills. Course topics in the Interior Design degree program include space planning, textiles, and lighting. Interior Design degree students develop a portfolio to showcase their work to potential employers. Graduates of the Interior Design degree program are prepared to pursue entry-level jobs like Interior Designer, space planner, and draftsperson.

FACILITIES
- Computer Labs
- Drafting Labs
- Lighitng Labs
- Materials Room
- Museums a few blocks away (SF Moma, Asian Art Museum, Yerba Buena , MoAD, to name a few)
- Full Scale plotters and printers on campus
- Wireless Internet Access throughout campus

ONLINE / DISTANCE LEARNING
Not reported

COURSES OF INSTRUCTION
- Residential Design
- Corporate Design
- Institutional Design
- Commercial Design
- Hospitality Design
- Retail Design
- Sustainable Design
- Lighting Design
- Building Codes
- Construction Documents and Detailing

INTERNSHIPS
Required of majors at 8th quarter. Students are typically placed at Gary Hutton Design, ASID Office, Donghia, and Gensler.

STUDY ABROAD
Twice a year, there is a study abroad opportunity that Interior Design students may elect to participate in.

NOTABLE ALUMNI
Not reported

STUDENT ACTIVITIES AND ORGANIZATIONS
Student-lead Interior Design Club

FACULTY SPECIALIZATIONS AND RESEARCH
Sustainable Design Focus for many faculty, incorporating sustainable and green design into all classes.

California State University, Sacramento

Department of Design, College of Arts & Letters

6000 J St., Sacramento, CA 95819 | 916-278-3962 | www.al.csus.edu/design/intd.html

UNIVERSITY PROFILE
Public
Urban
Commuter
Semester Schedule
Co-ed

STUDENT DEMOGRAPHICS
Undergraduate: 24,388
Graduate: 4,853

Male: 41%
Female: 59%

Full-time: 77%
Part-time: 23%

EXPENSES
Tuition: $4,026 (in-state)
$15,186 (out-of-state)
Room & Board: $9,472

ADMISSIONS
6000 J St.
Sacramento, CA 95819
916 278-7766
outreach@csus.edu

DEGREE INFORMATION

Major / Degree / Concentration	Enrollment	Requirements for entry	Graduation rate
Interior Design Bachelor of Science Interior Architecture	Not reported	A minimum grade of "C" is required in all lower + upper division courses. Portfolio Reviews occur once a year during Spring Semester and are required for students to take upper-division classes in the Interior Architecture concentration.	Not reported
Interior Design Certificate	Not reported	A minimum grade of "C" is required in all lower + upper division courses. Portfolio Reviews occur once a year during Spring Semester.	Not reported

TOTAL PROGRAM ENROLLMENT
Undergraduate: Not reported
Graduate: Not reported

Male: Not reported
Female: Not reported

Full-time: Not reported
Part-time: Not reported

International: Not reported
Minority: Not reported

Job Placement Rate: Not reported

SCHOLARSHIPS / FINANCIAL AID
Not reported

TOTAL FACULTY: 4
Full-time: Not reported
Part-time: Not reported
Online: Not reported

NCIDQ Certified: Not reported
Licensed Interior Designers: Not reported
LEED Certified: Not reported

INTERIOR DESIGN ADMINISTRATION
Sharmon Goff, Associate Professor, Department of Design Chair
Andrew Anker, Professor, Interior Design Program Coordinator

PROFESSIONAL / ACADEMIC AFFILIATIONS
American Society of Interior Designers
International Interior Design Association
Interior Design Educators Council
Environmental Design Research Association

CIDA ACCREDITATION
Bachelor of Arts Interior Design (2004, 2010)

PROGRAM DESCRIPTION AND PHILOSOPHY

The Interior Design Program at California State University, Sacramento has a regional reputation as a leading design school, and is recognized as a nationally-accredited program. The four-year program leads to a Bachelor of Arts degree in Interior Design and offers two concentrations: Interior Architecture and Interior Design Marketing.

The Interior Design Program provides students with the technical, creative, and critical thinking skills needed to enter the Interior Design profession. The breadth of courses in the program reflects the importance of both a liberal arts background and professional preparation in the design field. Courses encompass the study of design history and theory, aesthetics, graphics, lighting, space planning, computer-aided design, interior construction, and professional practice. The Interior Design curriculum provides comprehensive coverage in all the major areas of training, including concept development, design, communication, presentation, construction, and professional services. Many of the course assignments are based on actual design projects. Guest lecturers and professional panel critiques and discussions as well as building tours of outstanding projects are all important parts of the curriculum. Community service projects also help to maintain a strong connection to the community and profession.

The Interior Design major at California State University, Sacramento is one of the most highly sought after programs in Northern California and is considered an impacted program within the CSU system. As such, students entering the program are initially classified as Pre-Interior Design Majors. After completing the required lower division prerequisites, students may apply for admission to the upper division program by declaring their concentration in either Interior Architecture or Interior Design Marketing. Admission to the Interior Architecture concentration is limited and controlled by an annual portfolio review. Students interested in this concentration must submit a supplementary application including a portfolio of work.

FACILITIES
Not reported

ONLINE / DISTANCE LEARNING
Not reported

COURSES OF INSTRUCTION
- Introduction to Digital Design
- Visual Basics
- Introduction to Interior Design
- Design
- Design Fundamentals
- Introduction to Computer Aided Design
- Digital Imaging
- Art in the Western World: From Stone Age to End of Middle Ages
- Art in the Western Word: From Renaissance to Present
- History of Graphic Design
- Photography, a Social History
- Survey of Western Architecture and Interiors
- Interior Design Graphics I
- Interior Design Studio I
- Professional Practice I
- Interior Design Graphics II
- Interior Design Studio II
- Professional Practice II
- Interior Design Graphics III
- Interior Design Studio III
- Professional Practice III
- Interior Design Graphics IV
- Interior Design Studio IV
- Professional Practice IV—Internship
- American Design
- Asian Design
- Principles of House Design
- Film/Design

INTERNSHIPS
Required of majors at upper division. The internship program places students in professional organizations ranging from architecture and Interior Design firms to furniture companies, corporations, and government agencies.

STUDY ABROAD
Design and Architecture in Italy Travel Study Program: Trip participants will live in the city of canals, in fully equipped four-star apartments in the heart of the old city. Our apartments are within easy walking distance of the Rialto Bridge, San Marco, and other famous sites, but as we walk the streets, shop in the markets, and visit churches and palaces, we will also experience the Venice that tourists do not usually see. In addition to visiting the great works of Renaissance and Modern masters such as Palladio and Carlo Scarpa, students will learn about the history of the unique city. Our tour of Venice will be complemented by three full day excursions through the Veneto region that will include stops in Verona, Asolo, a Palladian villas tour and a day trip to the city of Vicenza.

NOTABLE ALUMNI
Not reported

STUDENT ACTIVITIES AND ORGANIZATIONS
The Interior Design program at Sacramento State has an active student club (PRINTS) representing the American Society of Interior Designers (ASID) and the International Interior Design Association (IIDA). Monthly meetings feature guest speakers from the professional community and include workshops and field trip events.

FACULTY SPECIALIZATIONS AND RESEARCH
Not reported

Cañada College

Interior Design Department

Bldg. 13-105, 4200 Farm Hill Blvd., Redwood City, CA 94061 | 650-306-3451 | http://canadacollege.edu/

UNIVERSITY PROFILE
Public
Suburban
Commuter
Semester Schedule
Co-ed

STUDENT DEMOGRAPHICS
Undergraduate: 6,000
Graduate: n/a

Male: 45%
Female: 55%

Full-time: 33%
Part-time: 67%

EXPENSES
Tuition: $26 per unit
   (resident); $208 per unit
   (non-resident)
Room & Board: n/a

ADMISSIONS
Admissions and Records
Office
Cañada College
4200 Farm Hill Blvd.
Redwood City , CA 94061
650-306-3226 (voice)
canadaadmissions@smccd
.edu

DEGREE INFORMATION

Major / Degree / Concentration	Enrollment	Requirements for entry	Graduation rate
Interior Design Associate of Arts	Not reported	Open enrollment	80%
Interior Design Certificate	Not reported	Open enrollment	80%
Residential & Commercial Design Certificate	Not reported	Open enrollment	80%
Kitchen & Bath Design Certificate* *NKBA accredited	Not reported	Open enrollment	80%
Green/Sustainable Design Certificate	Not reported	Open enrollment	80%
Re-design & Home Staging Certificate	Not reported	Open enrollment	80%

TOTAL PROGRAM ENROLLMENT
Undergraduate: 300
Graduate: n/a

Male: 12%
Female: 88%

Full-time: 25%
Part-time: 75%

International: 10%
Minority: 33%

Job Placement Rate: Approximately 75%, of those actually seeking employment in the field, highest among kitchen & bath design graduates; a majority of the graduates start or already have their own businesses.

SCHOLARSHIPS / FINANCIAL AID
See opposite page for more info

TOTAL FACULTY: 13
Full-time: 7%
Part-time: 93%
Online: 0%

NCIDQ Certified: 15%
Licensed Interior Designers: 30%
LEED Certified: 0%

INTERIOR DESIGN ADMINISTRATION
Nancy Wolford, Ph. D., Interior Design Program Coordinator & Professor
Linda Hayes, Dean, Business, Workforce, & Athletics
Sarah Perkins, Ph.D., Vice President of Instruction

PROFESSIONAL / ACADEMIC AFFILIATIONS
American Society of Interior Designers
International Interior Design Association
Interior Design Educators Council

PROGRAM DESCRIPTION AND PHILOSOPHY

The Cañada College program provides a solid foundation in Interior Design concepts and processes with opportunities for practical, hands-on project learning experiences, preparing students to directly enter the field or transfer to obtain a 4-year degree. It is well-known and highly respected for its certificate programs in Kitchen and Bath Design (NKBA Accredited Program — the first community college in the nation to receive this), Interior Design, and Green/Sustainable Design (the first regular academic program certificate in California). The Cañada program was one of the first Community College Interior Design programs in California (started more than 40 years ago), serving as a model for other programs in the state and region.

FACILITIES

Computer lab, smart classroom technology, extensive resource library, open studios, display space

ONLINE / DISTANCE LEARNING

Not at this time

COURSES OF INSTRUCTION

- Interior Architectural Drafting
- Introduction to Interior Design
- Color and Design
- Residential Design
- History of Interiors I & II
- Presentation Techniques I & II
- Professional Practices
- AutoCAD
- Lighting Design
- Residential & Commercial Construction
- Kitchen Design
- Bath Design
- Materials & Finishes
- Green/Sustainable Design

INTERNSHIPS

Required of majors. Required for Kitchen & Bath, Green/Sustainable Design, after completion of at least 12 units of Interior Design course work, recommended for all others. Interns are placed at various small design firms, mostly in the area of kitchen & bath, residential/small commercial design firms, design/build firms, sustainable/green design firms and suppliers, product retail and wholesale showrooms.

STUDY ABROAD

Not available

NOTABLE ALUMNI

Graduates are award-winning designers and leaders of local ASID & NKBA chapters as well as the national organizations.

STUDENT ACTIVITIES AND ORGANIZATIONS

Active student Interior Design club associated with ASID and NKBA national and local chapters, mentoring, networking, resource development, design competitions. Availability and close proximity of the San Francisco Design Center and the annual regional Interior Design Student Career Forum. Opportunities to work on real projects, both within the college and district, but also the community.

FACULTY SPECIALIZATIONS AND RESEARCH

Universal Design, Sustainable/Green Design, Color, History of Interiors, Kitchen and Bath Design

COMMUNITY COLLEGE TRANSFERS

Articulation with two local 4-year universities, San Francisco State and San Jose State Universities, for transfer to upper division program. We also have a unique agreement with the department at San Francisco State for students completing 31 semester units of required undergraduate courses at Cañada College and who already have a Bachelor's degree (about 50% of our students), to apply directly into their Master's degree program.

SCHOLARSHIPS / FINANCIAL AID

Student loans, BOG (Board of Governor's) tuition waivers for low income students, loans, grants and scholarships, both through the college, national, regional, and local organizations, several are Interior Design and college specific.

Students Receiving Scholarships or Financial Aid: 15%

Chabot College

Interior Design Department, School of the Arts

2555 Hesperian Blvd., Hayward, CA 94545 | 510-723-6600 | www.chabotcollege.edu

UNIVERSITY PROFILE
Public
Suburban

COMMUTER
Semester
Co-ed

STUDENT DEMOGRAPHICS
Undergraduate: 22,800
Graduate: n/a

Male: Not reported
Female: Not reported

Full-time: Not reported
Part-time: Not reported

EXPENSES
Tuition: $26 per unit
Room & Board: n/a

ADMISSIONS
2555 Hesperian Blvd.
Hayward, CA 94545
510-723-6700

DEGREE INFORMATION

Major / Degree / Concentration	Enrollment	Requirements for entry	Graduation rate
Interior Design Associate of Arts	Not reported	High school diploma or equivalent; 18 years of age or older	Not reported
Interior Design Certificate	Not reported	Same as above	Not reported
Kitchen & Bath Design Certificate	Not reported	Same as above	Not reported

TOTAL PROGRAM ENROLLMENT
Undergraduate: Not reported
Graduate: Not reported

Male: Not reported
Female: Not reported

Full-time: Not reported
Part-time: Not reported

International: Not reported
Minority: Not reported

Job Placement Rate: Not reported

SCHOLARSHIPS / FINANCIAL AID
Chabot offers Pell Grants, Federal Supplemental Educational Opportunity Grants, Federal Work Study Grants, Federal Stafford Loans, CA Grants, Bureau of Indian Affairs Grants, and other external scholarships. The CA Board of Governor's Fee Waiver program will waive fees for eligible CA residents.

TOTAL FACULTY: NOT REPORTED
Full-time: Not reported
Part-time: Not reported
Online: Not reported

NCIDQ Certified: n/a
Licensed Interior Designers: 2
LEED Certified: Not reported

INTERIOR DESIGN ADMINISTRATION
Celia Barberena, President
Gary Carter, Dean, School of the Arts
Adrian Huang, Architecture Instructor
Barbara Daher, Interior Design Instructor
Gus Vouchilis, Interior Design Instructor

PROFESSIONAL / ACADEMIC AFFILIATIONS
Not reported

PROGRAM DESCRIPTION AND PHILOSOPHY

Chabot College has facilities to take advantage of new approaches to learning, to facilitate the development of experimental programs, and to be adaptable to changes brought about by new technology. Our Interior Design curriculum includes Interior Design, architecture, art, and digital media. The Interior Design curriculum was updated and approved by the State of California in 2008. We are and NKBA Supported School and are working towards Endorsed NKBA Certification.

FACILITIES

Two years ago our building underwent a $1million renovation with the latest technologies. It has labs for architecture, Interior Design, photography, computer graphics, theater, etc. Within five years the entire campus will be reconfigured.

ONLINE / DISTANCE LEARNING

Not available, but planned.

COURSES OF INSTRUCTION

- Residential Space Planning
- History of Interiors & Furnishings
- Principles of Interior Design
- Introduction to Textiles
- Professional Practices
- Fundamentals of Lighting
- Materials & Resources
- Kitchen & Bathroom Design
- Special Needs Design
- Advanced Kitchen & Bathroom Design
- Commercial Design

INTERNSHIPS

Required for Kitchen & Bath Design certificate.

STUDY ABROAD

Not available

NOTABLE ALUMNI

Yuko Matsumoto recently became a member of NKBA. Feras Irikat is published in the national magazine for NKBA.

STUDENT ACTIVITIES AND ORGANIZATIONS

Interior Design Club, Architecture Club

FACULTY SPECIALIZATIONS AND RESEARCH

Not reported

COMMUNITY COLLEGE TRANSFERS

It is our goal to transfer as many students to San Francisco State University as interested, once they complete their AS in Interior Design. Many older or returning students get certificates with the intention of setting up their own businesses or going to work in related areas.

City College of San Francisco

Department of Architecture

50 Phelan Ave., Box L229, Batmale Hall 241, San Francisco, CA 94112 | 415-452-5293 | www.ccsf.edu/arch

UNIVERSITY PROFILE
Public
Urban
Commuter
Semester Schedule
Co-ed

STUDENT DEMOGRAPHICS
Undergraduate: Not reported
Graduate: 0

Male: Not reported
Female: Not reported

Full-time: Not reported
Part-time: Not reported

EXPENSES
Tuition: $26 per credit
(California resident); $209
per credit (Non-California
resident)
Room & Board: n/a

ADMISSIONS
Admissions & Records
50 Phelan Ave. Conlan Hall
Rm. 107
San Francisco, CA 94112
415-239-3285
admit@ccsf.edu

DEGREE INFORMATION

Major / Degree / Concentration	Enrollment	Requirements for entry	Graduation rate
Architectural Interiors Associate of Arts	150	Open enrollment	Not reported

TOTAL PROGRAM ENROLLMENT
Undergraduate: 500
Graduate: 0

Male: Not reported
Female: Not reported

Full-time: 35%
Part-time: 65%

International: Not reported
Minority: Not reported

Job Placement Rate: Not reported

SCHOLARSHIPS / FINANCIAL AID
Not reported

TOTAL FACULTY: 18
Full-time: 23%
Part-time: 77%
Online: 5%

NCIDQ Certified: Not reported
Licensed Interior Designers: Not reported
LEED Certified: 15%

INTERIOR DESIGN ADMINISTRATION
Andrew Chandler, AIA, Chair
Nestor Regino, Interiors Coordinator

PROFESSIONAL / ACADEMIC AFFILIATIONS
Not reported

PROGRAM DESCRIPTION AND PHILOSOPHY

The curriculum in Architectural Interiors, a two-year inter-departmental course of study, has a strong emphasis on both architecture and art.

The course of study includes instruction in the following: Orthographic projection, descriptive geometry, perspective, and shades and shadows; two-dimensional basic design; delineation and rendering; materials of construction; freehand drawing; professional practice/Interior Design; legal aspects of contracting; architectural technology (drafting); art history; basic design; basic drawing; structural analysis and design; industrial design fundamentals; art orientation; and graphic design.

The course of study is designed so that students may satisfy the requirements for graduation from the College. Students who satisfy these requirements and complete the curriculum with an average final grade of C (2.00 gpa) or higher receive the degree of Associate in Science and the Award of Achievement in Architectural Interiors.

Entry positions for which graduates who have received the Award of Achievement may qualify include those of draftsperson; delineator; salesperson; furniture designer; and assistant in coordination of colors, fabric, furniture, lighting systems, and exhibits.

FACILITIES
Computer lab, design studios

ONLINE / DISTANCE LEARNING
Not available

COURSES OF INSTRUCTION
- Design Fundamentals
- Archtectural Design
- Interior Design Studio
- Global History of Interior Design
- Interior Materials and Systems

INTERNSHIPS
Not required

STUDY ABROAD
City College of San Francisco Study Abroad programs include Australia, Cambodia, China, Costa Rica, Cuba, England, France, Indonesia, Italy, Japan, Laos, Mexico, Mongolia, Spain, Russia and Vietnam.

NOTABLE ALUMNI
Not reported

STUDENT ACTIVITIES AND ORGANIZATIONS
Not reported

FACULTY SPECIALIZATIONS AND RESEARCH
Not reported

COMMUNITY COLLEGE TRANSFERS
Students transfer to San Francisco State University, San Jose State University, California College of the Arts, Art Academy, and The Art Institute

Design Institute of San Diego

School of Interior Design

8555 Commerce Ave., San Diego, CA 92121 | 858-566-1200 | www.disd.edu

UNIVERSITY PROFILE

Private
Urban
Commuter
Semester Schedule
Co-ed

STUDENT DEMOGRAPHICS

Undergraduate: 6,000
Graduate: 0

Male: 1%
Female: 99%

Full-time: 75%
Part-time: 25%

EXPENSES

Tuition: $15,600
Room & Board: n/a

ADMISSIONS

Paula Parrish
Director of Admissions
Design Institute of San Diego
8555 Commerce Ave.
San Diego, California 92121
858-566-1200
pparrish@disd.edu

DEGREE INFORMATION

Major / Degree / Concentration	Enrollment	Requirements for entry	Graduation rate
Interior Design Bachelor of Fine Arts	400	C or better	85%

TOTAL PROGRAM ENROLLMENT

Undergraduate: Not reported
Graduate: Not reported

Male: Not reported
Female: Not reported

Full-time: Not reported
Part-time: Not reported

International: Not reported
Minority: Not reported

Job Placement Rate: Not reported

SCHOLARSHIPS / FINANCIAL AID

Financial aid comes from the federal government, States of California, and private scholarships. There are two types of aid: gift aid and self-help aid. Students may be awarded a combination of these or a "package."

TOTAL FACULTY: 40

Full-time: 10%
Part-time: 90%
Online: Not reported

NCIDQ Certified: 30%
Licensed Interior Designers: 20%
LEED Certified: 10%

INTERIOR DESIGN ADMINISTRATION

Margot Doucette, Director
Denise Homme, Program Director
Arthur Rosenstein, President

PROFESSIONAL / ACADEMIC AFFILIATIONS

American Society of Interior Designers
International Interior Design Association
Interior Design Educators Council

CIDA ACCREDITATION

Bachelor of Fine Arts in Interior Design
(2004, 2010)

PROGRAM DESCRIPTION AND PHILOSOPHY

Design Institute of San Diego is a private, independent college founded in 1977 and devoted to a single purpose: a professional education in Interior Design. The faculty, resources, administration, physical facilities, and educational activities of Design Institute are entirely committed to this purpose. The college seeks to educate students who are prepared for professional Interior Design practice immediately following graduation. General education courses provide the students with grounding in the liberal arts traditions, values, and critical thinking, and the Interior Design major offers a solid foundation of professional study for a career in Interior Design. The four-year program leads to the Bachelor of Fine Arts in Interior Design degree.

FACILITIES

CAD LAB—one building which contains four classrooms of computers, four large scale plotters, four color printers, four scanners, main building has display space for current student work.

ONLINE / DISTANCE LEARNING

Not reported

COURSES OF INSTRUCTION

- Elements of Design I
- History of interiors
- Architectural Drafting
- Color Theory and Application
- Textiles
- Building Codes and Standards
- Computer Aided Design
- Building Systems
- Lighting Design
- Business Practices
- Senior Project
- Portfolio & Presentation Techniques

INTERNSHIPS

Required of majors at third year level.

STUDY ABROAD

An annual trip abroad with program director, which includes architectural tours, and cultural events. Recent past trips include 10 days in Ireland, Spain, Italy, and France.

NOTABLE ALUMNI

Viveca Bissonette, Marge Dean, Lorena Gaxiola

STUDENT ACTIVITIES AND ORGANIZATIONS

American Society of Interior Designers, International Interior Design Association

FACULTY SPECIALIZATIONS AND RESEARCH

Lighting designer Cynthia Burke; *Research-Inspired Design* author, Lily Robinson; faculty members are mostly practicing, there are several faculty who specialize in fine art, history and building codes.

Fashion Institute of Design & Merchandising

Department of Interior Design

919 South Grand Ave., Los Angeles, CA 90015 | 213-624-1200 | www.fidm.edu//majors/interior-design/

UNIVERSITY PROFILE
Private
Urban
Commuter
Quarter Schedule
Co-ed

STUDENT DEMOGRAPHICS
Undergraduate: 151
Graduate: Not reported

Male: Not reported
Female: Not reported

Full-time: Not reported
Part-time: Not reported

EXPENSES
Tuition: $26,525
Room & Board: n/a

ADMISSIONS
919 South Grand Ave.
Los Angeles, CA 90015

OTHER CAMPUSES
San Francisco
San Diego
Orange County

DEGREE INFORMATION

Major / Degree / Concentration	Enrollment	Requirements for entry	Graduation rate
Interior Design Associate of Arts	151	GED/high school transcript, 3 recommendations, admissions essay, entrance requirement project	61%

TOTAL PROGRAM ENROLLMENT
Undergraduate: 151
Graduate: n/a

Male: 12%
Female: 88%

Full-time: 88%
Part-time: 12%

International: Not reported
Minority: 29%

Job Placement Rate: Not reported

SCHOLARSHIPS / FINANCIAL AID
Not reported

TOTAL FACULTY: 52
Full-time: 13%
Part-time: 87%
Online: NA

NCIDQ Certified: 7%
Licensed Interior Designers: NA
LEED Certified: 7%

INTERIOR DESIGN ADMINISTRATION
Tonian Hohberg, President
Barbara Bundy, Vice President of Education
Dina Morgan, Interior Design Department Chair

PROFESSIONAL / ACADEMIC AFFILIATIONS
American Society of Interior Designers
International Interior Design Association
Interior Design Educators Council

PROGRAM DESCRIPTION AND PHILOSOPHY

The Interior Design Program combines theoretical elements of Interior Design with practical creative approaches to the solution of functional and aesthetic design problems in the living, working, and recreational human environment. Competencies developed by the program include architectural drafting, CAD illustration and graphic presentation skills, and design proficiency. Students will also develop a working knowledge of the materials, resources, and business procedures pertaining to the Interior Design profession.

FACILITIES

FIDM has the largest fashion library on the West Coast with access to thousands of books, periodicals, trade publications, newspaper clipping files, trends reports, fabric swatch archives, fashion videos, and non-print reference material. The FIDM Museum and Galleries Permanent and Study Collection encompasses over 12,000 costumes, accessories, and textiles from the 18th century to the present, featuring top designers such as Chanel, Christian Dior, and Yves St. Laurent, to name a few.

ONLINE / DISTANCE LEARNING

Not available

COURSES OF INSTRUCTION

- Principles of Color
- Residential Design Concepts
- Lighting Design
- Commercial Design Practice

INTERNSHIPS

Not required of majors but available to students at the second year level. Interns are typically placed at Interior Design firms such as Kelly Wearstler.

STUDY ABROAD

Study abroad is available for study in Rome, New York, Paris, London and Milan.

NOTABLE ALUMNI

Michele Rose Coseo

STUDENT ACTIVITIES AND ORGANIZATIONS

FIDM's unique industry connections provide a valuable network for guest speakers and field trips. Also, using the FIDM network, Career Connections, held annually, is an opportunity for FIDM students on all four campuses to meet and interact with FIDM Alumni. Building a global network, FIDM's study tours to New York City, Rome, Paris, London, and Milan, allow students to meet with top industry professionals, tour major companies, and gather inspiration from some of the world's most exciting architecture and art.

FACULTY SPECIALIZATIONS AND RESEARCH

FIDM instructors are working professionals with invaluable industry connections.

COMMUNITY COLLEGE TRANSFERS

Students who wish to explore their transfer options should consult FIDM's Articulation Officer on the Los Angeles campus for assistance. Students graduating from FIDM must complete the graduation requirements for their specific degree. FIDM requirements, however, do not necessarily meet all lower division or general education requirements for other colleges. FIDM currently maintains articulation agreements with selected colleges with the intent of enhancing a student's transfer opportunities.

Interior Designers Institute

Interior Designers Institute

1061 Camelback St., Newport Beach, CA 92660 | 949-675-4451 | www.idi.edu

UNIVERSITY PROFILE
Private
Suburban
Commuter
Quarter Schedule
Co-ed

STUDENT DEMOGRAPHICS
Undergraduate: Not reported
Graduate: Not reported

Male: Not reported
Female: Not reported

Full-time: Not reported
Part-time: Not reported

EXPENSES
Tuition: $16,000
Room & Board: n/a

ADMISSIONS
1061 Camelback St.
Newport Beach, CA 92660
949-675-4451
contact@idi.edu

DEGREE INFORMATION

Major / Degree / Concentration	Enrollment	Requirements for entry	Graduation rate
Interior Design Associate of Arts	Not reported	High school diploma or GED	Not reported
Interior Design Bachelor of Arts	Not reported	High school diploma or GED	Not reported
Interior Design Master of Arts	Not reported	Candidates must have completed the BA program with a minimum 2.7 gpa. A portfolio review and personal interview are also required.	Not reported

TOTAL PROGRAM ENROLLMENT
Undergraduate: 350
Graduate: 7

Male: 10%
Female: 90%

Full-time: 30%
Part-time: 70%

International: 6%
Minority: 42%

Job Placement Rate: 87% (A.A.); 98% (B.A.)

SCHOLARSHIPS / FINANCIAL AID
Federal Direct Loans and Pell Grants are available

Students Receiving Scholarships or Financial Aid: 48%

TOTAL FACULTY: 22
Full-time: 32%
Part-time: 68%
Online: Not reported

NCIDQ Certified: NA
Licensed Interior Designers: NA
LEED Certified: NA

INTERIOR DESIGN ADMINISTRATION
Judy Deaton, ASID, IIDA, CID, Executive Director
Sharon Deaton, IDEC, Financial Director
Paul J. Rice, ASID, IIDA, CID, Director of Education

PROFESSIONAL / ACADEMIC AFFILIATIONS
American Society of Interior Designers
International Interior Design Association
Interior Design Educators Council

CIDA ACCREDITATION
Bachelor of Arts Degree in Interior Design (2005, 2011)

PROGRAM DESCRIPTION AND PHILOSOPHY

The Certificate Program may be taken for personal enrichment, to learn to design one's own home or as the prerequisite for the Associate of Arts Degree Program.

The Associate of Arts Degree in Interior Design is for the career-oriented Interior Design student. This program explores in-depth aspects of residential design as well as large commercial projects such as resorts and hotels, shopping centers, offices and hospitals, allowing students to consider a design career in many fields.

The CIDA-accredited Bachelor of Arts Degree in Interior Design creates a natural transition from college classroom to the workplace. To receive the B.A. Degree, the Certificate, A.A. Degree and B.A. Degree classes must be completed with a cumulative gpa of 2.0 or better and 45 quarter credit units of general education must be taken concurrently with or prior to completion of the design courses at the Institute.

The Master of Arts Degree Program is the highest degree offered. The Program is structured to allow the student or practicing designer to complete the Program in one year. Candidates must have completed the B.A. Program with a 2.7 or higher gpa. A portfolio review and personal interview are also required.

FACILITIES

Drafting and design studios with the latest equipment, student exhibition spaces, as well as a computer center and library with Internet access and inter-university research programs all facilitate learning and creativity in an air-conditioned setting of comfort and beauty. A Job Placement office with current student job listings and display boards is available as well as individual placement counseling. The Institute has aquired large, adjacent facilities for expansion to further enhance student activities. The Institute offers a student lounge and plenty of convenient parking, and administrative offices where students may seek help and attention.

ONLINE / DISTANCE LEARNING

Not available

COURSES OF INSTRUCTION

- Architectural Drafting I & II
- History of Interiors I & II
- Residential Design
- Commercial Design I & II
- Construction Principles
- Design Theory
- Color
- Perspective I & II
- Marker Rendering I & II
- Spaceplanning
- Business Principles
- Textiles
- Lighting Specifications
- Institutional Design
- Building Codes
- Environmental Design
- Computer Aided Drafting I & II

INTERNSHIPS

Required of majors in the B.A. program. Interns are with companies that are primarily higher-end commercial and residential Interior Design firms. Gensler, Barclay Butera, Inc., Kravet/Lee Jofa, Hirsch Bedner Associates, Haute Design Studio, Saddleback Interiors, Panaz U.S.A., Arch Interiors Design Group, Hospitality Plus, Inc., Herman Miller, Style Interiors, and NBC Studios.

STUDY ABROAD

Not available

NOTABLE ALUMNI

Wendi Young, California Designer of the Year; Rick Thompson, Recipient Yale R. Burge Award; ASID Orange County Chapter Presidents, Rick Thompson, David Rance and Diane Sparacino; television design celebrities featured on Fine Living & HGTV including Stephanie Cook (*Design Star*) and Sabina Vavra (A & E's *Tackling Design*).

STUDENT ACTIVITIES AND ORGANIZATIONS

Student Chapters of ASID, IIDA and Emerging Green Builders (EGB), part of the United States Green Building Council (USGBC). The EGB Group is for students dedicated to becoming future leaders of the green building movement.

FACULTY SPECIALIZATIONS AND RESEARCH

All professors are degreed professionals with an average of 15 years work experience in architecture and design. Faculty includes: a CBS Television set designer, winners of the coveted MAME Award, winner of the VAH National Kitchen Design Award, members of the California Board of Architectural Examiners and designers of many of the state's most prestigious projects. In addition, the faculty includes a number of Interior Designers who have been published in such magazines as *"Interior Design Magazine"*, *"Woman's Day"*, *"Profiles in Architecture"* and *"Coast Magazine"*. Most are professionally affiliated with ASID, IIDA or AIA.

Monterey Peninsula College

Department of Interior Design, Life Science Division

980 Fremont St., Monterey, CA 93940 | 831-646-4138 | www.mpc.edu/academics/**lifescience/interiordesign**

UNIVERSITY PROFILE
Public
Suburban
Commuter
Semester Schedule
Co-ed

STUDENT DEMOGRAPHICS
Undergraduate: 14,587
Graduate: n/a

Male: 48%
Female: 52%

Full-time: Not reported
Part-time: Not reported

EXPENSES
Tuition: $789
Room & Board: n/a

ADMISSIONS
980 Fremont St.
Monterey, CA 93940

DEGREE INFORMATION

Major / Degree / Concentration	Enrollment	Requirements for entry	Graduation rate
Interior Design Associate of Arts	22	Open enrollment	Not reported
Interior Design Certificate	25	Open enrollment	Not reported

TOTAL PROGRAM ENROLLMENT
Undergraduate: 70
Graduate: n/a

Male: 15%
Female: 85%

Full-time: 20%
Part-time: 80%

International: 10%
Minority: 31.5%

Job Placement Rate: 40%

SCHOLARSHIPS / FINANCIAL AID
See opposite page for more information

TOTAL FACULTY: 4
Full-time: 25%
Part-time: 75%
Online: Not reported

NCIDQ Certified: Not reported
Licensed Interior Designers: Not reported
LEED Certified: Not reported

INTERIOR DESIGN ADMINISTRATION
Sunshine Giesler, Department Chair
Julie Bailey, Division Office Manager

PROFESSIONAL / ACADEMIC AFFILIATIONS
American Society of Interior Designers
Interior Design Educators Council

PROGRAM DESCRIPTION AND PHILOSOPHY
The Interior Design program prepares students for employment in the many businesses that provide products and services for residential and commercial interiors.

FACILITIES
CAD lab with AutoCAD 2010, Revit, ArchiCAD, Google SketchUp and Adobe Photoshop; resource room that is constantly updated with donations from local Interior Design studios.

ONLINE / DISTANCE LEARNING
Not available.

COURSES OF INSTRUCTION
- Introduction to Interior Design
- Introduction to Drafting & Perspective
- Sustainable Environments
- History of Architecture & Interiors I and II
- Basic Materials and Finishes
- Fundamentals of Lighting
- Color Theory and Application
- Business Practices
- Textiles
- Rendering & Perspectives
- Introduction to Kitchen and Bath Design
- Introduction to Computer-Aided Drafting
- Introduction to Green Building and Design
- Interior Design Studio
- Portfolio

INTERNSHIPS
Not required

STUDY ABROAD
Not available

NOTABLE ALUMNI
Not reported

STUDENT ACTIVITIES AND ORGANIZATIONS
Student Interior Design Club

FACULTY SPECIALIZATIONS AND RESEARCH
Not reported

COMMUNITY COLLEGE TRANSFERS
The transfer program enables the student to complete the first two years in preparation for transfer to a baccalaureate-granting institution. MPC courses parallel those offered to Freshman and Sophomore students at the University of California, California State University, and private colleges and universities.

SCHOLARSHIPS / FINANCIAL AID
Federal Pell Grant: Applicants who meet all requirements will receive Federal Pell Grant based on need and number of units in which they are enrolled. Maximum Pell Grant for 2009-2010 = $5,350.

Federal Supplemental Educational Opportunity Grant (SEOG): Students who qualify for additional assistance may be offered an SEOG if eligible for the Pell Grant. Funds are awarded based on priority and need.

Cal Grants: Cal Grant recipients must be California residents. The Cal Grant application is separate from the FAFSA. To apply, the FAFSA and Cal Grant gpa Verification Form must be postmarked by March 2nd or September 2nd. The Cal Grant is a competitive grant and not all applicants receive funds. For more information, see www.csac.ca.gov.

District Grant in Aid (DGIA): Monterey Peninsula College provides institutional grants (while funds are available to undergraduate students who have completed less than 48 college units).

Orr Estate Grant: Monterey Peninsula College provides institutional grants (while funds are available) to students who have completed 12 units, are enrolled full-time, and have at least a 2.0 gpa.

Students Receiving Scholarships or Financial Aid: 40

Moorpark College

Department of Interior Design

7075 Campus Rd., Moorpark, CA 93021 | 805-378-1400 | **www.moorparkcollege.edu**

UNIVERSITY PROFILE
Public
Suburban
Residential
Semester Schedule
Co-ed

STUDENT DEMOGRAPHICS
Undergraduate: Not reported
Graduate: Not reported

Male: Not reported
Female: Not reported

Full-time: Not reported
Part-time: Not reported

EXPENSES
Tuition: $26 per unit
Room & Board: n/a

ADMISSIONS
7075 Campus Rd.
Moorpark, CA 93021
805-378-1400
tstewart@vcccd.edu

DEGREE INFORMATION

Major / Degree / Concentration	Enrollment	Requirements for entry	Graduation rate
Interior Design Associate of Science Residential Design	250	Open enrollment	Not reported

TOTAL PROGRAM ENROLLMENT
Undergraduate: Not reported
Graduate: Not reported
Male: Not reported
Female: Not reported

Full-time: Not reported
Part-time: Not reported

International: Not reported
Minority: Not reported

Job Placement Rate: Not reported

SCHOLARSHIPS / FINANCIAL AID
Not reported

TOTAL FACULTY: 5
Full-time: 50%
Part-time: 50%
Online: 0%

NCIDQ Certified: 0%
Licensed Interior Designers: 0%
LEED Certified: 0%

INTERIOR DESIGN ADMINISTRATION
Not reported

PROFESSIONAL / ACADEMIC AFFILIATIONS
American Society of Interior Designers

PROGRAM DESCRIPTION AND PHILOSOPHY

The Interior Design program at Moorpark College offers students a practical, "hands-on" experience. Students are engaged in coursework that involves community and campus projects. Internships are available throughout the professional design industry, including set design, product design, and residential and commercial design.

FACILITIES

Design studios (Sarah Bernhard Designs), wholesale and retail showrooms (Ethan Allen, Kravet, Innovations), set design firms, textile distributors (Pindler and Pindler), product design firms

ONLINE / DISTANCE LEARNING

Not reported

COURSES OF INSTRUCTION

- Beginning Interior Design
- Materials and Installations
- Textiles
- Intermediate Interior Design
- Space Planning
- History of Furniture
- Advanced Interior Design

INTERNSHIPS

Not required

STUDY ABROAD

Not reported

NOTABLE ALUMNI

Not reported

STUDENT ACTIVITIES AND ORGANIZATIONS

Not reported

FACULTY SPECIALIZATIONS AND RESEARCH

Not reported

COMMUNITY COLLEGE TRANSFERS

California State University-Northridge, Fashion Institute of Design and Merchandising (FIDM), Woodbury University, San Diego State University, California State University-Long Beach, University of California, Los Angeles (Extension)

Otis College of Art & Design

Department of Architecture / Landscape / Interiors

9045 Lincoln Blvd., Los Angeles, CA 90045 | 310-665-6867 | **www.otis.edu**

UNIVERSITY PROFILE
Private
Urban
Commuter
Semester
Co-ed

STUDENT DEMOGRAPHICS
Undergraduate: 1,154
Graduate: 67

Male: 33%
Female: 67%

Full-time: 97%
Part-time: 3%

EXPENSES
Tuition: $30,660
Room & Board: n/a

ADMISSIONS
9045 Lincoln Blvd.
Los Angeles, CA 90045
310-665-6826
admissions@otis.edu

DEGREE INFORMATION

Major / Degree / Concentration	Enrollment	Requirements for entry	Graduation rate
Architecture / Landscape / Interiors Bachelor of Fine Arts	51	2.0 gpa; average gpa is 3.0	72%

TOTAL PROGRAM ENROLLMENT
Undergraduate: 51
Graduate: Not reported

Male: 31%
Female: 69%

Full-time: 100%
Part-time: 0%

International: 25%
Minority: 55%

Job Placement Rate: 80%

SCHOLARSHIPS / FINANCIAL AID
Financial aid and scholarhips are awarded at entrance based upon a combination of artisitic/academic merit and financial need. Students may apply for Named Scholarships for their Sophomore, Junior, and Senior years. In the past students in this department have competed sucessfully for outside scholarships from foundations and organizations.

TOTAL FACULTY: 24
Full-time: 2
Part-time: 22
Online: 0

NCIDQ Certified: Not reported
Licensed Interior Designers: 60%
Licensed Architects: 14%
Licensed Landscape Architects: 10%
LEED Certified: 14%

INTERIOR DESIGN ADMINISTRATION
Linda Pollari, Chair
Mohamed Sharif, Assistant Chair
Wolf Herrera, Department Assistant

PROFESSIONAL / ACADEMIC AFFILIATIONS
American Society of Interior Designers
International Interior Design Association

PROGRAM DESCRIPTION AND PHILOSOPHY

Architecture/Landscape /Interiors seeks to contribute to the emergence of imaginative, contemporary practices through a synthetic curriculum of the spatial design fields: architecture (buildings), landscape (spaces between building), and interiors (spaces within buildings). Students study all three fields within a single, sequential curriculum. The department is focused on design empowered by technologies and theory. This focus on design, rather than craft, trains future architects and designers to communicate and collaborate with builders, crafts persons, and artisans working in any scale, material or technique. At the core of the curriculum are six comprehensive studio courses that combine or alternate between the related disciplines. Technologies and Ecologies courses focus on the materials and methods of building, landscape, and interior construction. Digital Media courses address digital communication skills (drafting, modeling, rendering, and fabrication). History and Theory courses provide the cultural and intellectual framework necessary for informed and articulate design proposals.

FACILITIES

Students have access to approximately 450 computers in ten labs college wide (approximately 300 Macs and 100 Windows PCs along with 15 Epson XL scanners, a 60" HP color printer, 44" & 24" Epson color printers, Xerox color and B/W laser printers, four 3D Printers, two Laser Cutter/Engravers, and a 3D scanner). Students also have access to approximately 50 computers in the Library. The computer center also provides an information sheet specifically intended to help guide students in the use of digital technology.

ONLINE / DISTANCE LEARNING

Not available

COURSES OF INSTRUCTION

- Studio I: Scale/Structure/Circulation
- Studio III: Interior/Display/Exchange
- Studio IV: Private/Interior Architecture
- Digital Media I: Communicating Information
- Technologies + Ecologies II: Interior Technology
- Detail Development
- Lighting Fundamentals
- Constructions
- History + Theory V: Corporate and Consumer Environments

INTERNSHIPS

Available, but not required. Students are typically placed at the following companies:
Ellerbe Beckett, San Francisco; Bennitt + Mitchell, Los Angeles; GRAFT LLC, Los Angeles; Chang Jo Architects, Seoul; Lighting Design Alliance, Long Beach; Mansilla + Tuñón Arquitectos, Madrid; Richard Meier & Partners Architects LLP, Los Angeles; Shubin + Donaldson Architects, Santa Barbara; Clive Wilkinson Architects, Los Angeles; Wolcott Architecture-Interiors, Culver

STUDY ABROAD

Mobility exchange program with a world wide network of independent colleges of art and deign

NOTABLE ALUMNI

As of fall 2009:
Boo Jang (07) has been working for Bennitt & Mitchell, an international landscape architecture firm, since 2005, when she was a Junior. David Orkand (04) received his Master of Architecture degree from Princeton University in 2007 and now is doing a Doctoral Research Fellowship at TIT while working for Atelier Bow-Wow, an internationally known architecture firm based Tokyo. Felicia Martin (02) received her Master of Architecture degree from Yale in 2009, with an award for Pursuit of Excellence In Residential Design, and is working for Franciso Mangado

Estudio in Pamplona, Spain. Patrick Ngo (05) graduated with a Master of Architecture from ULCA in 2008 and is working with Diller Scofidio + Renfro in New York. Gary Garcia (08) and Natalia Polunina (07) have each begun their second year in a Master of Landscape Architecture program. Gary is studying at USC while Natalia is at Harvard. Two A/L/I alums, Giselle Cabezut (06) and Dolly Davis (03) are studying at one of our +2 Master of Architecture programs. Giselle began her studies at USC in fall 2008. Dolly Davis started at UIC this fall, 2009, with a full scholarship. Dolly will graduate in two years, in spring 2011, with a Master of Architecture degree.

FACULTY SPECIALIZATIONS AND RESEARCH

Interior Design, Interior Architecture, Architecture, Landscape Architecture, Lighting Design

COMMUNITY COLLEGE TRANSFERS

Architecture/Landscape/Interiors has formal Articulation Agreements with the following community colleges (and will accept transfer credit from all regionally accredited institutions): Cerritos College, College of the Canyons, El Camino College, Fashion Institute of Design and Merchandising, Los Angeles Community College, Los Angeles Valley College, Mesa Community College, Mount San Antonio Community College, Orange Coast College, Pasadena City College, Pierce College, Rio Hondo College, Santa Monica College, West Los Angeles Community College, West Valley College.

In addition, Architecture/Landscape/Interiors graduates may receive advanced standing into the Master of Architecture programs at the University of Illinois at Chicago, the University of Southern California, and Woodbury University, Burbank, CA.

University of California, Los Angeles Extension

Architecture & Interior Design Program

10995 Le Conte Ave., Room 414, Los Angeles, CA 90024 | 310-825-9061 | www.uclaextension.edu/arc_id

UNIVERSITY PROFILE
Public
Urban
Commuter
Quarter Schedule
Co-ed

STUDENT DEMOGRAPHICS
Undergraduate: Not reported
Graduate: Not reported

Male: Not reported
Female: Not reported

Full-time: Not reported
Part-time: Not reported

EXPENSES
Tuition: Not reported
Room & Board: Not reported

ADMISSIONS
See Web site

DEGREE INFORMATION

Major / Degree / Concentration	Enrollment	Requirements for entry	Graduation rate
Foundation Level Certificate in Interior Design	Not reported	Open enrollment. Students may take up to five introductory classes before applying for admission.	Not reported
Advanced Level Master of Interior Architecture	Not reported	Completion of Foundation Level curriculum; minimum 3.0 gpa, application fee.	Not reported

TOTAL PROGRAM ENROLLMENT
Undergraduate: Not reported
Graduate: 250

Male: 10%
Female: 90%

Full-time: Not reported
Part-time: Not reported

International: Not reported
Minority: Not reported

Job Placement Rate: Not reported

SCHOLARSHIPS / FINANCIAL AID
Not reported

TOTAL FACULTY: NOT REPORTED
Full-time: Not reported
Part-time: Not reported
Online: Not reported

NCIDQ Certified: Not reported
Licensed Interior Designers: Not reported
LEED Certified: Not reported

INTERIOR DESIGN ADMINISTRATION
Not reported

PROFESSIONAL / ACADEMIC AFFILIATIONS
Not reported

PROGRAM DESCRIPTION AND PHILOSOPHY

The UCLA Extension Architecture and Interior Design Program (Arc_ID) has a tripartite mission:

1. To provide Southern California's best program in Interior Design for those individuals wanting a professional career in the Interior Design industry.
2. To offer the highest quality professional development opportunities for practicing architects and Interior Designers.
3. To provide members of the general public with a variety of classes through which they can deepen their knowledge and understanding in the areas of architecture and Interior Design.

If you are exploring the possibility of becoming an Interior Designer, you will want to consider the many benefits to our Interior Design Program, including:

- Open enrollment. As with all courses at UCLA Extension, you may register for your first course just prior to the beginning of any quarter throughout the year.
- An Instructor corps made up of distinguished practicing professionals from the fields of Interior Design, architecture, and fine art.
- Internship, mentorship, and job placement opportunities.

- Flexibility in course load and class scheduling. There are day and evening courses. A full-time student enrolls in three courses per quarter and will complete the program in a little over two years. Part-time students may take one or two courses per quarter. For more details, please consult the FAQ section of the UCLA extension Web site.
- Transfer credits. If you have taken art- and design-related courses at other institutions you may qualify for advanced standing in the program. To determine what transfer credits you may qualify for, you will need to make an appointment to meet with the Program Advisor.

FACILITIES
Not reproted

ONLINE / DISTANCE LEARNING
Not reported

COURSES OF INSTRUCTION
- Color Theory
- Interior Design Studio
- History of the Environmental Arts
- Elements of Design

INTERNSHIPS
An Internship is a very important step in the transition from "student status" to "professional status." The opportunity to participate in this practical experience in a design office or showroom is invaluable.

Internships are interesting and challenging positions available for students with varying degrees of technical skills and backgrounds.

The Internship serves as an elective course. There are internships available for students at all levels in our program. The student receives 6 units of credit after completing 136 hours. Firms are usually flexible and will work around a student's schedule. Generally, one full weekday (8 hours) is required. The beginning and ending dates do not have to coincide with those of the quarter.

STUDY ABROAD
Not reported

NOTABLE ALUMNI
Not reported

STUDENT ACTIVITIES AND ORGANIZATIONS
The UCLA Extension student chapter of the American Society of Interior Designers provides students with excellent networking opportunities, free peer tutoring, valuable career building support, and scholarship information. They also have lots of great special events planned. Visit their Web site: http://uclaextensionasid.homestead.com/

FACULTY SPECIALIZATIONS AND RESEARCH
Not reported

University of California, Berkeley Extension

Art & Design Program

95 Third St., San Francisco, CA 94103 | 415-284-1070 | **www.unex.berkeley.edu/art**

UNIVERSITY PROFILE
Public
Urban
Commuter
Semester Schedule
Co-ed

STUDENT DEMOGRAPHICS
Undergraduate: n/a
Graduate: 2,000

Male: 10%
Female: 90%

Full-time: 25%
Part-time: 75%

EXPENSES
Tuition: $6,500
Room & Board: n/a

ADMISSIONS
95 Third St.
San Francisco, CA 94103
415-284-1070

DEGREE INFORMATION

Major / Degree / Concentration	Enrollment	Requirements for entry	Graduation rate
Certificate in Interior Design & Interior Architecture	150	Bachelor degree or can petition for review of previous coursework	Not reported

TOTAL PROGRAM ENROLLMENT
Undergraduate: n/a
Graduate: 250

Male: 10%
Female: 90%

Full-time: Not reported
Part-time: Not reported

International: Not reported
Minority: Not reported

Job Placement Rate: 80%

SCHOLARSHIPS / FINANCIAL AID
Fran Kellogg Smith Scholarship for UCBerkeley CED student annually

TOTAL FACULTY: 35
Full-time: Not reported
Part-time: 100%
Online: Not reported

NCIDQ Certified: Not reported
Licensed Interior Designers: Not reported
LEED Certified: Not reported

INTERIOR DESIGN ADMINISTRATION
Rachael Hagner, M.Arch, AIA, IIDA Ed., Program Director

PROFESSIONAL / ACADEMIC AFFILIATIONS
American Society of Interior Designers
American Institute of Architects (AIA)
International Interior Design Association

PROGRAM DESCRIPTION AND PHILOSOPHY

Our goal is to provide the necessary educational preparation to enter the professional world of Interior Design. This encompasses:

- Providing theoretical and historical context as a basis of problem solving.
- Developing communication skills, both verbal and technical. This includes knowledge of the most current computer-aided drawing programs.
- Designing in a responsible way, abiding by the codes and producing designs that protect the health, welfare, and safety of the public.
- Creating a portfolio of work for students that illustrates their capabilities and readiness to perform the necessary tasks.
- Being informed on sustainability issues and ways to use materials in the most renewable ways.
- Understanding good business practices.
- Preparing students to gain professional status by being able to take and pass exams that give recognized credentials to Interior Designers: National Council for Interior Design Qualification Exam (NCIDQ); Interior Design Exam (IDEX)—California licensing in order for them to become a Ceritfied Interior Designer (CID); LEED Professional Accreditation, involveing sustainable aspects of design, is often required for designers on projects today.

FACILITIES

- Open computer labs
- Modern facility with student lounge
- Materials and Book Library
- Student and faculty work is featured rotating shows in our galleries
- School is easily accessed by public transportation
- Located near SFMOMA and Jewish Museum, Yerba Buena Center for the Arts and Moscone Center, Union Square.

ONLINE / DISTANCE LEARNING

Not available

COURSES OF INSTRUCTION

- Design Principles & Elements
- Graphic Communication (Drafting, Perspective, Rapid Visualization Techniques, Coloring with colored pencils, magic marker, and watercolors), Parts I & II
- AutoCAD
- Revit
- Design Studios I-IV
- Color Theory and Application for Interiors
- Building Components and Systems for Interior Architecture
- Fundamentals of Lighting Design
- Construction Documents Digital Presentation Techniques
- History of Architecture, Interiors, and Decorative Arts, Parts I & II
- Space Planning
- Interior Finishes and Materials
- Business Practices for Interior Designers

INTERNSHIPS

Not required. Interns are typically placed at companies such as HOK, Knoll, BAMO.

STUDY ABROAD

Not available

NOTABLE ALUMNI

Not reported

STUDENT ACTIVITIES AND ORGANIZATIONS

Student chapters of ASID and IIDA

FACULTY SPECIALIZATIONS AND RESEARCH

All faculty are working professionals with specialties in residential, commercial, hospitality or healthcare design. Our Advisory Committee consists of principals of promininent local firms—Gensler, BAMO, Orlando Diaz Design Asso., Barbara Scavullo, Huntsman Architectural Group, KDA Design Associates and the Executive Director of CCIDC (California Council for Interior Design Certification).

Woodbury University

Department of Interior Architecture

7500 Glenoaks Blvd.,Burbank, CA 91501 | 818-252-5144 | http://mcd.woodbury.edu/interiorarchitecture/

STUDENT DEMOGRAPHICS
Undergraduate: 1,300
Graduate: 250

Male: 45%
Female: 55%

Full-time: 85%
Part-time: 15%

EXPENSES
Tuition: $28,510
Room & Board: $8,978

ADMISSIONS
7500 Glenoaks Blvd
Burbank, CA 91510
818-252-5221
Cesar.Magallon@woodbury.edu

DEGREE INFORMATION

Major / Degree / Concentration	Enrollment	Requirements for entry	Graduation rate
Interior Architecture Bachelor of Fine Arts	95	2.85 gpa Portfolio review after Sophomore year	53%
Bachelor of Architecture	350	3.0 gpa Portfolio review after 3rd year	53%

TOTAL PROGRAM ENROLLMENT
Undergraduate: 95
Graduate: 0

Male: 15%
Female: 85%

Full-time: 15%
Part-time: 85%

International: 10%
Minority: 65%

Job Placement Rate: Not reported

SCHOLARSHIPS / FINANCIAL AID
To encourage and reward academic excellence, each year Woodbury University awards a number of undergraduate merit scholarships based upon the student's academic promise and personal accomplishments. Merit scholarships are awarded to students in their entering year at Woodbury. Your high school gpa and SAT scores, or college gpa for transfer students, are reviewed to determine awards. They are renewable each year up to an additional three years for standard programs or up to four years for architecture students, as long as the required grade point average is maintained. In addition there are State and Federal Financial aid programs available based on need.

Students Receiving Scholarships or Financial Aid: 85-90%

TOTAL FACULTY: 15
Full-time: 3
Part-time: 12
Online: 0

NCIDQ Certified: 15
Licensed Interior Designers: n/a
LEED Certified: 10

INTERIOR DESIGN ADMINISTRATION
Randy Stauffer, Chair, Professor, Interior Architecture

PROFESSIONAL / ACADEMIC AFFILIATIONS
American Society of Interior Designers
International Interior Design Association
Interior Design Educators Council

CIDA ACCREDITATION
Bachelor of Fine Arts in Interior Architecture (2005, 2011)

PROGRAM DESCRIPTION AND PHILOSOPHY

Interior architecture critically engages design as a progressive craft of form-making which transforms the individual and social ways we inhabit space. Design creatively orchestrates conflicting constraints creating meaningful solutions that fit into larger social and cultural contexts. Through the stories of our students, faculty and envisioned characters, the ephemeral and structured qualities of interior environments illuminate the human condition and its culturally rich spatial narratives. Students explore real and imagined geographies to critically produce space that researches technique and effect in order to develop new ways of seeing, building, and designing.

FACILITIES

Each student is provided dedicated studio space in which they have access to the studio 24/7. The University has an abundant number of computer labs both directly adjacent to the studios as well as through out the campus. In addition there are facilities available for making which include a shop, laser cutters and a new digital fabrication lab that houses 3D printers, laser cutters and a CNC milling machine. The campus has a library that has an extensive collection of design, art, and architecture books and journals. There is a materials library that mirrors the type of materials library found in many commercial Interior Design firms. In addition there is a lighting lab combined with photo shoot room.

ONLINE / DISTANCE LEARNING
Not available

COURSES OF INSTRUCTION
- Materials and Furnishings
- Space Planning
- Studio 1: 3D Design Principles I
- Studio 2: 3D Design Principles II
- Studio 3: IA Elements
- Studio 4: Branding and Identity
- Studio 5: Culture and Dwelling
- Studio 6: Typology and Community
- Studio 7: Narrative and Media
- Senior Project
- 3 History and Theory Courses
- Drawing 1 and 2
- Design and Color 1 and 2
- Lighting Design
- Detail Design
- Construction Documents
- Professional Practice
- Building Systems and Codes
- Human Factors Course
- Academic Writing 1 and 2
- Art History, Digital Communication

INTERNSHIPS
Required of majors after Sophomore year. Interns are typically placed at companies such as Gensler, Michael Beckson and Associates, Perkins and Will, The Thompson Collaborative, Studio Ma, Klawiter and Associates

STUDY ABROAD
Not reported

NOTABLE ALUMNI
Iva Kremsa, Karen Glik, Cassie Sanchez, Janine Tchilingarian

STUDENT ACTIVITIES AND ORGANIZATIONS
There is an active interior architecture student group called the Society of Interior Architecture Students (SOIAS) that puts on seminars, guest lectures, and student activities through out the academic year.

FACULTY SPECIALIZATIONS AND RESEARCH
Faculty are working professionals that bring their professional design experience into the courses. Several faculty are also actively researching design of the built environemnt and have received several design awards and fellowships by such noted organizations as the AIA and the American Academy in Rome.

COMMUNITY COLLEGE TRANSFERS
Woodbury University recognizes the value of student education in community colleges and has a robust relationship with local schools. Many community college courses transfer in through the review of student work developed in community college courses. A one-on-one meeting with the chair and articulation agreements determine those courses that are transferrable into the program.

The Art Institute of Colorado

Interior Design Department

1200 Lincoln, Denver, CO 80203 | 303-837-0825 | www.artinstitutes.edu/denver

UNIVERSITY PROFILE
Private
Urban
Commuter
Quarter Schedule
Co-ed

STUDENT DEMOGRAPHICS
Undergraduate: Not reported
Graduate: Not reported

Male: Not reported
Female: Not reported

Full-time: Not reported
Part-time: Not reported

EXPENSES
Tuition: Not reported
Room & Board: Not reported

ADMISSIONS
1200 Lincoln
Denver, CO 80203
303-837-0825

DEGREE INFORMATION

Major / Degree / Concentration	Enrollment	Requirements for entry	Graduation rate
Interior Design Bachelor of Arts	Not reported	Not reported	Not reported
Kitchen and Bath Design Associate of Applied Science	Not reported	Not reported	Not reported

TOTAL PROGRAM ENROLLMENT
Undergraduate: Not reported
Graduate: Not reported

Male: 10%
Female: 90%

Full-time: 75%
Part-time: 25%

International: 2%
Minority: 10%

Job Placement Rate: 96%

SCHOLARSHIPS / FINANCIAL AID
Not reported

TOTAL FACULTY: 17
Full-time: 5
Part-time: 12
Online: Not reported

NCIDQ Certified: 4
Licensed Interior Designers: Not reported
LEED Certified: 1

INTERIOR DESIGN ADMINISTRATION
Not reported

PROFESSIONAL / ACADEMIC AFFILIATIONS
American Society of Interior Designers
International Interior Design Association
Interior Design Educators Council

CIDA ACCREDITATION
Bachelor of Arts in Interior Design (2004, 2010)

PROGRAM DESCRIPTION AND PHILOSOPHY

Students can pursue an Interior Design degree at The Art Institute of Colorado. Our Interior Design degree program teaches students to take human elements into consideration when designing a space for living. The Interior Design degree program attracts creative individuals who want to improve quality of life through their designs. The Interior Design degree program emphasizes the design process with students developing concepts into functional designs. Interior Design degree students are taught in a hands-on environment with industry-related equipment and technology. The Interior Design degree program teaches traditional and computerized design skills. Course topics in the Interior Design degree program include space planning, textiles, and lighting. Interior Design degree students develop a portfolio to showcase their work to potential employers. Graduates of the Interior Design degree program are prepared to pursue entry-level jobs like Interior Designer, space planner, and draftsperson.

FACILITIES

Computer labs, library, resource rooms

ONLINE / DISTANCE LEARNING

Not reported

COURSES OF INSTRUCTION

- Architectural Drafting I
- Architectural Drafting II
- Elements of Interior Design
- History of Design and Architecture I
- Design Basics—Three-Dimensional
- Technical Perspective II
- Introduction to Space Planning
- Interior Design Communications
- Environmental and Sustainable Design
- History of Design and Architecture II
- Design Development—Residential and Commercial
- Interior Design Rendering
- Textiles/Finishes
- Advanced Rendering
- Kitchen and Bath Design
- Building and Environmental Systems
- Design Development—Commercial
- Corporate Programming and Design
- Digital Design
- Code—Barrier-Free Design
- Freehand Sketching for Interior Design
- Fundamentals of Working Drawings
- Hospitality Design
- Independent Study
- Computer Rendering
- Health Care/Senior Design
- Graduate Project—Programming
- Digital Presentation Techniques
- Advanced Construction Documents
- Advanced Residential Design
- Externship for Interior Design

INTERNSHIPS

Required of majors at 9th quarter

STUDY ABROAD

Not reported

NOTABLE ALUMNI

Not reported

STUDENT ACTIVITIES AND ORGANIZATIONS

Not reported

FACULTY SPECIALIZATIONS AND RESEARCH

Not reported

Colorado State University

Department of Design & Merchandising, College of Applied Human Sciences

Campus Delivery 1574, Fort Collins, CO 80538 | 970-491-1629 | www.dm.cahs.colostate.edu/

UNIVERSITY PROFILE
Public
Suburban
Residential
Semester Schedule
Co-ed

STUDENT DEMOGRAPHICS
Undergraduate: 19,653
Graduate: 3,555

Male: 49%
Female: 51%

Full-time: 86%
Part-time: 14%

EXPENSES
Tuition: $3,642.40 (Colorado resident, undergraduate); $4,731.40 (Colorado resident, graduate); $11,697.40 (non-resident, undergraduate); $10,525.15 (non-resident, graduate)
Room & Board: $8,324

ADMISSIONS
Colorado State University
1061 Campus Delivery
Fort Collins, CO 80523-1062

DEGREE INFORMATION

Major / Degree / Concentration	Enrollment	Requirements for entry	Graduation rate
Interior Design Bachelor of Arts	202	No requirements to declare Interior Design major. To move to Sophomore level, successful passing of Design Scenario + 2.5 gpa. Only 40 students accepted into Sophomore level	98%
Interior Design Master of Science Practitioner Track / Educator Track	14	Bachelor degree in Interior Design and acceptance in to program	85%

TOTAL PROGRAM ENROLLMENT
Undergraduate: 202
Graduate: 14

Male: 1%
Female: 14%

Full-time: 85%
Part-time: 15%

International: 2%
Minority: 2%

Job Placement Rate: 85%

SCHOLARSHIPS / FINANCIAL AID
Fellowships, scholarships, research assistantships, and graduate teaching assistantships are available.

Studnets Receiving Scholarships or Financial Aid: 25

TOTAL FACULTY: 5
Full-time: 100%
Part-time: 0%
Online: 0%

NCIDQ Certified: 2
Licensed Interior Designers: Not needed in Colorado
LEED Certified: 1

INTERIOR DESIGN ADMINISTRATION
Dr. Mary Littrell, Department Head
Dr. Stephanie A. Clemons, Coordinator and Professor, Interior Design

PROFESSIONAL / ACADEMIC AFFILIATIONS
American Society of Interior Designers
International Interior Design Association
Interior Design Educators Council

CIDA ACCREDITATION
Bachelor of Science in Interior Design (2009, 2015)

PROGRAM DESCRIPTION AND PHILOSOPHY

The Interior Design program embraces NCIDQ's definition of the professional Interior Designer; in addition, faculty value:

- learning as a collaborative effort inviting diversity: faculty bring to the program a range of experiences with substantial depth in their respective areas of expertise; diversity of approaches, language, practice regions and conceptual references make the learning environment challenging, vital and invites discourse about Interior Design.
- design research as the root of excellence in design practice: Interior Design research that appropriately informs decision-making in solving the challenges of the built environment is the foundation upon which faculty build their teaching and learning agendas.
- new models for learning to respond to new ways of working: faculty and students are engaged in methods of information delivery that embrace technology, time and the lessening importance of physical location for the generation of ideas.
- sustainable practice and green building: faculty and students advocate measures that reduce the impact of the built environment through effective construction methods, selection of materials and integrated practice strategies.

These values reinforce the institutional mission of CSU and provide a solid base from which to create unobstructed and unique opportunities for student learning and faculty growth.

Program Mission
The program guides students toward becoming dedicated Interior Designers [with]...strong communication [skills], who are active [as] team players, creative problem solvers, and...prepared

to make a positive impact in the practice of Interior Design through multidimensional practice opportunities in Interior Design. The program engages in its mission through research-based problem solving providing a solid transition from education to practice in a global community.

Goals: The Interior Design faculty strives to deliver program outcomes through six goals that maximize our location and resources and embrace change as a constant variable.

Goal 1: Apply research-based problem solving to the design of interiors to effect positive change in the health, welfare, and quality of life for people in home, work and leisure built environments;

Goal 2: Integrate an historical perspective in the study of environments for diverse populations that considers tradition, value, culture and heritage in the development of future environments;

Goal 3: Utilize Interior Design resources and technologies to affect the sustainability of communities in the Rocky Mountains;

Goal 4: Embrace technology as a resource and tool for innovation permitting the exploration of interior solutions of complexity to be envisioned as a dimension of design excellence at CSU;

Goal 5: Support learning outside the classroom to expand understanding of the profession and practice; and,

Goal 6: Maximize when possible and modify when needed departmental partnership with Construction Management, Art, Business and Psychology to continue to engage Interior Design students in the concepts and contributions of these disciplines to their practice knowledge.

FACILITIES

The most up-to-date hardware and software is available to Interior Design majors in over five computer labs. Students are taught: AutoCAD, Revit, InDesign, Sketchup, Max, Adobe products. Computer labs arely closed. The Department of Design and Merchandising also has the Avenir Museum with a renowned collection of historic costumes. Textile and studio labs available.

ONLINE / DISTANCE LEARNING

The Masters will be completely online by 2010.

COURSES OF INSTRUCTION

Available at Design and Merchandising Web site: www.dm.colostate.edu.

INTERNSHIPS

Required of majors at 3rd year level. Interns are typically placed at companies such as Gensler, RNL, Davis Parnership, Gallun Snow, Associates III, Boulder Associates, Lita Dirks & Company, Neenan & Company, Oglesby/Sherman, Fentress, etc.

STUDY ABROAD

Approximately 25-45% juniors complete a study abroad semester-long program to places such as Australia, Denmark, Great Britain, Italy. Currently investigating one to Egypt and India.

NOTABLE ALUMNI

Too many to indicate.

STUDENT ACTIVITIES AND ORGANIZATIONS

Active student chapters and student leadership opportunities.

FACULTY SPECIALIZATIONS AND RESEARCH

Universal design, sustainability, meaning of home (theory), various theories, creativity, infusion of Interior Design into K-12, preparing Interior Design educators.

Rocky Mountain College of Art & Design

Department of Interior Design

1600 Pierce St., Denver, CO 80214 | 800-888-ARTS | www.rmcad.edu/interior-design/overview

UNIVERSITY PROFILE
Private
Urban
Commuter
Trimester Schedule
Co-ed

STUDENT DEMOGRAPHICS
Undergraduate: 600
Graduate: n/a

Male: Not reported
Female: Not reported

Full-time: Not reported
Part-time: Not reported

EXPENSES
Tuition: Not reported
Room & Board: Not reported

ADMISSIONS
1600 Pierce St.
Denver, CO 80214
800-888-ARTS

DEGREE INFORMATION

Major / Degree / Concentration	Enrollment	Requirements for entry	Graduation rate
Interior Design Bachelor of Fine Arts	100	Not reported	Not reported
Interior Design Bachelor of Fine Arts Green Design Specialization	14	Not reported	Not reported

TOTAL PROGRAM ENROLLMENT
Undergraduate: Not reported
Graduate: Not reported

Male: Not reported
Female: Not reported

Full-time: Not reported
Part-time: Not reported

International: Not reported
Minority: Not reported

Job Placement Rate: Not reported

SCHOLARSHIPS / FINANCIAL AID
Not reported

TOTAL FACULTY: 10–15
Full-time: 4
Part-time: 1
Online: TBD

NCIDQ Certified: 80%
Licensed Interior Designers: n/a
LEED Certified: 30%

INTERIOR DESIGN ADMINISTRATION
Lauren Pillote, Dean of Design and
Applied Arts, Chair of Interior Design

PROFESSIONAL / ACADEMIC AFFILIATIONS
American Society of Interior Designers
International Interior Design Association
Interior Design Educators Council
U.S. Green Building Council

CIDA ACCREDITATION
Bachelor of Fine Arts (2008, 2014)

PROGRAM DESCRIPTION AND PHILOSOPHY

In order to create interiors that support the growing and diverse needs human beings have of their environments, it is essential that Interior Design students acquire and develop an understanding of the dynamic relationship between people and environments.

In RMCAD's Interior Design programs, you'll learn the theories and skills necessary for professional practice from faculty who are practicing design professionals and educators.

Our programs prepare students to contribute to society as skilled, ethical, environmentally responsible professional designers who are committed to improving the health, safety, and welfare of the public. We approach Interior Design as an extension of the arts while being grounded in the social and natural sciences of psychology, sociology, anthropology, ecology, and biology.

Program subject highlights include:
- Manual drafting + computer aided design (CAD)
- Space planning
- Interior materials + systems
- Environmental + human behavior
- Lighting design (CAD)
- Construction documents + contracts
- Business practices
- Senior-year internship

RMCAD also offers a unique program of study through our Green Design Area of Specialization. The Green Design Area of Specialization provides an in-depth exploration of the methods, processes, and principles of green design and sustainability.

When you graduate, you'll be prepared to work as a skilled, ethical, environmentally-responsible professional designer committed to improving the health, safety, and welfare of the public while embracing your own vision and creativity.

FACILITIES
Not reported

ONLINE / DISTANCE LEARNING
Both are planned

COURSES OF INSTRUCTION
- Drafting
- Design Process + Planning
- Residential Design
- Holistic Design
- Restaurant + Retail Design
- Office Design
- Special Use Design
- Senior Design Project
- Introduction to Green Design
- Survey of Interior Design
- Interior Materials
- Drafting
- Interior Design Sophomore/Junior Portfolio Review
- Building Codes + Regulations
- Introduction to Computer Aided Design (CAD)
- Architectural Perspective + Rendering Techniques
- Design Process and Planning
- Residential Design
- Holistic Design
- Building Structures + Systems
- Lighting Layout + Design
- Interior Design Professional Practices
- Intermediate CAD
- Construction Documents
- Restaurant + Retail Design
- Office Design
- Interior Design Senior Portfolio Review
- Green Design Senior Portfolio Review
- Interior Design Internship Program
- Design Research
- Special Use Design
- Senior Design Project
- Architectural Model Making
- Green Design II
- Interior Design Portfolio Development
- Custom Furnishings
- Green Design III

INTERNSHIPS
Required of majors

STUDY ABROAD
Not reported

NOTABLE ALUMNI
Not reported

STUDENT ACTIVITIES AND ORGANIZATIONS
Not reported

FACULTY SPECIALIZATIONS AND RESEARCH
Not reported

Paier College of Art

Department of Interior Design

20 Gorham Ave., Hamden, CT 06514 | 203-287-3031 | www.paiercollegeofart.edu

UNIVERSITY PROFILE
Private
Suburban
Commuter
Semester Schedule
Co-ed

STUDENT DEMOGRAPHICS
Undergraduate: 236
Graduate: n/a

Male: 41%
Female: 59%

Full-time: 75%
Part-time: 25%

EXPENSES
Tuition: $12,600
Room & Board: n/a

ADMISSIONS
20 Gorham Ave
Hamden, CT 06514
203-287-3031
paier.admission@snet.net

DEGREE INFORMATION

Major / Degree / Concentration	Enrollment	Requirements for entry	Graduation rate
Interior Design Bachelor of Fine Arts	40	Portfolio review 2.5 gpa SAT and ACT	73%

TOTAL PROGRAM ENROLLMENT
Undergraduate: 40
Graduate: n/a

Male: 10%
Female: 90%

Full-time: 67.5%
Part-time: 32.5%

International: 2.5%
Minority: 15%

Job Placement Rate: 93%

SCHOLARSHIPS / FINANCIAL AID
Students Receiving Scholarships or
Financial Aid: 62.5%

TOTAL FACULTY: 12
Full-time: 9%
Part-time: 91%
Online: 0%

NCIDQ Certified: 25%
Licensed Interior Designers: 25%
LEED Certified: 10%

INTERIOR DESIGN ADMINISTRATION
Jonathan Paier, President of the College
Francis Rexford Cooley, Dean of the
College
Pierre Strauch, Department Head of
Interior Design

PROFESSIONAL / ACADEMIC AFFILIATIONS
American Society of Interior Designers
Interior Design Educators Council
National Kitchen and Bath Association
American Institute of Architecture
Illuminating Engineering Society of
North America
OAQ L'ordre des Architectes du Quebec

114

PROGRAM DESCRIPTION AND PHILOSOPHY

The program emphasizes problem solving supported by professional technical courses.

FACILITIES

The Paier College of Art Interior Design Department has its own computer lab and materials library. The college also has three other computer labs. ID students may use for digital photography and other work.

ONLINE / DISTANCE LEARNING

Not available

COURSES OF INSTRUCTION

- Furniture Design and Theory
- Kitchen and Bath Design I and II
- Lighting and Mechanical Systems
- Residential Planning
- Residential Design
- The Corporate Building

INTERNSHIPS

Not required of majors. Interns are typically placed at contract Interior Design firms, architectural firms, and retailers.

STUDY ABROAD

Available through Central Connecticut State University and Southern Connecticut State University.

NOTABLE ALUMNI

Not reported

STUDENT ACTIVITIES AND ORGANIZATIONS

Student chapter of ASID, Student Council

FACULTY SPECIALIZATIONS AND RESEARCH

Architecture, Lighting Consultant, High End Residential Design, Museum and Gallery Installations

Brevard Community College

Interior Technology Program

3865 No. Wickham Rd., Melbourne, FL 32935 | 321-433-5861 | www.brevardcc.edu/careertech

UNIVERSITY PROFILE
Public
Suburban
Commuter
Semester Schedule
Co-ed

STUDENT DEMOGRAPHICS
Undergraduate: 75
Graduate: 0

Male: 10%
Female: 90%

Full-time: 80%
Part-time: 20%

EXPENSES
Tuition: Not reported
Room & Board: Not reported

ADMISSIONS
3865 N Wickham Rd.
Melbourne, Florida 32935
321-433-5550
brockertr@brevardcc.edu

DEGREE INFORMATION

Major / Degree / Concentration	Enrollment	Requirements for entry	Graduation rate
Interior Design Technology Associate of Science	Not reported	Not reported	Not reported
Kitchen and Bath Specialization Certificate	Not reported	Not reported	Not reported

TOTAL PROGRAM ENROLLMENT
Undergraduate: 75
Graduate: 0

Male: 10%
Female: 90%

Full-time: Not reported
Part-time: Not reported

International: Not reported
Minority: Not reported

Job Placement Rate: Not reported

SCHOLARSHIPS / FINANCIAL AID
Not reported

TOTAL FACULTY: 6
Full-time: 1
Part-time: 5
Online: 1

NCIDQ Certified: 4
Licensed Interior Designers: 4
LEED Certified: 0

INTERIOR DESIGN ADMINISTRATION
Dr. Katheryn Cobb, Provost

PROFESSIONAL / ACADEMIC AFFILIATIONS
International Interior Design Association

PROGRAM DESCRIPTION AND PHILOSOPHY

This program prepares students for employment in an Interior Design, architectural, or construction firm leading to state licensing and registration as an Interior Designer. Interior Design goes far beyond decorating. Interior Designers impact people's daily lives by creating custom residential, commercial, and leisure environments. This curriculum includes instruction in technical drafting skills, CAD programs, building materials, furnishings, and fixtures, utilizing a studio environment where students develop creative problem-solving skills. The skills garnered in design studios are necessary for developing and enhancing the spaces in which people live, work, and play. Education in the discipline and appropriate work experience along with passage of the state examination (NCIDQ) are the requirements to become a registered/licensed Interior Designer in Florida and in many other jurisdictions in the United States.

FACILITIES

Not reported

ONLINE / DISTANCE LEARNING

Not reported

COURSES OF INSTRUCTION

- Pictorial Drafting
- History of Interior Design 1
- Principles of Interior Design
- AutoCAD Fundamentals
- Building and Barrier Free Codes
- History of Design 2
- Architectural Drafting
- Residential Design 1
- Residential Design 2
- Materials and Sources
- Lighting
- Communications 1
- Kitchen and Bath Design 1
- Textiles for Interiors
- Interior Design Business Practices
- Kitchen and Bath Design 2
- Commercial Interior Design 1
- Why Preservation
- Social/Behavioral Science
- Inter-relationship of Design with Environments
- Commercial Interior Design 2
- Drawing
- Raster Graphics
- Survey of Materials and Resources
- Microcomputer Applications

INTERNSHIPS

Instructor signature required for registration, at second year level.

STUDY ABROAD

Available as a humanities course

NOTABLE ALUMNI

Not reported

STUDENT ACTIVITIES AND ORGANIZATIONS

Not reported

FACULTY SPECIALIZATIONS AND RESEARCH

Not reported

Florida State University

Department of Interior Design, College of Visual Arts, Theatre and Dance

302 Eppes Hall, Tallahassee, FL 32306 | 850-644-1436 | http://interiordesign.fsu.edu

UNIVERSITY PROFILE
Public
Suburban
Residential
Semester Schedule
Co-ed

STUDENT DEMOGRAPHICS
Undergraduate: 30,000
Graduate: 8,400

Male: 44.3%
Female: 55.7%

Full-time: 90%
Part-time: 10%

EXPENSES
Tuition: $3,156.30 (in-state):
$17,690.70 (out-of-state)
Room & Board: $8,390

ADMISSIONS
A2500 UCA
Tallahassee, FL 32306
850-644-6200
admissions@fsu.edu

DEGREE INFORMATION

Major / Degree / Concentration	Enrollment	Requirements for entry	Graduation rate
Interior Design Bachelor of Science	177	Passage of First Year Review	100%
Interior Design Post Professional Master of Science	Not reported	See Web site for current requirements	100%
Interior Design Post Professional Master of Fine Arts	Not reported	See Web site for current requirements	100%
Interior Design First Professional Master of Science	Not reported	See Web site for current requirements	100%

TOTAL PROGRAM ENROLLMENT
Undergraduate: 177
Graduate: 38

Male: 4%
Female: 96%

Full-time: 100%
Part-time: 0%

International: 3%
Minority: 13%

Job Placement Rate: 90%

SCHOLARSHIPS / FINANCIAL AID
General scholarships for
undergraduates are university funded,
not through the department. Check
University Admissions for further
information. Assistantships and stipends
available for Graduate Students.

TOTAL FACULTY: 13
Full-time: 62%
Part-time: 38%
Online: 0%

NCIDQ Certified: 50%
Licensed Interior Designers: 25%
LEED Certified: 12%

INTERIOR DESIGN ADMINISTRATION
Sally McRorie, Dean, College of Visual
Arts, Theatre and Dance
Eric Wiedegreen, Chair, Department of
Interior Design

PROFESSIONAL / ACADEMIC AFFILIATIONS
American Society of Interior Designers
International Interior Design Association
Interior Design Educators Council
Environmental Design Research
Association

CIDA ACCREDITATION
B.S. and B.A.—Interior Design (2009,
2015)

PROGRAM DESCRIPTION AND PHILOSOPHY

The mission of the Florida State University Interior Design program is to educate students to contribute to and advance the discipline and profession of Interior Design. The program will instill in students technological and graphic proficiencies including an understanding and sensitivity to history, environment, codes and standards, and human response. The program's academic objective is to promote the application of knowledge and skills to positively impact human culture. Long-term accreditation through CIDA.

FACILITIES

Program will move to the $49.2-million renovated William Johnston Building in Fall 2011. The new building will allow for some of the best design facilities in the nation, including cold desks for most studios, wood, working shop, CAD and Print labs, gallery, public critique space, subject specific library, and student networking areas.

ONLINE / DISTANCE LEARNING

Not available

COURSES OF INSTRUCTION

See Web site

INTERNSHIPS

Required of majors. Interns are placed at generally larger, multidisciplinary firms in urban areas.

STUDY ABROAD

23 years history of Summer Abroad study in Interior Design focused at the FSU Study Center in Florence, Italy. Also summer program at the Ringling Museum of Art (Sarasota, FL) on the restoration and preservation of the decorative arts.

NOTABLE ALUMNI

Kim Marks (President of NCIDQ); Sue Markham (Facility Manager for Gulf Power); 25 graduates of the program are now educators in university design programs across the country.

STUDENT ACTIVITIES AND ORGANIZATIONS

Active Interior Design Student Organization recognized by the university and aligned with both ASID and IIDA.

FACULTY SPECIALIZATIONS AND RESEARCH

Faculty represent a good mix of researchers and designers. The national presidents in the past five years of the Interior Design Educators Council (IDEC) have been FSU faculty. Strong faculty and program commitment to social justice issues and sustainability.

International Academy of Design & Technology–Tampa

Department of Interior Design

5104 Eisenhower Blvd., Tampa, FL 33634 | 813-880-8087 | www.academy.edu

UNIVERSITY PROFILE
Private
Urban
Commuter

STUDENT DEMOGRAPHICS
Undergraduate: Not reported
Graduate: Not reported

Male: Not reported
Female: Not reported

Full-time: Not reported
Part-time: Not reported

EXPENSES
Tuition: Not reported
Room & Board: Not reported

ADMISSIONS
5104 Eisenhower Blvd.
Tampa, FL 33634
1-800-ACADEMY

DEGREE INFORMATION

Major / Degree / Concentration	Enrollment	Requirements for entry	Graduation rate
Interior Design **Associate of Science**	Not reported	Completion of high school / GED equivalency	Not reported
Interior Design **Bachelor of Fine Arts**	Not reported	Completion of high school / GED equivalency	Not reported

TOTAL PROGRAM ENROLLMENT
Undergraduate: Not reported
Graduate: Not reported

Male: Not reported
Female: Not reported

Full-time: Not reported
Part-time: Not reported

International: Not reported
Minority: Not reported

Job Placement Rate: Not reported

SCHOLARSHIPS / FINANCIAL AID
Financial Aid is available for those who qualify. A complete listing of scholarship opportunities and financial aid options is available in the campus Catalog.

TOTAL FACULTY: NOT REPORTED
Full-time: Not reported
Part-time: Not reported
Online: Not reported

NCIDQ Certified: Not reported
Licensed Interior Designers: Not reported
LEED Certified: Not reported

INTERIOR DESIGN ADMINISTRATION
Dr. Karen O'Donnell, President
Phil Bulone, Dean of Education
Pat Johnston, Chair Interior Design

PROFESSIONAL / ACADEMIC AFFILIATIONS
American Society of Interior Designers
International Interior Design Association
Interior Design Educators Council

CIDA ACCREDITATION
Bachelor of Fine Arts in Interior Design
(2009, 2015)

PROGRAM DESCRIPTION AND PHILOSOPHY

The Interior Design program prepares students to develop creative and technical solutions for interior spaces that meet the aesthetic and functional requirements while addressing safety, regulatory, and environmental concerns. Students will apply the fundamentals of art and design, theories of design, "green design," and an understanding of human behavior to their design solutions. Critical thinking, research, analysis, documentation, and drawing and presentation skills are incorporated in the design process. Students have an opportunity to explore creativity through the selection of colors, materials and finishes, textiles, lighting solutions, furnishings, and other interior elements to solve design problems.

FACILITIES

Computer, drafting, resource room, lighting lab and copy facilities are on site. All computer labs are equipped with plotters.

ONLINE / DISTANCE LEARNING

Not reported

COURSES OF INSTRUCTION

See Web site

INTERNSHIPS

Required of majors

STUDY ABROAD

Available

NOTABLE ALUMNI

Not reported

STUDENT ACTIVITIES AND ORGANIZATIONS

Active chapters of ASID; IIDA and EGB

FACULTY SPECIALIZATIONS AND RESEARCH

Specialists in area of course assignments; full-time and adjunct

Miami International University of Art & Design

Department of Interior Design

1501 Biscayne Blvd., Suite 100, Miami, FL 33132 | 305-428-5673 | www.aii.edu/miami/

UNIVERSITY PROFILE
Private
Urban
Residential
Commuter
Quarter Schedule
Co-ed

STUDENT DEMOGRAPHICS
Undergraduate: Not reported
Graduate: Not reported

Male: Not reported
Female: Not reported

Full-time: Not reported
Part-time: Not reported

EXPENSES
Tuition: $80,000
Room & Board: $14,000

ADMISSIONS
1501 Biscayne Blvd., Suite 100
Miami, FL 33132
305-428-5600
aimiamifadm@aii.edu

DEGREE INFORMATION

Major / Degree / Concentration	Enrollment	Requirements for entry	Graduation rate
Interior Design Bachelor of Fine Arts	200	Application and interview	80%
Interior Design Master of Fine Arts	12	3.0 gpa Interior Design undergraduate degree. Portfolio, entry essay.	100%

TOTAL PROGRAM ENROLLMENT
Undergraduate: 200
Graduate: 12

Male: 10%
Female: 90%

Full-time: 70%
Part-time: 30%

International: 15%
Minority: 20%

Job Placement Rate: 90%

SCHOLARSHIPS / FINANCIAL AID
Miami International University of Art and Design has Student Financial Services to help students and their families develop a financial plan to ensure program completion. Specialists from this department help students complete applications for grants and loans applicable to students' circumstances. Once a student's eligibility is determined, the student and the specialist develop a plan for meeting educational expenses. Various loans are available to assist with educational costs as well as scholarships and grants.

Students Receiving Scholarships or Financial Aid: 80

TOTAL FACULTY: 14
Full-time: 60%
Part-time: 40%
Online: n/a

NCIDQ Certified: 40%
Licensed Interior Designers: 60%
LEED Certified: 10%

INTERIOR DESIGN ADMINISTRATION
Ricardo Navarro, Academic Department Director, Interior Design

PROFESSIONAL / ACADEMIC AFFILIATIONS
American Society of Interior Designers
International Interior Design Association
Interior Design Educators Council

CIDA ACCREDITATION
Bachelor of Fine Arts (2004, 2010)

PROGRAM DESCRIPTION AND PHILOSOPHY

The Philosophy of the Interior Design program is to foster the ability to create built environments through a full awareness and understanding of design. The program provides each student with the foundation to think critically, strategically, and creatively. The Interior Design Program is based on the premise that Interior Design is both an art and a science. As a professional discipline that interfaces between architecture and the end user, the Interior Design program strives to educate students in enhancing the quality of life and facilitate human activity within the built environment.

FACILITIES

- Computer Labs
- Drafting Labs
- Materials/Resource Room
- Museums and Miami Art District
- Full Scale plotters and printers on campus
- Wireless Internet Access throughout campus
- Student lounge

ONLINE / DISTANCE LEARNING

Not available

COURSES OF INSTRUCTION

- Interior Design Studio: Residential
- Interior Design Studio Commercial: Retail Design
- Interior Design Studio Commercial: Institutional Design
- Interior Design Studio Commercial: Office Design
- Interior Design Studio Commercial: Hospitality Design
- Human Factors
- Lighting Design
- Building Codes
- Fundamentals and Advanced Construction Documents
- Revit, Autocad, 3Dmax
- History of Architecture and Furniture
- Furniture Design
- Professional Practice and Administration

INTERNSHIPS

Required of majors at 12th quarter level. Students have been employed at many commercial and residential markets. Students have been able to seek employment at architectural firms, interior design firms, procurements firms, development companies, and manufacturing companies.

STUDY ABROAD

Not available

NOTABLE ALUMNI

Not reported

STUDENT ACTIVITIES AND ORGANIZATIONS

Student-lead Interior Design Club IDG (Interior Design Group), ASID/IIDA student chapters

FACULTY SPECIALIZATIONS AND RESEARCH

Sustainable Design Focus for many faculty, Residential Design, Office Design, Rendering (digital and hand), Sketching, Design Process

University of Florida

Department of Interior Design, College of Design, Construction & Planning

336 Architecture Building, Gainesville, FL 32611 | 352-392-0252 | www.dcp.ufl.edu/interior

UNIVERSITY PROFILE
Public
Suburban
Residential
Semester Schedule
Co-ed

STUDENT DEMOGRAPHICS
Undergraduate: 36,386
Graduate: 15,885

Male: 47%
Female: 53%

Full-time: 92%
Part-time: 8%

EXPENSES
Annual Tuition: $5,020 (in-state)
Room and Board: $7,500 (in-state); tuition/room & board $22,280 (out-of-state)

ADMISSIONS
201 Criser Hall
Gainesville, FL 32611
352-392-1365

DEGREE INFORMATION

Major / Degree / Concentration	Enrollment	Requirements for entry	Graduation rate
Bachelor of Design	100	2.8 gpa with selective admission after Sophomore year	95%
Master of Interior Design	25	3.0 gpa + minimum 1,000 GRE (see UFL Web site for most current information)	90%
Doctor of Philosophy	8	Master's in Interior Design or allied field, 3.0 gpa + minimum 1,000 GRE (see UFL Web site for most current information)	96%

TOTAL PROGRAM ENROLLMENT
Undergraduate: 100
MID: 25
PhD: 8

Male: 5
Female: 95

Full-time: 95
Part-time: 5

International: 7
Minority: 10

Job Placement Rate: 95%

SCHOLARSHIPS / FINANCIAL AID
Scholarships are available to upper division Interior Design students--see the department Web site for the most current information.

Students Receiving Scholarships or Financial Aid: 75%

TOTAL FACULTY
Full-time: 100%

NCIDQ Certified: 43%
Licensed Interior Designers: 43%
LEED Certified: 43%

INTERIOR DESIGN ADMINISTRATION
Margarget Portillo, Ph.D., Professor and Chair
Candy Carmel-Gilfilen, Assistant Professor and Undergraduate Coordinator
Maruja Torres-Antonini, Ph.D., Associate Professor and Graduate Coordinator

PROFESSIONAL / ACADEMIC AFFILIATIONS
American Society of Interior Designers
International Interior Design Association
Interior Design Educators Council
Environmental Design Research Association

CIDA ACCREDITATION
Bachelor of Design
(2005, 2011)

PROGRAM DESCRIPTION AND PHILOSOPHY

We see graduates from our Interior Design programs as becoming thought leaders in the field. Our well-recognized reputation stems from a commitment to the role of research in guiding the design process and informing design decisions. A dynamic studio-based learning approach only strengthened by:

- Being part of a multidisciplinary design college, affording interaction with historic preservation, architecture, landscape architecture, building construction, and urban and regional planning
- Being part of leading Association of American Universities (AAU) public institution offering exposure to many specialized programs, resources and learning experiences
- Being part of a large, dynamic campus with great involvement in in design planning and building projects with real clients who have real needs

The department also offers a 4+1 master's program, enabling students to complete a Master's of Interior Design with a specialization. Further, the program also has a unique design field experience requirment with four track options: (1) Internship within Florida, U.S. or overseas; (2) Study Abroad Program or Domestic Field School; (3) Service Learning Experience; (4) Design Research Project.

FACILITIES

Students have access to dedicated studios 24/7 with digital sketch tablets, plotters for large scale color printing as well as a college fabrication shop which affords students a cutting edge in manipulating materials and form. Our program also utilizes the College gallery, state-of-the-art computer lab, Harn Museum of Art as well as the Architecture & Fine Arts Library.

COURSES OF INSTRUCTION
- History of Interior Design I & II
- Design Innovation
- Architectural Design 1,2,3
- Introductional to Architectural Interiors
- Design Communications
- Interior Design Materials
- Computer Applications
- Interior Lighting
- Interior Design Construction Documents
- Environmental Technologies
- Professional Practice of Interior Design
- Advanced Design Detailing
- Preservation of Historic Interiors; Color Theory
- Interior Design Studios--focusing on on campus projects (i.e., Stadium Skybox, Art Museum staff offices and major exhibition space, Honors program offices and learning environiments); projects completed in partnership with design firms (international airports; healthcare facilities; corporate headquarters); national competition-based projects.

INTERNSHIPS

Interns are placed coast to coast in the United States and Internationally (ie. China and London) in leading Interior Design and architectural firms. Recently students have been placed in '100 design giant firms' and '100 green design firms' including Gensler, Perkins + Will, RTKL, VOA Associates, TPG Architecture, TVS Design, RMJM, HKS, Looney Ricks Kiss Architects, Heery International, Smallwood Reynolds Stewart Stewart & Associates, Gresham Smith and Partners, Haskell, Callison, Marc-Michaels Interior Design, Bilkey Llinas Design, Arquitectonica, and Nelson.

STUDY ABROAD
Available

NOTABLE ALUMNI
Juliana Catlin, FASID; Robert John Dean, FASID; Hugh Latta, FASID; Holmes Newman, FASID; Robert Blakeslee; Sally Burkhard; Leith Oatman; E. Camille Puckett; Jennifer Ramski; Susan Schuyler Smith; Robert Smith; Howard Snoweiss; Paula Stafford; Phyllis Taylor; James West; Larry Wilson

STUDENT ACTIVITIES AND ORGANIZATIONS
The university has student organizations including the American Society of Interior Designers (ASID), International Interior Design Association (IIDA), and Architecture College Council (ACC) with 60-80 members ranging from Freshman-graduate students. The organizations have monthly meetings, mixer events, educational seminars, and guest speakers. Projects include community outreach, philanthrophy, and design scholarship.

FACULTY SPECIALIZATIONS AND RESEARCH
Environmental and Social Sustainability; Historic Preservation and Adaptive Reuse; Environmental Lighting and Color; Creativity and Organizational Innovation; Design Security; Design Pedagogy; Narrative Studies; Cross-Cultural Design Research

COMMUNITY COLLEGE TRANSFERS
Community college students who wish to transfer to the University of Florida's Interior Design Department should complete 60 credit hours or have an A.A. degree and have earned a minimum overall gpa of 2.85 to be considered eligible for admission to the program.

The Art Institute of Atlanta

Interior Design Department

6600 Peachtree Dunwoody Rd. N.E., 100 Embassy Row, Atlanta, GA 30328 | 770-394-8300 | www.artinstitutes.ed

UNIVERSITY PROFILE
Private
Urban
Commuter
Quarter Schedule
Co-ed

STUDENT DEMOGRAPHICS
Undergraduate: 3,408
Graduate: 0

Male: Not reported
Female: Not reported

Full-time: Not reported
Part-time: Not reported

EXPENSES
Tuition: $22,656
Room & Board: $24,500

ADMISSIONS
6600 Peachtree Dunwoody
Rd. N.E., 100 Embassy Row
Atlanta, GA 30328
770-394-8300
jmmclure@aii.edu

DEGREE INFORMATION

Major / Degree / Concentration	Enrollment	Requirements for entry	Graduation rate
Bachelor of Fine Arts	238	Application for admission, a 150-word essay, a signed notice regarding transferability for credit earned, and high school transcripts or GED test scores. Official reports of SAT, ACT, ASSET, or COMPASS scores must be given to the school. Students are required to complete an interview with an assistant director of admissions and to present a portfolio of their work. There is a $50 application fee.	31%

TOTAL PROGRAM ENROLLMENT
Undergraduate: 252
Graduate: 0

Male: 12%
Female: 88%

Full-time: 82%
Part-time: 18%

International: 5%
Minority: 34%

Job Placement Rate: 86.5% (2008)

SCHOLARSHIPS / FINANCIAL AID
See opposite page for more info.

TOTAL FACULTY: 14
Full-time: 8
Part-time: 6
Online: varies

NCIDQ Certified: 40%
Licensed Interior Designers: 14%
LEED Certified: 7%

INTERIOR DESIGN ADMINISTRATION
Paul M. Black, Department Chair

PROFESSIONAL / ACADEMIC AFFILIATIONS
American Society of Interior Designers
International Interior Design Association
Interior Design Educators Council

CIDA ACCREDITATION
Bachelor of Fine Arts in Interior Design
(2010, 2016)

PROGRAM DESCRIPTION AND PHILOSOPHY

The philosophy of the Interior Design department is based on the premise that Interior Design is both an art and a science. As the discipline that interfaces between architecture and the user, its purpose is to enhance the quality of life and facilitate human activity in the built environment. The study of this discipline is best served by a multi-disciplinary approach, which combines the critical thinking skills and broad, cultural knowledge inherent in the liberal arts with the creative and technical skills necessary for Interior Design practice. The program combines theoretical considerations with practical experiences to integrate knowledge and its application.

The mission of the Interior Design department is to prepare students to function as trained professionals who can conceive and develop viable, creative design solutions within the realities of a global market. The development of realistic expectations for individual achievement within the field enables students to contribute successfully at many diverse levels. By meeting the education goals, students should develop an attitude of flexibility and a desire for life-long learning that will enable them to become contributing members of the design profession. They should recognize their responsibility to meet the evolving needs of individuals, to the global community and to the principles of sustainable design.

FACILITIES

Alternate Campus Location in Decatur, GA, Bookout Collection (special ID collection in Library) CAD Labs, Drafting Studios, Lighting Lab, Resource Room, Gallery.

ONLINE / DISTANCE LEARNING

Up to 20% of the degree can be earned through online courses at The Art Institute of Pittsburgh, online division. In addition, most classes have an online component.

COURSES OF INSTRUCTION
- Architectural Drafting
- Interior Space
- Human Factors
- Design Process
- Design Development
- Lighting Design
- Corporate Design
- Specialty Design
- Problems in Residential Design
- Advanced Corporate
- Hospitality Design
- Historic Preservation

INTERNSHIPS
Available for 3rd year and above

Placement:
Hirsch Bedner & Associates
Design Continuum
Gensler
Peace Design
Stan Topal Associates
Steinmetz Associates
Ferry Hayes and Allan
McAlpine Booth & Ferrier Interiors
Dekalb Office Environments
Ivan Allan Workspace
Teknion
Lodgian Hotels
Haverty's Funiture

STUDY ABROAD
Available

NOTABLE ALUMNI
Jackie Naylor, ASID
Ann Platz, ISID
Barbara Westmoreland, ASID
Sue Whisler, ASID

STUDENT ACTIVITIES AND ORGANIZATIONS
ASID Student Chapter, IIDA Student Chapter, Retail Design Insitute

FACULTY SPECIALIZATIONS AND RESEARCH
LEED, Commercial, Retail Design, Design for Aging, Design for Health Care, Computer Applications, Hand Rendering, Residential, Housing

SCHOLARSHIPS / FINANCIAL AID
Evelyn Keedy Memorial Scholarship
Congressional Art Competition Scholarships
National Art Honor Society Scholarship
Georgia Equalizaton Tuiton Grant
President's Award for Perfect Attendance
President's Scholarship
Scholastics Arts Competition
Technology Student Association Competition
VICA (Vocational Industrial Clubs of America)
The Art Institute of Atlanta High School Scholarship Competition
The Art Institute of Atlanta 50th Anniversary Scholarship
The Art Institute of Atlanta Merit Award
Bookout Scholarship
NEWH Scholarships

Bauder College

Department of Interior Design

384 Northyards Blvd., Atlanta, GA 30313 | 404-237-7573 | http://atlanta.bauder.edu

UNIVERSITY PROFILE
Private
Urban
Commuter
Quarter Schedule
Co-ed

STUDENT DEMOGRAPHICS
Undergraduate: Not reported
Graduate: Not reported

Male: 50%
Female: 50%

Full-time: 80%
Part-time: 20%

EXPENSES
Tuition: Not reported
Room & Board: Not reported

ADMISSIONS
384 Northyards Blvd.,
Suite 190
Atlanta, GA 30313

DEGREE INFORMATION

Major / Degree / Concentration	Enrollment	Requirements for entry	Graduation rate
Interior Design Associate of Arts	238	Not reported	95%

TOTAL PROGRAM ENROLLMENT
Undergraduate: 1,400

Male: 20%
Female: 80%

Full-time: 90%
Part-time: 10%

International: Not reported
Minority: Not reported

Job Placement Rate: 95%

SCHOLARSHIPS / FINANCIAL AID
Not reported

TOTAL FACULTY: Not reported
Full-time: Not reported
Part-time: Not reported
Online: Not reported

NCIDQ Certified: Not reported
Licensed Interior Designers: Not reported
LEED Certified: Not reported

INTERIOR DESIGN ADMINISTRATION
Karen Driskell, Department Chair

PROFESSIONAL / ACADEMIC AFFILIATIONS
American Society of Interior Designers
Interior Design Educators Council

PROGRAM DESCRIPTION AND PHILOSOPHY

A degree in Interior Design from Bauder College can help you launch an exciting new career. Our Interior Design program includes the training and opportunity to design several interior environments. You will be presented with the principles of space planning, material selection, drafting, and presentation. In addition, our program includes education in the creative use of color, lighting, style, and fabrics. Technical design capabilities can be enhanced through the use of computer-aided design software. You can learn how to effectively communicate with clients and vendors by using industry-recognized visual tools, strategic planning, and effective problem-solving techniques.

Upon successful completion of the program graduates are awarded an associate's degree.

Program Features Include
- A curriculum that develops both design and technical skills
- An ideal environment for students who are creative and outgoing
- Training in the use of basic drafting equipment
- Available externships that allow students to participate in project design
- Field trips to destinations of design interest

Potential Career Opportunities
As a graduate of this program you may find future entry-level employment opportunities such as:
- Interior Designer
- Home interior consultant
- Kitchen/bath designer
-

Additional opportunities for Interior Design graduates are found in both the retail and wholesale industries as manufacturers' representatives, showroom personnel, and in furniture sales.

FACILITIES
Drawing/Drafting labs, Large Resource/Sample room, designated CAD lab

ONLINE / DISTANCE LEARNING
Not available

COURSES OF INSTRUCTION
Not reported

INTERNSHIPS
Required of majors

STUDY ABROAD
Not available

NOTABLE ALUMNI
Not reported

STUDENT ACTIVITIES AND ORGANIZATIONS
Student chapter of ASID

FACULTY SPECIALIZATIONS AND RESEARCH
Kitchen and Bath design, CAD operator, Hospitality design, Residential and model home design, Retail design

COMMUNITY COLLEGE TRANSFERS
SACS accredited, credits may transfer

Brenau University–Evening Weekend College

Department of Interior Design

500 Washington St. S.E., Campus Box 10, Gainesville, GA 30501 | 770-534-6240 | www.brenau.edu

UNIVERSITY PROFILE
Private
Urban
Commuter
Semester Schedule
Co-ed

STUDENT DEMOGRAPHICS
Undergraduate: 859
Graduate: 592

Male: 19%
Female: 81%

Full-time: Not reported
Part-time: Not reported

EXPENSES
Tuition: $411 (undergraduate credit); $515 (graduate credit)
Room & Board: n/a

ADMISSIONS
500 Washington St. S.E.
Gainesville, GA 30501
770-534-6100
admissions@brenau.edu

DEGREE INFORMATION

Major / Degree / Concentration	Enrollment	Requirements for entry	Graduation rate
Interior Design Bachelor of Fine Arts / Master of Interior Design (5-year program)	28	Open entry with Sophomore portfolio review and entry portfolio review for the MID	98%
Interior Design Master of Fine Arts	Starting Fall 2010	Not reported	Not reported

TOTAL PROGRAM ENROLLMENT
Undergraduate: 24
Graduate: 6

Male: 0%
Female: 100%

Full-time: 90%
Part-time: 10%

International: Not reported
Minority: Not reported

Job Placement Rate: Not reported

SCHOLARSHIPS / FINANCIAL AID
Not reported

TOTAL FACULTY: 7
Full-time: 2
Part-time: 5
Online: 2

NCIDQ Certified: 7
Licensed Interior Designers: 3
LEED Certified: 2

INTERIOR DESIGN ADMINISTRATION
Dr. Andrea Birch, Dean of the School of Fine Art and Humanities
Lynn Jones, Chair of Interior Design
Noreen Connelly, Interior Design Program Director

PROFESSIONAL / ACADEMIC AFFILIATIONS
American Society of Interior Designers
International Interior Design Association
Interior Design Educators Council

CIDA ACCREDITATION
Bachelor of Fine Arts/ Master of Interior Design (2007, 2013)

PROGRAM DESCRIPTION AND PHILOSOPHY

The North Atlanta campus is a campus primarily for the older, non-traditional student, many of whom have previous degrees. The mission statement and the curriculum are the same for both locations.

FACILITIES

Computer classrooms and labs with AutoCAD and Adobe software, large format plotter, printer, scanner, blueprint machine, material resource room

ONLINE / DISTANCE LEARNING

Online courses are available but no online Interior Design degree is offered.

COURSES OF INSTRUCTION

Not reported

INTERNSHIPS

Required of majors

STUDY ABROAD

Available through the art history courses

NOTABLE ALUMNI

Not reported

STUDENT ACTIVITIES AND ORGANIZATIONS

Student chapter of ASID

FACULTY SPECIALIZATIONS AND RESEARCH

Commercial Design, Facilities Design, Historical Preservation, Universal Design, Sustainability, Rendering, 2D and 3D AutoCAD

Brenau University–Women's College

Department of Interior Design

500 Washington St. SE., Campus Box 10, Gainesville, GA 30501 | 770-534-6240 | www.brenau.edu

UNIVERSITY PROFILE
Private
Urban
Residential
Semester Schedule
Women Only

STUDENT DEMOGRAPHICS
Undergraduate: 833
Graduate: 58

Male: 0%
Female: 100%

Full-time: 95%
Part-time: 5%

EXPENSES
Tuition: $19,870
Room & Board: $10,065

ADMISSIONS
500 Washington St. S.E.
Gainesville, GA 30501
770-534-6100
admissions@brenau.edu

DEGREE INFORMATION

Major / Degree / Concentration	Enrollment	Requirements for entry	Graduation rate
Interior Design Bachelor of Fine Arts / Master of Interior Design (5-year program)	18	Open entry with Sophomore portfolio review and entry portfolio review for the MID	98%

TOTAL PROGRAM ENROLLMENT
Undergraduate: 18
Graduate: 0

Male: 0%
Female: 100%

Full-time: 100%
Part-time: 0%

International: Not reported
Minority: Not reported

Job Placement Rate: Not reported

SCHOLARSHIPS / FINANCIAL AID
Art and Design scholarship with a portfolio review. Other options available university-wide.

TOTAL FACULTY: 7
Full-time: 2
Part-time: 5
Online: 2

NCIDQ Certified: 7
Licensed Interior Designers: 3
LEED Certified: 2

INTERIOR DESIGN ADMINISTRATION
Dr. Andrea Birch, Dean of the School of Fine Art and Humanities
Lynn Jones, Chair of Interior Design
Noreen Connelly, Interior Design Program Director

PROFESSIONAL / ACADEMIC AFFILIATIONS
American Society of Interior Designers
International Interior Design Association
Interior Design Educators Council

CIDA ACCREDITATION
Bachelor of Fine Arts/Master of Interior Design (2007, 2013)

PROGRAM DESCRIPTION AND PHILOSOPHY

The Interior Design department of Brenau University supports the four Learning Portals of the Institutional Strategic Plan and is committed to the goals set forth in the University's mission statement and principles of practice. The mission of the Interior Design department, consistent with the University's stated mission, is to provide excellence in Interior Design education in a student-centered environment grounded in a liberal arts tradition that prepares students to practice Interior Design in the twenty-first century.

FACILITIES

Computer classrooms and labs with AutoCAD and Adobe software, large format plotter, printer, scanner, blueprint machine, material resource room

ONLINE / DISTANCE LEARNING

Online courses are available but no online Interior Design degree is offered.

COURSES OF INSTRUCTION

Not reported

INTERNSHIPS

Required of majors

STUDY ABROAD

Available through the art history courses

NOTABLE ALUMNI

Not reported

STUDENT ACTIVITIES AND ORGANIZATIONS

Student chapter of ASID

FACULTY SPECIALIZATIONS AND RESEARCH

Commercial Design, Facilities Design, Historical Preservation, Universal Design, Sustainability, Rendering, 2D and 3D AutoCAD

Georgia Southern University

Department of Hospitality, Tourism, & Family & Consumer Sciences

1110 IT Dr., P.O. Box 8057, Statesboro, GA 30460 | 912-478-5544 | www.georgiasouthern.edu/

UNIVERSITY PROFILE
Public
Suburban
Residential
Semester Schedule
Co-ed

STUDENT DEMOGRAPHICS
Undergraduate: 19,000
Graduate: 2,574

Male: 35%
Female: 65%

Full-time: 36%
Part-time: 64%

EXPENSES
Tuition: $3,996 (in-state);
$15,972 (out-of-state)
Room & Board: $7,900

ADMISSIONS
P.O. Box 8024
Statesboro, GA 30460
912-478-5391

DEGREE INFORMATION

Major / Degree / Concentration	Enrollment	Requirements for entry	Graduation rate
Interior Design Bachelor of Science	112	2.25 gpa and a C or better in four required major courses and the completion of 30 credit hours, an application and a letter of intent. 18 students are selected each semester.	85%

TOTAL PROGRAM ENROLLMENT
Undergraduate: 112
Graduate: 0

Male: 2%
Female: 98%

Full-time: 95%
Part-time: 5%

International: 2%
Minority: 8%

Job Placement Rate: 90%

SCHOLARSHIPS / FINANCIAL AID
Georgia Southern University offers over fourteen different scholarship opportunities based on a variety of qualifications. Scholarships related to Interior Design are made available by faculty through professional organizations. Interior Design students have been consistently awarded scholarships from the Network of Executive Women in Hospitality, GA, chapter and the Statesboro Home Builders Association.

TOTAL FACULTY: 4
Full-time: 100%
Part-time: Not reported
Online: Not reported

NCIDQ Certified: 75%
Licensed Interior Designers: 25%
LEED Certified: 25%

INTERIOR DESIGN ADMINISTRATION
Dr. Jean Bartels, Dean of the College of Health and Human Sciences
Dr. Diana Cone, Chair of the Department of Hospitality, Tourism, and Family and Consumer Sciences
Ms. Patricia M. Walton, ASID, IDEC, Interior Design Program Coordinator

PROFESSIONAL / ACADEMIC AFFILIATIONS
American Society of Interior Designers
International Interior Design Association
Interior Design Educators Council

CIDA ACCREDITATION
Bachelor of Science, Major in Interior Design (2010, 2016)

8률88ível8

8 seq88

88ческого8

PROGRAM DESCRIPTION AND PHILOSOPHY

The mission of the program is to provide a professional undergraduate education that develops entry-level designers able to formulate practical and creative solutions relevant to the needs of the individual, family, organization, and community; to provide a broad range of Interior Design experiences which give the opportunity to develop practical, technical, and organizational skills along with aesthetic judgment; to prepare the graduate to be an entry-level professional and competent Interior Designer in the region and the global community.

The Interior Design program has a myriad of strengths supported by CIDA's assertion that it is worthy of national accreditation and national recognition since 2000 (*Council for Interior Design Accreditation). The curriculum is extremely contemporary, utilizing technology effectively and efficiently. The thrust of the curriculum is focused on design projects, with students graduating with real world skills and experiences. Learning extends beyond the classroom with historic tours (Savannah, Charleston); the New York Interior Study Tour, the Las Vegas Hospitality Expo, classes and exhibits in Atlanta; guest speakers and special events on campus who share worldly knowledge and professional wisdom. The curriculum meets the standards for Interior Design licensure in the State of Georgia and Georgia Southern graduates are in demand in the design workforce.

FACILITIES

The Interior Design program offers two computer labs dedicated to our majors. One 36-seat teaching lab with new furnishings and computers as of 2009 with specialized software such as Revit and Architectural Desktop and AutoCAD. A dedicated student resource center with large format plotter, printers and scanners, and work space for project assembly. A 500 sf resource library is maintained by student workers with organized samples for student use. Design resources include catalogs and extensive samples for all types of finishes and fabrics for both commercial and residential design. The program facilities are conveniently located in the center of our beautiful campus with easy access o the new comprehensive university library, student center, and bookstore.

ONLINE / DISTANCE LEARNING
Not at this time

COURSES OF INSTRUCTION
- Art Foundation 2D, 3D, Drawing
- Art History
- Interior Design Graphics
- Design Studio I Presentation
- Interior Materials
- Decorative Accessories
- History of Interiors I and II
- Lighting
- CAD I and CAD II
- Building Codes
- Textiles for Interiors
- Studio II Residential
- Studio III Hospitality
- Professional Practices I and II
- Studio IV Commercial
- Studio V Thesis Capstone
- Interior Design Practicum

INTERNSHIPS
Required of majors at the Junior level. Graduates are well prepared to adapt to work in a variety of firms; commercial, hospitality and residential companies that range from large nationally known architectural and design firms to smaller sole proprietor businesses. Graduates continue to successfully pursue additional certifications such as NCIDQ, LEED AP, CKD, CBD and professional status in many of the professional Interior Design organizations.

STUDY ABROAD
Available.

NOTABLE ALUMNI
Not reported

STUDENT ACTIVITIES AND ORGANIZATIONS
Interior Design related student chapters for American Society of Interior Designers. Several students join the International Interior Design Association and the National Association of Kitchens and Baths. The campus offers many opportunities for student organizations emphasizing personal interests and abilities.

FACULTY SPECIALIZATIONS AND RESEARCH
All faculty are tenure-track, full-time professors who have earned an MFA or MA degree in Interior Design with professional membership in ASID, IIDA, and IDEC. The majority are NCIDQ qualified with specializations in residential design with a focus on Universal Design and Aging in Place; in design communication techniques both technology driven and hand skills; in sustainable design practices; in specialized upscale restaurant design and in corporate spaces including open office systems. All faculty are current in professional practice field as well.

Savannah College of Art & Design

Department of Interior Design, School of Building Arts

Savannah Campus: P.O. Box 3146, Savannah, GA 31411 | 912-525-6911 | www.scad.edu/interior-design
Atlanta Campus: 1600 Peachtree St., Atlanta, GA 30309 | 912-525-5100 | www.scad.edu/interior-design

UNIVERSITY PROFILE
Private
Urban
Commuter
Quarter Schedule
Co-ed

STUDENT DEMOGRAPHICS
Undergrad & Grad: approx.
7,500 in Savannah campus

Male: Not reported
Female: Not reported

Full-time: Not reported
Part-time: Not reported

EXPENSES
Tuition: $29,070
Room & Board: $7,460

ADMISSIONS
P.O. Box 3146
Savannah, GA 31411
912-525-5152
admissions@scad.edu

DEGREE INFORMATION

Major / Degree / Concentration	Enrollment	Requirements for entry	Graduation rate
Interior Design **Bachelor of Fine Arts**	Not reported	Not reported	Not reported
Interior Design **Master of Fine Arts**	Not reported	Not reported	Not reported
Interior Design **Master of Arts**	Not reported	Not reported	Not reported

TOTAL PROGRAM ENROLLMENT
Undergraduate: 435
Graduate: 89

Male: Unknown
Female: Unknown

Full-time: Not reported
Part-time: Not reported

International: 10%
Minority: Not reported

Job Placement Rate: Not reported

SCHOLARSHIPS / FINANCIAL AID
Hank Stembridge Scholarship is
specifically for Interior Design students.

TOTAL FACULTY: 30
Full-time: 75%
Part-time: 25%
Online: 5%

NCIDQ Certified: 75%
Licensed Interior Designers: Not
reported
LEED Certified: 50%

INTERIOR DESIGN ADMINISTRATION
Khoi Vo, Chair, (Savannah Campus)
Rebekah Adkins, Chair, (Atlanta
Campus)
Sandi Haggberg, Admin. Assistant

PROFESSIONAL / ACADEMIC AFFILIATIONS
American Society of Interior Designers
International Interior Design Association
Interior Design Educators Council

CIDA ACCREDITATION
Bachelor of Fine Arts in Interior Design
(2009, 2015) - Atlanta
Bachelor of Fine Arts in Interior Design
(2009, 2015) - Savannah

PROGRAM DESCRIPTION AND PHILOSOPHY

Interior Designers identify, research, and creatively solve problems pertaining to the function, safety and quality of interior environments. SCAD offers one of the largest and most professionally-engaged Interior Design programs in the United States. Students benefit from the expertise of full-time faculty who hold terminal degrees in the field and who share a common belief that a holistic educational framework guides future professional development and inspires life-long learning.

The Interior Design program challenges students to become innovative designers who are capable of critical thinking and effective communication. Professional ethics and values are stressed within the context of social, environmental, and global design practice. Projects include commercial, residential, and institutional design, and address a wide range of behavioral, environmental, decorative, and technical issues. Social responsibility and sustainability are emphasized.

SCAD Interior Design students work with electronic design software including Revit, AutoCAD, MicroStation, SketchUp, Adobe CS5 Master Collection, 3Ds Max, SURFCAM, and Autodesk Maya. A fully integrated intranet system offers online help, shared drive space, downloadable 3D models, building-use maps, and access to online resources.

In the B.F.A. program, students gain a strong foundation in drawing, design and technology, and also study design history, human responses to the environment, construction, materials, furnishings, lighting, building codes, barrier-free design, sustainable design and professional practices. The M.A. degree offers advanced study for those who wish to gain knowledge of design theory and the Interior Design profession with an emphasis on emerging materials, human response, and research methods.

The M.F.A. is a terminal degree that emphasizes design inquiry, in-depth investigation, and communication for students who wish to become design practitioners and/or earn the credentials to teach at the college level.

The DesignIntelligence 2010 Deans Survey named the SCAD graduate program in Interior Design one of the top three most admired for "preparing students for practice," noting SCAD's "excellent faculty and rigorous application of theory."

FACILITIES
Cutting-edge software; multiple computer labs; museums; historic sites; archives, etc.

ONLINE / DISTANCE LEARNING
Master of Arts only

COURSES OF INSTRUCTION
- Intro. to Interior Design
- Form, Space, and Order
- Interior Materials
- History of Interior Design
- Lighting for the Interior
- Human Responses to the Built Environment
- Portfolio Prep.
- Professional Practices
- Studios I, II, III, IV, V, VI.

INTERNSHIPS
Required of majors. Interns are typically placed at companies such as HOK, HIRSCH BEDNER, Gulfstream Aerospace, The Moderns, Ltd., Gensler Architecture, Staybridge Suites.

STUDY ABROAD
Available

NOTABLE ALUMNI
Not reported

STUDENT ACTIVITIES AND ORGANIZATIONS
Not reported

FACULTY SPECIALIZATIONS AND RESEARCH
Healthcare Design

University of Georgia

Lamar Dodd School of Art

270 River Rd., Athens, GA 30602 | 706-542-1511 | www.art.uga.edu/interiordesign

UNIVERSITY PROFILE
Public
Urban
Residential
Semester Schedule
Co-ed

STUDENT DEMOGRAPHICS
Undergraduate: 26,142
Graduate: 8,743

Male: Not reported
Female: Not reported

Full-time: Not reported
Part-time: Not reported

EXPENSES
Tuition: $7,530
Room & Board: $8,046

ADMISSIONS
Terrell Hall
Athens, GA 30602
706-542-1466
undergrad@admissions.uga
.edu

DEGREE INFORMATION

Major / Degree / Concentration	Enrollment	Requirements for entry	Graduation rate
Interior Design Bachelor of Fine Arts	102	School or Art Portfolio Review first semeste.r, ID Progression Review third semester, including portfolio, gpa, and assigned weekend-long project	99%
Interior Design Master of Fine Arts	5	Portfolio review	99%

TOTAL PROGRAM ENROLLMENT
Undergraduate: 102
Graduate: 5

Male: 2%
Female: 98%

Full-time: 100%
Part-time: 0%

International: 3%
Minority: 1%

Job Placement Rate: Historically: 95% with 5% going directly into graduate school for architecture

SCHOLARSHIPS / FINANCIAL AID
Nearly all in-state students receive HOPE Scholarships, which cover the tuition and provides a book allowance. The program offers two scholarships annually for studying in Athens. The UGA Cortona Studies abroad program offers two more annually for Interior Design students.

Students Receiving Scholarships or Financial Aid: 95%

TOTAL FACULTY: 10
Full-time: 4
Part-time: 6
Online: 0

NCIDQ Certified: 2
Licensed Interior Designers: 1
LEED Certified: 2

INTERIOR DESIGN ADMINISTRATION
Georgia Strange, Director
Thom Houser, Associate Director and
  Interior Design Chair

PROFESSIONAL / ACADEMIC AFFILIATIONS
American Society of Interior Designers
Interior Design Educators Council

CIDA ACCREDITATION
Bachelor of Fine Arts/Interior Design
(2006, 2012)

138

PROGRAM DESCRIPTION AND PHILOSOPHY

Students are encouraged to develop a personal style in the area or the materials they specialize in. The B.F.A. candidate should achieve an insight into and an understanding of the nature of the materials they choose to work with. In most areas, students are required to present an exhibition before graduation that demonstrates their achievement in developing a mature and cohesive body of work.

FACILITIES

The Lamar Dodd School of Art has all of the facilities one expects in a major research institution, including wood and metal shops, laser cutter and CNC router, diverse fine art and design studios. The campus includes the Georgia Museum of Art and the State of Georgia Botanical Gardens.

ONLINE / DISTANCE LEARNING

Not available

COURSES OF INSTRUCTION

- Drawing, I and II
- Color Comp
- Art History
- Studio I-V
- Concepts Studio
- Concepts Lecture
- CAD
- Building Systems
- Materials
- Lighting
- Furniture Design
- Professional Practices
- Internship or Study Abroad
- ID History
- Exit Studio

INTERNSHIPS

Required of majors between 3rd and 4th year. Nationally and regionally students have interned at Gensler, Perkins+Will, Hirsch Bedner Associates, Design Continuum, Image Design, plus many more prominent firms. Internationally students have interned in London, Paris, Amsterdam, Sydney, and Seoul.

STUDY ABROAD

Students may study on the UGA campus during spring of their third year or take the same classes at our campus in Cortona, Italy, that same summer. Typically 40-60% of our students have a residential study abroad experience.

NOTABLE ALUMNI

Not reported

STUDENT ACTIVITIES AND ORGANIZATIONS

Student Chapter of ASID

FACULTY SPECIALIZATIONS AND RESEARCH

Interior Design, architecture, photography, time-based media, installation art

Westwood College

School of Design

1100 Spring St., NW, Atlanta, GA 30309 | 404-898-9321 | **www.westwood.edu**

UNIVERSITY PROFILE
Private
Urban
Commuter
Quarter Schedule
Co-ed

STUDENT DEMOGRAPHICS
Undergraduate: 800
Graduate: 0

Male: 45%
Female: 55%

Full-time: 95%
Part-time: 5%

EXPENSES
Tuition: Not reported
Room & Board: Not reported

ADMISSIONS
1100 Spring St., NW
Atlanta, GA 30309
404-898-9321

DEGREE INFORMATION

Major / Degree / Concentration	Enrollment	Requirements for entry	Graduation rate
Interior Design Bachelor of Science	15	Not reported	80%
CAD Associate of Science	15	Portfolio review	90%

TOTAL PROGRAM ENROLLMENT
Undergraduate: 30
Graduate: 0

Male: 45%
Female: 55%

Full-time: 95%
Part-time: 5%

International: 5%
Minority: 80%

Job Placement Rate: Not reported

SCHOLARSHIPS / FINANCIAL AID
Not reported

TOTAL FACULTY: 6
Full-time: 2
Part-time: 4
Online: Not reported

NCIDQ Certified: 3
Licensed Interior Designers: 2
LEED Certified: 2

INTERIOR DESIGN ADMINISTRATION
Not reported

PROFESSIONAL / ACADEMIC AFFILIATIONS
Not reported

PROGRAM DESCRIPTION AND PHILOSOPHY
Not reported

FACILITIES
Not reported

ONLINE / DISTANCE LEARNING
Available, through our online school

COURSES OF INSTRUCTION
- Color Theory
- Design Theory
- Drawing and Perspective
- Residential Interiors
- Space Planning
- Commercial Interiors
- CAD I
- Residential CAD
- Commercial CAD
- 3D CAD
- Residential Comm.

INTERNSHIPS
Not reported

STUDY ABROAD
Not reported

NOTABLE ALUMNI
Not reported

STUDENT ACTIVITIES AND ORGANIZATIONS
Not reported

FACULTY SPECIALIZATIONS AND RESEARCH
Not reported

Iowa State University

Interior Design Program, College of Design

146 College of Design, Ames, IA 50011 | 515-294-6983 | www.design.iastate.edu/interiordesign/index.php

UNIVERSITY PROFILE
Public
Rural
Residential
Semester Schedule
Co-ed

STUDENT DEMOGRAPHICS
Undergraduate: 22,521
Graduate: 5,424

Male: 56.3%
Female: 43.7%

Full-time: 88.5%
Part-time: 11.5%

EXPENSES
Tuition: $18,500
Room & Board: $7,500

ADMISSIONS
Office of Admissions
100 Enrollment Services
Center
Ames, IA 50011-2011
800-262-3810
admissions@iastate.edu

DEGREE INFORMATION

Major / Degree / Concentration	Enrollment	Requirements for entry	Graduation rate
Interior Design **Bachelor of Fine Arts**	240	2.5 gpa Portfolio Review & written essay after Sophomore year	98%
Interior Design **Master of Fine Arts**	5	Interior Design BA or BFA Portfolio Review & Faculty approval	98%
Interior Design **Master of Arts** **First- Professional Degree**	10	Interior Design BA or BFA Portfolio Review & Faculty approval	98%

TOTAL PROGRAM ENROLLMENT
Undergraduate: 240
Graduate: 20

Male: 7%
Female: 93%

Full-time: 100%
Part-time: 0

International: 10%
Minority: 6%

Job Placement Rate: 100%

SCHOLARSHIPS / FINANCIAL AID
Financial aid and scholarships are available through the Office of Student Financial Aid at ISU for both merit and need (see financialaid.iastate.edu), as well as a large number of scholarships through the College of Design that apply specifically to Design students, and even more available to assist in the cost of study abroad in our Rome Program.

TOTAL FACULTY: 8
Full-time: 7
Part-time: 1
Online: 0

NCIDQ Certified: 3
Licensed Interior Designers: 1
LEED Certified: 3

INTERIOR DESIGN ADMINISTRATION
Lee Cagley, Director of Interior Design
Linda Galvin, Admistrative Specialist

PROFESSIONAL / ACADEMIC AFFILIATIONS
American Society of Interior Designers
International Interior Design Association
Interior Design Educators Council

CIDA ACCREDITATION
Bachelor of Fine Arts in Interior Design (2009, 2015)

PROGRAM DESCRIPTION AND PHILOSOPHY

Interior Design at ISU is focussed on the creative pursuit of bettering the interface between man and his surroundings. We believe strongly in a humanist approach to interior design, and support it with in-depth study of human factors, systems, universal design, globally and locally sustainable design methods, and socially responsible solutions for every inhabited space, from intimate and personal to macrocosmic and communal. Our goal is to help students create environments that support aspiration, desire, beauty, and hope.

FACILITIES

Computer Labs (and laptop leasing available); Brunnier Museum & Furniture Collection; Interdisciplinary opportunities in Architecture, Graphic Design, Digital Media, Integrated Studio Arts, Industrial Design, Art History & Critical Theory, Business & Management, Entrepreneurial Studies, and Human Computer Interface, to name only a few.

ONLINE / DISTANCE LEARNING

Not available

COURSES OF INSTRUCTION

Interior Design Studio Sophomore, Junior, & Senior Level; Human Factors; Building Systems; Lighting & HVAC Interior Systems; History of Interior Design; and a variety of option studios and electives allowing students to specialize in a broad spectrum of areas such as healthcare and wellness, hospitality, entrepreneurial studies, industrial design and product design, sustainability and biorenewables, color theory and application, and a constantly changing series of interdisciplinary studios dealing with collaborative solutions to global issues.

INTERNSHIPS

Required of majors at Junior level. Our internship students are required to locate with firms that have at least one Professional or Principal who has passed the NCIDQ exam, and we prefer them to be practicing Licensed Professionals. We have an excellent working relationship with a large number of firms both within the state of Iowa, as well as national and international interior design studios in a wide range of fields of specialization.

STUDY ABROAD

Junior year Fall semester can be spent in our facilities in Rome.

NOTABLE ALUMNI

Rachelle Schlosser-Lynn, Lee Cagley, Lori Brunner, Mary Anne Beecher, Susan Hoffman, Carol Moore, Deeia Topp, Rod Forslund, Lauri Tredinnick, Jennifer Nemec

STUDENT ACTIVITIES AND ORGANIZATIONS

Interior Design Student Association; IIDA Student chapter, ASID Student Chapter

FACULTY SPECIALIZATIONS AND RESEARCH

Humanics and Human Factors, Health, Safety, & Welfare Issues, Color Theory & Application, Research & Critical Theory in Interior Design, Hospitality, Wellness, and Environments for the Aging, Interior Architecture, Sustainable Environments, & Methods, Wayfinding, and a strong support system for Independent Study.

College of DuPage

Interior Design Program

425 Fawell Blvd., Glen Ellyn, IL 60137 | www.cod.edu/interior_design/index.htm

UNIVERSITY PROFILE
Public
Suburban
Commuter
Semester Schedule
Co-ed

STUDENT DEMOGRAPHICS
Undergraduate: 30,000
Graduate: 0

Male: 50%
Female: 50%

Full-time: 40%
Part-time: 60%

EXPENSES
Tuition: $129 per credit hour (District 502 residents); $316 per credit hour (out-of-district Illinois residents); $386 per credit hour (non-residents of the state of Illinois); $65 per credit hour (Senior citizens who are residents of District 502)

Room & Board: n/a

ADMISSIONS
Admissions and Information
College of DuPage
Student Resource Center (SRC), Room 2046
Glen Ellyn, IL 60137
630-942-3081
admissions@cod.edu

DEGREE INFORMATION

Major / Degree / Concentration	Enrollment	Requirements for entry	Graduation rate
Interior Design Associate of Applied Science	225	Open enrollment	90%
Advanced Kitchen & Bath Design Certificate* *NKBA accredited	20+	Required course per certificate	95%
Advanced Computer Application Certificate	20+	Required course per certificate	95%
Advanced Lighting Design Certificate	20+	Required course per certificate	95%
Sustainable Interior Design Certificate	New in Fall 2010	Required course per certificate	Not reported

TOTAL PROGRAM ENROLLMENT
Undergraduate: 275
Graduate: 0

Male: 10%
Female: 90%

Full-time: 30%
Part-time: 70%

International: 30%
Minority: 10%

Job Placement Rate: 85%

SCHOLARSHIPS / FINANCIAL AID
Not reported

TOTAL FACULTY: 12
Full-time: 2
Part-time: 10
Online: Not reported

NCIDQ Certified: 80%
Licensed Interior Designers: 80%
LEED Certified: 20%

INTERIOR DESIGN ADMINISTRATION
Karen Randall, Dean
Professor M. Ann Cotton, Coordinator

PROFESSIONAL / ACADEMIC AFFILIATIONS
American Society of Interior Designers
International Interior Design Association
Interior Design Educators Council

PROGRAM DESCRIPTION AND PHILOSOPHY
Intelligent Creativity

FACILITIES
New LEED Certified building with State-of-the-Art classrooms and dedicated CAD lab with plotters, lighting lab, gallery, and materials lab.

ONLINE / DISTANCE LEARNING
Not available

COURSES OF INSTRUCTION
Courses vary according to AAS degree and/or certificates

INTERNSHIPS
Required of majors per cooperative education credits or as NKBA certificate program

STUDY ABROAD
Field studies and cultural exchanges for credit

NOTABLE ALUMNI
Not reported

STUDENT ACTIVITIES AND ORGANIZATIONS
Kitchen and Bath student group / NKBA

FACULTY SPECIALIZATIONS AND RESEARCH
Lighting, history, green/LEED, contract, office, residential

COMMUNITY COLLEGE TRANSFERS
Various 2+2 degree transfer options to "CIDA" Illinois schools for completion of ID Bachelors after graduation with AAS ID degree.

Columbia College Chicago

Department of Art & Design

600 S. Michigan Ave., Chicago, IL 60605 | 312-369-7380 | www.colum.edu/Academics/Art_and_Design/

UNIVERSITY PROFILE
Private
Urban
Residential
Semester Schedule
Co-ed

STUDENT DEMOGRAPHICS
Undergraduate: 20,000
Graduate: Not reported

Male: Not reported
Female: Not reported

Full-time: Not reported
Part-time: Not reported

EXPENSES
Tuition: $20,190
(undergraduate); $16,966
(graduate)
Room & Board: $2,550

ADMISSIONS
600 S. Michigan Ave.
Chicago, IL 60605
312-369-7130
(undergraduate)
312-369-7260 (graduate)
admissions@colum.edu
(undergraduate)
gradstudy@colum.edu
(graduate)

DEGREE INFORMATION

Major / Degree / Concentration	Enrollment	Requirements for entry	Graduation rate
Interior Architecture Bachelor of Fine Arts	Not reported	Not reported	Not reported
Interior Architecture Master of Fine Arts	Not reported	Not reported	Not reported

TOTAL PROGRAM ENROLLMENT
Undergraduate: Not reported
Graduate: Not reported

Male: Not reported
Female: Not reported

Full-time: Not reported
Part-time: Not reported

International: Not reported
Minority: Not reported

Job Placement Rate: Not reported

SCHOLARSHIPS / FINANCIAL AID
Not reported

TOTAL FACULTY: 27
Full-time: 3
Part-time: Not reported
Online: Not reported

NCIDQ Certified: Not reported
Licensed Interior Designers: Not reported
LEED Certified: Not reported

INTERIOR DESIGN ADMINISTRATION
Joclyn Oats, Director
Tim Cozzens, Coordinator of the BFA Interior Architecture Program

PROFESSIONAL / ACADEMIC AFFILIATIONS
American Society of Interior Designers
International Interior Design Association
Interior Design Educators Council
Interior Design Associations Foundation

CIDA ACCREDITATION
Bachelor of Fine Arts in Interior Architecture (2005, 2011)

PROGRAM DESCRIPTION AND PHILOSOPHY

Interior Architecture is a three-dimensional response to a client's environmental requirements. The Interior Architect is cognizant of building systems (structural, mechanical, etc.) and manipulates interior space, furniture, and finishes to serve functional requirements and conceptual/artistic ends. The program focuses almost exclusively on commercial/non-residential interior spatial solutions.

Students are prepared to enter the architecture and design profession as an entry-level designer by matriculating through the rigorous, CIDA-accredited foundation/advanced/professional-level coursework and participating in the mandatory internship program during their Senior year. Graduates typically join firms as active team members working on a variety of project typologies.
Following two years of professional experience, graduates are qualified to undertake the National Council for Interior Design Accreditation (NCIDQ) exam, leading to licensed/titled status.

FACILITIES
- 10th Floor Fine Art Studios
- The Shop
- Classrooms
- Ceramics Lab
- Digital Output Center
- Fashion Lab
- A+D Computer Lab
- Metals Lab
- Model Shop
- Printmaking Studio
- Resource Room
- Visual Media Center
- Wood Shop

ONLINE / DISTANCE LEARNING
Not reported

COURSES OF INSTRUCTION
- History of Art I: Stone Age to Gothic
- History of Art II: Renaissance to Modern
- Interior Architecture: Drawing I
- Drawing I
- Fundamentals of 2-D Design
- Fundamentals of 3-D Design
- Foundations of Photography I
- Darkroom Workshop I
- Digital Photography for Non-Majors
- Photography for Interior Architecture Majors
- History of Architecture I
- History of Architecture II
- Interior Architecture/Design Theory I
- Architectural Drafting and Detailing I
- AutoCAD Fundamentals
- Sources and Materials
- Color for Interiors
- Design Studio II
- History of Furniture Seminar
- Architectural Drafting and Detailing II
- Design Studio III: Code Compliance
- Design Studio IV: Adaptive Reuse
- Design Studio V: Global Issues
- Senior Project A: Research and Programming
- Senior Project B: Schematic Design
- Senior Project C: Design Development
- Senior Project D: Working Drawing
- Senior Project E: Presentation and Critique
- AutoCAD Detailing III
- AutoCAD Detailing IV
- Rendering and Presentation
- Fundamentals of Lighing
- Business Practice for Designers
- Portfolio Development Workshop

INTERNSHIPS
Required of major. You must have a cumulative gpa of 3.0 or better, and 60 or more credits earned to sign up for an Internship. Students have previously held internship with the following companies:
- Getty's Group Inc.
- McBride & Kelly Architects, Inc.
- Mekos Studios
- O'Donnell, Wicklund, Pigozzi & Peterson Architects, Inc.,
- Perkins & Will
- Skidmore Owings Merrill
- Vertex Architects
- VOA Associates, Inc.

STUDY ABROAD
Not reported

NOTABLE ALUMNI
Not reported

STUDENT ACTIVITIES AND ORGANIZATIONS
Not reported

FACULTY SPECIALIZATIONS AND RESEARCH
Not reported

Harper College

Department of Interior Design

CTP Division, 1200 W. Algonquin Rd., Palatine, IL 60067 | 847-925-6894 | www.harpercollege.edu/ind

UNIVERSITY PROFILE
Public
Suburban
Commuter
Semester Schedule
Co-ed

STUDENT DEMOGRAPHICS
Undergraduate: 26,000
Graduate: 0

Male: 45%
Female: 55%

Full-time: 44%
Part-time: 56%

EXPENSES
Tuition: $3,000
Room & Board: n/a

ADMISSIONS
2300 W. Algonquin Rd.
Palatine, IL 60067
847-925-6707

DEGREE INFORMATION

Major / Degree / Concentration	Enrollment	Requirements for entry	Graduation rate
Interior Design Associate of Applied Science	125	High school graduation	80%

TOTAL PROGRAM ENROLLMENT
Undergraduate: Not reported
Graduate: Not reported

Male: Not reported
Female: Not reported

Full-time: Not reported
Part-time: Not reported

International: 1%
Minority: 40%

Job Placement Rate: 50%

SCHOLARSHIPS / FINANCIAL AID
Not reported

TOTAL FACULTY: 16
Full-time: 1
Part-time: 15
Online: Not reported

NCIDQ Certified: 6
Licensed Interior Designers: 16
LEED Certified: 3

INTERIOR DESIGN ADMINISTRATION
Jacque Mott, Department Coordinator
Sally Griffith, Dean

PROFESSIONAL / ACADEMIC AFFILIATIONS
American Society of Interior Designers
Interior Design Educators Council
National Kitchen and Bath Association
International Furnishings and Design
 Association
Association for the Advancement of
Sustainability in Higher Education
U.S. Green Building Council

PROGRAM DESCRIPTION AND PHILOSOPHY

Interior Design at Harper provides you with a global education in visual and design subjects. We focus on your success by providing a learning-centered environment to help you transform raw creativity into style, communication, and function. The program offers creative, artistic, and challenging career opportunities. We offer state-of-the-art curriculum produced by experienced and dedicated design professionals. The Faculty is comprised of practicing designers who bring real-life experiences into the classroom. The curriculum has a focus on the technical aspects of design including space planning, computer-assisted drafting, design communication, lighting, sustainable and universal design. We include artistic composition and design process along with historic interior coursework. Our program is suited to both the complete beginner and for those with some basic knowledge of design. We have maintained our accreditation from the National Kitchen and Bath Association since 1997. The curriculum prepares our students for national registration and licensing exams.

FACILITIES

Computer labs, drafting labs, library, resource room, lighting labs, design/build space, and state-of-the-art technology.

ONLINE / DISTANCE LEARNING

We have two required courses offered online. We have several other non-required courses online.

COURSES OF INSTRUCTION

- Design I
- Theory and Fundamentals of Design
- Interior Design Studio I
- History of Furniture and Interior Architecture
- Materials and Sources
- Problem Solving and Design Communication
- History of Art I, II, and III
- Architectural CAD I
- Interior Design Studio II
- Interior Perspective and Rendering
- Codes for Interior Designers
- Interior Detailing and Construction Drawing
- Fundamentals of Speech Communication
- 3D Design Studio
- Historic Styles Studio
- Lighting for Interior Design
- CAD Studio
- Kitchen Design Studio
- Contract Design Studio
- Professional Practices for Interior Design
- Bathroom Design Studio
- Portfolio Review
- Digital Imaging I
- 3-Dimensional CAD for Interior Designers
- 3-Dimensional Presentation
- Kitchen and Bath CAD Studio
- Materials and Sources
- Problem Solving and Design Communication
- Bath Design Studio
- Advanced Sketching and Perspective Drawing
- Topics in Interior Design
- Environmental Design Studio

INTERNSHIPS

Required of majors during their 2nd year. Interns are typically placed at kitchen and bath designers, retail, lighting designers, and trade showrooms as design assistants.

STUDY ABROAD

Available through the college, not the department.

NOTABLE ALUMNI

Not reported

STUDENT ACTIVITIES AND ORGANIZATIONS

Harper College NKBA Student Club

FACULTY SPECIALIZATIONS AND RESEARCH

Health Care, Codes, Computer Graphics, Residential, Commercial, Kitchen & Bath, Hospitality, Flooring, Facilities Management, Perspective and Rendering

COMMUNITY COLLEGE TRANSFERS

2+2 agreements established with:
- Rhodec International
- Harring College of Design
- Illinois Institute of Art Schaumburg
- International Academy of Merchandising and Design
- Southern Illinois University

Most of our credits transfer to 4-year institutions.

We are NKBA accredited school, so our students may sit for the AKBD exam in their last semester.

Harrington College of Design

Department of Interior Design

200 West Madison St., Chicago, IL 60606 | 312-697-3310 | www.interiordesign.edu

UNIVERSITY PROFILE
Private
Urban
Commuter
Semester Schedule
Co-ed

STUDENT DEMOGRAPHICS
Undergraduate: 1,102
Graduate: 72

Male: 15%
Female: 85%

Full-time: 38%
Part-time: 62%

EXPENSES
Tuition: Not reported
Room & Board: n/a

ADMISSIONS
200 West Madison St.,
5th Floor
Chicago, IL 60606
877-939-4975

DEGREE INFORMATION

Major / Degree / Concentration	Enrollment	Requirements for entry	Graduation rate
Interior Design Associate of Applied Science	125	2.0 cumulative gpa	Not reported
Interior Design Bachelor of Fine Arts	528	2.0 cumulative gpa	Not reported
Interior Design Master of Arts	53	3.0 cumulative gpa or GRE, interview	Not reported
Interior Design Master of Interior Design	19	3.0 cumulative gpa, interview, portfolio review	Not reported

TOTAL PROGRAM ENROLLMENT
Undergraduate: 653
Graduate: 72

Male: 15%
Female: 85%

Full-time: 39%
Part-time: 61%

International: 2%
Minority: 23%

Job Placement Rate: Not reported

SCHOLARSHIPS / FINANCIAL AID
See opposite page for more info

TOTAL FACULTY: 45
Full-time: 16%
Part-time: 84%
Online: n/a

NCIDQ Certified: 31%
Licensed Interior Designers: licensed in
  both ID and AIA
LEED Certified: 28%

INTERIOR DESIGN ADMINISTRATION
Dr. John Martin-Rutherford, Department
  Chair
Sue Kirkman, VP of Academic Affairs/
  Dean of Education

PROFESSIONAL / ACADEMIC AFFILIATIONS
American Society of Interior Designers
International Interior Design Association
Interior Design Educators Council
Interior Design Associations Foundation

CIDA ACCREDITATION
Bachelor of Fine Arts in Interior Design
(2008, 2014)

PROGRAM DESCRIPTION AND PHILOSOPHY

Bachelor of Fine Arts in Interior Design—This bachelor's level program is a 130-credit program that combines the core requirements of 94 semester credit hours in interior-design-related curriculum known as the Professional Studies and 36 semester credit hours of diverse academic Liberal Arts and Sciences coursework. This program assists students in the first phase of preparation toward becoming a qualified, licensed professional. Upon completion of the Bachelor of Fine Arts in Interior Design program, students should be able to:

- Understand how to work with a variety of design project types and users.
- Develop the attitudes, traits, and values of professional responsibility, accountability, and effectiveness.
- Understand the fundamentals of art and design, theories of design, green design, human behavior, and discipline-related history.
- Understand and apply the knowledge, skills, processes, and theories of Interior Design.
- Communicate effectively.
- Develop skills in computer applications used in the Interior Design industry.
- Design within the context of building systems and to use appropriate materials and products.
- Apply the laws, codes, regulations, standards, and practices that protect the health, safety, and welfare of the public.
- Understand the foundations of business and professional practice.

FACILITIES

Harrington's six-story vertical campus within a glass-and-granite high-rise reflecting the surrounding cityscape serves as a learning laboratory. Structural elements, plumbing, HVAC and even some walls are left exposed or dissected to exemplify to students the inner workings of the built environment. A unique three-story display space connects floors designed to hold a mix of classrooms, galleries, offices, and spaces for conversation and collaboration on projects. A specialized design library with extensive traditional archival holdings and continuously updated digital resources supports student research. Harrington's technology delivers a flexible and innovated education in studio, computer, and lecture classrooms while its faculty of practicing professionals expands the learning experience to the rich design and cultural community of Chicago.

ONLINE / DISTANCE LEARNING
Not available

COURSES OF INSTRUCTION
Foundation art classes, specified general education to enhance program objectives, skill-building course work, integration and application of knowledge through studios based on process through specializations, thesis work, international study, and internship opportunities

INTERNSHIPS
Required of majors trying to attain their BFA. Interns are typically placed at architectural and Interior Design firms, kitchen and bath retailers, construction firms and showrooms.

STUDY ABROAD
Greece, Italy, Spain, France, England, and Japan.

NOTABLE ALUMNI
Barbara Pallet former NCIDQ President, Kara Mann, Todd Hase, Janet Blutter-Shiff, Leah Bolger, Chris Coldoff, Sophie Custer, Madeline Gelis, Shelly Handman, Dennis Kluge, Robert Marks, Sheryl Ann Schulze, Maribeth Schwind, Cynthia Vranas

STUDENT ACTIVITIES AND ORGANIZATIONS
ASID, IIDA, AIGA, PSMA, Student Government, Osmosis, Green Design, Architecture Club

FACULTY SPECIALIZATIONS AND RESEARCH
Practicing professionals

COMMUNITY COLLEGE TRANSFERS
Articulation agreements with selected community colleges.

SCHOLARSHIPS / FINANCIAL AID
- Federal Pell Grant: This grant program is designed to assist needy undergraduate students who desire to continue their education beyond high school.
- Federal Supplemental Educational Opportunity Grant (FSEOG): The FESG is a grant program for undergraduate students with exceptional need with priority given to students with Federal Pell Grant Eligibility.
- Federal Stafford Loans: Federal Stafford loans, available through the Federal Family Education Loan program (FFELP), are low-interest loans that are made to the student by a lender, such as a bank, credit union, or savings and loan association.
- Federal Parent-PLUS: The Federal Parent-PLUS loan is available to graduate students.
- Academic Competitiveness Grant (ACG): The Academic Competitiveness Grant (ACG) is available to students who complete a rigorous high school curriculum (as defined by the Secretary of Education).
- Federal Work Study (FWS): FWS is a financial-aid program designed to assist students in meeting the cost of their education by working part-time while attending school.
- Private Loans: Various lending institutions offer loans to help cover the gap between the cost of education and the amount of federal eligibility.
- Harrington Scholarship Programs: Harrington offers scholarship opportunities to its new and continuing students through its institutional scholarship programs.
- Receiving Scholarships or Financial Aid: 70%

Illinois State University

Department of Family & Consumer Sciences

Campus Box 5060, Normal, IL 61790 | 309-438-2517 | http://fcs.illinoisstate.edu

UNIVERSITY PROFILE
Public
Suburban
Residential
Semester Schedule
Co-ed

STUDENT DEMOGRAPHICS
Undergraduate: 18,344
Graduate: 2,512

Male: 43%
Female: 57%

Full-time: 94%
Part-time: 6%

EXPENSES
Tuition: $2,795
Room & Board: $2,118

ADMISSIONS
Campus Box 2200
Normal, IL 61790

DEGREE INFORMATION

Major / Degree / Concentration	Enrollment	Requirements for entry	Graduation rate
Family & Consumer Sciences Bachelor of Arts Interior & Environmental Design	3	Application to University or application to major if already admitted	Not reported
Family & Consumer Sciences Bachelor of Science Interior & Environmental Design	139	Application to University or application to major if already admitted	Not reported

TOTAL PROGRAM ENROLLMENT
Undergraduate: 142
Graduate: 2

Male: 3%
Female: 97%

Full-time: 95%
Part-time: 5%

International: 0%
Minority: 14%

Job Placement Rate: Not reported

SCHOLARSHIPS / FINANCIAL AID
11 departmental scholarships available after Freshman year is completed, ranging in value from $350 to $2000. College and university scholarships also available, as well as student on-campus jobs, federal work study, and other traditional financial aid.

TOTAL FACULTY: 4
Full-time: 75%
Part-time: 25%
Online: 0%

NCIDQ Certified: 75%
Licensed Interior Designers: 100%
LEED Certified: 0%

INTERIOR DESIGN ADMINISTRATION
Dr. Randy Winter, Acting Department chair
Ms. Connie Dyar, Interior & Environmental Design Sequence Coordinator
Mr. Richard Kane, Departmental Academic Advisor

PROFESSIONAL / ACADEMIC AFFILIATIONS
American Society of Interior Designers
International Interior Design Association
Interior Design Educators Council

CIDA ACCREDITATION
BA or BS in Family and Consumer Sciences (2008, 2014)

PROGRAM DESCRIPTION AND PHILOSOPHY

The Interior and Environmental Design sequence prepares students to design innovative, functional, supportive, and responsible interior environments that positively impact the quality of life.

The curriculum develops students' skills and knowledge in color and design, drafting, space planning, building and interior systems, materials and finishes, historical interiors, building and barrier-free codes, and Auto-CAD. The needs of special populations and the mandates that regulate the field of Interior Design are emphasized.

Our undergraduate program is accredited by the Council for Interior Design Accreditation (CIDA), formerly FIDER, and emphasizes commercial Interior Design. Our graduates are typically employed by one of the Top 100 Design firms, such as Gensler, SpAce, Callison, IA Interior Architects, The Gettys Group, Design Forum and Environments Group in Chicago, St. Louis, and other major cities.

Course content is based on the knowledge and skills needed to pass the National Council for Interior Design Qualification (NC10Q) licensing exam.

FACILITIES

Interior Design Drafting laboratory, CAD Drafting Lab, Interior Finishes Sample Library, Textile Laboratory

ONLINE / DISTANCE LEARNING

Not available.

COURSES OF INSTRUCTION

- Environmental Design Elements
- Interior Construction and Building Systems
- Drafting for Interior Design
- Environmental Lighting Design
- Rendering for Interior Designers
- History of Interior and Environmental Design I & II
- Interior Design Studio I - III

INTERNSHIPS

Required of majors at Junior or Senior level. Interns are typically placed at companies such as Gensler, SpAce, Callison, IA Interior Architects, The Gettys Group, Design Forum, and Environments Group

STUDY ABROAD

Biannual study tour to Europe visiting London, Paris, and Florence. Domestic study tours to New York and Los Angeles on other years.

NOTABLE ALUMNI

Not reported

STUDENT ACTIVITIES AND ORGANIZATIONS

Student Chapter of International Interior Design Association (IIDA)

FACULTY SPECIALIZATIONS AND RESEARCH

Colonialism, Historic Preservation and Community Development, Design Theory, Design for Children, Design for the Elderly, Healthcare Design

International Academy of Design & Technology–Chicago

Department of Interior Design

One North State St., Suite 500, Chicago, IL 60602 | 312-980-9200 | www.iadtchicago.edu

UNIVERSITY PROFILE
Private
Urban
Rural
Commuter
Quarter Schedule
Co-ed

STUDENT DEMOGRAPHICS
Undergraduate: 1,311
Graduate: 0

Male: 43%
Female: 57%

Full-time: 83%
Part-time: 17%

EXPENSES
Tuition: Not reported
Room & Board: Not reported

ADMISSIONS
One North State St.,
Suite 500
Chicago, IL 60602
312-980-9200
www.iadtchicago.edu

DEGREE INFORMATION

Major / Degree / Concentration	Enrollment	Requirements for entry	Graduation rate
Interior Design Bachelor of Fine Arts	116	Completion of high school or GED equivalency. All applicants are assessed in order to determine their readiness for college level coursework. Assessment may include reading comprehension, writing, and/or math. The Academy-Chicago has both conditional and unconditional acceptance, determined by assessment scores.	Not reported

TOTAL PROGRAM ENROLLMENT
Undergraduate: Not reported
Graduate: Not reported

Male: Not reported
Female: Not reported

Full-time: Not reported
Part-time: Not reported

International: Not reported
Minority: Not reported

Job Placement Rate: Not reported

SCHOLARSHIPS / FINANCIAL AID
Financial Aid is available for those who qualify. A complete listing of scholarship opportunities and financial aid options is available in the campus Catalog.

TOTAL FACULTY:
Full-time: Not reported
Part-time: Not reported
Online: Not reported

NCIDQ Certified: Not reported
Licensed Interior Designers: Not reported
LEED Certified: Not reported

INTERIOR DESIGN ADMINISTRATION
Robert Nachtsheim, President
Kathleen Embry, Vice President of Academic Affairs
Deborah Craig, Program Chair - Interior Design

PROFESSIONAL / ACADEMIC AFFILIATIONS
American Society of Interior Designers
International Interior Design Association
Interior Design Educators Council

CIDA ACCREDITATION
Bachelor of Fine Arts in Interior Design (2010, 2016)

PROGRAM DESCRIPTION AND PHILOSOPHY

The CIDA-accredited Bachelor of Fine Arts in Interior Design combines the elements and principles of design with practical applications, incorporating space planning and problem-solving, supplemented with general education coursework. The curriculum will help students explore creative design, business skills and computer-aided design technology. The BFA degree in Interior Design can help prepare students for an entry-level position in the Interior Design industry.

FACILITIES

The Interior Design department offers students two PC computer labs with computer aided design software, Adobe software, Microsoft suite; two dedicated drafting labs; a dedicated interiors resource and materials library and lighting lab. IADT Chicago also offers students an educational resource lab; a portfolio enrichment resource lab and an open computer lab in conjunction with the college's library.

ONLINE / DISTANCE LEARNING

General Education courses are offered online.

COURSES OF INSTRUCTION

- Interior Design Principles
- Space Planning
- Perspective & Sketch Rendering
- Computer Aided Design
- Commercial Design
- Lighting Fundamentals
- Contract Interiors
- Sustainable Practices
- Residential Design
- Senior Design Project for Interior Design

INTERNSHIPS

Required of majors at Senior level.

STUDY ABROAD

Study Abroad opportunities are available for earned credit at American Intercontinental University.

NOTABLE ALUMNI

Not reported

STUDENT ACTIVITIES AND ORGANIZATIONS

Interior Design students have the opportunity to join IADT Chicago's Interior Design Student Association (IDSA).

FACULTY SPECIALIZATIONS AND RESEARCH

Several faculty members (both full-time and adjunct) are certified by NCIDQ or NCARB and hold Illinois state licensing in their respective disciplines. Two faculty members are also LEED accredited professionals. One faculty member is a Certified Kitchen Designer (CKD).

International Academy of Design & Technology–Schaumburg

Department of Interior Design

915-A National Parkway, Schaumburg, IL 60173 | 847-969-2800 | www.iadtschaumburg.com

UNIVERSITY PROFILE
Private
Suburban
Commuter
Quarter Schedule
Co-ed

STUDENT DEMOGRAPHICS
Undergraduate: 232
Graduate: 0

Male: 29%
Female: 71%

Full-time: 64%
Part-time: 36%

EXPENSES
Tuition: $13,860
Room & Board: n/a

ADMISSIONS
915-A National Parkway
Schaumburg, IL 60173
847-969-2800

DEGREE INFORMATION

Major / Degree / Concentration	Enrollment	Requirements for entry	Graduation rate
Interior Design Bachelor of Fine Arts	27	Completion of high school or GED equivalency. All applicants are assessed in order to determine their readiness for college level coursework. Assessment may include reading comprehension, writing, and/or math.	Not reported

TOTAL PROGRAM ENROLLMENT
Undergraduate: Not reported
Graduate: Not reported

Male: Not reported
Female: Not reported

Full-time: Not reported
Part-time: Not reported

International: Not reported
Minority: Not reported

Job Placement Rate: Not reported

SCHOLARSHIPS / FINANCIAL AID
Financial Aid is available for those who qualify. A complete listing of scholarship opportunities and financial aid options is available in the campus Catalog.

TOTAL FACULTY: Not reported
Full-time: Not reported
Part-time: Not reported
Online: Not reported

NCIDQ Certified: Not reported
Licensed Interior Designers: Not reported
LEED Certified: Not reported

INTERIOR DESIGN ADMINISTRATION
Mark Holroyd, Campus President
Shelly Pierce, Program Chair

PROFESSIONAL / ACADEMIC AFFILIATIONS
American Society of Interior Designers
International Interior Design Association
Interior Design Educators Council

PROGRAM DESCRIPTION AND PHILOSOPHY

The Bachelor of Fine Arts in Interior Design combines the elements and principles of design with practical applications, incorporating space planning and problem-solving, supplemented with general education coursework. The curriculum will help students explore creative design, business skills and computer aided design technology. The BFA degree in Interior Design can help prepare students for an entry-level position in the Interior Design industry.

FACILITIES

The Interior Design department offers students a drafting lab with PC's containing computer aided design software, Adobe software, Microsoft suite; a dedicated interiors resource and materials library. IADT Schaumburg also offers students an open computer lab in conjunction with the college's library.

ONLINE / DISTANCE LEARNING

General Education courses are offered online.

COURSES OF INSTRUCTION

- Interior Design Principles
- Space Planning
- Perspective & Sketch Rendering
- Computer Aided Design
- Commercial Design
- Lighting Fundamentals
- Contract Interiors
- Sustainable Practices
- Residential Design
- Senior Design Project for Interior Design

INTERNSHIPS

Required of majors at Senior level

STUDY ABROAD

Study Abroad opportunities are available for earned credit at American Intercontinental University.

NOTABLE ALUMNI

Not reported

STUDENT ACTIVITIES AND ORGANIZATIONS

Interior Design students have the opportunity to join IADT-Schaumburg's Interior Design Student Association (IDSA).

FACULTY SPECIALIZATIONS AND RESEARCH

Several faculty members (adjunct) are certified by NCIDQ and hold Illinois state licensing in their respective disciplines.

Ball State University

Department of Family & Consumer Sciences

200 University Ave., Muncie, IN 47306 | 765-285-5000 | www.bsu.edu/fcs

UNIVERSITY PROFILE
Public
Suburban
Residential
Semester
Co-ed

STUDENT DEMOGRAPHICS
Undergraduate: 20,000
Graduate: 4,000

Male: 50%
Female: 50%

Full-time: Not reported
Part-time: Not reported

EXPENSES
Tuition: $7,500
Room & Board: $7,900

ADMISSIONS
Admission Office
Muncie, IN 47306
765-285-8300

DEGREE INFORMATION

Major / Degree / Concentration	Enrollment	Requirements for entry	Graduation rate
Interior Design Bachelor of Science or Arts	120	Application to University or application to major if already admitted	90%
Interior Design Master of Science or Arts	5	Letters of recommendation and portfolio review	Not reported

TOTAL PROGRAM ENROLLMENT
Undergraduate: Not reported
Graduate: Not reported

Male: 5%
Female: 95%

Full-time: 100%
Part-time: 0%

International: 4%
Minority: 5%

Job Placement Rate: 92%

SCHOLARSHIPS / FINANCIAL AID
Visit www.bsu.edu/fcs

TOTAL FACULTY:
Full-time: 90%
Part-time: 10%
Online: n/a

NCIDQ Certified: 20%
Licensed Interior Designers: n/a
LEED Certified: n/a

INTERIOR DESIGN ADMINISTRATION
Reza Ahmadi, Program Director

PROFESSIONAL / ACADEMIC AFFILIATIONS
American Society of Interior Designers
International Interior Design Association
Interior Design Educators Council

CIDA ACCREDITATION
BA or BS in Family and Consumer Sciences (2007, 2013)

PROGRAM DESCRIPTION AND PHILOSOPHY
Not reported

FACILITIES
24/7 access to Resource Library, Computer lab, and Studio

ONLINE / DISTANCE LEARNING
The graduate program is 100% online. Visit www.bsu.edu/distance/interiordesign

COURSES OF INSTRUCTION
- Universal Design
- Professional Practice
- Color and Light
- Six Design Studios
- Four Graphic Communications
- Interior Construction Detailing
- Interior Finishes
- Sustainable Interiors
- Programming
- Design History and Theory

INTERNSHIPS
Required of majors at the Junior level

STUDY ABROAD
Available

NOTABLE ALUMNI
Not reported

STUDENT ACTIVITIES AND ORGANIZATIONS
American Society of Interior Designers, International Interior Design Association

FACULTY SPECIALIZATIONS AND RESEARCH
Universal Design

Indiana University, Bloomington

Department of Apparel Merchandising & Interior Design

Memorial Hall East 232, Bloomington, IN 47405 | 812-855-5497 | http://design.iub.edu/dsg/degree.shtml

UNIVERSITY PROFILE
Public
Urban
Residential
Semester Schedule
Co-ed

STUDENT DEMOGRAPHICS
Undergraduate: Not reported
Graduate: Not reported

Male: Not reported
Female: Not reported

Full-time: Not reported
Part-time: Not reported

EXPENSES
Tuition: Contact Admissions
Room & Board: Contact
Admissions

ADMISSIONS
300 N. Jordan Ave.
Bloomington, IN 47405
812-855-0661
iuadmit@indiana.edu

DEGREE INFORMATION

Major / Degree / Concentration	Enrollment	Requirements for entry	Graduation rate
Interior Design Bachelor of Science	125	Minimum C- grade in Beginning Interior Design	80-90%

TOTAL PROGRAM ENROLLMENT
Undergraduate: 125
Graduate: 0

Male: 4%
Female: 96%

Full-time: 89%
Part-time: 11%

International: 5% and growing
Minority: 2%

Job Placement Rate: 80-90%

SCHOLARSHIPS / FINANCIAL AID
Outstanding Senior Recognition,
Outstanding Service, Ruth Mary Griswold
Scholarhip, Opal Conrad Scholarship,
Dorothy G. Hemer Competitive Prize, La
Verda Graham Rood Scholarship, and
Pygmalion Prize.

TOTAL FACULTY: 9
Full-time: 89%
Part-time: 11%
Online: 0%

NCIDQ Certified: 3
Licensed Interior Designers: 3
LEED Certified: 1

INTERIOR DESIGN ADMINISTRATION
C. Thomas Mitchell, Ph.D.: Department
Chair + Design Studies Group Program
Director
Terri Shockley, Department
Administration

PROFESSIONAL / ACADEMIC AFFILIATIONS
International Interior Design Association
Interior Design Educators Council

CIDA ACCREDITATION
Bachelor of Science in Interior Design
(2005, 2011)

PROGRAM DESCRIPTION AND PHILOSOPHY

Indiana University's Interior Design program is multidisciplinary, focusing on integrating user-needs through the use of state-of-the-art design methods. There is an emphasis on collaboration and creative use of technology in the program. From the outset students are encouraged to see themselves as preparing to enter the design profession—using their education as a model for their subsequent work experience. In addition, IU's Design Studies is at the forefront of Sustainability in design. CIDA Accreditation: IU's program is accredited by CIDA (the Council for Interior Design Accreditation), along with about 150 others nationwide and in Canada. The program has been continuously accredited since 1992; our next accreditation visit is in Spring 2011.

FACILITIES

The Design Studies group moved into a newly renovated studio complex in Smith Research Center designed specifically to support our program. The complex features one 3,000-square-foot studio space dedicated to the first two years and a pair of 1,500-square-foot studios for the exclusive use of students in the upper two years. There are three desktop computers in each studio for student use, along with other resources to support their work.

In addition there is a student work room, a plotter room featuring black and white and color printers and plotters and scanner facilities, an office featuring our growing collection of iconic chairs, and faculty offices. All Interior Design classes are held at Smith Research Center, easily accessible by a free bus and with ample parking for students. The facility is open until 10:00 pm on weeknights and is accessible on the weekend, as well.

ONLINE / DISTANCE LEARNING
Not available

COURSES OF INSTRUCTION
- Beginning Interior Design
- Design Methods
- Digital Architectural Drawing
- Architectural Theories and Concepts, Interior Design I—Three-Dimensional Interior Design
- Interior Design II—Space Design
- Interior Design II—Space Design
- Materials and Components of Interior Design
- Lighting Interior Spaces I & II
- Architectural, Interior, and Furniture Design Studies
- Interior Design III—The Dwelling
- Interior Design IV—The Workplace
- Advanced Digital Architectural Drawing
- Professional Practices in Interior Design
- Interior Design V—Comprehensive Design
- Interior Design VI—Special Populations
- Plus several elective classes in ID.

INTERNSHIPS
Not required but highly recommended during the summer between Junior and Senior year.

STUDY ABROAD
Many options available to students. We have a very active overseas studies office at the IUB campus. DIS Summer Program in Copenhagen—Interior Design as well as programs to study architecture, finish languages, study history, etc.

NOTABLE ALUMNI
Not reported

STUDENT ACTIVITIES AND ORGANIZATIONS
The Design Studies Student Organization offers opportunities for all levels of Interior Design students to broaden and apply their classroom knowledge and studio skills, and pursue professional development and networking opportunities with design industry firms. Among other programs and initiatives, the group organizes special studio projects, participates in design competitions, supports the Bloomington chapter of Habitat for Community, and works with such local institutions as the Monroe County Historical Society to provide design support and expertise. Design Studies Group professor Barb Young provide faculty guidance to the organization.

FACULTY SPECIALIZATIONS AND RESEARCH
Not reported

Ivy Tech Community College of Indiana

School of Fine Arts and Design

4475 Central Ave., Columbus, IN 47203 | 812-374-5148 | www.ivytech.edu/columbus

UNIVERSITY PROFILE
Public
Urban
Commuter
Semester Schedule
Co-ed

STUDENT DEMOGRAPHICS
Undergraduate: 6,524
Graduate: NA

Male: 36%
Female: 62%

Full-time: 35%
Part-time: 65%

EXPENSES
Tuition: $2,509.20
Room & Board: n/a

ADMISSIONS
4475 Central Ave.
Columbus, IN 47203
812-374-5255
kbaker17@ivytech.edu

DEGREE INFORMATION

Major / Degree / Concentration	Enrollment	Requirements for entry	Graduation rate
Interior Design Associate of Applied Science	Not reported	Not reported	Not reported
Kitchen and Bath Design Associate of Applied Science	New in Fall 2010	Not reported	Not reported
Interior Design Associate of Arts Transfer Degree to Indiana University-Purdue University Indianapolis	Not reported	Not reported	Not reported

TOTAL PROGRAM ENROLLMENT
Undergraduate: 15
Graduate: n/a

Male: Not reported
Female: Not reported

Full-time: Not reported
Part-time: Not reported

International: 0%
Minority: 0%

Job Placement Rate: Not reported

SCHOLARSHIPS / FINANCIAL AID
Grants, Loans and scholarships available to students. Based on Financial need as reported by the FAFSA.

TOTAL FACULTY: 3
Full-time: 33%
Part-time: 66%
Online: Not reported

NCIDQ Certified: 1
Licensed Interior Designers: 1
LEED Certified: 0

INTERIOR DESIGN ADMINISTRATION
John Hogan, Chancellor
Dr. Rosalie Hine, Vice Chancellor Academic Affairs
Jonathan Wilson, Dean School of Fine Arts & Design

PROFESSIONAL / ACADEMIC AFFILIATIONS
American Society of Interior Designers

PROGRAM DESCRIPTION AND PHILOSOPHY

Program prepares students for the residential or commercial job market, or for a transfer to a four-year college. Classes are small and hands-on, instructors are all design practitioners. New Kitchen and Bath concentration.

FACILITIES

Computer labs, drafting lab, resource room, University Library

ONLINE / DISTANCE LEARNING

Not the entire major, but substantial number of classes available online through Columbus or two other Ivy Tech campuses (South Bend or Evansville, Indiana)

COURSES OF INSTRUCTION

- Design Theory
- Drafting and Construction
- Introduction to Interior Design
- Design Presentation
- CAD for Environmental Designers
- Textiles for Interiors
- Interior Design II
- History of Interiors and Furniture
- Lighting and Building Systems
- Interior Materials
- Professional Practice
- Portfolio Preparation/Internship

INTERNSHIPS

Not required

STUDY ABROAD

Not available

NOTABLE ALUMNI

Not reported

STUDENT ACTIVITIES AND ORGANIZATIONS

ASID Student members at large, NKBA Student Members

FACULTY SPECIALIZATIONS AND RESEARCH

Residential construction and small scale commercial

COMMUNITY COLLEGE TRANSFERS

AS Degree transferable to IUPUI, many courses transfer to other public/private colleges

Johnson County Community College

Department of Interior Design

12345 College Blvd. Box 37, Overland Park, KS 66210 | 913-469-8500 | www.jccc.edu/home/depts.php/1223

STUDENT DEMOGRAPHICS
Undergraduate: 20,401
Graduate: 0

Male: 46%
Female: 54%

Full-time: 36%
Part-time: 64%

EXPENSES
Tuition: $1,680
Room & Board: n/a

ADMISSIONS
12345 College Blvd. Box 41
Overland Park, KS 66210
913-469-3803
jcccadmissions@jccc.edu

DEGREE INFORMATION

Major / Degree / Concentration	Enrollment	Requirements for entry	Graduation rate
Interior Design Associate of Applied Science	175	Not reported	Not reported
Interior Entrepreneurship Associate of Applied Science	15	Not reported	Not reported
Interior Merchandising Associate of Applied Science	10	Not reported	Not reported

TOTAL PROGRAM ENROLLMENT
Undergraduate: 213
Graduate: 0

Male: Not reported
Female: Not reported

Full-time: Not reported
Part-time: Not reported

International: Not reported
Minority: Not reported

Job Placement Rate: Not reported

SCHOLARSHIPS / FINANCIAL AID
JCCC Interior Design Scholarships:
Jack Harris, Harris Polsky, Bill
and June Bailey JCCC Foundation
scholarships; Interior Design Student
Association Design Merit Awards—
Design Presentation, Space Planning,
Residential Design, Commercial Design
and Kitchen and Bath Design

TOTAL FACULTY: 14
Full-time: 28%
Part-time: 72%
Online: 0%

NCIDQ Certified: 14
Licensed Interior Designers: 0
LEED Certified: 14

INTERIOR DESIGN ADMINISTRATION
Jan Cummings, Department Chair
Lindy Robinson, Dean of Business
Terry Calaway, President of JCCC

PROFESSIONAL / ACADEMIC AFFILIATIONS
American Society of Interior Designers
International Interior Design Association
Interior Design Educators Council
Environmental Design Research
Association

PROGRAM DESCRIPTION AND PHILOSOPHY

The mission of JCCC's Interior Design department is to provide relevant curriculum with experiential learning. Theory and application dovetail in the classroom and community providing exposure to business/ industry standards. These contribute to developing professionalism in the student.

FACILITIES

Manual drafting lab, computer lab, textile library, materials and resources library, sample lab

ONLINE / DISTANCE LEARNING

Not available

COURSES OF INSTRUCTION

- Interior Design
- Architectural Drafting for ID
- Space Planning
- Design Presentation
- Interior Textiles
- Materials & Resources
- AutoCAD
- Practices & Procedures
- Budgeting & Estimating
- Furniture & Ornamentation (Antiquity to Renaissance, Renaissance to Twentieth Century)
- Internship (I and II for a total of 480 hours)
- Lighting Design & Planning
- Residential Design
- Leadership in Design
- Asian Furniture and Design
- Capstone: Portfolio & Presentation

INTERNSHIPS

Required of majors. Student internships are available at retail establishments, design firms and to the trade businesses.

STUDY ABROAD

We offer spring break or summer options—one or two week travel.

NOTABLE ALUMNI

Not reported

STUDENT ACTIVITIES AND ORGANIZATIONS

Student chapters of ASID, IIDA, NKBA

FACULTY SPECIALIZATIONS AND RESEARCH

LEED AP; CKD; industry professionals in window treatments, furniture— casegoods and upholstery, weaving, and faux finish painting

COMMUNITY COLLEGE TRANSFERS

JCCC Interior Design students can transfer credits to several area universities to complete a BS or BA degree.

Kansas State University

Department of Apparel, Textiles & Interior Design, College of Human Ecology

ATID, 225 Justin Hall, Manhattan, KS 66506 | 785-532-6993 | www.humec.k-state.edu/atid/

UNIVERSITY PROFILE
Public
Suburban
Residential
Semester Schedule
Co-ed

STUDENT DEMOGRAPHICS
Undergraduate: 19,000
Graduate: 4,800

Male: 52%
Female: 48%

Full-time: 88%
Part-time: 12%

EXPENSES
Tuition: $6,456
Room & Board: $6,752

ADMISSIONS
Kansas State University
119 Anderson Hall
Manhattan, KS 66506-0102
1-800-432-827
k-state@k-state.edu

DEGREE INFORMATION

Major / Degree / Concentration	Enrollment	Requirements for entry	Graduation rate
Interior Design Bachelor of Science	125	Selective admissions of best-qualified based on comparisons of ACT/SAT scores, un-weighted high school gpa, and high school class rank	Not reported

TOTAL PROGRAM ENROLLMENT
Undergraduate: 125
Graduate: n/a

Male: 4%
Female: 96%

Full-time: 100%
Part-time: 0%

International: 2%
Minority: 8%

Job Placement Rate: 90%

SCHOLARSHIPS / FINANCIAL AID
There are multiple endowed scholarships for students in the ATID department and additional scholarships and aid available at the college and university level.

Students Receiving Scholarships or Financial Aid: 75%

TOTAL FACULTY: 6
Full-time: 100%
Part-time: Not reported
Online: Not reported

NCIDQ Certified: 66%
Licensed Interior Designers: Not reported
LEED Certified: Not reported

INTERIOR DESIGN ADMINISTRATION
Barbara G. Anderon, Associate Professor and ID Program Coordinator

PROFESSIONAL / ACADEMIC AFFILIATIONS
International Interior Design Association
Interior Design Educators Council
Environmental Design Research Association

CIDA ACCREDITATION
Bachelor of Science in Interior Design (2010, 2016)

PROGRAM DESCRIPTION AND PHILOSOPHY

The Interior Design program in the Department of Apparel, Textiles, and Interior Design in the College of Human Ecology focuses on developing the appropriate skills and knowledge base to prepare graduates for an entry-level position in the profession of Interior Design. Each semester of the ID Program is structured to introduce, or enhance through interrelationship and reinforcement, the knowledge and skills that will prepare students for subsequent courses, learning outside of the classroom, and the competence necessary to begin professional practice. Student learning within the curriculum begins with general knowledge and design fundamentals and progressively increases in difficulty and complexity.

In addition to preparing graduates for a productive career, the Interior Design curriculum is designed to prepare graduates for their personal and community lives. The expectation is that through study of Interior Design, human ecology, and general education courses, graduates will be engaged in the world and aware of the opportunities they have to affect positive outcomes through person involvement.

FACILITIES

Design studios, printing and plotting, material/sample resources, classic modern chair collection, historic textiles collection, K-State's Beach Museum of Art, excellent Library services including an Architecture Library with special collections/rare books.

ONLINE / DISTANCE LEARNING
Not available

COURSES OF INSTRUCTION
- Interior Design Studios 1-8
- Design & Behavior in the Interior Environment
- History of Interior Design I and II
- Construction Methods and Materials for Interior Design
- Building Systems for Interior Design
- Computer-Aided Visual Communication in Interior Design
- Textiles
- Interior Design Practices and Procedures
- Designing for Supportive Environments

INTERNSHIPS

Not required. Within the last three years, our students have interned or gained employment with top firms such as Callison in Seattle, Perkins + Will in Dallas & Washington, D.C., Hersch Bedner Associates in Santa Monica, SOM in Washington, D.C., and Gensler in Dallas and San Francisco. Our students are also employed by leading firms in other metropolitan areas including Denver, Chicago, Kansas City, Omaha, St. Louis, and Wichita.

STUDY ABROAD

At least every other year our faculty lead study tours. Students who choose to study abroad for a summer or semester receive guidance from the faculty.

NOTABLE ALUMNI
Jo Heinz
Kristin Goodman
Aaron Anderson

STUDENT ACTIVITIES AND ORGANIZATIONS

Student are actively involved with student chapters of ASID and IIDA. ID students are leaders in, and members of, the KSU chapter of Emerging Green Builders. Each year students organize the Annual Interior Design Student Symposium. The Interior Design Professional Advisory Board provides significant support for the Symposium.

FACULTY SPECIALIZATIONS AND RESEARCH

The Interior Design faculty members have diverse areas of expertise including: human behavior in interior environments, gerontology, design theory, history of interiors and architecture, historic preservation, commercial interiors, residential interiors, healthcare, energy efficiency, sustainability, design education, ethical professional practice, digital technology, and symbology.

University of Kansas

School of Architecture, Design & Planning

1467 Jayhawk Blvd., Lawrence, KS 66045 | 785-864-4401 | www.sadp.ku.edu/design

UNIVERSITY PROFILE
Public
Suburban
Residential
Semester Schedule
Co-ed

STUDENT DEMOGRAPHICS
Undergraduate: 23,000
Graduate: 6,500

Male: 47%
Female: 53%

Full-time: 78%
Part-time: 22%

EXPENSES
Tuition: $7,400 (in-state),
$19,300 (out-of-state)
Room & Board: $6,000-
$10,000

ADMISSIONS
Office of Admissions
1502 Iowa Street
Lawrence, KS 66045
adm@ku.edu

DEGREE INFORMATION

Major / Degree / Concentration	Enrollment	Requirements for entry	Graduation rate
Environmental/ Interior Design Bachelor of Fine Arts	75	In-state 3.0 gpa KBOR curriculum or 23 ACT and 10-20 image portfolio and essays	75%

TOTAL PROGRAM ENROLLMENT
Undergraduate: 550
Graduate: 40

Male: 40%
Female: 60%

Full-time: 80%
Part-time: 20%

International: 15%
Minority: 15%

Job Placement Rate: 65-70%

SCHOLARSHIPS / FINANCIAL AID
Scholarships are two fold, in that
Academic-only scholarships are
offered from the Office of Admissions
& Scholarships and departmental
scholarships are also offered and
include the portfolio review.

Students Receiving Scholarships or
Financial Aid: 70%

TOTAL FACULTY: 22
Full-time: 68%
Part-time: 30%
Online: 2

NCIDQ Certified: Not reported
Licensed Interior Designers: Not
reported
LEED Certified: Not reported

INTERIOR DESIGN ADMINISTRATION
Lois Greene, Associate Dean
Brian Hanabury, Coordinator of Student
Success
Samantha Raines, Coordinator of
Admissions

PROFESSIONAL / ACADEMIC AFFILIATIONS
American Society of Interior Designers

PROGRAM DESCRIPTION AND PHILOSOPHY
Students gain specialized knowledge of building systems, general construction, furniture, furnishing and equipments (FF&E), building codes, accessible requirements (ADA), and sustainable design. All Design Department students attend the Hallmark Symposium, which brings 7 design professionals to campus each semester.

FACILITIES
Full-scale professional grade print labs and common shops, the Spencer Museum of Art (only comprehensive art museum in the state), as well as a student supply store, snack bar, and lockers all within the building.

ONLINE / DISTANCE LEARNING
Not available, studio course work requires students be on campus.

COURSES OF INSTRUCTION
- Environmental Graphics
- Fiber Properties
- Interior Programming
- Sustainable Design
- Building Technology
- Environmental Systems
- Interior Specifications
- Human Factors

INTERNSHIPS
Required of majors at the Junior-Senior level. Interns are typically placed in a wide variety of settings from Architectural firms in the area, to alumni and emeritus faculty across the world. Students are required to complete either an internship or Intra-design problems course as part of their professional requirements.

STUDY ABROAD
Faculty-led study abroads over the Summer across the world.

NOTABLE ALUMNI
Not reported

STUDENT ACTIVITIES AND ORGANIZATIONS
Over 500 clubs and organizations across campus for students to be apart of and augment their in class experience. Also over 50 minor areas of study to enhance a student's marketability.

FACULTY SPECIALIZATIONS AND RESEARCH
Not reported

COMMUNITY COLLEGE TRANSFERS
We typically only transfer the Foundation-level studio classes and Liberal Arts requirements. Upper level studios are generally non-transferrable.

Wichita Area Technical College

Interior Design Program

4501 E 47th St. S. Wichita, KS 67210 | 316-677-1833 | www.watc.edu

UNIVERSITY PROFILE
Public
Suburban
Commuter
Semester Schedule
Co-ed

STUDENT DEMOGRAPHICS
Undergraduate: 30
Graduate: n/a

Male: 1%
Female: 99%

Full-time: 80%
Part-time: 20%

EXPENSES
Tuition: $7,000
Room & Board: n/a

ADMISSIONS
4501 E 47th St.
S. Wichita, KS 67210
316-677-9520
amcfayden@watc.edu

DEGREE INFORMATION

Major / Degree / Concentration	Enrollment	Requirements for entry	Graduation rate
Interior Design Associate of Applied Science	30	COMPASS Testing scores: Math: 26 Reading: 70 English: 23	80%
Kitchen and Bath Technical Certificate	7	COMPASS Testing scores: Math: 26 Reading: 70 English: 23	80%
Painted & Faux Finishes Certificate of Completion	10	COMPASS Testing scores: Math: 26 Reading: 70 English: 23	100%
Floral Design Certificate of Completion	10	COMPASS Testing scores: Math: 26 Reading: 70 English: 23	100%

TOTAL PROGRAM ENROLLMENT
Undergraduate: 35
Graduate: n/a

Male: 3%
Female: 97%

Full-time: 69%
Part-time: 31%

International: 0%
Minority: 18%

Job Placement Rate: 98%

SCHOLARSHIPS / FINANCIAL AID
Students Receiving Scholarships or
Financial Aid: 49%

TOTAL FACULTY: 3
Full-time: 100%
Part-time: 50%
Online: 10%

NCIDQ Certified: 80%
Licensed Interior Designers: 100%
LEED Certified: Not reported

INTERIOR DESIGN ADMINISTRATION
Bridget Mack, IIDA, IDEC, Interior
Design Program Coordinator

PROFESSIONAL / ACADEMIC AFFILIATIONS
International Interior Design Association
Interior Design Educators Council

PROGRAM DESCRIPTION AND PHILOSOPHY

By profession, an Interior Designer is qualified by education, experience, and examination to enhance the function and quality of interior spaces for the purpose of improving the quality of life, increasing productivity, and protecting the health, safety, and welfare of the public. Interior Designers integrate their findings with their knowledge of the field and formulate plans to be practical and aesthetic to improve the lifestyle of the occupants.

The Interior Design program provides competency-based training in research techniques, problem solving, proficiencies, and presentation skills required to be a successful professional Interior Designer. The program focuses on creativity and critical thinking.

Students of this program will learn the basics of Interior Design, including the principles and elements of design, blueprint reading, building technology, color theory, materials, fabrics, history of furniture and architecture, lighting technologies, drawing for interiors, business law for interiors, and gain practical experience. Throughout the program, students will be building a professional portfolio. Upon successful completion of the program, students will be able to:

- Analyze the clients' needs, goals, and life and safety requirements.
- Integrate findings with knowledge of Interior Design.
- Formulate preliminary design concepts that are appropriate, functional, and aesthetic.
- Develop and present final design recommendations through appropriate presentation media.
- Prepare working drawings and specifications of non-load-bearing interior construction, materials, finishes, space planning, furnishings, fixtures, and equipment.
- Collaborate with professional services of other licensed practitioners in the technical areas of mechanical, electrical, and load-bearing design as required for regulatory approval.
- Prepare and administer dibs and contract documents as the clients' agent.
- Review and evaluate design solutions during implementation and upon completion of projects.
- Improve the quality of life, increase productivity, and protect the health, safety, and welfare of the public.
- Develop an appropriate budget for the client.

FACILITIES

Computer Labs with software: Visio, 20/20 Technologies, Minutes Matter, CAD, and Chief Architect. Student Material Library features sample books, carpets, solid surface materials, wallpapers, and paint chips that are residential and commercial grade.

ONLINE / DISTANCE LEARNING

Some of the Interior Design courses are presently being offered online. All core courses will be offered online by 2012 with the exception of hands on classes. [Painted and Faux Finishes and Floral Design.]

Floral Design is offered as a hybrid course. 90% of the material is covered online and two hours a week in a traditional setting for hands-on work.

COURSES OF INSTRUCTION

- Interior Design Fundamentals
- Blueprint Reading for Interiors
- Color Theory
- Materials & Resources I
- Materials & Resources II
- History of Furniture & Architecture I
- History of Furniture & Architecture II
- Lighting Technologies
- Design Studio I
- Design Studio II
- Business Practices and Portfolio Development
- Seminars
- Mentorship
- Drafting for Interiors
- Interior Design Codes and Standards
- Intro to CAD
- Public Speaking
- Computer Applications
- Composition I
- Collage Algebra
- General Psychology
- Art Appreciation

INTERNSHIPS

Required of majors at second year. Interns are typically placed at Aircraft Firms, Architecture Firms, Office Design Firms, Residential Design Firms, Kitchen and Bath Firms, Designers for Builders, Window Treatment Design Co., Drafting Co., Flooring Co., Lighting Co., Various Retailers as Merchandisers, Event Planners, Painted and Faux Finishing Co., and Floral Design Shops.

STUDY ABROAD

Not available

NOTABLE ALUMNI

Not reported

STUDENT ACTIVITIES AND ORGANIZATIONS

Not reported

FACULTY SPECIALIZATIONS AND RESEARCH

Not reported

COMMUNITY COLLEGE TRANSFERS

All general elective courses transfer to four-year institutions. Core course transferance will depending on the four-year insitution being applied for.

Sullivan College of Technology & Design

Department of Interior Design

3901 Atkinson Square Dr., Louisville, KY 40218 | 502-254-3545 | **www.sctd.edu**

UNIVERSITY PROFILE
Private
Suburban
Commuter
Quarter Schedule
Co-ed

STUDENT DEMOGRAPHICS
Undergraduate: 609
Graduate: 0

Male: 69%
Female: 31%

Full-time: 73%
Part-time: 27%

EXPENSES
Tuition: $31,140 (FULL 18
month program AAS degree)
Room & Board: $550

ADMISSIONS
3901 Atkinson Square Dr.
Louisville, KY 40218
502-254-3545

DEGREE INFORMATION

Major / Degree / Concentration	Enrollment	Requirements for entry	Graduation rate
Interior Design Diploma	Not reported	High school diploma or GED, personal interview campus tour, and adequate scores on the school's entrance exam are required.	Not reported
Interior Design Associate of Applied Science	Not reported	High school diploma or GED, personal interview campus tour, and adequate scores on the school's entrance exam are required.	Not reported
Interior Design Bachelor of Arts	Not reported	Completion of Associate of Applied Science degree in Interior Design at the Sullivan College of Technology and Design or at a comparable accredited institution.	Not reported

DEGREE INFORMATION
Not reported

TOTAL PROGRAM ENROLLMENT
Undergraduate: 118
Graduate: 0

Male: 85%
Female: 15%

Full-time: 58%
Part-time: 42%

International: Not reported
Minority: 30%

Job Placement Rate: 100%

SCHOLARSHIPS / FINANCIAL AID
We are a Title IV school and our students access all related federal grants and loans, Pell, Stafford, Perkins etc. We have several funding pools in Kentucky students also access. The college provides an array of academic scholarships.

Students Receiving Scholarships or Financial Aid: 8%

TOTAL FACULTY: 19
Full-time: 26%
Part-time: 74%
Online: 0%

NCIDQ Certified: 16%
Licensed Interior Designers: Not reported
LEED Certified: Not reported

INTERIOR DESIGN ADMINISTRATION
David Winkler, Executive Director
Sheree P. Koppel, Ed.D., Academic Dean
Terri George, Program Chairperson

PROFESSIONAL / ACADEMIC AFFILIATIONS
American Society of Interior Designers
International Interior Design Association
Interior Design Educators Council

PROGRAM DESCRIPTION AND PHILOSOPHY

The objectives of this program are to provide competence in performing the basic skills necessary to implement a design, including taking measurements, providing cost estimates, preparing drawings and business documents, assisting clients with the selection and arrangement of interior furnishings and materials, space planning, and working with installers, contractors, and other specialists. Upon completion of this program, graduates will be able to analyze and conceptualize a residential or contract design based on the principles of design. If students go on to pursue the bachelor's degree, they will further develop a broad base of skills and qualifications needed to implement designs for residential and commercial clients. The BA graduate will gain further discernment and application of kitchen and bath design, lighting techniques, construction and building codes and a variety of other Interior Design specializations. Of special note is the emphasis on green design issues throughout the program.

FACILITIES

Multiple computer labs; drafting rooms with professional drafting tables; 2D/3D laboratory; full-service media center with 18,000 available resources, a residential resource room and a commercial resource room

ONLINE / DISTANCE LEARNING

Not available

COURSES OF INSTRUCTION

- Mechanical and Electrical Systems
- Historic Preservation and Adaptive Use
- Introduction to Interior Design
- Rendering
- Perspective Drawing
- Art History; Design History
- 2D/3D Design Foundations
- Advanced Rendered Perspectives
- Housing, Urban Development and Sustainable Design
- Lighting Techniques I
- Sales and Business
- Contract Interiors
- Kitchen and Bath
- Space Planning, Healthcare, and Universal Design
- Interior Finishes
- Architectural Drafting
- Custom Casework and Furniture Design
- CAD for Interior Design
- Residential Interiors
- Textiles
- Project and Facilities Management
- Portfolio

INTERNSHIPS

Required of majors at BA level. Students are responsible for locating their own externships so locations vary. Lowe's, Liz at Home, Rue La La, Munsen Business, and Office Environmental Corporation are some possibilities for externships as well as permanent employment.

STUDY ABROAD

Not available

NOTABLE ALUMNI

Abbey Thonen is notable for her work history and efforts to establish her own business. Samantha Green is our first BA graduate. Stacey Barczak and her unique business, Decoupage Interiors.

STUDENT ACTIVITIES AND ORGANIZATIONS

Student chapters of ASID, IIDA, and SkillsUSA; numerous service learning opportunities.

FACULTY SPECIALIZATIONS AND RESEARCH

LEED, NKBA certifications, NCIDQ certifications, visual arts

University of Kentucky

School of Interior Design, College of Design

110 Pence Hall, Lexington, KY 40506 | 859-257-7617 | www.uky.edu/Design/interiordesign.html

UNIVERSITY PROFILE
Public
Urban
Residential
Semester Schedule
Co-ed

STUDENT DEMOGRAPHICS
Undergraduate: 19,241
Graduate: 7,859

Male: 52% (undergrad), 42% (grad)
Female: 48% (undergrad), 48% (grad)

Full-time: 89%
Part-time: 11%

EXPENSES
Tuition: $4,305 (resident per semester) $8,839 (non-resident per semester)
Room & Board: $2,822–$3,765 per semester

ADMISSIONS
100 Admissions Office
Funkhouser Bldg.
Lexington, KY 40506
859-257-2000
www.uky.edu/Admission/

DEGREE INFORMATION

Major / Degree / Concentration	Enrollment	Requirements for entry	Graduation rate
Interior Design Bachelor of Arts	100	Selective admission at the Freshman year. Review of high school performance and portfolio	90%
Interior Design Master of Arts	6	Undergraduate degree in Interior Design or related area	90%

TOTAL PROGRAM ENROLLMENT
Undergraduate: 70
Graduate: 6

Male: 3%
Female: 97%

Full-time: 91%
Part-time: 9%

International: 15%
Minority: 2%

Job Placement Rate: 80%

SCHOLARSHIPS / FINANCIAL AID
Scholarships from the School of ID are available after the first year. University-wide diversity scholarships are available beginning first year as well scholarships for financial need and academic merit. Non-resident applicants whoses parent are graduates of the University of KY can qualify for a partitial tuition award. More information can be found at www.uky.edu

TOTAL FACULTY: 6
Full-time: 6
Part-time: 0
Online: 0

NCIDQ Certified: 85%
Licensed Interior Designers: 100%
LEED Certified: 0%

INTERIOR DESIGN ADMINISTRATION
Ann W. Dickson, Director, School of Interior Design, College of Design

PROFESSIONAL / ACADEMIC AFFILIATIONS
American Society of Interior Designers
International Interior Design Association

CIDA ACCREDITATION
Bachelor of Arts in Interior Design (2009, 2015)

PROGRAM DESCRIPTION AND PHILOSOPHY

The School of Interior Design at the University of Kentucky focuses on creating design innovation in the way people work and enjoy life by enhancing business performance through creative, sustainable, and technical solutions for interior environments that address the human needs unique to users and setting. The CIDA accredited degree program provides professional training for entry into the practice of interior design. The program focuses on cultivating graduates with unique design thinking skills and the ability to design utilizing multidisciplinary knowledge in solving complex organizational issues associated with work, place, experience, and the relationalship to business performance.

FACILITIES

Computer Lab, Design & Consruction Shop, Design Library in College, Museum on Campus, Materials Lab

ONLINE / DISTANCE LEARNING

Not available

COURSES OF INSTRUCTION

- Color Theory
- Environmental Theory
- Lighting Design & Theory
- Digital Media
- History & Theory of Interior Environments
- Interior Construction Systems
- Seminars in architecture

INTERNSHIPS

Not required. Internship must be full-time work experience under the supervision of a certified Interior Designer.

STUDY ABROAD

Summer program in Dessau, Germany

NOTABLE ALUMNI

Debra Lehaman-Smith, Eileen Jones, Bill Peace, Wayne Braun

STUDENT ACTIVITIES AND ORGANIZATIONS

Student Design Association which combines both ASID & IIDA, Beau Arts Charity Ball sponsored by students of the college, Dance Blue Dancathon for the Children's Hospital at UK initiated by an ID student, College Student Council, University Student Government, numerous sororities & fraternities.

FACULTY SPECIALIZATIONS AND RESEARCH

- Light Design & Technology
- Design for the Elderly
- Workplace Innovation
- Professionalism and Education

Western Kentucky University

Department of Family & Consumer Sciences

1906 College Heights Blvd., #11037, Bowling Green, KY 42101 | 270-745-4352 | www.wku.edu/Dept/Academic/chhs/c

UNIVERSITY PROFILE
Public
Urban
Residential
Semester Schedule
Co-ed

STUDENT DEMOGRAPHICS
Undergraduate: 19,000
Graduate: 3,000

Male: 40%
Female: 60%

Full-time: Not reported
Part-time: Not reported

EXPENSES
Tuition: $7,200
Room & Board: Not reported

ADMISSIONS
1906 College Heights Blvd
Bowling Green, KY 42101
270-745-0111
CFS@wku.edu

DEGREE INFORMATION

Major / Degree / Concentration	Enrollment	Requirements for entry	Graduation rate
Design, Merchandising & Textiles Bachelor of Science Interior Design	90	Not reported	Not reported

TOTAL PROGRAM ENROLLMENT
Undergraduate: 90
Graduate: Not reported

Male: 10%
Female: 90%

Full-time: 90%
Part-time: 10%

International: 5%
Minority: 5%

Job Placement Rate: 90%

SCHOLARSHIPS / FINANCIAL AID
- Marie Adams - Home Economics Alumni Association Scholarship
- Beta Delta - Phi Upsilon Omicron Scholarships
- Bernice King Doublas Scholarship
- Evadine Parker - Phi Upsilon Omicron Scholarship
- Fashion, Inc., Scholarship
- Susie Pate Scholarship
- Warren County Homemakers Association - Melissa Bohannon Clemmons Scholarship

TOTAL FACULTY: 3
Full-time: 3
Part-time: Not reported
Online: Not reported

NCIDQ Certified: 1
Licensed Interior Designers: 1
LEED Certified: Not reported

INTERIOR DESIGN ADMINISTRATION
Doris Sikora, Department Head

PROFESSIONAL / ACADEMIC AFFILIATIONS
American Society of Interior Designers
International Interior Design Association
Interior Design Educators Council

PROGRAM DESCRIPTION AND PHILOSOPHY

The central purpose of this program is to prepare graduates who can successfully design interior spaces which satisfy the functional and aesthetic needs of the users. Specifically, graduates will be able to identify, research, and creatively solve problems pertaining to the function and quality of the interior environment and perform services relative to its design, including programming, analysis, space planning and aesthetics based on specialized knowledge of interior construction, building codes, equipment, materials and furnishings. Graduates will have skills for preparing drawings and documents relative to the design in order to enhance and protect the health, safety, and welfare of the public.

FACILITIES
Not reported

ONLINE / DISTANCE LEARNING
Not reported

COURSES OF INSTRUCTION
- Materials and Finishes
- Studio I-VII
- Environmental Controls
- History of Architecture and Interior Design
- Business Principles and Practice
- Textiles
- CAD for the Human Environment
- Portfolio

INTERNSHIPS
Required of majors at the Senior level

STUDY ABROAD
Yearly Interior Design trip to Australia or Europe through the department and opportunities with KIIS, CSSA, and Semester at Sea.

NOTABLE ALUMNI
Not reported

STUDENT ACTIVITIES AND ORGANIZATIONS
American Society of Interior Designers, International Interior Design Association, National Kitchen and Bath Association

FACULTY SPECIALIZATIONS AND RESEARCH
Not reported

Delgado Community College

Arts Department, Division of Arts & Humanities

615 City Park Ave., New Orleans, LA 70119 | 504-671-6372 | www.dcc.edu

UNIVERSITY PROFILE
Public
Urban
Commuter
Semester
Co-ed

STUDENT DEMOGRAPHICS
Undergraduate: 17,208
Graduate: n/a

Male: 32.5%
Female: 67.5%

Full-time: 48%
Part-time: 52%

EXPENSES
Tuition: $845
Room & Board: n/a

ADMISSIONS
615 City Park Ave.,
New Orleans, LA 70119

DEGREE INFORMATION

Major / Degree / Concentration	Enrollment	Requirements for entry	Graduation rate
Interior Design Associate of Arts Degree	Not reported	Not reported	Not reported
Interior Design Technical Diploma	Not reported	Not reported	Not reported

TOTAL PROGRAM ENROLLMENT
Undergraduate: Not reported
Graduate: n/a

Male: Not reported
Female: Not reported

Full-time: Not reported
Part-time: Not reported

International: Not reported
Minority: Not reported

Job Placement Rate: Not reported

SCHOLARSHIPS / FINANCIAL AID
We offer student scholarships sponsored
by the ASID student chapter.

TOTAL FACULTY: 3
Full-time: 100%
Part-time: n/a
Online: Not reported

NCIDQ Certified: 0
Licensed Interior Designers: 0
LEED Certified: 0

INTERIOR DESIGN ADMINISTRATION
Patrice Moore, Dean of Art & Humanities
Erin Sanders, Chair of Visual Arts, INTD
  Program Coordinator

PROFESSIONAL / ACADEMIC AFFILIATIONS
America Society of Interior Designers
Interior Design Educator's Council

PROGRAM DESCRIPTION AND PHILOSOPHY

Delgado Community College offers the Associate of Arts Degree in Interior Design. This degree program is appropriate for students who wish to prepare for the National Council of Interior Design preparation.

FACILITIES

The Interior Design Department has a dedicated computer lab, materials resource library,studio classrooms.

ONLINE / DISTANCE LEARNING

Select courses are offered online.

COURSES OF INSTRUCTION

- Drawing I
- Computers for Int. Design
- Painting I
- History of Interior Design I
- Interior Design IV
- Drafting for Interior Design
- Color for Interior Space
- Two-Dimensional Design
- Interior Materials, Finishes, & Furnishings
- Interior Design I
- Interior Design II
- Lighting Design
- History of Interior Design II
- Interior Construction Systems
- Interior Design III
- Professional Practices for Interior Design

INTERNSHIPS

Not required

STUDY ABROAD

Available

NOTABLE ALUMNI

Not reported

STUDENT ACTIVITIES AND ORGANIZATIONS

The Interior Design Department has a student chapter of the American Society of Interior Designers.

FACULTY SPECIALIZATIONS AND RESEARCH

Not reported

Louisiana State University

Department of Interior Design

402 Design Building, Baton Rouge, LA 70803 | 225-578-8422 | http://design.lsu.edu/Interior_Design

UNIVERSITY PROFILE
Public
Urban
Residential
Semester Schedule
Co-ed

STUDENT DEMOGRAPHICS
Undergraduate: Not reported
Graduate: Not reported

Male: Not reported
Female: Not reported

Full-time: Not reported
Part-time: Not reported

EXPENSES
Tuition: $5,400
Room & Board: $9,400

ADMISSIONS
Undergraduate Admissions
1146 Pleasant Hall
Baton Rouge, LA 70803
225-578-1175
admissions@lsu.edu

DEGREE INFORMATION

Major / Degree / Concentration	Enrollment	Requirements for entry	Graduation rate
Interior Design Bachelor of Interior Design	120	Controlled admission of 60 Freshmen and selective admission of 40 into the second year through portfolio review and gpa	85%

TOTAL PROGRAM ENROLLMENT
Undergraduate: 210
Graduate: 0

Male: 8%
Female: 92%

Full-time: 91%
Part-time: 9%

International: 1.5%
Minority: 4.5%

Job Placement Rate: 89%

SCHOLARSHIPS / FINANCIAL AID
Interior Design awards 10 - 15 internal scholarships per year ranging from $300 - $1000 each. The scholarship requirements vary from academic merit, financial need, travel and study proposals to portfolio review. LSU offers many scholarship and finacial aid packages through the admissions and finacial aid offices. Our students also compete for various outside scholarships, such as the NEWH (The Hospitality Industry Network) award for $1700 and the IALD (International Association of Lighting Designers) Student Stipend for $1000. The professional organizations also provide scholarship opportunities.

TOTAL FACULTY: 10
Full-time: 70%
Part-time: 30%
Online: 0%

NCIDQ Certified: 60%
Licensed Interior Designers: 60%
LEED Certified: 20%

INTERIOR DESIGN ADMINISTRATION
T.L. Ritchie, Chair

PROFESSIONAL / ACADEMIC AFFILIATIONS
American Society of Interior Designers
International Interior Design Association
Interior Design Educators Council
Environmental Design Research Association

CIDA ACCREDITATION
Bachelor of Interior Design (B.I.D.) (2008, 2014)

PROGRAM DESCRIPTION AND PHILOSOPHY

At the heart of the Interior Design curriculum is the core design studio sequence. There are six consecutive core design studios. The intense core studios concentrate on design, design process, and design theory issues. Within this design sequence there remains the investigation of different practice and interest layers, such as residential, office, hospitality, health care, institutional, adaptive reuse, and retail. The studios are problem-based explorations which develop creative and critical inquiry to resolve increasingly complex projects. As the student progresses through the core design sequence there is a systematic investigation and application of the design process in increasing intensity culminating in the Senior capstone project which is the most comprehensive inquest and resolution.

Linked to the design studio sequence are a series of focus or support studios. In this sequence the students learn, in concentration, the knowledge and skills necessary to support the design process. Within the focus sequence is a technical stream of courses that informs the student in industry methodologies. There is a professional sequence also. Internship and Professional Practice are the backbone of this sequence. To encourage interdisciplinary knowledge, skills, and perspective, the program is enriched by the requirement of nine hours of Art and Design electives.

FACILITIES

CADGIS: The Computer Aided Design and Geographic Information Systems Laboratory is a teaching, research, and service unit that is jointly supported by the College of Art & Design and the Department of Geography/Anthropology. CADGIS has been funded with grants of over $150,000.00 per year.

Lumen Laboratory: The Interior Design Computer Support Area is available with workstations, scanners, printers, and plotters. This area is a support facility for the more extensive CADGIS Laboratory.

Design Workshop: The Design Shop is an interdisciplinary facility that is available within the College of Art & Design. The shop provides equipment, suitable work space, and appropriate technical assistance to students who are working on projects that require large scale power tools, laser cutters and 3D printers.

Interior Design Materials Library: The material resource library contains product information on an extensive array of finishes, furniture and accessories. Sample books, specification information, product displays, Sweets Catalogues, Code and Regulatory Manuals, and other reference material are available. A computer station, Internet access, and scanner are provided. The materials library represents a donation value of $100,000-$180,000.

ONLINE / DISTANCE LEARNING
Not available

COURSES OF INSTRUCTION
- Introduction to Interior Design
- Principles And Elements Of Two-Dimensional Design
- Drawing and Composition, and Technical Drawing
- Design I-VI, Senior Seminar, Research and Capstone
- Graphics, Color, and Illumination I & II, Construction Documents
- Component Design
- Computer Visualization
- Advanced Computer Visualization
- Field Studies and Special Studies
- Art I&II, Architecture I&II and Interior Design I&II History
- Interior Construction and Systems and Interior Materials, Finishes and Furnishings
- Professional Sequence: Internship and Professional Practice
- Art and Design electives

INTERNSHIPS
Required of majors at 3rd year level. Our students consistently secure internships with the leading design and architecture firms nationally and internationally. Recent examples are Hirsch Bedner Associates, Smith Group, Metropolitan Museum of Art (NY- lighting division), HKS, HOK, RTKL and Tilottson Lighting Design.

STUDY ABROAD
Available

NOTABLE ALUMNI
Jacque St. Dizier, Kenneth Brown, Susan Tilotson, Greg Switzer

STUDENT ACTIVITIES AND ORGANIZATIONS
Community outreach and the scholarship of engagement are of critical importance to professional education and this program. The Department has been active with the Center for Community Engagement, Learning, and Leadership (CCELL) since its inception. Interior Design was also the earliest supporter of the Office of Community Design and Development (OCDD), the an outreach office for the college. Interior Design faculty and students work and intern on numerous research and outreach projects for the office.

FACULTY SPECIALIZATIONS AND RESEARCH
The Steelcase [LSU] Research Partnership which is a research/ applied scholarship activity initiated by Interior Design faculty has interesting engagement opportunities. The faculty's work with the Louisiana House and sustainable living research which commenced ten years ago has developed into an additional community activity especially after Hurricanes Katrina, Rita, and Gustav. The Department faculty also has a history of collaboration with the Louisiana Main St. Program. Numerous community projects have been implemented. A highlight for the department came in 2002 when a third year studio project became the first all Interior Design team to receive the prestigious Historic American Buildings Survey (HABS) national Charles E. Peterson Prize.

Boston Architectural College

School of Interior Design

320 Newbury St., Boston, MA 02115 | 617-585-0285 | www.the-bac.edu

UNIVERSITY PROFILE
Private
Urban
Commuter
Semester Schedule
Co-ed

STUDENT DEMOGRAPHICS
Undergraduate: 640
Graduate: 476

Male: 63%
Female: 37%

Full-time: 98.7%
Part-time: 1.3%

EXPENSES
Tuition: $16,129
(undergraduate); $18,312
(graduate)
Room & Board: n/a

ADMISSIONS
320 Newbury St.
Boston, MA 02115
617-262-5000

DEGREE INFORMATION

Major / Degree / Concentration	Enrollment	Requirements for entry	Graduation rate
Interior Design **Bachelor of Interior Design**	69	High school diploma	25%
Interior Design **Master of Interior Design**	62	Bachelor degree	34%

TOTAL PROGRAM ENROLLMENT
Undergraduate: 69
Graduate: 62

Male: 14%
Female: 86%

Full-time: 100%
Part-time: 0%

International: 8%
Minority: 30%

Job Placement Rate: 95%

SCHOLARSHIPS / FINANCIAL AID
Institutional Aid: grants & scholarships;
Federal Aid: Pell Grant, Federal
Academic Competitiveness Grant (ACG),
Federal Supplemental Educational
Opportunity Grant (FSEOG), Stafford
Loan (Subsidized & Unsubsidized; PLUS
Loan (undergraduate & graduate);
Veterans Benefits; State Aid: state
grants, state no-interest loan;
Alternative Private Loans

Students Receiving Scholarships or
Financial Aid: 92%

TOTAL FACULTY: 23
Full-time: 5%
Part-time: 95%
Online: 5%

NCIDQ Certified: 41%
Licensed Interior Designers: NA
LEED Certified: 20%

INTERIOR DESIGN ADMINISTRATION
David B. Harrison, ASID, IIDA, IDEC,
Head of School

PROFESSIONAL / ACADEMIC AFFILIATIONS
American Society of Interior Designers
International Interior Design Association
Interior Design Educators Council

CIDA ACCREDITATION
Bachelor or Master of Interior Design
(2009, 2015)

PROGRAM DESCRIPTION AND PHILOSOPHY

Interior designers transform clients' ideas of their needs into aesthetically pleasing, comfortable, productive, and safe interior spaces.

The Interior Design program at the Boston Architectural College teaches the thought processes and pragmatic skills necessary to program, design, build, and assess the comfort, productivity, safety and sustainability of spaces directly experienced by human inhabitants. New research suggests that programs like those at the BAC that provide practice-based knowledge and analytical tools that enable graduates to enter the traditional roles of designers and managers, space planners, healthcare designers, historic preservationists, retail and hospitality specialists, exhibition designers, and lighting designers also provide the basis for careers as environmental graphics designers, industrial designers, marketing and media specialists, theater designers as well as others in emerging careers that provide physical and aesthetic solutions for clients seeking improvements in their enclosed built environments.

The BAC's Interior Design program stresses innovative design thinking and the ability to work creatively with clients to transform ideas into solid, material form. Practicing designers serve as faculty in studios and practice settings as well as in the classroom teaching the history and theory of design, ergonomics and accessibility, lighting and color theory, furniture, building technologies, the properties and coordination of materials, and methods of professional Interior Design practice.

The Undergraduate Interior Design program develops conceptualization; freehand and digital visualization and rendering; human factors and universal codes; building engineering; lighting and furniture design; model making; textiles and materials; and the presentation skills necessary to be a successful practitioner. The program has been recognized as a "Hidden Gem among Interior Design programs in America." The Graduate program adds related research, analytical thinking, global learning, business practices, and collaborative management skills that enable graduates to be successful and innovative practitioners, teachers, and leaders in society-at-large. Both programs focus on commercial, health care, educational, hospitality and residential design, and provide opportunities for hands-on furniture-making and travel within the United States and abroad.

In conjunction with the BAC's Architecture, Landscape Architecture, Design Studies, Preservation, Sustainability, and Technology programs, the Interior Design program applies design thinking toward the achievement of comfort, productive efficiency, safety, and delight through the art and science of designing better interior environments.

FACILITIES

Boston is itself a museum; computer labs; photography lab; laser model making lab; Museum of Fine Arts; Isabel Stewart Gardner Museum; Institute of Contemporary Art; Museum of Science; Boston Children's Museum; Aquarium; Otis House; Nichols House; Gibson House; Paul Revere House; Gropius House; MIT; Harvard

ONLINE / DISTANCE LEARNING

The entire program is not offered online but specific courses are.

COURSES OF INSTRUCTION

Minimum of two semesters of foundation including studio, orthogonal drawing, perspective drawing, computer aided drawing; five studios; Mechanical/Electrical/Plumbing/Structural; Introduction to Art History & Criticism; Human Factors & Codes; Lighting Design; Color & Color Theory; Textiles; ID Materials; History of ID & Furniture; Professional Practice; Thinking Green; two semesters of Design Degree Project (BID); two semesters of Thesis (MID)

INTERNSHIPS

Not required of majors.

All of the BAC's disciplines are "concurrent curricula," meaning that students work in their chosen field while also attending classes. This requires a reduced academic load which results in a longer time in school, but upon graduation the students are far beyond "entry level" as they have already become managers. While employed, the students accrue "practice credits," with each discipline determining the number of practice credits required for graduation. Students find their own positions with area architectural and Interior Design firms with assistance from the College and have regular contact with the Practice Department about their progress in the work place.

STUDY ABROAD

Available

NOTABLE ALUMNI

Not reported

STUDENT ACTIVITIES AND ORGANIZATIONS

ASID Student Chapter; Atelier (student government); NOMA; Studio Q; golf team; soccer team; curling club; running club

FACULTY SPECIALIZATIONS AND RESEARCH

Our faculty are practicing professional Interior Designers specializing in health care, hospitility, government, education, corporate, and residential design.

Endicott College

School of Visual and Performing Arts

376 Hale St., Beverly, MA 01915 | 978-232-2250 | www.endicott.edu

UNIVERSITY PROFILE
Private
Suburban
Residential
Semester Schedule
Co-ed

STUDENT DEMOGRAPHICS
Undergraduate: 2,400
Graduate: 800

Male: 44%
Female: 56%

Full-time: 99%
Part-time: 1%

EXPENSES
Tuition: $25,848
Room & Board: $12,388

ADMISSIONS
376 Hale St.
Beverly, MA 01915
978-921-1000
800-325-1114
admission@endicott.edu

DEGREE INFORMATION

Major / Degree / Concentration	Enrollment	Requirements for entry	Graduation rate
Interior Design Bachelor of Science	110	Portfolio review	25%

TOTAL PROGRAM ENROLLMENT
Undergraduate: 110
Graduate: 8 (this is the first year)

Male: 0%
Female: 100%

Full-time: 100%
Part-time: 0%

International: 0%
Minority: 0%

Job Placement Rate: Not reported

SCHOLARSHIPS / FINANCIAL AID
Not reported

TOTAL FACULTY: 12
Full-time: 33%
Part-time: 66%
Online: 0%

NCIDQ Certified: 25%
Licensed Interior Designers: NA
LEED Certified: 17%

INTERIOR DESIGN ADMINISTRATION
Kevin Renz, Assistant Dean

PROFESSIONAL / ACADEMIC AFFILIATIONS
Not reported

CIDA ACCREDITATION
Bachelor of Science in Interior Design
(2010, 2016)

PROGRAM DESCRIPTION AND PHILOSOPHY

The four-year degree program offered by the Department of Interior Design is fully accredited by the Council for Interior Design Accreditation (formerly FIDER). Graduates are prepared to enter the working world as professional Interior Designers capable of creating interior architectural environments. They also receive the academic credentials to sit for the National Council Interior Design Qualification (NCIDQ) examination upon completion of two years of work experience. Successful completion of the exam is necessary for professional membership in national and international Interior Design service organizations.

Emphasis is placed on the development of creative skills and problem-solving strategies necessary for designing within the built environment. The philosophy and principles of design are combined with three-dimensional space planning, human factors, building technology, and environmental considerations for an educational experience that balances the theoretical and practical.

FACILITIES

Laptop program, printing lab

ONLINE / DISTANCE LEARNING

Not available

COURSES OF INSTRUCTION

The curriculum is comprehensive and includes courses in institutional, residential, and commercial design, the history of Interior Design, historic preservation, drawing, rendering, drafting, computer-aided design and drafting, construction technology, materials, furniture, color, lighting, detailing, and business practice. The Interior Design curriculum has fully integrated traditional and digital media. To facilitate this Endicott College provides state-of-the-art, network-ready laptop computers to first-year students entering the Interior Design program. All students entering the program are required to participate in this Laptop Program. The computers are fully loaded with software, protected with warranties against loss from theft or damage, and supported by on-campus technical staff with loaners available when needed. Further information is available at Academic Resources' statement, Laptop Requirement in Interior Design.

INTERNSHIPS

Through the Internship Program, students actually work for Interior Designers and experience first hand the challenges of the design profession. There are three internship experiences and these occur in January of the Freshman and Sophomore years, and for the entire fall semester of the Senior year. The following are just some of the internship sites with which the college enjoys an on-going relationship:
- Currier & Associates, Newburyport, MA
- Carpenter & MacNeille Architects
- Schwartz/Silver Architects, Inc., Boston, MA
- Jung Brannen Associates, Inc., Boston, MA
- D'Agostino Izzo Quirk Architects, Somerville, MA
- Graham-Kim International, Inc., Woburn, MA
- Olson, Lewis, Dioli and Doktor Architecture, Manchester, MA
- Winter St. Architects, Inc., Salem, MA
- Symmes, Maini & McKee Associates, Cambridge, MA
- The Stubbins Associates, Cambridge, MA
- Siemasko + Verbridge, Inc.

STUDY ABROAD

Denmark and Italy

NOTABLE ALUMNI

Not reported

STUDENT ACTIVITIES AND ORGANIZATIONS

The department's Student Interior Design Focus Group engages in activities such as Career Day where the students attend seminars offered by design professionals. Membership in professional organizations such as the American Society of Interior Designers and the International Interior Design Association is encouraged in order that students begin networking within the design community.

FACULTY SPECIALIZATIONS AND RESEARCH

Electronic workflow

New England School of Art & Design at Suffolk University

Interior Design Department

75 Arlington St., Boston, MA 02116 | 617-573-8785 | www.suffolk.edu/nesad

UNIVERSITY PROFILE
Private
Urban
Commuter
Semester Schedule
Co-ed

STUDENT DEMOGRAPHICS
Undergraduate: 3,341
Graduate: 634

Male: 33%
Female: 67%

Full-time: 87%
Part-time: 13%

EXPENSES
Tuition: $27,100
Room & Board: $14,294

ADMISSIONS
73 Tremont St.
Boston, MA 02116
617-573-8785
admission@suffolk.edu

DEGREE INFORMATION

Major / Degree / Concentration	Enrollment	Requirements for entry	Graduation rate
Interior Design Bachelor of Fine Arts	100	2.5 gpa Portfolio review	100%
Interior Design Master of Arts	75	2.9 gpa Portfolio review	90%

TOTAL PROGRAM ENROLLMENT
Undergraduate: 100
Graduate: 75

Male: 20%
Female: 80%

Full-time: 70%
Part-time: 30%

International: 10%
Minority: 10%

Job Placement Rate: 85%

SCHOLARSHIPS / FINANCIAL AID
Federal Student Aid, Federal Work Study Aid, PLUS (parent loan for undergraduate students), Vendome Scholarship, President's Incentive Loan/ Grant Program, Miller Scholarship program, check out www.suffolk.edu/ finaid

Students Receiving Scholarships or Financial Aid: 60%

TOTAL FACULTY: 31
Full-time: 6
Part-time: 25
Online: 0

NCIDQ Certified: 5%
Licensed Interior Designers: NA
LEED Certified: 5%

INTERIOR DESIGN ADMINISTRATION
Karen Clarke, Co-program Director of Interior Design
Nancy Hackett, Co-program Director of Interior Design

PROFESSIONAL / ACADEMIC AFFILIATIONS
American Society of Interior Designers
International Interior Design Association
Interior Design Educators Council
Interior Design Associations Foundation

CIDA ACCREDITATION
BFA in Interior Design and MA in Interior Design (2008, 2014)

PROGRAM DESCRIPTION AND PHILOSOPHY

The Interior Design program at NESADSU educates Interior Designers in ways in which they may use their talents to transform society. They possess the intellectual background, the practical skills, and the passion for design that allows them to impact the ways in which we live our lives- at home, in the office and in restaurants, hotels, hospitals, and schools. Create problem-solving, attention to the rule of law, the protection of our planet, and an understanding of human behavior: they all play a role in the work of an interior.

FACILITIES

Interior Design students have access to a design library of current resources, a materials library modeled on those in professional design firms, and a professional-quality lighting lab. Along with the required internship, these tools will provide the skills necessary in order to secure meaningful and remunerative employment in the field. There are five electronic studio classrooms, two lecture rooms, open computer workstations, access to three large scale plotters, lazer color printers and ink-jet color printers.

ONLINE / DISTANCE LEARNING

Not at this time

COURSES OF INSTRUCTION

The Interior Design curriculum at NESADSU involves a comprehensive study of design theory, history, communication and design skills, sustainable design and code adherence, and professional practices. Students will also gain a solid understanding of the computer as a tool for 2- and 3-dimensional presentation. The Interior Design studio and lecture courses are:

- Interior Design Studio I
- Residential Design
- Contract I & II
- Furniture Design
- Orthogonal Drawing
- Materials and Finishes
- Marketing and Contracts
- Codes and Construction
- History and Theory of Interior Architecture
- Environmental Systems
- Lighting
- Perspective & Rendering
- Interior Design Communication & Advanced IDC
- Programming
- Art History I & II
- History of Furniture and Architecture I & II
- Senior Studio
- Construction Documents

INTERNSHIPS

Required of majors. The students intern at local Interior Design or architectural firms in the city of Boston. A list of some of the architectural firms: Gensler, CBT Architects, Sheply Bullfinch Abbott Architects, Cannon Associates, Bergmeyer Associates, Tsoi Kobus Architects.

STUDY ABROAD

Available

NOTABLE ALUMNI

Not reported

STUDENT ACTIVITIES AND ORGANIZATIONS

Interior Design Council - student organization that organizes student events such as guest speakers, tours, volunteering services to non-profit organizations, and participating in the IIDA yearly fashion show.

FACULTY SPECIALIZATIONS AND RESEARCH

Karen Clarke, LEED AP, NCIDQ certified, specializes in Sustainable Design, Nancy Hackett, IIDA, NCIDQ certified, specializes in Commercial and Institutional Interior Design Studio, Sean Solley, IDEC, specializes in Human Centered Design and Drawing Communication, Mark Brus, AIA, specializes in Architectural History and Theory, Nasser Benkaci, IDEC, specializes in thesis design, resarch and architectural construction. Anna Gitelman, specializes in lighting and digital drawings.

Wentworth Institute of Technology

Department of Design & Facilities

550 Huntington Ave., Boston, MA 02115 | 617-989-4050 | www.wit.edu/df/DF_Home_page.html

UNIVERSITY PROFILE
Private
Urban
Residential
Semester Schedule
Co-ed

STUDENT DEMOGRAPHICS
Undergraduate: 3,808
Graduate: 84

Male: 81%
Female: 19%

Full-time: 89%
Part-time: 11%

EXPENSES
Tuition: $22,870
Room & Board: $11,000

ADMISSIONS
550 Huntington Ave.
Boston, MA 02115
617-989-4000
admissions@wit.edu

DEGREE INFORMATION

Major / Degree / Concentration	Enrollment	Requirements for entry	Graduation rate
Interior Design Bachelor of Science	117	Portfolio review and gpa after Sophomore year	67%
Facilities Planning & Management	70	Interdisciplinary first two years with Interior Design or Architecture	72%

TOTAL PROGRAM ENROLLMENT
Undergraduate: 171
Graduate: 0

Male: 8%
Female: 92%

Full-time: 99%
Part-time: 1%

International: 4%
Minority: 5%

Job Placement Rate: Not reported

SCHOLARSHIPS / FINANCIAL AID
Students Receiving Scholarships or
Financial Aid: 72%

TOTAL FACULTY: 23
Full-time: 26%
Part-time: 74%
Online: 0%

NCIDQ Certified: 2
Licensed Interior Designers: NA
LEED Certified: 4

INTERIOR DESIGN ADMINISTRATION
Suzanne Kennedy, Department Head
Herb Fremin, Program Coordinator

PROFESSIONAL / ACADEMIC AFFILIATIONS
American Society of Interior Designers
Interior Design Educators Council

CIDA ACCREDITATION
Bachelor of Science - Interior Design
(2005, 2011)

PROGRAM DESCRIPTION AND PHILOSOPHY

The program recognizes that academic preparation is the foundation of lifelong learning in a dynamic and evolving profession. It seeks to develop student fluency and competence in an array of basic skills and processes with equal insight into the artistic, technical, and managerial competencies of practice. More precisely, the program graduates students with a broad overview of the profession by balancing a curriculum equally weighted in creativity—the art of design—and rudimentary technical knowledge and business acumen required to realize their conceptions.

The program orientation and the structure of the curriculum rest on a tripartite base: Wentworth's 'Student Learning Outcomes,' CIDA accreditation standards, and the NCIDQ definition of the professional Interior Designer. These three standards recognize the reality of the specialized, diverse knowledge, and skills required in practice and affords graduates substantial preparation for professional licensure.

To achieve this balanced orientation, the program seeks:
- to foster creativity and artistic vision
- to develop fluency with a design process
- to broaden intellectual depth
- to develop technical skills and the craft of making
- to introduce students to the business of design
- to offer the opportunity to work efficiently both independently and collaboratively in teams
- to recognize the broad professional fiduciary responsibilities to the general public including, but not limited to ethical practice, regulatory requirements, and growing public concerns for resource conservation and sustainability.

FACILITIES

Individual studio work stations are available starting in the Sophomore year. All students receive laptops fully loaded with software at the Freshman and Junior years. Printers are available in studios. Printers, plotters, and scanners are available in labs. WIT is a member of the Colleges of the Fenway consortium which provides cross-registration and extra curricular opportunities and the Fenway Libraries Online which provides access to sixteen libraries incuding the Boston Public Library. Wentworth is adjacent to the Boston Museum of Fine Arts and Isabella Stewart Gardner Museum and has memberships allowing students free access.

ONLINE / DISTANCE LEARNING

Not available

COURSES OF INSTRUCTION

Design Studios (each semester)
Interior Architectural Lighting
Behavioral Aspects of Design
Textiles
Materials & Construction Methods
Construction Documents

INTERNSHIPS

Required of majors. 2 coop semesters (1 Junior, 1 Senior). Interns are typically placed at companies such as Gensler, Nelson, Sasaki Associates, TRO/Jung Brannen, Meichi Peng Design Studio, Hutker Architects, Harvard Business School, Office Environments of New England, Creative Office Pavilion.

STUDY ABROAD

Not available

NOTABLE ALUMNI

Meichi Peng, Patrick Planeta

STUDENT ACTIVITIES AND ORGANIZATIONS

Wentworth's Division III athletics programs include 15 varsity, two club and six intramural sports, emphasizing both men's and women's sports. The Center for Community Partnerships provides opportunities for students to participate in service learning projects with the local community. The Office of Student Leadership oversees 48 academic and social clubs and provides formal leadership training opportunities. The Student Association for Interior Design (SAID) organizes local, regional, and national trips to design offices, historic houses, and professional conferences such as NeoCon.

FACULTY SPECIALIZATIONS AND RESEARCH

Not reported

Anne Arundel Community College

Interior Design Department

101 College Parkway, Arnold, MD 21012 | 410-777-2442 | www.aacc.edu

UNIVERSITY PROFILE
Public
Suburban
Commuter
Semester Schedule
Co-ed

STUDENT DEMOGRAPHICS
Undergraduate: 16,741
Graduate: n/a

Male: 39%
Female: 61%

Full-time: 36%
Part-time: 64%

EXPENSES
Tuition: $88/Credit Hr
Room & Board: n/a

ADMISSIONS
101 College Parkway
Arnold, MD 21012
410-777-2246
admissions@aacc.edu

DEGREE INFORMATION

Major / Degree / Concentration	Enrollment	Requirements for entry	Graduation rate
Interior Design Associate of Arts	107	Open enrollment	Not reported
Interior Design Certificate	29	Open enrollment	Not reported
Interior Design Advanced Certificate	New in 2010	Completion of courses listed as pre-requisites in the AAS degree option or the equivalent industry experience	Not reported

TOTAL PROGRAM ENROLLMENT
Undergraduate: 109
Graduate: n/a

Male: 9%
Female: 91%

Full-time: 34%
Part-time: 66%

International: 1%
Minority: 22%

Job Placement Rate: 85%

SCHOLARSHIPS / FINANCIAL AID
The college believes that no student should be restricted from attending college because of limited financial resources. AACC offers grants, scholarships, loans, and/or employment programs to eligible full-time and part-time students in all degree programs and most certificate programs. Our Financial Aid Office will assist students with all services related to scholarships, student loans, grants, and Veteran's Benefits.

Students Receiving Scholarships or Financial Aid: 32%

TOTAL FACULTY: 8
Full-time: 60%
Part-time: 40%
Online: 25%

NCIDQ Certified: 30%
Licensed Interior Designers: 43%
LEED Certified: 43%

INTERIOR DESIGN ADMINISTRATION
Michael Ryan, Department Chair

PROFESSIONAL / ACADEMIC AFFILIATIONS
American Society of Interior Designers
Interior Design Educators Council

PROGRAM DESCRIPTION AND PHILOSOPHY

Prepares students in the field of Interior Design while developing essential skills required in the workforce. Program focuses on both residential and commercial aspects of design and construction such as; illustration, color, lighting, textiles, finishes, and furnishings. Equips students with employable skills in research, client relations, programming, contract documentation, design analysis, presentation, CAD (computer aided design), building-information modeling [BIM] and interior material specifications. In addition to both the creative and functional aspects of design the program focuses on health, safety, and welfare issues required by the industry. These issues include sustainable design based on the LEED system (Leadership in Energy and Environmental Design) through the USGBC (United States Green Building Council), ADA (American Disability Act) and human factors in design such as anthropometrics, ergonomics, and color psychology. Credits may be transferred to schools offering bachelors's degrees in Interior Design. See department chair regarding specific college and university requirements and department transfer agreements. Program satisfies minimum credit requirements for ASID (American Society of Interior Designers) Allied or professional membership. Also satisfies the minimum educational requirement for NCIDQ (National Council for Interior Design Qualification) certification. Provides pathways to industry required internships, entry-level positions, and the advanced certificate options.

FACILITIES

The department is in a new state of the art LEED certified facility. Students have access to over 85 computers, 6 scanners (2 full sized), 5 full-sized plotters, 10 color laser printers, blueprint machine, large document copier, 3D printer, and a fully equipped wood shop. Students have access to the latest releases of AutoCAD, Revit, SketchUp, Photoshop, and 3D Studio Max. Our close location to Annapolis, Baltimore and Washington, DC, make it an ideal location for local resources, businesses and museums.

ONLINE / DISTANCE LEARNING
Not available.

COURSES OF INSTRUCTION
- Introduction to Interior Design
- Materials and Methods for Interior Design 1
- Textiles and Textile Applications
- Residential Design Studio
- Architectural Design 1, 2
- Architectural Materials and Methods 1
- History of Interior Design
- Space Planning
- Commercial Design Studio
- Interior Construction Detailing
- Advanced Residential Studio
- Kitchen and Bath Design
- Portfolio and Visual Presentations
- History of Ornament, Textiles, and Color
- Lighting for Interior Design
- Sustainable Interiors
- Professional Practices in Interior Design
- Environmental Systems for Design
- Computer Applications for Design
- Color
- Drawing 1
- CAD Electives (AutoCAD, Revit, SketchUp, 3D Studio Max)

INTERNSHIPS
Required of majors for the advanced certificate. Students are placed in local and regional design firms and allied businesses.

STUDY ABROAD
The department offers a travel study program every other summer to Paris where students can earn three credits. The course is called ACH 261-Paris by Design and is transferable.

NOTABLE ALUMNI
Not reported

STUDENT ACTIVITIES AND ORGANIZATIONS
The college has over 75 student clubs and organizations. The department maintains an active ASID student club and students have won an unprecedented number of statewide ASID awards.

FACULTY SPECIALIZATIONS AND RESEARCH
Full and part-time faculty are active practicing professionals with specialties in a variety of different areas, adding strength and diversity to the program.

COMMUNITY COLLEGE TRANSFERS
The department maintains several formal and informal agreements with various prestigious institutions. Students have successfully transferred to these universities and colleges, often being awarded scholarships for their work completed at AACC. Students are encouraged to check the department's transfer web page and department chair for updated information.

Baker College Auburn Hills

Interior Design Program

1500 University Dr., Auburn Hills, MI 48326 | 248-340-0600 | **www.baker.edu**

UNIVERSITY PROFILE
Private
Suburban
Commuter
Quarter Schedule
Co-ed

STUDENT DEMOGRAPHICS
Undergraduate: 4,200
Graduate: 1,500

Male: 30%
Female: 70%

Full-time: 70%
Part-time: 30%

EXPENSES
Tuition: $198 per credit hour
Room & Board: n/a

ADMISSIONS
1500 University Dr.
Auburn Hills, MI 48326
248-340-0600

DEGREE INFORMATION

Major / Degree / Concentration	Enrollment	Requirements for entry	Graduation rate
Interior Design Associate of Applied Science	85	3.5 gpa	90%
Interior Design Bachelor of Interior Design	60	3.5 gpa	90%
Kitchen and Bath Design Advanced Certificate	20	3.5 gpa	90%

TOTAL PROGRAM ENROLLMENT
Undergraduate: Not reported
Graduate: Not reported

Male: Not reported
Female: Not reported

Full-time: Not reported
Part-time: Not reported

International: Not reported
Minority: Not reported

Job Placement Rate: 95%

SCHOLARSHIPS / FINANCIAL AID
Not reported

TOTAL FACULTY: NOT REPORTED
Full-time: Not reported
Part-time: Not reported
Online: Not reported

NCIDQ Certified: Not reported
Licensed Interior Designers: Not reported
LEED Certified: Not reported

INTERIOR DESIGN ADMINISTRATION
Not reported

PROFESSIONAL / ACADEMIC AFFILIATIONS
American Society of Interior Designers
National Kitchen and Bath Association

PROGRAM DESCRIPTION AND PHILOSOPHY
We prepare students to be employed.

FACILITIES
Technology, computer, drafting labs, resource room, library

ONLINE / DISTANCE LEARNING
Not available

COURSES OF INSTRUCTION
- Textiles
- Building Systems
- Space Planning
- CAD

INTERNSHIPS
Required of majors at all levels.

STUDY ABROAD
Not available

NOTABLE ALUMNI
Not reported

STUDENT ACTIVITIES AND ORGANIZATIONS
National Kitchen and Bath Association and American Society of Interior Designers

FACULTY SPECIALIZATIONS AND RESEARCH
Commercial, residential, kitchen, bath and CAD

COMMUNITY COLLEGE TRANSFERS
Not reported

Central Michigan University

Department of Human Environmental Studies

Wightman Hall 205, Mt. Pleasant, MI 48859 | 989-774-3218 | www.ehs.cmich.edu/hev

UNIVERSITY PROFILE
Public
Suburban
Residential
Semester Schedule
Co-ed

STUDENT DEMOGRAPHICS
Undergraduate: 20,450
Graduate: 1,900

Male: 45%
Female: 55%

Full-time: 90%
Part-time: 10%

EXPENSES
Tuition: $10,170 (in-state)
$23,670 (out-of-state)
Room & Board: $8,092

ADMISSIONS
Admissions Office,
Warriner Hall
Mount Pleasant, MI 48859
989-774-3076
cmuadmit@cmich.edu

DEGREE INFORMATION

Major / Degree / Concentration	Enrollment	Requirements for entry	Graduation rate
Interior Design Bachelor of Applied Arts	85	Completion of 12 credits of Art and/or portfolio review	90%
Interior Design Bachelor of Arts	Not reported	Completion of 12 credits of Art and/or portfolio review	Not reported
Interior Design Bachelor of Science	Not reported	Completion of 12 credits of Art and/or portfolio review	Not reported

TOTAL PROGRAM ENROLLMENT
Undergraduate: 100
Graduate: Not reported

Male: Not reported
Female: Not reported

Full-time: Not reported
Part-time: Not reported

International: 3%
Minority: 8%

Job Placement Rate: Approximately
70%, although it was close to 100% prior
to the recession. The percentage is
currently higher for graduates willing to
leave the state.

SCHOLARSHIPS / FINANCIAL AID
See opposite page for more info.

TOTAL FACULTY: 6
Full-time: 66%
Part-time: 33%
Online: 1

NCIDQ Certified: 50%
Licensed Interior Designers: N/A
LEED Certified: 1

INTERIOR DESIGN ADMINISTRATION
Dr. Megan Goodwin, PhD Department
Chairperson

PROFESSIONAL / ACADEMIC AFFILIATIONS
American Society of Interior Designers
International Interior Design Association
Interior Design Education Council
Environmental Design Research
    Association

CIDA ACCREDITATION
Bachelor of Applied Arts (2008, 2014)

PROGRAM DESCRIPTION AND PHILOSOPHY

The Interior Design program at Central Michigan University involves the detailed design of interiors drawing on diverse knowledge from various disciplines emphasizing an integrated approach that relates Interior Design to society and architecture. Students in the program are prepared to excel in a wide range of careers including commercial and residential design as well as other related areas. The program is nationally accredited by the Council for Interior Design Accreditation (CIDA) and the National Association of Schools of Art and Design (NASAD).

FACILITIES

Our students have access to two drafting laboratories/classrooms, a materials/resource space, and a CAD lab. The library on campus has won numerous awards and provides students with study rooms and spaces. The seniors hold an annual exhibition, which will be held in the new LEED certified College of Education and Human Services next year. We maintain close contact with alumni who assist the program by providing internships, job shadow experiences, serve as jurors, etc.

ONLINE / DISTANCE LEARNING

We offer an online course on green building principles.

COURSES OF INSTRUCTION

- Drafting
- Visual Communications
- Introduction to Interior Design
- Beginning and Advanced CAD, Residential
- Contract
- Design for Special Groups
- Textiles
- Materials and Components of Interior Design
- Design History and Precedent
- Design History and Criticism
- Human Shelter and Environment
- Internship
- Construction Documents
- Lighting and Mechanical Systems
- Professional Business Practices
- Seminar in Interior Design
- Thesis

INTERNSHIPS

Required of majors at Senior level. We place interns in diverse areas of the industry around the country such as Kitchen and Bath, Residential, Interiors Division of an Architectural firm, Commercial design dealership, Corporate Design such as Steelcase, Herman Miller, or Haworth.

STUDY ABROAD

Available

NOTABLE ALUMNI

We have the most awesome students who are all notable for very diverse reasons.

STUDENT ACTIVITIES AND ORGANIZATIONS

American Society of Interior Design (ASID) student chapter. Many students are co-members of the Home Builders Association student chapter or other organizations related to their minors such as Leadership, Business, etc.

FACULTY SPECIALIZATIONS AND RESEARCH

- Media and Technology
- Lighting for Older Adults
- Supportive Environments for Older Adults in Assisted Living Facilities
- Sustainability

SCHOLARSHIPS / FINANCIAL AID

Helen Lohr Scholarship:
This $1,000 scholarship is based upon merit and is to go to a student for use in the Junior or Senior year. The applicant must be a major or minor in the Department of Human Environmental Studies.

Charlotte Trout Scholarship
This $500 scholarship is awarded to a Junior or Senior majoring in Human Environmental Studies. Preference is given to a student who gives promise of becoming outstanding in the field and who is dedicated to the preservation of the family. The student must demonstrate excellent performance in scholastic achievement.

Tracey Marie Rondy Memorial Endowment Award:
This scholarship was established by Tracey Rondy's family and friends in her memory. It will be awarded to an outstanding CMU student who has demonstrated leadership, service, academic achievement and commitment to his or her chosen field. The recipient will also exemplify dedication and a positive attitude. The student must be a resident from the Mt. Pleasant area and enrolled as a full-time CMU student, with an overall G.P.A. of 3.0 or better. Priority will be given to students majoring in Interior Design and/or have worked on the Mt. Pleasant vocational education house during high school.

Receiving Scholarships or Financial Aid: 87% of full-time, first-time, degree-seeking undergrads (new Freshman) receive aid—this includes Work Study, loans to students, grants or scholarship aid. 54% of all undergrads receive grant or scholarship aid—this percentage does not include Work Study or loans to students.

Eastern Michigan University

Interior Design Program, College of Technology

206 Roosevelt Hall, Ypsilanti, MI 48187 | 734-262-5712 | www.emich.edu/cot/undergrad_intdes.htm

UNIVERSITY PROFILE
Public
Urban
Commuter
Semester Schedule
Co-ed

STUDENT DEMOGRAPHICS
Undergraduate: Not reported
Graduate: Not reported

Male: Not reported
Female: Not reported

Full-time: Not reported
Part-time: Not reported

EXPENSES
Tuition: Not reported
Room & Board: Not reported

ADMISSIONS
Office of Undergraduate
Admissions
P.O. Box 921
Ypsilanti, MI 48197
undergraduate.admissions@
emich.edu
transfer.admissions@emich
.edu

DEGREE INFORMATION

Major / Degree / Concentration	Enrollment	Requirements for entry	Graduation rate
Interior Design Bachelor of Science	130	C or better grades in all the Interior Design courses	90%

TOTAL PROGRAM ENROLLMENT
Undergraduate: 130
Graduate: 25

Male: 8%
Female: 92%

Full-time: 93%
Part-time: 7%

International: 25%
Minority: 25%

Job Placement Rate: Many different architecture and Interior Design firms.

SCHOLARSHIPS / FINANCIAL AID
There are 7 students that receive scholarship from the college every year. There are 4 specific scholarships designated to the Interior Design students.

TOTAL FACULTY: 17
Full-time: 4
Part-time: 13
Online: 0

NCIDQ Certified: 2
Licensed Interior Designers: Not reported
LEED Certified: 1

INTERIOR DESIGN ADMINISTRATION
Bob Lahidji, School Head
Jiang Lu, Program Coordinator

PROFESSIONAL / ACADEMIC AFFILIATIONS
American Society of Interior Designers
International Interior Design Association
Interior Design Educators Council

CIDA ACCREDITATION
Bachelor of Science in Interior Design (2008, 2014)

PROGRAM DESCRIPTION AND PHILOSOPHY

Academic preparation of students will enable them to creatively solve problems related to the function and quality of interior environments that meet human needs and fulfill human aspirations. Central to this mission is evidence-based design that integrates theory, knowledge, and technical skills with a holistic view of people, their environments, and global factors; a sensitivity to environmentally responsible design issues; consideration of the needs of all users regardless of age, physical stature, or current capability/disability status.

FACILITIES

Computer labs, fieldtrips to Steelcase, Herman Miller, art museums, and NeoCon

ONLINE / DISTANCE LEARNING

Not available

COURSES OF INSTRUCTION

Revit, 3DMax

INTERNSHIPS

Required of majors at the Junior level. Interns are typically placed at companies such as Hobbs + Black Architecture + Interior Design; Newmann Smith Architecture + Interior Design; The VA hospital in Ann Arbor; The University of Michigan Interior Design department, hall residential department, and hospital department; facility planning and design of EMU, etc.

STUDY ABROAD

Not available

NOTABLE ALUMNI

Not reported

STUDENT ACTIVITIES AND ORGANIZATIONS

Not reported

FACULTY SPECIALIZATIONS AND RESEARCH

Architectural and Interior Design environment and culture study, sustainable design, facility management, material and design, SOLT study.

International Academy of Design & Technology–Detroit

Department of Interior Design

1850 Research Dr., Troy, MI 48083 | 248-457-2721 | www.iadtdetroit.com/

UNIVERSITY PROFILE

Private
Suburban
Commuter
Quarter Schedule
Co-ed

STUDENT DEMOGRAPHICS

Undergraduate: 879
Graduate: 0

Male: Not reported
Female: Not reported

Full-time: Not reported
Part-time: Not reported

EXPENSES

Tuition: Not reported
Room & Board: Not reported

ADMISSIONS

1850 Research Dr.
Troy, MI 48083
248-457-2700
bmarini@iadtdetroit.com

DEGREE INFORMATION

Major / Degree / Concentration	Enrollment	Requirements for entry	Graduation rate
Interior Design Bachelor of Fine Arts	76	High school diploma or GED, personal interview campus tour, and adequate scores on the school's entrance exam are required.	Not reported

TOTAL PROGRAM ENROLLMENT

Undergraduate: 879
Graduate: 0

Male: Not reported
Female: Not reported

Full-time: Not reported
Part-time: Not reported

International: Not reported
Minority: Not reported

Job Placement Rate: Not reported

SCHOLARSHIPS / FINANCIAL AID

Financial Aid is available for those who qualify. A complete listing of scholarship opportunities and financial aid options is available in the campus Catalog.

TOTAL FACULTY: 10–12

Full-time: 2
Part-time: 10
Online: 0

NCIDQ Certified: 50%
Licensed Interior Designers: n/a
LEED Certified: 10%

INTERIOR DESIGN ADMINISTRATION

Cynthia Bechill, President
Dr. Julia Smetanka, Director of
Education
Barbara S. Marini FASID/IDEC Interior
Design Program Chair

PROFESSIONAL / ACADEMIC AFFILIATIONS

American Society of Interior Designers
International Interior Design Association
Interior Design Educators Council

CIDA ACCREDITATION

Bachelor of Fine Arts in Interior Design
(2009, 2015)

PROGRAM DESCRIPTION AND PHILOSOPHY

The Interior Design program prepares students to develop creative and technical solutions for interior spaces that meet aesthetic and functional requirements while addressing safety, regulatory, and environmental concerns. Students will apply the fundamentals of art and design, theories of design, "green design," and an understanding of human behavior to their design solutions. Critical thinking, research, analysis, documentation, and drawing and presentation skills are incorporated in the design process. Students have an opportunity to explore creativity through the selection of colors, materials and finishes, textiles, lighting solutions, furnishings, and other interior elements to solve design problems. Skills in time management, budgeting, project management, business practices, and resource allocation will contribute to student readiness for employment in positions such as:

- Space planner;
- Materials and resource librarian;
- Design assistant;
- Showroom consultant;
- Design sales representative;
- Facilities planner;
- Interior Design consultant;
- Computer-aided designer; and
- Exhibit and visual merchandiser.

This program of study assists students in the first phase of preparation toward becoming a qualified Interior Design professional. Education, experience, and examination are needed to become a certified or licensed Interior Designer in some states. The Interior Design program prepares students for entry-level positions in the profession (subject to state licensing).

FACILITIES

All of the computer labs are equipped with state of the art software, including Revit, AutoCAD, and Studio Max. Locally we are in close proximity to museums such as the Detroit Institute of Arts as well as the Michigan Design Center. Students take advantage of such cultural jewels as the Cranbrook Academy and The Henry Ford Museums.

ONLINE / DISTANCE LEARNING

Some of the General Education courses are offered on line; at this point Interior Design courses are not on-line.

COURSES OF INSTRUCTION

- Drafting
- Perspective and Rendering
- Textiles
- Materials and Resources
- Lighting
- AutoCAD
- Digital Media for Interior Design
- Revit
- Sustainable Design
- Studio courses

INTERNSHIPS

Required of majors at Senior Level. Interns are typically placed at companies such as Michigan Design Center, Macy's, IPG, JGA, Hamilton Anderson, NBS, Interior Environments.

STUDY ABROAD

Students are eligible to travel abroad through American Intercontinental University with programs in London and Italy for Interior Design students.

NOTABLE ALUMNI

Not reported

STUDENT ACTIVITIES AND ORGANIZATIONS

Student Chapter of ASID (American Society of Interior Designers) and IIDA (International Interior Design Association) provide students with opportunities to be involved in such design community activities as Student Career Day, Interim House, and Finish 2 Fashion.

FACULTY SPECIALIZATIONS AND RESEARCH

Most of the faculty specialize in Interior Design as practitioners, in both residential and commercial Interior Design. Several faculty are registered architects and practice in those areas as well.

COMMUNITY COLLEGE TRANSFERS

Most community college courses tranfer into our program as well as university courses in both General Education and Interior Design. We offer portfolio review opportunities in addition to considering professional work experience and proficiency testing for some courses.

Lawrence Technological University

College of Architecture & Design

21000 W. Ten Mile Rd., Southfield, MI 48075 | 248-204-2805 | http://ltu.edu/architecture_and_design/

UNIVERSITY PROFILE
Private
Suburban
Commuter
Semester Schedule
Co-ed

STUDENT DEMOGRAPHICS
Undergraduate: 4,500
Graduate: Not reported

Male: Not reported
Female: Not reported

Full-time: Not reported
Part-time: Not reported

EXPENSES
Tuition: $25,450-$29,140
Room & Board: $5,210-9,610

ADMISSIONS
21000 W. Ten Mile Rd.
Southfield, MI 48075
248-204-3160
admissions@ltu.edu

DEGREE INFORMATION

Major / Degree / Concentration	Enrollment	Requirements for entry	Graduation rate
Interior Architecture Bachelor of Science	60	2.5 gpa	Not reported

TOTAL PROGRAM ENROLLMENT
Undergraduate: 80
Graduate: 20

Male: 12%
Female: 88%

Full-time: Not reported
Part-time: Not reported

International: Not reported
Minority: Not reported

Job Placement Rate: 93%

SCHOLARSHIPS / FINANCIAL AID
Buell Honor Scholarships
Lawrence Tech Scholarships
University Honor Scholarships
Trustee Scholarships (first-time
    students)
Trustee Transfer Scholarships (full-time
    transfer students)
Trustee Transfer Scholarships (part-time
    transfer students)

A number of partial scholarship awards
are available each year to on-campus
students who have a minimum of two
full-time semesters and have attained a
qualifying gpa.

TOTAL FACULTY: 15
Full-time: 20%
Part-time: 75%
Online: 5%

NCIDQ Certified: 40%
Licensed Interior Designers: 0 - No
licensing req. in Michigan
LEED Certified: 30%

INTERIOR DESIGN ADMINISTRATION
Glen LeRoy, Dean
Ralph Nelson, Assistant Dean and
Director of Graduate programs
Dan Faoro, Chair of Architecture
Department

**PROFESSIONAL / ACADEMIC
AFFILIATIONS**
American Society of Interior Designers
International Interior Design Association
Interior Design Educators Council

CIDA ACCREDITATION
Bachelor of Interior Architecture (2008,
2014)

PROGRAM DESCRIPTION AND PHILOSOPHY

The Bachelor of Interior Architecture at Lawrence Tech is strongly integrated with the undergraduate program in architecture. You will comprehensively respond to human needs embodied in interior spaces through the exploration and appreciation of technical, social, psychological, cultural, and environmental factors. The program incorporates architectural education, giving you the strong interdisciplinary foundation required in professional practice.

Lawrence Tech's Bachelor of Interior Architecture program is known for:

- A comprehensive design curriculum, allowing you to integrate design history and theory, color theory, lighting, furniture design and construction, and materials to help you develop your unique approach to interior architecture.
- A studio-based program, giving you the ability to comprehensively pull your course work together and build a strong portfolio with which to enter the profession.
- A strong technical emphasis, providing you the advanced tools used in the profession.

The only undergraduate interior architecture program in Michigan, the Lawrence Tech degree program is accredited by the Council for Interior Design Accreditation and the National Association for Schools of Art and Design. The program has been named one of the "Top 20" Interior Design programs in the United States by Design Intelligence.

FACILITIES

The Academic Achievement Center (AAC) provides free academic support services to all students. Students come to the AAC to get help with homework or test preparation, compare notes, meet with study groups, or study quietly. Tutoring is provided in person and online for core classes in architecture and design, biology, chemistry, computer science, engineering, ESL, mathematics, physics, and writing. Students can walk in any day and see if a tutor is available; they can also guarantee time with a tutor by scheduling an appointment online.

Testing Services (proctored testing) are offered for students who are unable to complete quizzes or exams during regularly scheduled class time. When not in use for testing, private rooms are open for general student use.

Study skills workshops, individual study habit consultations, and study strategy handouts are available. Students also can access first-year academic support programs and Writing Proficiency exam and prep workshops. The AAC also offers computer workstations, a photocopier, other electronic resources, and conference rooms that can be reserved.

ONLINE / DISTANCE LEARNING

Some courses are available online.

COURSES OF INSTRUCTION

- Art/Architecture Awareness
- World Masterpieces 1 & 2
- History of the Designed Env. 1 & 2
- Integrated Design Studio 1 & 2
- Structures 1
- Building Systems 1 & 2
- Furniture and Millwork
- Interior Architecture Studio 1, 2, & 3
- Environmental Systems 1
- Graphic Design 1
- Interior Materials, Textiles, & Components
- Allied Design: Interior Architecture
- Interior Design Practice
- History of Interiors and Furniture
- Advanced Lighting
- Preservation Technology
- Internship Studies
- Environmental Psychology

INTERNSHIPS

Required of Junior and Senior Interior Architecture majors

STUDY ABROAD

The Summer Abroad Program is intended to provide the opportunity to explore the architectural and urban fabric and literature of the internationally renowned city, and to expose students to the rich history and culture of the Paris environment. Students will explore Paris and late-twentieth-century architecture through an international architectural design studio and seminar. A Paris-based design project will be initiated in the studio and the seminar will seek to give an understanding of the history of architecture and planning, particularly the insertion of the Late 20th Century, contemporary architecture into the historical fabric. Design process explorations, on site studies, guides walking tours, lectures and discussions are part of the Study Abroad Program.

This is a life learning experience that cannot be duplicated through the normal class process on campus. Part of the total study abroad experience is diverse European travel possibilities during the month-long stay in Paris.

The Paris Program experience can be used to fufill the Allied Studio for Architecture students, the Junior/Senior Literature Elective for all majors, and there is also an Art History elective open to all majors and graduate students.

NOTABLE ALUMNI

Not reported

STUDENT ACTIVITIES AND ORGANIZATIONS

IASO (Interior Architecture Student Organization), IIDA (International Interior Design Association), ASID (American Society of Interior Designers)

FACULTY SPECIALIZATIONS AND RESEARCH

Not reported

The Art Institutes International Minnesota

Interior Design Department

15 South 9th St., Minneapolis, MN 55402 | 612-332-3361 | www.artinstitutes.edu/minneapolis

UNIVERSITY PROFILE
Private
Urban
Commuter
Quarter Schedule
Co-ed

STUDENT DEMOGRAPHICS
Undergraduate: 2,008
Graduate: n/a

Male: 40%
Female: 60%

Full-time: 55%
Part-time: 45%

EXPENSES
Tuition: $22,416
Room & Board: $6480 per year

ADMISSIONS
15 South 9th St.
Minneapolis,MN 55402
612-332-3361
aimadm@aii.edu

DEGREE INFORMATION

Major / Degree / Concentration	Enrollment	Requirements for entry	Graduation rate
Interior Design Associate of Applied Science	Not reported	Not reported	Not reported
Interior Design Bachelor of Science	Not reported	Not reported	Not reported

TOTAL PROGRAM ENROLLMENT
Undergraduate: 287
Graduate: n/a

Male: 4%
Female: 96%

Full-time: 75%
Part-time: 25%

International: 0%
Minority: Not reported

Job Placement Rate: 80-85%

SCHOLARSHIPS / FINANCIAL AID
The Art Institues Internal Minnesota Merit and Need Scholarship

Student Success Scholarship

EDMC Education Foundation Scholarship

Students Receiving Scholarships or Financial Aid: 94%

TOTAL FACULTY: 15
Full-time: 7
Part-time: 8
Online: 0

NCIDQ Certified: 4
Licensed Interior Designers: Not reported
LEED Certified: 3

INTERIOR DESIGN ADMINISTRATION
Gina Carlson, Academic Director for the Interior Design programs

PROFESSIONAL / ACADEMIC AFFILIATIONS
American Society of Interior Designers
International Interior Design Association

PROGRAM DESCRIPTION AND PHILOSOPHY

The mission of the Interior Design program is to provide students with relevant skills preparing them for their profession of choice. Students will be able to conceive and execute viable and creative design solutions for diverse clients.

FACILITIES

Several computer labs, library, Academic Achievement Center which offers tutoring, Career Services Department

ONLINE / DISTANCE LEARNING

Some of the program's courses and general education courses are available online, but the majority of this program is in a traditional classroom setting.

COURSES OF INSTRUCTION

- Textiles & Fabrics
- History of Architecture
- History of Design to 1830
- Civilization & the Arts
- History of Design from 1830 to Present
- 19th & 20th Century Architecture
- Architectural Drafting
- Perspectives
- Mixed Media
- Building Materials and Mechanical Systems
- Computer Aided Drafting
- Revit Applications
- Lighting
- Interior Tectonics & Codes
- Interior Detailing
- Advanced Detailing
- 3D Design
- Introduction to Space Planning
- Design Process
- Specialty Design
- Elements of Interior Design
- Design Development: Residential
- Problems in Residential Design
- Advanced Residential Design
- Design Development: Commercial
- Advanced Corporate Design
- Advanced Specialty Design
- Professional Practice
- Senior Design Project
- Career Development
- Internship

INTERNSHIPS

Required of majors at third year

STUDY ABROAD

Available

NOTABLE ALUMNI

Holly Bayer of HautHaus, Inc.

STUDENT ACTIVITIES AND ORGANIZATIONS

American Sociate of Interior Designers, Cinnamon Toast (The focus of this club is strengthening student's rendering, presentation, board layout and technical skills.)

FACULTY SPECIALIZATIONS AND RESEARCH

Not reported

University of Minnesota

Department of Design, Housing, and Apparel; College of Design

1985 Buford Ave., Saint Paul, MN 55108 | 612-624-9700 | http://dha.design.umn.edu

UNIVERSITY PROFILE
Public
Urban
Commuter
Semester Schedule
Co-ed

STUDENT DEMOGRAPHICS
Undergraduate: 29,978
Graduate: 21,738

Male: 47%
Female: 53%

Full-time: 82%
Part-time: 28%

EXPENSES
Tuition: $11,542 (in state undergrad)
Room & Board: $7,280

ADMISSIONS
231 Pillsbury Dr. S.E.
Minneapolis, MN 55455
612-625-2008

DEGREE INFORMATION

Major / Degree / Concentration	Enrollment	Requirements for entry	Graduation rate
Interior Design **Bachelor of Science**	152	Portfolio review at end of first year as a pre-Interior Design student; overall gpa of at least 2.5; Minimum of C- in five required courses	78%
Design **Master of Arts, Science, PhD** **Interior Design Track**	8	A first professional degree in Interior Design; overall academic record; GRE scores; goal statement; letters of reference; TOEFL scores if applicable; portfolio; writing sample	Not reported

TOTAL PROGRAM ENROLLMENT
Undergraduate: 152
Graduate: 8

Male: 4%
Female: 96%

Full-time: 82%
Part-time: 28%

International: 4%
Minority: 8%

Job Placement Rate: 71%

SCHOLARSHIPS / FINANCIAL AID
Incoming Freshman scholarships based on need and merit; continuing student scholarships based on merit.

TOTAL FACULTY: 10
Full-time: 4
Part-time: 6
Online: 0

NCIDQ Certified: 5
Licensed Interior Designers: 7
LEED Certified: 3

INTERIOR DESIGN ADMINISTRATION
Becky Yust, Department Head
Denise Guerin, Interior Design Program Director
Stephanie Zollinger, Director of Graduate Studies

PROFESSIONAL / ACADEMIC AFFILIATIONS
American Society of Interior Designers
International Interior Design Association
Interior Design Educators Council
Interior Design Associations Foundation
Environmental Design Research Association

CIDA ACCREDITATION
Bachelor of Science (2006, 2012)

PROGRAM DESCRIPTION AND PHILOSOPHY

The Interior Design undergraduate Program integrates teaching, research, and outreach efforts to improve human well being through the design of interior environments. The designed environment influences people's behavior and well being. Guided by society's informal and formal regulations, such as cultural norms, laws, and policies, it can support or hinder people's physical, social, or psychological needs. Interior Designers who understand this relationship can create environments that support and improve people's quality of life in the settings in which they lead their lives. By identifying and creatively solving problems related to the interior environment, we contribute to the life, health, safety, and welfare of diverse individuals, groups, or communities. Through its goals to produce graduates who design holistically, think critically, and act responsibly, the program prepares students for excellence in professional practice and professional leadership. The program has been CIDA-accredited since 1972.

FACILITIES

PC and Mac computer labs with unique software related to Interior Design; wood & metal workshop; architecture library; Goldstein Museum of Design

ONLINE / DISTANCE LEARNING

Not available

COURSES OF INSTRUCTION

- Eight sequential Interior Design studio courses
- CAD
- Drawing & Design
- Color & Design
- Textile Analysis
- Interior Materials & Specifications
- Lighting Design & Life Safety Issues
- Interior Design Ethics & Professional Practice
- Intro to Business or Management
- History of Interiors & Furnishings
- Interior Design Research & Thesis for Graduate Degrees: Quantitative and/or Qualitative & Mixed Research Methods
- Evidence-Based Design; Design Theory and Criticism
- Teaching and Assessment
- Innovation Theory and Analysis
- Research Ethics

INTERNSHIPS

Required of majors in upper division (jr/sr). Interns are typically placed at various Interior Design firms and architectural firms in the Minneapolis-Saint Paul area.

STUDY ABROAD

Students are encouraged to study abroad for a semester and faculty have identified appropriate international programs related to the major; faculty also lead short-term study abroad trips.

NOTABLE ALUMNI

Not reported

STUDENT ACTIVITIES AND ORGANIZATIONS

Student chapter of A.S.I.D.; mentor program

FACULTY SPECIALIZATIONS AND RESEARCH

- Occupant issues in the designed environment
- Culture and design
- Development of the Interior Design profession
- Design pedagogy
- Cultural aspects of space
- Identity construction
- Non-western traditions
- Evidence-based design
- Interior Design profession's body of knowledge
- Legislation and regulation of design practitioners
- Interior Design
- Regional and vernacular interior architecture
- Interior Design student learning styles

Maryville University

College of Arts and Sciences

650 Maryville University Dr., St. Louis, MO 63141 | 314-529-9300 | www.maryville.edu/

DEGREE INFORMATION

Major / Degree / Concentration	Enrollment	Requirements for entry	Graduation rate
Interior Design Bachelor of Fine Arts	99	Entrance portfolio and portfolio review at the end of each semester	95%

TOTAL PROGRAM ENROLLMENT
Undergraduate: 96
Graduate: n/a

Male: 4%
Female: 96%

Full-time: 86%
Part-time: 14%

International: 1%
Minority: 19%

Job Placement Rate: 96%

SCHOLARSHIPS / FINANCIAL AID
The Art & Design Scholarship Program provides recognition and financial support for undergraduate students with outstanding artistic talent who enter Maryville University directly from high school or as a transfer student. Scholarship amounts range from $500 - $5000. Students must submit a portfolio for review.

TOTAL FACULTY: 26
Full-time: 39%
Part-time: 61%
Online: n/a

NCIDQ Certified: 20%
Licensed Interior Designers: 93%
LEED Certified: 1%

INTERIOR DESIGN ADMINISTRATION
Darlene Davison, Interior Design Program Director

PROFESSIONAL / ACADEMIC AFFILIATIONS
American Society of Interior Designers
International Interior Design Association

CIDA ACCREDITATION
Bachelor of Fine Arts in Interior Design (2010, 2016)

PROGRAM DESCRIPTION AND PHILOSOPHY

Our program strives to develop 'practice ready' students who combine creativity and critical thinking skills through a rigourous curriculum structured to facilitate development of a diverse, creative and competitive portfolio. We prepare students to enter the Interior Design profession and become contributing members of a global market with a spirit of service and commitment to sustainable design prctices.

FACILITIES

Each studio is equipped with a 15 student workspaces which include a computer and drafting table. Each computer has Microsoftro sofffice and Windows XP, Adobe Creative Suite 4 Design Premium, Sketch Up, Podium Artlantis Studio 2, Kerkythea 2008, 3DS Max Design 2010. Each studio has screen w/ ceiling mounted digital projector, HP Laser Jet 5100, HP Color Laser Jet, Cannon Imageprograf IPF 700.

ONLINE / DISTANCE LEARNING

Not available

COURSES OF INSTRUCTION

- Interior Design Foundations
- Interior Design Studio I-IV
- Architectural Graphics & Technology I-IV
- Lighting
- Interior Detailing
- Interior Materials
- Hisitory of Interior Design I & II
- Modern Art & Architecture

Electives:
- Revit
- Advanced CAD
- Rendering
- Issues in Sustainable Design
- Universal Design

INTERNSHIPS

Required of majors at Junior level. Interns are typically placed at companies such as HOK, Arcturis, Lawrence Group, Hastings and Chivetta, NewGround, ColliersTurely and others.

STUDY ABROAD

Available

NOTABLE ALUMNI

Not reported

STUDENT ACTIVITIES AND ORGANIZATIONS

American Society of Interior Designers, International Interior Design Association

FACULTY SPECIALIZATIONS AND RESEARCH

- Design
- Space Planning
- Sustainable Design
- Universal Design
- Detailing

COMMUNITY COLLEGE TRANSFERS

Matriculation agreement w/ Meramec Community College

Missouri State University

Department of Fashion and Interior Design

901 S. National, Springfield, MO 65897 | 417-836-5136 | www.missouristate.edu/fid

UNIVERSITY PROFILE
Public
Urban
Residential
Semester Schedule
Co-ed

STUDENT DEMOGRAPHICS
Undergraduate: 12,908
Graduate: 2,600

Male: Not reported
Female: Not reported

Full-time: Not reported
Part-time: Not reported

EXPENSES
Tuition: Not reported
Room & Board: Not reported

ADMISSIONS
Not reported

DEGREE INFORMATION

Major / Degree / Concentration	Enrollment	Requirements for entry	Graduation rate
Interior Design Bachelor of Science	110	Not reported	75%

TOTAL PROGRAM ENROLLMENT
Undergraduate: 110
Graduate: 0

Male: 5%
Female: 95%

Full-time: Not reported
Part-time: Not reported

International: Not reported
Minority: Not reported

Job Placement Rate: Not reported

SCHOLARSHIPS / FINANCIAL AID
In addition to general scholarships offered through the university, four scholarships are offered exclusively to Interior Design majors by the Springfield Design Association and the Home Builders Association.

TOTAL FACULTY: 6
Full-time: 2
Part-time: 4
Online: Not reported

NCIDQ Certified: 50%
Licensed Interior Designers: Not reported
LEED Certified: 50%

INTERIOR DESIGN ADMINISTRATION
Dr. Paula Kemp, Acting Department Head

PROFESSIONAL / ACADEMIC AFFILIATIONS
American Society of Interior Designers
Interior Design Educators Council

PROGRAM DESCRIPTION AND PHILOSOPHY
Not reported

FACILITIES
Computer lab with current version of AutoCAD, digital plotter, well-stocked sample room for students to use for projects.

ONLINE / DISTANCE LEARNING
Not reported

COURSES OF INSTRUCTION
- AutoCAD
- Specifications
- Residential Design 1 and 2
- Contract Design 1 and 2
- Presentation Techniques
- History of Furniture and Decorative Arts
- Color and Light
- Environmental Living
- Internship

INTERNSHIPS
Required of majors

STUDY ABROAD
At least one trip a year is taken overseas. We have taken students to France, Italy, Greece, and China.

NOTABLE ALUMNI
Not reported

STUDENT ACTIVITIES AND ORGANIZATIONS
ASID-Student Chapter is an active group with monthly meetings, guest speakers, and service projects in the community.

FACULTY SPECIALIZATIONS AND RESEARCH
Not reported

University of Central Missouri

Department of Art and Design

Art Center 120, Warrensburg, MO 64093 | 660-543-4481 | www.ucmo.edu/art/

UNIVERSITY PROFILE
Public
Rural
Residential
Semester Schedule
Co-ed

STUDENT DEMOGRAPHICS
Undergraduate: 9,088
Graduate: 2,103

Male: 43%
Female: 57%

Full-time: 73%
Part-time: 27%

EXPENSES
Tuition: $859
Room & Board: $4,520

ADMISSIONS
Ward Edwards 1400
Warrensburg, MO 64093
1-877-729-8266
admit@ucmo.edu

DEGREE INFORMATION

Major / Degree / Concentration	Enrollment	Requirements for entry	Graduation rate
Interior Design Bachelor of Fine Arts	117	Not reported	75%

TOTAL PROGRAM ENROLLMENT
Undergraduate: 513
Graduate: 0

Male: 22%
Female: 78%

Full-time: 90%
Part-time: 10%

International: 2%
Minority: 12%

Job Placement Rate: Not reported

SCHOLARSHIPS / FINANCIAL AID
Students receive financial aid from Federal and State Loans and several scholarship opportunities at the departmental level. Annual student art scholarship event - Student Citation Art Show

Students Receiving Scholarships or Financial Aid: 84%

TOTAL FACULTY: 22
Full-time: 73%
Part-time: 27%
Online: Not reported

NCIDQ Certified: 1
Licensed Interior Designers: Not reported
LEED Certified: 1

INTERIOR DESIGN ADMINISTRATION
Dr. Mick Luehrman, Department Chair
Dr. Susan Stevenson, Program Director

PROFESSIONAL / ACADEMIC AFFILIATIONS
American Society of Interior Designers
Interior Design Educators Council
Environmental Design Research Association

PROGRAM DESCRIPTION AND PHILOSOPHY

The University Of Central Missouri (UCM), located 30 miles east of the Kansas City Metropolitan area, is a comprehensive university providing a small-college learning environment coupled with large-university opportunities. The Department of Art & Design is a NASAD-accredited department with over 500 majors. The Interior Design BFA at UCM is a dynamic growing program (100+ majors) that is progressive, industry focused, and actively pursuing CIDA accreditation.

FACILITIES

25 MAC Computer Lab, plotters, AutoCAD, Revit, 3D Max, Adobe CS, Sketchup, Model and Mat cutting room, Art Center Gallery

ONLINE / DISTANCE LEARNING

Not available but the following courses are offered as online—Ideas and the Visual Arts, Design with Digital Media

COURSES OF INSTRUCTION

- Introduction to Interior Design
- Residential Interior Design
- Presentation Techniques
- Restaurant and Store Planning
- Corporate and Institutional Design
- Materials for Interiors
- History of Interiors
- Furniture Design and Detailing

INTERNSHIPS

Not required but available for those with Junior standing. Interns are typically placed at companies such as Focus Architecture, WSKF Architecture, Hollis and Miller.

STUDY ABROAD

Paris Art History Tour, Middleburg Center for Transatlantic Studies

NOTABLE ALUMNI

Not reported

STUDENT ACTIVITIES AND ORGANIZATIONS

Student Chapter of ASID, Service Learning Opportunities.

FACULTY SPECIALIZATIONS AND RESEARCH

NCIDQ Certificate Holder, LEED AP, National Kitchen and Bath Association Certified Kitchen and Bath Designer, Research in the area of place attachment, Creative efforts in Fiber Arts

University of Missouri

Department of Architectural Studies, College of Human Environmental Sciences

137 Stanley Hall, Columbia, MO 65211 | 573-882-7224 | http://arch.missouri.edu/

UNIVERSITY PROFILE
Public
Urban
Residential
Semester Schedule
Co-ed

STUDENT DEMOGRAPHICS
Undergraduate: 23,000—total university
Graduate: Not reported

Male: Not reported
Female: Not reported

Full-time: primarily
Part-time: Not reported

EXPENSES
Tuition: see Web site
Room & Board: see Web site

ADMISSIONS
Admissions Office
Jesse Hall
Columbia, MO 65211

DEGREE INFORMATION

Major / Degree / Concentration	Enrollment	Requirements for entry	Graduation rate
Human Environmental Sciences Bachelor of Science Interior Design	170	2.0 gpa	95%
Human Environmental Sciences Bachelor of Science Architectural Studies	70	2.0 gpa	95%
Architectural Studies Master of Arts or Science	60	3.0 gpa	75%

TOTAL PROGRAM ENROLLMENT
Undergraduate: 220
Graduate: 50

Male: 40%
Female: 60%

Full-time: 90%
Part-time: 10%

International: 10%
Minority: 6%

Job Placement Rate: 1/3 go to grad school; most of remaining get jobs

SCHOLARSHIPS / FINANCIAL AID
http://arch.missouri.edu/career/scholarships.htm

Students Receiving Scholarships or Financial Aid: 10%

TOTAL FACULTY: NOT REPORTED
Full-time: 7
Part-time: Not reported
Online: Not reported

NCIDQ Certified: 40%
Licensed Interior Designers: 40%
LEED Certified: 25%

INTERIOR DESIGN ADMINISTRATION
Not reported

PROFESSIONAL / ACADEMIC AFFILIATIONS
International Interior Design Association
Interior Design Educators Council
Environmental Design Research Association

CIDA ACCREDITATION
BS HES Architectural Studies (2006, 2012)

PROGRAM DESCRIPTION AND PHILOSOPHY
See http://arch.missouri.edu/

FACILITIES
Computer labs, technology, museum, resources of a major university

ONLINE / DISTANCE LEARNING
Available for MA, MS, PhD

COURSES OF INSTRUCTION
See http://arch.missouri.edu/

INTERNSHIPS
Not required. Interns are placed mostly at architectural firms.

STUDY ABROAD
Available

NOTABLE ALUMNI
Beth Harmon Vaughn, John Fulton, Tracy Stearns, Wendy Gray, Jane Ganz

STUDENT ACTIVITIES AND ORGANIZATIONS
Student chapters of ASID, IIDA, CSI, AIAS, and many campus organizations

FACULTY SPECIALIZATIONS AND RESEARCH
Environment and behavior; design with digital media

Mississippi State University

College of Architecture, Art & Design: Interior Design Program

449 Hardy Rd., Mississippi State, MS 39762 | 662-325-0530 | http://caad.msstate.edu

UNIVERSITY PROFILE
Public
Rural
Residential
Semester Schedule
Co-ed

STUDENT DEMOGRAPHICS
Undergraduate: 14,602
Graduate: 3,999

Male: 51%
Female: 49%

Full-time: Not reported
Part-time: Not reported

EXPENSES
Tuition: $5,150
Room & Board: $6,690

ADMISSIONS
P.O. Box 622
Mississippi State, MS 39762
1-662-325-2224
admit@msstate.edu

DEGREE INFORMATION

Major / Degree / Concentration	Enrollment	Requirements for entry	Graduation rate
Interior Design Bachelor of Science	109	2.5 gpa Portfolio review after 2nd year	80%

TOTAL PROGRAM ENROLLMENT
Undergraduate: 109
Graduate: 0

Male: 4%
Female: 96%

Full-time: 98%
Part-time: 2%

International: 0%
Minority: 11%

Job Placement Rate: 85%

SCHOLARSHIPS / FINANCIAL AID
Other than typical university financial aid, the department awards between 4 and 6 scholarships a year for our 3rd- and 4th-year students. A scholarship for 2nd-year students is being currently investigated.

TOTAL FACULTY: 5
Full-time: 100%
Part-time: 0%
Online: 0%

NCIDQ Certified: 2
Licensed Interior Designers: 2
LEED Certified: 1

INTERIOR DESIGN ADMINISTRATION
Beth Miler, Director Interior Design
Jim West, Dean of the College of Architecture, Art and Design

PROFESSIONAL / ACADEMIC AFFILIATIONS
American Society of Interior Designers
Interior Design Educators Council

CIDA ACCREDITATION
Bachelor of Science in Interior Design (2007, 2013)

PROGRAM DESCRIPTION AND PHILOSOPHY

The Interior Design faculty have established educational and professional goals for the First Professional Degree Level Program. These goals are reviewed and adjustments are made as universal, national, local advancements, and changes of technology occur which may impact the goals. The overall program goals are to:

- Prepare students who can identify, research, and creatively solve problems pertaining to the function and quality of the interior environment.
- Prepare students to perform services relative to interior spaces including programming; design analysis; space planning; aesthetics and inspection of work on site; using specialized knowledge of interior construction, building systems and components; building regulations; equipment; and materials and furnishings.
- Prepare students to produce drawings and documents relative to the design of interior spaces.
- Enhance the quality of life for individuals and families.
- Protect the health, safety, and welfare of the public.

FACILITIES

1st and 2nd year students share studio space. 3rd and 4th year students have a designated space in the building. Interior Design students in our program must have their own laptop by the second semester of their first year. The building has wireless connection available for all students.

We have plotter and printer capabilites in our building for the students to use as well as other technology such as large flat-bed scanners in the another building. MSU has numerous computer labs across campus and all of their computers have software for our students to use in their courses. We have archival space on the network within the department for students to store images of their projects. Students have access to a large campus library as well as a college library that is specific to architecture, art, interiors, and construction.

ONLINE / DISTANCE LEARNING
Not available

COURSES OF INSTRUCTION
- Interior Design Graphics
- Studio 1-6
- Furniture Design
- Environments for Special Needs
- Rendering
- CAAD
- 3D CADD Modeling
- Professional Practice
- Materials
- Details & Construction
- Color & Lighting
- History of Interiors 1 & 2
- Portfolio

INTERNSHIPS
Required of majors during the summer of third and fourth years. Interns are placed in many of the top 100 A & D firms in the country as well as firms in the state. Interns are also placed in high-end residential firms, furniture manufacturing firms as product designers, dealerships, hospitals, and others. Interns are employed geographically in areas from Dallas, Texas, to New York.

STUDY ABROAD
London every two years, Italy every year, other study abroad opportunities through the university

NOTABLE ALUMNI
Not reported

STUDENT ACTIVITIES AND ORGANIZATIONS
We have a student chapter of ASID for students and encourage them to attend functions and workshops offered by the other departments in the College: Architecture, Art, and Building Construction Science.

FACULTY SPECIALIZATIONS AND RESEARCH
Faculty research varies with each faculty member but all of the faculty are interested in K-12 curriculum for Interior Design. Other areas are summer camps and design experiences for the underserved students in the state. E-learning and technology as well as online education in the design field are also faculty research areas. Research is ongoing in studying and examining studio experiences with mixed disciplines such as Interior Design students and architecture students.

University of Southern Mississippi

School of Construction

118 College Dr. #5138, Hattiesburg, MS 39406 | 601-266-6358 | http://construction.usm.edu/

UNIVERSITY PROFILE
Public
Urban
Residential
Commuter
Semester Schedule
Co-ed

STUDENT DEMOGRAPHICS
Undergraduate: 11,464
Graduate: 2,878

Male: Not reported
Female: Not reported

Full-time: Not reported
Part-time: Not reported

EXPENSES
Tuition: $5,096 (in-state)
Room & Board: $5,818

ADMISSIONS
118 College Dr
Hattiesburg, MS 39406
601-266-1000
admissions@usm.edu

DEGREE INFORMATION

Major / Degree / Concentration	Enrollment	Requirements for entry	Graduation rate
Interior Design Bachelor of Science	70	2.5 gpa Course pre-requisites Portfolio review after Sophomore year	Not reported

TOTAL PROGRAM ENROLLMENT
Undergraduate: 70
Graduate: 0

Male: 5%
Female: 95%

Full-time: 100%
Part-time: Not reported

International: 0%
Minority: 10%

Job Placement Rate: 84%

SCHOLARSHIPS / FINANCIAL AID
Scholarships are available at the Junior
and Senior Level.

TOTAL FACULTY: 4
Full-time: 50%
Part-time: 50%
Online: Not reported

NCIDQ Certified: 50%
Licensed Interior Designers: Not
reported
LEED Certified: 25%

INTERIOR DESIGN ADMINISTRATION
Dr. Martha Saunders, President
Dr. Robert Lyman, Provost

PROFESSIONAL / ACADEMIC AFFILIATIONS
American Society of Interior Designers
International Interior Design Association
Interior Design Educators Council

CIDA ACCREDITATION
Bachelor of Science (2004, 2010)

PROGRAM DESCRIPTION AND PHILOSOPHY

The mission of the Interior Design program at Southern Miss is to provide an educational experience that prepares graduates for professional careers in the Interior Design field. The program provides a diverse, challenging, and multidisciplinary perspective that encourages creative, professional, and environmentally responsible design solutions for residential, commercial, and institutional facilities. The Interior Design program acknowledges the definition of a professional designer endorsed by the National Council for Interior Design Qualifications (NCIDQ) and other design associations of North America and strives to meet the following goals: 1) To support the University mission "to cultivate intellectual development and creativity through the generation, dissemination, application and preservation of knowledge." 2) To maintain high-quality standards for Interior Design education through professional accreditations. 3) To provide opportunities for students to interact with multiple disciplines in collaborative environments both on and off campus. 4) To promote evidence-based design research in order to solve problems related to the needs of people in all environments. 5) To cultivate effective communication skills, knowledge of design theory, history, sustainability, and codes along with creative, abstract and critical thinking skills. 6) To instill a sense of service, lifelong learning and social obligation.

FACILITIES

24/7 studio, computer lab with oversized scanner, plotters, resource library, lecture rooms, drafting studios and student lounge.

ONLINE / DISTANCE LEARNING

Some courses are taught as hybrid, no ID courses are fully online.

COURSES OF INSTRUCTION

- Building Systems
- Design I and II
- 3D Design
- Visual Communication
- Textiles
- History of Furniture
- Computer Aided Design I and II
- Portfolio Development
- Interior Materials
- Residential Design I and II
- Commercial Design I and II
- Senior Capstone
- Cultural Systems in the Environment

INTERNSHIPS

Required of majors at Junior or Senior levels. Interns are typically placed at Architecture firms in the Southeast, local and regional Interior Design firms, Design/Build firms, Kitchen and Bath firms.

STUDY ABROAD

British Studies Program, undergraduate and graduate level.

NOTABLE ALUMNI

Melissa Birdsong, VP for Trend, Forcasting and Design, Lowes Home Improvement

STUDENT ACTIVITIES AND ORGANIZATIONS

Student Chapter of the American Society of Interior Designers and the National Kitchen and Bath Association. Students participate in the regional ASID Career Day with schools in LA, AR, and MS and consistently win awards in residential, commercial, hospitality, and beginning design categories.

FACULTY SPECIALIZATIONS AND RESEARCH

Aging in Place, Historic Preservation, BIM, and Sustainable Design

Appalachian State University

Department of Technology

397 Rivers St., ASU Box 32122, Boone, NC 28608 | 828-262-3110 | www.tec.appstate.edu

UNIVERSITY PROFILE
Public
Rural
Residential
Semester Schedule
Co-ed

STUDENT DEMOGRAPHICS
Undergraduate: 14,872
Graduate: 2,096

Male: 46.2%
Female: 53.8%

Full-time: 96.7%
Part-time: 3.3%

EXPENSES
Tuition: $4,854
Room & Board: $5,560

ADMISSIONS
287 Rivers St., Suite A
ASU Box 32004
Boone, NC 28608
828-262-2120
admissions@appstate.edu

DEGREE INFORMATION

Major / Degree / Concentration	Enrollment	Requirements for entry	Graduation rate
Interior Design Bachelor of Science	167	University admission; Portfolio review after Freshman year; Minimum grade of C is required for each major course	88%

TOTAL PROGRAM ENROLLMENT
Undergraduate: 167
Graduate: 0

Male: 4%
Female: 96%

Full-time: 98%
Part-time: 2%

International: 2%
Minority: 10%

Job Placement Rate: 100%

SCHOLARSHIPS / FINANCIAL AID
Please see the following Web sites for scholarship opportunities: www.tec.appstate.edu/students/scholarships.htm and www.admissions.appstate.edu/scholarships/view-all
The program also offers the Stephanie V. Blank Diversity Scholarship to a qualifing incoming Freshman student from NC, SC, or GA [please contact Admissions for details].

Students Receiving Scholarships or Financial Aid: 59%

TOTAL FACULTY: 5
Full-time: 80%
Part-time: 20%
Online: 0%

NCIDQ Certified: 80%
Licensed Interior Designers: 20%
LEED Certified: 20%

INTERIOR DESIGN ADMINISTRATION
Jeff Tiller, Chairperson
Jeanne Mercer-Ballard, Interior Design Program Coordinator

PROFESSIONAL / ACADEMIC AFFILIATIONS
American Society of Interior Designers
International Interior Design Association
Interior Design Educators Council

CIDA ACCREDITATION
Bachelor of Science in Interior Design (2009, 2015)

PROGRAM DESCRIPTION AND PHILOSOPHY

The Interior Design curriculum focuses on integrating theory and application through individual and collaborative problem-solving strategies within the context of the design process. The program places particular emphasis on community service, environmental responsibility, global issues, and universal design in order to prepare students for the challenges of the ever-changing profession. Through practical and aesthetically appropriate design solutions, students actively engage in the development of interior spaces from an ethically responsible perspective for the purpose of improving the quality of life, increased productivity, and protecting the health, safety, and welfare of the public. The program is dedicated to creating a supportive learning environment that allows students to develop individual expression of knowledge and skills to create resonance and connection with the practice of Interior Design.

FACILITIES

Studios (accessible 24-7), media, and technology equipment, computer labs, construction labs, wood shop, libraries

ONLINE / DISTANCE LEARNING

Not available

COURSES OF INSTRUCTION

- Visual Literacy I-III
- Studio I-VII
- Systems I and II
- History of Interior Design & Architecture I & II
- Construction Documents and Detailing
- Environmental and Human Behavior
- Field Study
- Internship Workshop
- Professional Practice
- Construction Technology
- Building Mechanical Systems
- Internship

INTERNSHIPS

Required of majors after 3rd year

Placement: architecture and design firms (residential and commercial), corporate and institutional facilities departments; commercial furniture dealerships; product distributor showrooms; manufacturers; commercial photography studios and other related types of firms.

STUDY ABROAD

The University and program have many formal relationships with study abroad opportunities. The program encourages this experience during the Junior year.

NOTABLE ALUMNI

Stephanie Blank, Jill Pable, Ruth Cline

STUDENT ACTIVITIES AND ORGANIZATIONS

ASIDS [Appalachian Student Interior Design Society]

FACULTY SPECIALIZATIONS AND RESEARCH

- Lighting Design
- Environmentally-Sensitive Design
- Economically-Sensitive Design
- Service-Learning
- Community Design
- Kitchen and Bath Design
- Communication
- Sacred Space
- Universal Design

COMMUNITY COLLEGE TRANSFERS

Transfer students with previous design coursework at the college level will be placed in the appropriate level of the program after assessment of their transcript and portfolio.

Carteret Community College

Department of Interior Design

Donald B. Student Center - 3505 Arendell St., Morehead City, NC 28557 | 252-222-6260 | **www.carteret.edu**

UNIVERSITY PROFILE
Public
Rural
Commuter
Semester Schedule
Co-ed

STUDENT DEMOGRAPHICS
Undergraduate: $2,410
Graduate: n/a

Male: Not reported
Female: Not reported

Full-time: Not reported
Part-time: Not reported

EXPENSES
Tuition: $69.25 per semester hour
Room & Board:n/a

ADMISSIONS
Carteret Community College
Attn: Admissions Office
3505 Arendell St.
Morehead City, NC 28557

DEGREE INFORMATION

Major / Degree / Concentration	Enrollment	Requirements for entry	Graduation rate
Interior Design Associate of Applied Science	35	High school diploma or GED	Not reported

TOTAL PROGRAM ENROLLMENT
Undergraduate: 35
Graduate: n/a

Male: 32%
Female: 68%

Full-time: 40%
Part-time: 60%

International: 0%
Minority: 19%

Job Placement Rate: 90%

SCHOLARSHIPS / FINANCIAL AID
Bernice Bienenstock Furniture Library Scholarship, amongst a wide range of other available financial aid offerings

TOTAL FACULTY: NOT REPORTED
Full-time: Not reported
Part-time: Not reported
Online: Not reported

NCIDQ Certified: Not reported
Licensed Interior Designers: Not reported
LEED Certified: Not reported

INTERIOR DESIGN ADMINISTRATION
Dr. Kerry Youngblood, President of Carteret Community College
Dr. Fran Emory, VP of Instruction and Student Support

PROFESSIONAL / ACADEMIC AFFILIATIONS
Not reported

PROGRAM DESCRIPTION AND PHILOSOPHY

The Interior Design curriculum of Carteret Community College, located on beautiful Bogue Sound in North Carolina, prepares students for a variety of job opportunities in the fields of both residential & commercial design. The course of study is diverse, exposing students to the elements and principles of interior design, first through study on a abstract level to assure a thorough understanding, then applying this knowledge base to the field of interior design. Two full-time faculty totally 40 years of teaching experience, plus adjuncts teach classes that are limited to 16, enabling valuable one-on-one instruction.

FACILITIES

Computer Labs, extensive Product Library, Beaufort Historical Grounds, Nearby Historic Tryon Palace in New Bern, NC is the home of the world-renowned International Home Furnishings Center (annual field trip)

ONLINE / DISTANCE LEARNING

Many of the courses are Hybrid (partially on-line). Presently, two of our courses, DES 265 Lighting and DES 255 History of Interiors & Furnishings I are totally on-line.

COURSES OF INSTRUCTION

- Architectural Graphics
- CAD
- Products
- Textiles
- Graphic Presentation I & II
- Store Planning
- Materials & Calculations
- Lighting
- Contract Design
- Residential Design

INTERNSHIPS

Required of majors. Companies where interns are typically placed include Flooring, Architectural Firms, Marine Interiors, AutoCAD, Window Treatment, Cabinetry, Lowes, Sherwin-Williams, Ashley Furniture, and Design Shops.

STUDY ABROAD

Not available

NOTABLE ALUMNI

Not reported

STUDENT ACTIVITIES AND ORGANIZATIONS

Interior Design Club, Interior Design Alumni Network (Facebook presence)

FACULTY SPECIALIZATIONS AND RESEARCH

Not reported

COMMUNITY COLLEGE TRANSFERS

Carteret's AAS degree is a two-year degree preparing students to enter the work field upon completion. Most four-year universities will provide a portfolio review upon request for individuals that hold an interest in transferring.

Central Piedmont Community College

Department of Interior Design

AU 120, Central Campus, Charlotte, NC 28235 | 704-330-6189 | http://arts.cpcc.edu/academics/interior-design

UNIVERSITY PROFILE
Public
Urban
Commuter
Semester Schedule
Co-ed

STUDENT DEMOGRAPHICS
Undergraduate: Not reported
Graduate: Not reported

Male: Not reported
Female: Not reported

Full-time: 80%
Part-time: 20%

EXPENSES
Tuition: $1,600 (in-state);
$4,672 (out-of-state)
Room & Board: n/a

ADMISSIONS
Central Piedmont Community
College
PO Box 35009
Charlotte, NC 28235
704-330-2722

DEGREE INFORMATION

Major / Degree / Concentration	Enrollment	Requirements for entry	Graduation rate
Interior Design Associate of Applied Science	190	High school diploma and placement tests in math and English	64%
Residential Decoration Diploma	8	High school diploma and placements tests in math and English	Not reported

TOTAL PROGRAM ENROLLMENT
Undergraduate: 198
Graduate: n/a
Male: 7%
Female: 93%

Full-time: 30%
Part-time: 70%

International: Not reported
Minority: 37%

Job Placement Rate: 90%

SCHOLARSHIPS / FINANCIAL AID
Not reported

TOTAL FACULTY: 7
Full-time: 50%
Part-time: 50%
Online: 5%

NCIDQ Certified: Not reported
Licensed Interior Designers: Not
 reported
LEED Certified: Not reported

INTERIOR DESIGN ADMINISTRATION
Michell W. Campbell, AIA, Chair

PROFESSIONAL / ACADEMIC AFFILIATIONS
Not reported

PROGRAM DESCRIPTION AND PHILOSOPHY

The Interior Design program at Central Piedmont Community College is designed to prepare students for a variety of job opportunities in the field of both residential and non-residential Interior Design. The focus of the studies is technical knowledge, professional practices, and aesthetic principles.

FACILITIES

Not reported

ONLINE / DISTANCE LEARNING

Not reported

COURSES OF INSTRUCTION

- Graphic Presentation
- Principles & Elements of Design
- Principles of Interior Design
- History/Interior & Furnishings
- Architectural CAD
- Residential Design
- Comm/Contract Design
- Textiles/Fabrics
- Codes & Standards/Int. Design

INTERNSHIPS

Not required

STUDY ABROAD

Not reported

NOTABLE ALUMNI

Not reported

STUDENT ACTIVITIES AND ORGANIZATIONS

Not reported

FACULTY SPECIALIZATIONS AND RESEARCH

Not reported

East Carolina University

Department of Interior Design and Merchandising

249 Rivers Building, ECU, Greenville, NC 27858 | 252-328-6929 | www.ecu.edu/che/idmr/

UNIVERSITY PROFILE
Public
Rural
Residential
Semester Schedule
Co-ed

STUDENT DEMOGRAPHICS
Undergraduate: 29,000
Graduate: 2,500

Male: Not reported
Female: Not reported

Full-time: Not reported
Part-time: Not reported

EXPENSES
Tuition: $4,300
Room & Board: $7,200

ADMISSIONS
Not reported

DEGREE INFORMATION

Major / Degree / Concentration	Enrollment	Requirements for entry	Graduation rate
Interior Design Bachelor of Science	140	2.5 gpa; C or better in five ID courses; Sophomore portfolio review	Not reported

TOTAL PROGRAM ENROLLMENT
Undergraduate: 300
Graduate: 0

Male: 5%
Female: 95%

Full-time: 95%
Part-time: 5%

International: 3%
Minority: 3%

Job Placement Rate: Not reported

SCHOLARSHIPS / FINANCIAL AID
Students Receiving Scholarships or
Financial Aid: 60

TOTAL FACULTY: 11
Full-time: 11
Part-time: 0
Online: 0

NCIDQ Certified: 2
Licensed Interior Designers: 2
LEED Certified: 1

INTERIOR DESIGN ADMINISTRATION
Katherine Swank, Chair Department of
Interior Design and Merchandising

PROFESSIONAL / ACADEMIC AFFILIATIONS
American Society of Interior Designers
International Interior Design Association
Interior Design Educators Council

CIDA ACCREDITATION
Bachelor of Science (2009, 2015)

PROGRAM DESCRIPTION AND PHILOSOPHY

Our shared value of design for human needs provides a common purpose connecting the practice of Interior Design to the consequential issues of society (e.g., environmental degradation, human health and well-being, cultural diversity, social justice, and sustainable community). As such, the program is a catalyst for fostering connections with communities while preparing students for assuming diverse roles in professional practice.

The mission of the ECU Interior Design program is to prepare students to be creative problem-solvers with a strong sense of social responsibility. Our program integrates addressing the human condition in interior environments.

FACILITIES

State of the art computer-aided design labs, sample resource room, manual drafting studios, textiles lab, master classrooms, and exhibition space.

ONLINE / DISTANCE LEARNING

The Interior Design program is offered face-to-face.

COURSES OF INSTRUCTION

- Interior Design Fundamentals
- Color and Light
- Manual Graphics
- Historic Interiors
- Digital Graphics
- Residential Interiors
- Commercial Interiors
- Materials and Specification
- Building Systems
- Professional Procedures
- Universal Design
- Capstone Studio
- Problems in Interiors

INTERNSHIPS

Required of majors rising to Senior level. Interns are typically placed at firms with certified designers affiliated with ASID, IIDA, NKBA, AIA.

STUDY ABROAD

Summer programs are offered alternating European with Asian studies. Interior Design has partnered with Bilkent University, Ankara, Turkey, to offer a student exchange program.

NOTABLE ALUMNI

Not reported

STUDENT ACTIVITIES AND ORGANIZATIONS

Student organizations affiliated with ASID and NKBA. Service learning and community engagement projects including: design of cultural heritage centers for the Native American Woodland Indians of eastern North Carolina; universal design of the barracks of the future for Wounded Warriors Battalion-East, USMC; greening tourist destinations of the North Carolina Outer Banks; and volunteer home modification and repair services for elderly homeowners in partnership with Rebuilding Together Pitt Country, NC, Inc.

FACULTY SPECIALIZATIONS AND RESEARCH

- Environmental interior poetics
- Universal design
- Design for special populations and human health
- Sustainable design
- Teaching and learning
- Teaching through technology
- Interdisciplinary service-learning

High Point University

Department of Interior Design

833 Montlieu Ave., High Point, NC 27262 | 336-841-9376 | http://homefurnishings.highpoint.edu/

UNIVERSITY PROFILE
Private
Urban
Residential
Semester Schedule
Co-ed

STUDENT DEMOGRAPHICS
Undergraduate: 3,300
Graduate: 350

Male: 41%
Female: 59%

Full-time: 99%
Part-time: 2%

EXPENSES
Tuition: Not reported
Room & Board: Not reported

ADMISSIONS
833 Montlieu Ave.
High Point, NC 27262

DEGREE INFORMATION

Major / Degree / Concentration	Enrollment	Requirements for entry	Graduation rate
Interior Design Bachelor of Science	100	Sophomore review	99%

TOTAL PROGRAM ENROLLMENT
Undergraduate: 100
Graduate: n/a

Male: 1%
Female: 99%

Full-time: 99%
Part-time: 1%

International: 1%
Minority: 1%

Job Placement Rate: NA

SCHOLARSHIPS / FINANCIAL AID
Variety of targeted scholarships,
including full-tuition, from many sources
within the home furnishings industry.

Students Receiving Scholarships or
Financial Aid: 50%

TOTAL FACULTY: 4
Full-time: 4
Part-time: n/a
Online: n/a

NCIDQ Certified: 1
Licensed Interior Designers: n/a
LEED Certified: 0

INTERIOR DESIGN ADMINISTRATION
Cathy Nowicki, Program Coordinator

PROFESSIONAL / ACADEMIC AFFILIATIONS
International Interior Design Association
Interior Design Educators Council
Interior Design Associations Foundation

CIDA ACCREDITATION
Bachelor of Science in Interior Design
(2007, 2013)

PROGRAM DESCRIPTION AND PHILOSOPHY

The Interior Design program at High Point University focuses on uniting knowledge and skills for a practical approach to Interior Design education. Projects are client-oriented, providing students opportunities to develop innovative solutions to real-world design problems. Special attention is paid to the availability of manufacturers' showrooms and the High Point Furniture market.

FACILITIES

Computer labs, design studios, showrooms, and manufacturers in the High Point area.

ONLINE / DISTANCE LEARNING

Not available

COURSES OF INSTRUCTION

- CAD, Visual Presentation
- Contract Design
- Residential Interiors
- Building Systems
- Architectural Detailing
- Textiles
- Furniture Fundamentals
- Senior Seminar

INTERNSHIPS

Not required of majors. Interns are typically placed at small design firms, photography studios, and furniture showrooms.

STUDY ABROAD

Available

NOTABLE ALUMNI

Not reported

STUDENT ACTIVITIES AND ORGANIZATIONS

Design and Furnishings Club, variety of campus-sponsored clubs

FACULTY SPECIALIZATIONS AND RESEARCH

- Commercial
- Residential
- History of furnishings

Meredith College

Department of Human Environmental Sciences

3800 Hillsborough St., Raleigh, NC 27607 | 919-760-8395 | www.meredith.edu/hes/interior-design/default.htm

UNIVERSITY PROFILE
Private
Urban
Residential
Semester Schedule
Women Only

STUDENT DEMOGRAPHICS
Undergraduate: 2,001
Graduate: 249

Male: 0%
Female: 100 undergraduate%

Full-time: 80%
Part-time: 20%

EXPENSES
Tuition: $24,490
Room & Board: $7,020

ADMISSIONS
3800 Hillsborough St.
Raleigh, NC 227607
919-760-8581
admissions@meredith.edu

DEGREE INFORMATION

Major / Degree / Concentration	Enrollment	Requirements for entry	Graduation rate
Interior Design Bachelor of Science	86	Not reported	90%

TOTAL PROGRAM ENROLLMENT
Undergraduate: 86
Graduate: 0

Male: 0%
Female: 100%

Full-time: 90%
Part-time: 10%

International: .04%
Minority: .07%

Job Placement Rate: 72%

SCHOLARSHIPS / FINANCIAL AID
Award approximately 21 scholarships per year ranging in amounts from $500 to $3000. These awards are given to freshmen to seniors.

Students receiving Scholarships or Financial Aid: 20%

TOTAL FACULTY: 5
Full-time: 60%
Part-time: 40%
Online: 0%

NCIDQ Certified: 60%
Licensed Interior Designers: NA
LEED Certified: 20%

Interior Design ADMINISTRATION
Dr. Deborah Tippett, Head of HES
Dr. Martha Burpitt, Program Coordinator—Interior Design

PROFESSIONAL / ACADEMIC AFFILIATIONS
American Society of Interior Designers
International Interior Design Association
Interior Design Educators Council

CIDA ACCREDITATION
Bachelor of Science (2007, 2013)

PROGRAM DESCRIPTION AND PHILOSOPHY

Operating within the context of a liberal arts college the Interior Design program seeks to enable its students to become creative, critical thinkers. The Interior Design Program strives to provide students with an awareness of the needs of people, their dependence and their interactions with the larger environment. The full-time faculty and adjunct faculty in the Interior Design program represents several professional points of view, background, and experiences, thereby enriching the learning environment for students. The faculty support and collaborate with student in undergraduate research and creative activities. Meredith College's location in Raleigh, NC, offers diverse internships and employment opportunities for students throughout their college careers. Raleigh's professional design organizations welcomes students' participation in programs, Continuing Education Units, and workshops.

FACILITIES

Resource Room, Computer labs with applicable software, printer-plotter room, Lighting Lab

ONLINE / DISTANCE LEARNING

Not available

COURSES OF INSTRUCTION

- Interior Design I, II, III, IV
- Contract Interiors
- Interior Lighting Design
- Technology Applications in Interior Design
- Special Problems in AutoCADD
- Professional Practice for Interior Design

INTERNSHIPS

Not required. Students intern with office dealerships (Storr Office Environments, Alfred Williams), architectural firms (Phillips Architecture, Cline Design Associates), design firms (Schelfe Associates, Design Lines Ltd.), showrooms (Karen Saks, A. Hoke) and a variety of retail establishments (Norwalk Furniture, Traditions in Tile, Eatmans Carpet).

STUDY ABROAD

Denmark International School, Sansepolcro, Italy (Meredith Campus), and other Meredith-sponsored study abroad opportunities.

NOTABLE ALUMNI

Jennifer Eanes Foster(2000) published in *Better Homes & Gardens*.
Kaitlin Quinlivan Phelps (2003) winner of DOC award for carpet design for Mannington.

STUDENT ACTIVITIES AND ORGANIZATIONS

Student Chapter of American Society of Interior Designers

FACULTY SPECIALIZATIONS AND RESEARCH

- Evolution of Home Design
- Green/Sustainable Design
- Office Design, Commercial Design, and Historic Preservation

University of North Carolina at Greensboro

Department of Interior Architecture

102 Gatewood Building, 527 Highland Ave., Greensboro, NC 27402 | 336-334-5320 | www.uncg.edu/iar/

UNIVERSITY PROFILE
Public
Urban
Residential
Semester Schedule
Co-ed

STUDENT DEMOGRAPHICS
Undergraduate: 14,000
Graduate: 4,000

Male: 33%
Female: 67%

Full-time: 89%
Part-time: 11%

EXPENSES
Tuition: $2,600 (in-state)
Room & Board: $4,800

ADMISSIONS
Office of Admissions
PO Box 26170
Greensboro, NC 27402
336-334-5000
pcrowlan@uncg.edu

DEGREE INFORMATION

Major / Degree / Concentration	Enrollment	Requirements for entry	Graduation rate
Interior Architecture Bachelor of Science	185	Acceptance to University; Department open house or interview with Department Chair; Department application process that includes a design exercise	95%
Interior Architecture Master of Science* *Concentrations in Historic Preservation, Interior Product Design, and Museum Studies available	25	Acceptance to Graduate School; GRE scores; Design degree	90%

TOTAL PROGRAM ENROLLMENT
Undergraduate: 185
Graduate: 25

Male: 15%
Female: 85%

Full-time: 95%
Part-time: 5%

International: 5%
Minority: 15%

Job Placement Rate: 80+%

SCHOLARSHIPS / FINANCIAL AID
See opposite page for more info.

TOTAL FACULTY: 10–12
Full-time: 90%
Part-time: 10%
Online: 0%

NCIDQ Certified: 30%
Licensed Interior Designers: 0%
LEED Certified: 10%

INTERIOR DESIGN ADMINISTRATION
Anna Marshall-Baker, Professor and Chair
Tommy Lambeth, Undergraduate Coordinator
Tina Sarawgi, Graduate Coordinator

PROFESSIONAL / ACADEMIC AFFILIATIONS
Interior Design Educators Council
Environmental Design Research Association

CIDA ACCREDITATION
Bachelor of Science in Interior Architecture (2006, 2012)

PROGRAM DESCRIPTION AND PHILOSOPHY

The Department of Interior Architecture is a community of scholars active in design theory and practice. We transcend the accepted definitions of interior spaces, their appearances, their functions, human interactions within and outside them, and their impact on the world. Within the IARC Department, students and faculty engage in regional, national, and international design discourses, practices, and processes to unite interior spaces with enclosing architecture and the objects contained within them.

FACILITIES

Digital Lab (Mac), Wood Shop And Fabrication Lab (For Metal And Plastic), IAR Library. Natuzzi Student Lounge.

ONLINE / DISTANCE LEARNING

Not Available

COURSES OF INSTRUCTION

- Social And Behavioral Aspects of Interior Architecture
- Materials, Methods, And Technologies Of Interior Architecture I & II
- Design Visualization I & II
- Visual Communication I & II
- Internship in Interior Architecture

INTERNSHIPS

Required of majors at 3rd-4th level. Interns are typically placed at companies such as Gensler, O'Brien Atkins, Little and Associates, Calloway Johnson Moore and West, Workplace Strategies, HBF

STUDY ABROAD

We have established residential programs in places such as Finland, Australia, and Great Britain although students have also studied in Mexico, China, Hong Kong, and Italy. We also have travel abroad programs that have occurred in India, Greece and Italy, and throughout western Europe.

NOTABLE ALUMNI

Jon Clegg, Callie Narron

STUDENT ACTIVITIES AND ORGANIZATIONS

Student chapter of IIDA, Dept membership in USGBC

FACULTY SPECIALIZATIONS AND RESEARCH

- History and Theory
- Historic Preservation
- Design/Build (Urban Studio)
- Community Engagement
- Product and Furniture Design
- Digital Technologiesl
- Lighting

COMMUNITY COLLEGE TRANSFERS

UNCG has a 2+ articulation agreement with community colleges. Students enter our program as 2nd year students and have 6 semesters of work to complete before graduating.

SCHOLARSHIPS / FINANCIAL AID

In addition to financial aid at the level of the university, students in the Dept of Interior Architecture are among many selected for scholarships and awards from the School of Human Environmental Sciences which distributes over 80 scholarships each spring. The amounts of the awards vary and some are desginated specifically for students in Interior Architecture. This year more than 10% of students in Interior Architecutre received awards.

Students Receiving Scholarships or Financial Aid: 50%

Western Carolina University

School of Art & Design

Fine & Performing Arts Center Office, Cullowhee, NC 28723 | 877-WCU-4YOU | **www.wcu.edu**

UNIVERSITY PROFILE
Public
Rural
Residential
Semester Schedule
Co-ed

STUDENT DEMOGRAPHICS
Undergraduate: 9,500
Graduate: 150

Male: 47%
Female: 53%

Full-time: Not reported
Part-time: Not reported

EXPENSES
Tuition: Not reported
Room & Board: Not reported

ADMISSIONS
102 Camp Building
Western Carolina University
Cullowhee, NC 28723
1-877-WCU-4YOU
admiss@wcu.edu

DEGREE INFORMATION

Major / Degree / Concentration	Enrollment	Requirements for entry	Graduation rate
Interior Design **Bachelor of Science**	85	2.0 gpa	95%

TOTAL PROGRAM ENROLLMENT
Undergraduate: 100
Graduate: 20

Male: 40%
Female: 60%

Full-time: 80%
Part-time: 20%

International: 2%
Minority: 1%

Job Placement Rate: Not reported

SCHOLARSHIPS / FINANCIAL AID
Roberta Buckner Scholarship; Wilma Cosper Scholarship

TOTAL FACULTY: 4
Full-time: 4
Part-time: 0
Online: 0

NCIDQ Certified: 3
Licensed Interior Designers: Not reported
LEED Certified: 1

Interior Design ADMINISTRATION
Richard Tichich, School Director
Robert Kehrberg, Dean of College of Fine & Performing Arts
Jane Nichols, Interior Design Program Coordinator

PROFESSIONAL / ACADEMIC AFFILIATIONS
American Society of Interior Designers
International Interior Design Association
Interior Design Educators Council
Environmental Design Research Association

CIDA ACCREDITATION
Bachelor of Science (2006, 2012)

PROGRAM DESCRIPTION AND PHILOSOPHY

Interior Design program stresses environmental and social sustainability, design for aging, health and wellness, and provides unique opportunities for service learning, real-world projects and travel studies abroad.

FACILITIES

Design studios, ACAD & plotter labs, library, sample rooms and Senior studio w/ 24-hour access and designated work-stations.

ONLINE / DISTANCE LEARNING

Not available

COURSES OF INSTRUCTION
- Space Planning
- Contract Design 1 and 2
- Residential Design 1 & 2
- ACAD
- Lighting Design
- Senior Capstone

INTERNSHIPS

Required of majors at Junior level. Interns are placed at commerical, residential, and kitchen design firms.

STUDY ABROAD

Summer studies abroad (Europe)

NOTABLE ALUMNI

Not reported

STUDENT ACTIVITIES AND ORGANIZATIONS

Interior Design Club

FACULTY SPECIALIZATIONS AND RESEARCH
- Sustainable Design
- LEED
- Design for Aging
- Healthcare Design
- Hospitality Design
- Kitchen & Bath Design
- Frank Lloyd Wright & Organic Architecture
- Housing for Aging-In-Place

COMMUNITY COLLEGE TRANSFERS

Transcript and portfolio review

North Dakota State University

Department of Apparel, Design and Hospitality Management

EML 178, Dept # 2610, PO Box 6050, Fargo, ND 58108-6050 | 701-231-8604 | www.ndsu.edu/adhm/

UNIVERSITY PROFILE
Public
Suburban
Residential
Semester Schedule
Co-ed

STUDENT DEMOGRAPHICS
Undergraduate: 11,666
Graduate: 1,835

Male: Not reported
Female: Not reported

Full-time: Not reported
Part-time: Not reported

EXPENSES
Tuition: $6,455 (ND resident)
Room & Board: $6,568

ADMISSIONS
Ceres 114 - Dept 5230
PO Box 6050
Fargo, ND 58108
1-800-488-NDSU
NDSU.Admission@ndsu.edu

DEGREE INFORMATION

Major / Degree / Concentration	Enrollment	Requirements for entry	Graduation rate
Interior Design Bachelor of Science or Arts	100	3.0 gpa Portfolio review at end of Sophomore year	100%

TOTAL PROGRAM ENROLLMENT
Undergraduate: 100
Graduate: 0

Male: 5%
Female: 95%

Full-time: 80%
Part-time: 20%

International: 1%
Minority: 5%

Job Placement Rate: 75-80%

SCHOLARSHIPS / FINANCIAL AID
NDSU Student Chapter of ASID provides 2 $250 scholarships to Interior Design majors accepted into the program. The College of Human Development provides a variety of yearly scholarship opportunties to all majors in the college.

Students Receiving Scholarships or Financial Aid: 90%

TOTAL FACULTY: 5
Full-time: 5
Part-time: 0
Online: 0

NCIDQ Certified: 60%
Licensed Interior Designers: 20%
LEED Certified: 0%

INTERIOR DESIGN ADMINISTRATION
Dr. Holly Bastow-Shoop, Department Head
Dr. Susan Ray-Degges, ASID, Program Coordinator

PROFESSIONAL / ACADEMIC AFFILIATIONS
American Society of Interior Designers
International Interior Design Association
Interior Design Educators Council
Environmental Design Research Association

CIDA ACCREDITATION
BA or BS in Interior Design (2010, 2016)

PROGRAM DESCRIPTION AND PHILOSOPHY

Students leaving the NDSU Interior Program are technically proficient in communicating design solutions through various media and have extensive background in materials and material applications. Faculty collaborate to create more consistent project guidelines and requirements to increase student understanding of the Interior Design process.

With a great need to support design solutions with evidence, students develop an understanding of human behavior early in the program and it is reinforced across the curriculum. Student work demonstrates a clear understanding of the design process as students are able to develop multiple design solutions to address a given project scenario. Students have also developed the necessary skills to locate research data/ findings and make informed design decisions based on facts rather than preferences or intuition Collaboration and teamwork (students and faculty) are key features of the program and imperative for a successful learning experience in Interior Design. Student teamwork in collecting information, critiquing work, and analyzing design solutions improves the quality of the finished product. Collaborative Senior capstone projects represent the "best" of the joint efforts of our students and faculty. Faculty mentor the students through the design process rather than "teach" them.

FACILITIES

All studio spaces are wired to access the University network system. Students accepted into the Interior Design program have access to computers, plotting equipment, color printers, scanners, and additional software for design production in the Junior and Senior studio spaces. Individual workstations are provided at the Junior and Senior level and large open spaces promote interaction, discussion, and mentorship between students. Surrounding tackable wall spaces in the studio encourage project pinup and discussion.

Studios are available 7 days a week. Students have card-key access that allows them to enter the studios outside of daily operational hours. Open discussion areas are provided in the Freshman and Sophomore studio spaces with large pin-up areas. Student exhibition space is available in the Memorial Union, two glass display cases adjacent to the Design Center, two glass display cases on the 2nd floor corridor of Family Life Center and in the Departmental office area.

The program maintains a high-quality Design Center staffed by students. The collection includes recent discontinued or current residential and commercial catalogs, and interior finish materials. An online database and search engine is also maintained in the design library to stay abreast of new products. These acquisitions are made possible through generous donations of local, regional, and national manufacturers and design firms. In addition, the program subscribes to computer services for student access to resources through the Internet. The Design Center is strategically located adjacent to the Junior and Senior studio and one floor below the Freshman and Sophomore studio.

ONLINE / DISTANCE LEARNING

Not available

COURSES OF INSTRUCTION

- Design Fundamentals
- Interior Design Careers
- Interior Graphics
- Interior Environmental Analysis
- Residential and Commercial Design Studios
- Residential and Commercial Systems
- Codes
- Professional Practice

INTERNSHIPS

Required of majors between Junior/ Senior year. Interns are typically placed with companies such as Target Corporation, Wold, BWBR, Gunkelman/Flescher.

STUDY ABROAD

Offered through the international office

NOTABLE ALUMNI

Tama Duffy Day; Sandra Strand

STUDENT ACTIVITIES AND ORGANIZATIONS

Students may become a member of the NDSU Student ASID Chapter. They may also become a student member of the North Dakota Interior Designer's organization.

FACULTY SPECIALIZATIONS AND RESEARCH

Faculty research areas include gerontology, environment & behavior, lighting, technology, and digital media.

University of Nebraska, Lincoln

Department of Interior Design

232 Architecture Hall, Lincoln, NE 68588-0107 | 402-472-9233 | http://archweb.unl.edu

UNIVERSITY PROFILE
Public
Urban
Residential
Semester Schedule
Co-ed

STUDENT DEMOGRAPHICS
Undergraduate: 25,000
Graduate: Not reported

Male: Not reported
Female: Not reported

Full-time: Not reported
Part-time: Not reported

EXPENSES
Tuition: Not reported
Room & Board: Not reported

ADMISSIONS
Office of Admissions
232 Architecture Hall
Lincoln, NE 68588-0107
402-472-9233

DEGREE INFORMATION

Major / Degree / Concentration	Enrollment	Requirements for entry	Graduation rate
Interior Design Bachelor of Science in Design	150	2.6 gpa Portfolio review after Sophomore year 3.0 gpa for transfer students	Not reported

TOTAL PROGRAM ENROLLMENT
Undergraduate: 145
Graduate: 30

Male: 7%
Female: 93%

Full-time: 69%
Part-time: 31%

International: 0%
Minority: 2%

Job Placement Rate: 90%

SCHOLARSHIPS / FINANCIAL AID
In addition to University scholarships, there are a number of scholarships available at the 3rd and 4th year levels of the program.

TOTAL FACULTY: 8
Full-time: 80%
Part-time: 20%
Online: Not reported

NCIDQ Certified: Not reported
Licensed Interior Designers: Not reported
LEED Certified: 16%

INTERIOR DESIGN ADMINISTRATION
R. Wayne Drummond, FAIA, Dean
Betsy S. Gabb, IIDA, FIDEC, Program Director Interior Design

PROFESSIONAL / ACADEMIC AFFILIATIONS
American Society of Interior Designers
International Interior Design Association
Interior Design Educators Council
Environmental Design Research Association

CIDA ACCREDITATION
Bachelor of Science in Design (2007, 2013)

PROGRAM DESCRIPTION AND PHILOSOPHY

As a land grant institution, the University is committed to teaching, research, and service. Thus, all have a part in the development of the curriculum and extra curricular activities of the Program and the College. The College has chosen to interweave all three within the delivery of the curriculum.

A unique feature of undergraduate education on the University of Nebraska campus is the UCARE Program, sponsored by Pepsi. UCARE stands for Undergraduate Creative Activity and Research Experience. All undergraduates are eligible to apply to work with faculty on a creative activity or research experience for a two year time period. Participating students receive a stipend of $2,000 in their first year, and $2,400 in their second year.

The integration of the Interior Design program within the College of Architecture has provided a collaborative teaching and learning environment for all. The common core of courses shared by students in Interior Design, architecture, and landscape architecture through the first two years of the program has given the program a strong grounding in both two and three dimensional design providing our graduates with not only strong interdisciplinary working relationships but strength in three dimensional thinking/visioning as well.

FACILITIES

Architecture Hall is located within the southwestern "Fine Arts" quadrant of the City Campus, with convenient access to the Lincoln central business district. All College lecture classrooms, design and planning studios, computer, media and shop facilities; the professional library; exhibit spaces; and other ancillary facilities are located within this building. Architecture Hall was renovated and remodeled in 1987 at a cost of $4.4 million. The project joined two historic buildings (the original Law College and the original Library) to provide 101,662 square feet.

Studios
The third floor of the west building, commonly referred to as the "barn" accommodates first and second year studio classes. The Interior Design studios that house third and fourth year design studios are located on the first floor of the of the west building. Each studio is accessible 24 hours a day and accommodates approximately 12-16 students.

Archives
The College maintains an archival facility to preserve selected student design projects (drawings and models), as well as selected projects from non-design classes.

Shop
The college shop is located on the west side of the lower level, in the same area as the media center and computer classroom. Over 3,000 square feet house power and hand tools and accessories necessary for wood and metal working and some plastics operations. This comprehensive, hands-on learning facility is used by students at all levels of the program and is staffed by work-study students and teaching assistants.

Media Center
The Media Center is located on the lowest level of the building. Equipment includes oversize plotters, color printers, laser cutters, a 3D printer, and a CNC machine.

ONLINE / DISTANCE LEARNING

A post professional Master of Science in Architecture with a Specialization in Interior Design is available online or in residence.

COURSES OF INSTRUCTION

Not reported

INTERNSHIPS

Required of majors after completion of third year. Interns are typically placed at companies such as Gensler, HDR, Leo A Daly, and the Interior Design Firm,

STUDY ABROAD

A wide number of options are available, including a London semester.

NOTABLE ALUMNI

Not reported

STUDENT ACTIVITIES AND ORGANIZATIONS

ASID Student Chapter, IIDA Student Center, Emerging Green Builders, Alpha Rho Chi, Tau Sigma Delta, AIAS

FACULTY SPECIALIZATIONS AND RESEARCH

Not reported

Kean University

Robert Bush School of Design

Vaughn Eames Building, Union, NJ 07083　|　908-737-5326　|　www.kean.edu/~design/interior_design/

UNIVERSITY PROFILE
Public
Urban
Commuter
Semester Schedule
Co-ed

STUDENT DEMOGRAPHICS
Undergraduate: 12,000
Graduate: 3,000

Male: 45%
Female: 55%

Full-time: 75%
Part-time: 25%

EXPENSES
Tuition: Not reported
Room & Board: Not reported

ADMISSIONS
Office of Admissions
1000 Morris Ave.
Union, NJ 07083
908-737-0000

DEGREE INFORMATION

Major / Degree / Concentration	Enrollment	Requirements for entry	Graduation rate
Interior Design Bachelor of Fine Arts	185	3.0 gpa Portfolio review after Sophmore year	95%

TOTAL PROGRAM ENROLLMENT
Undergraduate: 185
Graduate: Not reported

Male: 5%
Female: 95%

Full-time: 75%
Part-time: 25%

International: 5%
Minority: 35%

Job Placement Rate: 90%

SCHOLARSHIPS / FINANCIAL AID
Five specific Interior Design Scholarships are awarded through endowments and/or the RBSD and the College of Visual & Performing Arts.

Receiving Scholarships or Financial Aid: 10

TOTAL FACULTY: 9
Full-time: 3
Part-time: 6
Online: 0

NCIDQ Certified: 5
Licensed Interior Designers: 3
LEED Certified: 1

INTERIOR DESIGN ADMINISTRATION
Linda O'Shea, IIDA, LEED AP. IDEC, Professor of Interior Design, Interior Design Program Coordinator

PROFESSIONAL / ACADEMIC AFFILIATIONS
American Society of Interior Designers
International Interior Design Association
Interior Design Educators Council

CIDA ACCREDITATION
Bachelor of Fine Arts in Interior Design (2006, 2012)

PROGRAM DESCRIPTION AND PHILOSOPHY

The educational philosophy of the BFA Interior Design program is to develop a creative professional that can synthesize information and analyze problems from many perspectives. Program emphasis is on creative development, aesthetic awareness, and effective design solutions based on human needs in the contemporary environment.

FACILITIES

Kean University offers the Thinking Creatively Conference, Liberty Hall Museum, the Center for Human Rights, Kean Stage, NJ Center for Technology and Mathematics, and numerous computer labs and art galleries.

ONLINE / DISTANCE LEARNING

Not available

COURSES OF INSTRUCTION

- Architectural Lighting Design
- Design & the Built Environment
- Architectural Rendering & Perspective
- Critical Perspectives in Design
- Manual & ACAD Drafting
- Understanding Images
- Visual Thinking
- Design Studio I-V
- Life Safety Codes for Interior Designers
- Building Materials & Methods
- Materials and Finishes
- Business Practices

INTERNSHIPS

Not required. Intern opportunities are available at regional Interior Design and architectural firms.

STUDY ABROAD

Annual Travel Learn Experiences Abroad

NOTABLE ALUMNI

All of our alumni are notable

STUDENT ACTIVITIES AND ORGANIZATIONS

Interior Design Student Association, Interior Design Collaborative

FACULTY SPECIALIZATIONS AND RESEARCH

The Interior Design faculty, through teaching and research, specialize in deisgn for special populations, sustainable design, healthcare design, creative problem solving and design psychology.

COMMUNITY COLLEGE TRANSFERS

Articulation Agreements with regional community colleges, and State of NJ transfer guidelines for acceptance of credits. All transfer students are requied to submit an entry design portfolio.

New Jersey Institute of Technology

School of Art & Design, College of Architecture & Design

Newark, NJ 07102 | 973-596-3080 | http://design.njit.edu

UNIVERSITY PROFILE
Public
Urban
Residential & Commuter
Semester Schedule
Co-ed

STUDENT DEMOGRAPHICS
Undergraduate: 5,924
Graduate: 2,916

Male: 76%
Female: 24%

Full-time: 73%
Part-time: 27%

EXPENSES
Tuition: $12,856 in-state;
$22,600 out-of-state
Room & Board: $4,850

ADMISSIONS
NJIT Office of Admissions
Fenster Hall
Newark, NJ 07102-1982
1-800-925-NJIT or 973-596-3300
admissions@njit.edu

DEGREE INFORMATION

Major / Degree / Concentration	Enrollment	Requirements for entry	Graduation rate
Interior Design Bachelor of Arts	75	Average composite score of 1140 SAT (combined critical reading and math sections only); optional portfolio review. (Note: admissions to Honors College is more competitive.)	Not reported

TOTAL PROGRAM ENROLLMENT
Undergraduate: 75
Graduate: 0

Male: 37%
Female: 67%

Full-time: 100%
Part-time: 0%

International: Not reported
Minority: Not reported

Job Placement Rate: Not reported

SCHOLARSHIPS / FINANCIAL AID
Need-based aid available; merit aid available to students admitted to Honors College.

TOTAL FACULTY: 10
Full-time: 20%
Part-time: 80%
Online: 0%

NCIDQ Certified: 2
Licensed Interior Designers: Not reported
LEED Certified: 0

INTERIOR DESIGN ADMINISTRATION
Urs P. Gauchat, Dean of the College of Architecture & Design
John Cays, Associate Dean for Academics of the College of Architecture & Design
Glenn Goldman, Director - School of Art & Design

PROFESSIONAL / ACADEMIC AFFILIATIONS
American Society of Interior Designers
International Interior Design Association
Interior Design Educators Council

PROGRAM DESCRIPTION / PHILOSOPHY

The Interior Design program is a perfect complement to the architecture and design programs at NJIT. Located within College of Architecture and Design, the focus of the Interior Design program is to elevate the human experience through the design and enhancement of interior environments. Through the cross-fertilization of design disciplines that also include industrial design, digital design, and architecture, students in the Interior Design program learn how to address issues of interior architecture as well as human ergonomics and aesthetics.

Building on a legacy of innovation in the pedagogical and professional uses of digital media, the Interior Design program at NJIT exists within a strong digital culture committed to the use of information technology, including Building Information Modeling, in the processes and products of design.

The College of Architecture and Design is positioned to produce Interior Design graduates capable of designing and rehabilitating residential, commercial and institutional interior spaces and facilities with an understanding of building systems, lighting design, sustainability, aesthetics and spatial excitement for a variety of clients, design professionals, and user groups in the twenty-first century.

FACILITIES

Foundation Labs for first year students (3 labs - 20 Windows 7/64 bit workstations per lab - 8 to 12 GB RAM per machine); Digital Fabrication Lab (3D printing); Shop (traditional material/media); Animation Lab; Library; Materials Library.

ONLINE / DISTANCE LEARNING

Not available

COURSES OF INSTRUCTION

- Interior Design Studio (5 semesters)
- Collaborative Design Studio
- History of Furniture
- Introduction to Structures
- Building & Interior Systems (I-II)
- Building Information Modeling
- Construction Documents
- Methods and Materials
- Principles of Psychology
- Principles of Management
- Economics
- Human Factors & Ergonomics
- General Physics
- Color & Composition
- History of Art & Design (I-II)
- Communication in Art & Design
- Cultural History

INTERNSHIPS

Not required

STUDY ABROAD

NJIT College of Architecture and Design has a summer program in Italy

NOTABLE ALUMNI

Not reported

STUDENT ACTIVITIES AND ORGANIZATIONS

Design Student Union (student group with Architecture, Interior Design, Industrial Design, and Digital Design students at NJIT)

FACULTY SPECIALIZATIONS AND RESEARCH

Furniture design, building systems, lighting/luminaire design, digital media, building information modeling, design of educational environments

COMMUNITY COLLEGE TRANSFERS

Community college students may receive credit for general education courses, traditional media graphics (drawing), and other work on a case-by-case basis. Spring transfers into the first year are accepted.

International Academy of Design & Technology– Las Vegas

Department of Interior Design

2495 Village View Dr., Henderson, NV 89074 | 702-990-0150 | www.iadtvegas.com/

UNIVERSITY PROFILE
Private
Suburban
Commuter
Quarter Schedule
Co-ed

STUDENT DEMOGRAPHICS
Undergraduate: 64
Graduate: n/a

Male: Not reported
Female: Not reported

Full-time: Not reported
Part-time: Not reported

EXPENSES
Tuition: $405 per credit
Room & Board: n/a

ADMISSIONS
2495 Village View Dr.
Henderson, NV 89074
702-990-0150

DEGREE INFORMATION

Major / Degree / Concentration	Enrollment	Requirements for entry	Graduation rate
Interior Design Bachelor of Fine Arts	180	High school diploma or GED	Not reported

TOTAL PROGRAM ENROLLMENT
Undergraduate: 64
Graduate: n/a

Male: Not reported
Female: Not reported

Full-time: Not reported
Part-time: Not reported

International: Not reported
Minority: Not reported

Job Placement Rate: Not reported

SCHOLARSHIPS / FINANCIAL AID
Please see detailed information provided in the catalog, in the Financial Aid Information section, located on the Web site.

TOTAL FACULTY: 11
Full-time: 50%
Part-time: 50%
Online: Not reported

NCIDQ Certified: 45%
Licensed Interior Designers: 36%
LEED Certified: 18%

INTERIOR DESIGN ADMINISTRATION
Trampas Johnston, Program Chair

PROFESSIONAL / ACADEMIC AFFILIATIONS
American Society of Interior Designers

PROGRAM DESCRIPTION AND PHILOSOPHY

The Interior Design Program prepares students to develop creative and technical solutions for interior spaces that meet aesthetic and functional requirements while addressing safety, regulatory, and environmental concerns. Students will apply the fundamentals of art and design, theories of design, "green design," and an understanding of human behavior to their design solutions. Critical thinking, research, analysis, documentation, and drawing and presentation skills are incorporated in the design process. Students have an opportunity to explore creativity through the selection of colors, materials and finishes, textiles, lighting solutions, furnishings, and other interior elements to solve design problems. Skills in time management, budgeting, project management, business practices, and resource allocation will contribute to student readiness for entry level employment in positions.

FACILITIES

The students have access to both an on-ground library as well as on-line library resources (CECybrary); they also have computer labs—one dedicated to the program—a resource room with donated manufacturer samples.

ONLINE / DISTANCE LEARNING

The Interior Design program has some of the required courses offered online from IADT Online through a consortium agreement.

COURSES OF INSTRUCTION

- Design Fundamentals, Introduction to Drawing
- Drafting
- Sketching and Rendering
- History of Interior Design
- Textiles
- Interior Design Issues and Programming
- Computer Aided Design
- Resources and Materials
- Digital Media for Interior Design
- Building Sytems and Codes
- Sustainable Design for a Global Society
- Interior Design I, II, III, & IV (allowing study on a variety of Residential and Commercial projects.)

INTERNSHIPS

Required of majors at the Senior level.

STUDY ABROAD

London and Paris.

NOTABLE ALUMNI

Not reported

STUDENT ACTIVITIES AND ORGANIZATIONS

An ASID student chapter has been established, biannual markets at the World Market Center, and other related Trade Shows that are held annually in Las Vegas.

FACULTY SPECIALIZATIONS AND RESEARCH

We haved faculty with specializations in residential , hospitality design, manufacturer rep experience and national home builder industry experience.

University of Nevada, Reno

Interior Design Program

Interior Design, MS 0092, Reno, NV 89557 | 775-784-1780 | www.unr.edu

UNIVERSITY PROFILE
Public
Urban
Residential
Commuter
Semester Schedule
Co-ed

STUDENT DEMOGRAPHICS
Undergraduate: 13,300
Graduate: 3,500

Male: 46%
Female: 54%

Full-time: 83%
Part-time: 17%

EXPENSES
Tuition: Not reported
Room & Board: Not reported

ADMISSIONS
Admissions Office, MS 120
Reno, NV 89557
775-784-4700
smaples@unr.edu
(Steve Maples, Director of
Admissions)

DEGREE INFORMATION

Major / Degree / Concentration	Enrollment	Requirements for entry	Graduation rate
Interior Design Bachelor of Science	100+	3.0 weighted gpa in high school English, math, social sciences, and natural sciences; or a combined score from the SAT critical reading and math section of at least 1040; or an ACT composite score of at least 22	80%

TOTAL PROGRAM ENROLLMENT
Undergraduate: 100+
Graduate: 0 (no graduate program)

Male: 10%
Female: 90%

Full-time: 47%
Part-time: 53%

International: 1%
Minority: 15%

Job Placement Rate: virtually all those who seek positions related to Interior Design find them

SCHOLARSHIPS / FINANCIAL AID
Interior Design Scholarship (Portfolio), Lighting Essay Scholarship, and a wide variety of college and university scholarships

Receiving Scholarships or Financial Aid: The University does not track this information by individual major. However, in the past 5 years, department records indicate Interior Design students have been awarded approximately 250 scholarships. University-wide, 34% full-time undergraduate students receive financial aid.

TOTAL FACULTY: 6
Full-time: 17%
Part-time: 83%
Online: 0%

NCIDQ Certified: 66%
Licensed Interior Designers: 50%
LEED Certified: 33%

INTERIOR DESIGN ADMINISTRATION
LuAnn Nissen, Director

PROFESSIONAL / ACADEMIC AFFILIATIONS
American Society of Interior Designers

PROGRAM DESCRIPTION AND PHILOSOPHY

A design education is a broadly-based study of human experience and interaction with the built environment, rooted in the liberal arts and design fundamentals, with a focus on purposeful problem solving. It provides a broadly based, process oriented, professionally relevant course of study which addresses aesthetic, spatial, behavioral, and environmental factors.

Students majoring in Interior Design at the University of Nevada, Reno learn principles of design, the design process, critical thinking and problem-solving skills, and methods of presenting design concepts. They complete a number of professional projects, prepare a portfolio of their design work and participate in a Senior internship, applying concepts learned in the classroom while gaining valuable on-the-job experience in a professional setting. The intrinsic goal of the Interior Design program is to nurture each student's creative, applied, communication, and critical thinking skills through an interdisciplinary curriculum which balances human well-being and quality of life with functional, aesthetic, behavioral, and pragmatic approaches to solving design problems.

FACILITIES

Computer labs, large format printer, photo equipment, department resource & materials library, design studio

ONLINE / DISTANCE LEARNING

Not available

COURSES OF INSTRUCTION

- Foundations for Design
- Architectural Drafting
- Construction Drawings & Detailing
- Computer Applications
- Interior Presentation Techniques
- Textiles
- Materials & Resources
- Housing
- Space, Light, & Color
- History of Interiors
- Building Codes
- Design I (Residential Design Studio)
- Design II (Contract Design Studio)
- Contemporary Design Concepts
- Design III (Senior Studio)
- Professional Practices
- Portfolio Development
- Internship
- World Architecture
- Art History I & II, Business & Professional Speaking
- Effective Business Writing

INTERNSHIPS

Required of majors at Senior level. Interns are typically placed at Interior Design firms, architectural firms, retailers and wholesalers of furnishings & materials, office furnishing dealerships, cabinetry & appliance companies, manufacturers, andcontractors/builders & developers.

STUDY ABROAD

Available

NOTABLE ALUMNI

Not reported

STUDENT ACTIVITIES AND ORGANIZATIONS

ASID Student Chapter, NKBA Student Membership

FACULTY SPECIALIZATIONS AND RESEARCH

Not reported

Alfred State College

Interior Design Department

10 Upper College Dr., Alfred, NY 14802 | 607-587-4696 | www.alfredstate.edu/academics/programs/interior-design

UNIVERSITY PROFILE
Public
Rural
Residential
Semester
Co-ed

STUDENT DEMOGRAPHICS
Undergraduate: 3,200
Graduate: 0

Male: 65.3%
Female: 34.7%

Full-time: Not reported
Part-time: Not reported

EXPENSES
Tuition: $4,970
Room & Board: $5,000

ADMISSIONS
10 Upper College Dr.
Alfred, NY 14802
1-800-425-3733
admissions@alfredstate.edu

DEGREE INFORMATION

Major / Degree / Concentration	Enrollment	Requirements for entry	Graduation rate
Interior Design Associate of Arts	24	Math & Algebra	Not reported

TOTAL PROGRAM ENROLLMENT
Undergraduate: Not reported
Graduate: n/a

Male: Not reported
Female: Not reported

Full-time: Not reported
Part-time: Not reported

International: Not reported
Minority: Not reported

Job Placement Rate: 90%

SCHOLARSHIPS / FINANCIAL AID
See opposite page for more info

TOTAL FACULTY: Not reported
Full-time: Not reported
Part-time: Not reported
Online: Not reported

NCIDQ Certified: Not reported
Licensed Interior Designers: Not reported
LEED Certified: 1

INTERIOR DESIGN ADMINISTRATION
Dr. John M. Anderson, President
Craig Clark, Interim VP for Academic Affairs
Valerie Nixon, VP for Administration & Enrollment

PROFESSIONAL / ACADEMIC AFFILIATIONS
American Society of Interior Designers

PROGRAM DESCRIPTION AND PHILOSOPHY

This program is designed to provide a basic education and skills so students can find work in an entry-level position or continue on in their Interior Design education. The program consists of a core of graphics sequence leading to a studio sequence that concentrates on Interior Design issues. These are supplemented by courses in appropriate technical areas related to the discipline. Computer applications are integrated throughout the four semesters with a strong component in 2D and 3D computer graphics. The faculty consists of Interior Designers as well as licensed architects and engineers.

FACILITIES

We are a wireless facility. We have an architectural design library, an Interior Design library loaded with finishes and manufacturer's binders. We have two laser cutters for building models. There is an archive room filled with past student work. There are five computer labs/studios.

ONLINE / DISTANCE LEARNING
Not available

COURSES OF INSTRUCTION
- Color
- Lighting & Acoustics
- Furniture, Fabrics, and Finishes
- History of Interiors
- Studio I & II
- Computer Graphics
- Portfolio
- Geometry
- Literature
- Architectural History

INTERNSHIPS
Not required

STUDY ABROAD
Semester in Sorrento, Italy

NOTABLE ALUMNI
Maryia Boykins, Sarah Tice, Sarah Norton

STUDENT ACTIVITIES AND ORGANIZATIONS

Interior Design Club which plans field trips. We have attended NeoCon East in Baltimore, visited Toronto, and visited Rochester, NY, Strong Museum of Play. There is also an Architecture Club with recently visited Philadelphia, PA and Frank Lloyd Wright's Falling Water in Bear Run, PA. Other active organizations are the Student Senate, Intercollegiate Sports Program, the Alfred State Response Team, the Drama Club, the Sustainability Club, the Visual Impact Club, and the Radio Station.

FACULTY SPECIALIZATIONS AND RESEARCH
Not reported

Cornell University

Department of Design and Environmental Analysis, College of Human Ecology

3M13 MVR Hall, Ithaca, NY 14853-4401 | 607-255-2168 | www.human.cornell.edu/che/DEA/index.cfm

UNIVERSITY PROFILE
Private
Suburban
Residential
Semester
Co-ed

STUDENT DEMOGRAPHICS
Undergraduate: 13,931
Graduate: 4,689

Male: 51%
Female: 49%

Full-time: 100%
Part-time: 0%

EXPENSES
Tuition: $37,750
(undergraduate); $29,500
(graduate)
Room & Board: $12,650

ADMISSIONS
Undergraduate Admissions
Cornell University
410 Thurston Ave.
Ithaca, NY 14850
607-255-5241
admissions@cornell.edu

Graduate School
Cornell University
143 Caldwell Hall
Ithaca, NY 14853
607-255-5820
gradschool@cornell.edu

DEGREE INFORMATION

Major / Degree / Concentration	Enrollment	Requirements for entry	Graduation rate
Interior Design Bachelor of Science First professional degree	52	Class average of 90 or higher; SAT or ACT test results; portfolio submission	Not reported
Design Master of Arts 2 year professional degree*	2	GRE, TOEFL Porfolio 3.0 gpa	Not reported

*Concentration in Design History & Criticism, Design Leadership, Special Populations, Sustainable & Regenerative Design

TOTAL PROGRAM ENROLLMENT
Undergraduate: 90
Graduate: 20

Male: 13% (undergraduate); 20% (graduate)
Female: 87% (undergraduate); 80% (graduate)

Full-time: 100%
Part-time: 0%

International: Not reported
Minority: Not reported

Job Placement Rate: 100%

SCHOLARSHIPS / FINANCIAL AID
Not reported

TOTAL FACULTY: 17
Full-time: 88%
Part-time: 12%
Online: 0%

NCIDQ Certified: Not reported
Licensed Interior Designers: Not reported
LEED Certified: Not reported

INTERIOR DESIGN ADMINISTRATION
Sheila Danko, Professor and Department Chair
Jack Elliott, Professor and Director of Graduate Studies
Paul Eshelman, Professor and Director of Undergraduate Studies

PROFESSIONAL / ACADEMIC AFFILIATIONS
American Society of Interior Designers
Interior Design Educators Council
Environment Design Research Association

CIDA ACCREDITATION
Bachelor of Science (2010, 2016)

PROGRAM DESCRIPTION AND PHILOSOPHY

The Interior Design (ID) option is accredited by the Council for Interior Design Accreditation (CIDA) as a first professional degree program. It is the only Interior Design program in the Ivy League.

With an emphasis on problem-solving design studios, students learn not just technical design skills, but also ways to think imaginatively and constructively about design and its role in our lives. That includes understanding the impact of design decisions on the environment and our planet, as well as on the people who inhabit the settings we help create. Small classes and faculty who are both leaders in their field and deeply committed to undergraduate education, make Interior Design in DEA as rewarding as it is challenging.

FACILITIES

Studios, CAD lab, computer labs, City NYC trip, field trips

ONLINE / DISTANCE LEARNING

Not available

COURSES OF INSTRUCTION

- Digital Graphics
- Interior Design Studio I - VIII
- Theory and Practice
- Ecological Literacy and Design
- Furniture as Social Art
- Design Graphics and Visualization
- Construction Documents and Detailing
- Design Theory and Criticism Seminar
- Intro to Professional Practice of Interior Design
- Digital Communications
- Intro to REVIT and Building Info Modeling (BIM)
- Making a Difference: By Design
- Design City (field study)
- Interior Materials and Sustainable Elements
- History and Theory of the Interior

INTERNSHIPS

Not required

STUDY ABROAD

Hong Kong Polytech and University of New South Wales, Australia

NOTABLE ALUMNI

Jan Stensland
Nancy Darling

STUDENT ACTIVITIES AND ORGANIZATIONS

ASID Student Chapter, HFES Student Chapter, IFMA Student Chapter

FACULTY SPECIALIZATIONS AND RESEARCH

Sheila Danko: Design leadership, and sustainable & regenerative design; Jan Jennings & Kathleen Gibson: Design history, theory & criticism; Paul Eshelman: Special populations; Jack Elliott: Sustainable & regenerative design

Fashion Institute of Technology

Department of Interior Design

Seventh Ave. and 27th St., New York, NY 10001 | 212-217-3760 | www.fitnyc.edu/interiordesign

UNIVERSITY PROFILE
Public
Urban
Residential
Semester Schedule
Co-ed

STUDENT DEMOGRAPHICS
Undergraduate: 10,207
Graduate: 206

Male: 16%
Female: 84%

Full-time: 70%
Part-time: 30%

EXPENSES
Tuition: $3,714 (Freshman year, in-state)
Room & Board: $9,650–$17,520

ADMISSIONS
Seventh Ave. and 27th St.
New York, NY 10001
212-217-3760
fitinfo@fitnyc.edu

DEGREE INFORMATION

Major / Degree / Concentration	Enrollment	Requirements for entry	Graduation rate
Interior Design Associate of Applied Science	Not reported	Portfolio and a high school diploma or a GED	Not reported
Interior Design Bachelor of Fine Arts	Not reported	AAS from FIT or Associate degree or at least 60 credits toward a Bachelor degree in an equivalent program at a regionally accredited college	Not reported

TOTAL PROGRAM ENROLLMENT
Undergraduate: 373
Graduate: NA

Male: 13%
Female: 87%

Full-time: 93%
Part-time: 7%

International: 10%
Minority: 24%

Job Placement Rate: Not reported

SCHOLARSHIPS / FINANCIAL AID
See opposite page for more info.

TOTAL FACULTY: 62
Full-time: Not reported
Part-time: Not reported
Online: Not reported

NCIDQ Certified: Not reported
Licensed Interior Designers: Not reported
LEED Certified: Not reported

INTERIOR DESIGN ADMINISTRATION
Takashi Kamiya, Chair

PROFESSIONAL / ACADEMIC AFFILIATIONS
Not reported

CIDA ACCREDITATION
Bachelor of Fine Arts (2007, 2013)

PROGRAM DESCRIPTION AND PHILOSOPHY

Interior Design is a multifaceted profession dealing with complete environments that not only please but also enhance the health and safety of the user. Like other Interior Design programs, FIT encourages students to develop a creative vision and hone their design skills—but creativity alone won't make a successful Interior Designer. Our curriculum also emphasizes the practical skills students need to envision great spaces—and to know how to build them, too. FIT's Interior Design program has been preparing students for success for more than 50 years. This rigorous, multidisciplinary program combines the academic study of the history and theory of Interior Design with practical, hands-on projects. Each undergraduate program also includes a core of traditional liberal arts courses, providing students with a global perspective, critical-thinking skills, and the ability to communicate effectively, and students have the option of completing a liberal arts minor.

FACILITIES

FIT's campus provides its students with classrooms, laboratories, and studios that reflect the most advanced educational and industry practices. The Fred P. Pomerantz Art and Design Center houses drawing, painting, photography, printmaking, and sculpture studios; display and exhibit design rooms; a model-making workshop; and a graphics printing service bureau. The Peter G. Scotese Computer-Aided Design and Communications facility provides the latest technology in computer graphics, photography, and the design of advertising, fashion, interiors, textiles, and toys. Other facilities include a design/research lighting laboratory, and 23 computer labs, in addition to several other labs with computers reserved for students in specific programs.

ONLINE / DISTANCE LEARNING

Not reported

COURSES OF INSTRUCTION

- Interior Design Studio
- Perspective Drawing
- Presentation Techniques
- Interior Architectural Detail
- Ecology and the Built Environment
- Furniture Design

INTERNSHIPS

Required of majors. Past sponsors include Gensler, Interior Architects, and the Rockwell Group.

STUDY ABROAD

The study abroad experience provides students with the opportunity to immerse themselves in divers cultures and prepares them to live and work in a global community. Interior Design students can study in countries such as England and Italy.

NOTABLE ALUMNI

Interior Designers Tony Chi and Matthew Patrick Smyth

STUDENT ACTIVITIES AND ORGANIZATIONS

The college is home to more than 60 clubs, societies, and athletic teams—everything from major-related organizations to hobby groups to a ski and snowboard club. Each organization is open to all students who have paid their activity fee. The Student Council, the governing body of the Student Association, grants all students the privileges and responsibilities of citizens in a self-governing college community. FIT has intercollegiate teams in basketball, cross-country, half-marathon, outdoor track, dance, table tennis, tennis, swimming and diving, and volleyball.

FACULTY SPECIALIZATIONS AND RESEARCH

FIT's faculty is drawn from top professionals in academia, art, design, communications, and business, providing a curriculum rich in real-world experience and traditional educational values. Student-instructor interaction is encouraged, with a maximum class size of 25, and courses are structured to foster participation, independent thinking, and self-expression.

COMMUNITY COLLEGE TRANSFERS

Transfer students must submit official transcripts for credit evaluation. Students seeking admission to a baccalaureate program must hold an AAS degree from FIT or an equivalent college degree, or at least 60 credits toward a bachelor's degree in an equivalent program at a regionally accredited college.

SCHOLARSHIPS / FINANCIAL AID

The college directly administers its own institutional grants and scholarships, which are provided by The Educational Foundation for the Fashion Industries. College-administered federal funding includes Federal Pell Grants, Federal Perkins Loans, Federal Supplemental Educational Opportunity Grants, Federal Work-Study Program awards, and the Federal Family Educational Loan Program, which includes student and parent loans. New York State residents who meet state guidelines for eligibility may also receive Tuition Assistance Program (TAP) and/or Educational Opportunity Program (EOP) grants. Financial aid applicants must file the Free Application for Federal Student Aid (FAFSA), through which they apply for the Federal Pell Grant, and should also apply to all available outside sources of aid.

New York Institute of Technology

School of Architecture & Design

Northern Blvd., Midge Karr Fine Arts, Old Westbury, NY 11568 | 516-686-7786 | **www.nyit.edu/architecture**

UNIVERSITY PROFILE
Private
Suburban
Residential
Commuter
Semester Schedule
Co-ed

STUDENT DEMOGRAPHICS
Undergraduate: Not reported
Graduate: Not reported

Male: Not reported
Female: Not reported

Full-time: Not reported
Part-time: Not reported

EXPENSES
Tuition: $24,670
Room & Board: $5,858

ADMISSIONS
P.O. Box 8000, Northern Blvd.
Old Westbury, NY 11568
800-345-NYIT
admissions@nyit.edu

DEGREE INFORMATION

Major / Degree / Concentration	Enrollment	Requirements for entry	Graduation rate
Interior Design Bachelor of Fine Arts	96	Not reported	Not reported

TOTAL PROGRAM ENROLLMENT
Undergraduate: Not reported
Graduate: Not reported

Male: Not reported
Female: Not reported

Full-time: Not reported
Part-time: Not reported

International: Not reported
Minority: Not reported

Job Placement Rate: 90%

SCHOLARSHIPS / FINANCIAL AID
Not reported

TOTAL FACULTY: 13
Full-time: 3
Part-time: 10
Online: 1

NCIDQ Certified: 50%
Licensed Interior Designers: 30%
LEED Certified: 30%

INTERIOR DESIGN ADMINISTRATION
Judith DiMaio, Dean, School of
  Architecture and Design
Frank Mruk, Associate Dean, School of
  Architecture and Design
Martha Siegel, Chairperson, Department
  of Interior Design

**PROFESSIONAL / ACADEMIC
AFFILIATIONS**
American Society of Interior Designers
International Interior Design Association
Interior Design Educators Council

CIDA ACCREDITATION
Bachelor of Fine Arts in Interior Design
(2010, 2016)

PROGRAM DESCRIPTION AND PHILOSOPHY
Not reported

FACILITIES
3 Computer/large-format print labs, woodshop/laser cuter lab, lighting lab, materials lab, architectural library, 2 galleries, lecture center

ONLINE / DISTANCE LEARNING
Not available

COURSES OF INSTRUCTION
- Fundamentals of Design I
- Visualization I
- Fundamentals of Design II
- Visualization II
- Intro History-Theory-Crit-in Arch. & Design
- Materials I
- Materials II
- History of Interiors I
- History of Interiors II, Working Drawings
- ID CAD I
- ID CAD II
- Structures
- Color in Space
- Interior Design I
- Interior Design II
- ID Problems I
- ID Problems II
- Building Codes & Regulations
- Business Procedures

INTERNSHIPS
Required of majors at Junior level. Interns are typically placed at companies such as Bentel & Bentel, JJ Falk, InARCH, Nugent Designs, Inc., Sherwin-Williams, Z-Squared, etc.

STUDY ABROAD
Available

NOTABLE ALUMNI
Not reported

STUDENT ACTIVITIES AND ORGANIZATIONS
Interior Design Club, Lecture Series (Arch & Design), various campus clubs and associations not specific to Interior Design

FACULTY SPECIALIZATIONS AND RESEARCH
Not reported

New York School of Interior Design

New York School of Interior Design

170 E 70th St., New York, NY 10021 | 212-472-1500 | www.nysid.edu

UNIVERSITY PROFILE
Private
Urban
Commuter
Semester Schedule
Co-ed

STUDENT DEMOGRAPHICS
Undergraduate: 657
Graduate: 58

Male: 11%
Female: 89%

Full-time: 36%
Part-time: 64%

EXPENSES
Tuition: $25,000
Room & Board: n/a

ADMISSIONS
170 E 70th St.
New York, NY 10021
212-472-1500 ext. 204
admissions@nysid.edu

DEGREE INFORMATION

Major / Degree / Concentration	Enrollment	Requirements for entry	Graduation rate
Interior Design Certificate	157	3.0 gpa Recommendations Essay	Not reported
Interior Design Associate of Applied Science	211	3.0 gpa Recommendations Essay Fine Arts Portfolio	Not reported
Interior Design Bachelor of Fine Arts	164	3.0 gpa Recommendations Essay	Not reported
Interior Design Master of Fine Arts Professional level	38	3.0 gpa Recommendations Essay Fine Arts Portfolio	Not reported
Interior Design Master of Fine Arts Post-professional level	20	3.0 gpa Recommendations Essay Design Portfolio	Not reported
History of the Decorative Arts Bachelor of Arts	0	3.0 gpa Recommendations Essay	Not reported

TOTAL PROGRAM ENROLLMENT
Undergraduate: 657
Graduate: 58

Male: 11%
Female: 81%

Full-time: 36%
Part-time: 64%

International: 11%
Minority: 28%

Job Placement Rate: 85%

SCHOLARSHIPS / FINANCIAL AID
See opposite page for more info.

TOTAL FACULTY: 80
Full-time: 10%
Part-time: 90%
Online: 0%

NCIDQ Certified: 11%
Licensed Interior Designers: 26%
LEED Certified: 3%

INTERIOR DESIGN ADMINISTRATION
Scott Ageloff, Dean
Ellen Fisher, Associate Dean

PROFESSIONAL / ACADEMIC AFFILIATIONS
American Society of Interior Designers

CIDA ACCREDITATION
Bachelor of Fine Arts (2006, 2012)

PROGRAM DESCRIPTION AND PHILOSOPHY

NYSID offers three undergraduate degree programs: the Bachelor of Arts in the History of the Interior and Decorative Arts (BA), the professional-level Bachelor of Fine Arts in Interior Design (BFA), and the preprofessional Associate in Applied Science in Interior Design (AAS). Both the BFA and AAS programs, together with the requisite work experience, prepare graduates to sit for the NCIDQ exam leading to state certification.

A nondegree certificate program, Basic Interior Design, is offered for those who need to develop a portfolio for the AAS or BFA programs, or for those seeking personal enrichment and entry-level job opportunities in fields related to Interior Design.

NYSID also offers three Graduate-Level Programs. The Professional-Level Master of Fine Arts in Interior Design (MFA-1) program provides students with a prior Bachelor's degree in an unrelated field with professional-level Interior Design training.

The Post-Professional Master of Fine Arts in Interior Design (MFA-2) program is for students who already have an undergraduate degree in architecture or Interior Design, and focuses on advanced studio and academic research.

The Master of Professional Studies in Sustainable Interior Environments (MPS) is a post-professional program focused on specialized knowledge, thinking, and skills in the growing world of design sustainability.

FACILITIES

Library, atelier (workspace/resource room), computer labs, plotters, fabric collection

ONLINE / DISTANCE LEARNING

Not available

COURSES OF INSTRUCTION

- Color for Interiors
- Basic Drafting
- Residential Design
- Contract Design
- Lighting
- Modern Architecture
- Design

INTERNSHIPS

Not required of majors. Students have interns with companies such as David Scott, Mica Ertegun, Anne Eisenhower, Rick Shaver, and Mariette Himes Gomez

STUDY ABROAD

Not available

NOTABLE ALUMNI

Susan Nagle, David Scott, Alberto Villalobos, Mariette Himes Gomez, Laurie Hicks Smith, Mercedes Desio

STUDENT ACTIVITIES AND ORGANIZATIONS

Not reported

FACULTY SPECIALIZATIONS AND RESEARCH

Not reported

SCHOLARSHIPS / FINANCIAL AID

Students Receiving Scholarships or Financial Aid: 23%

All Applicants must complete the Free Application for Federal Student Aid (FAFSA) online at www.fafsa.ed.gov. This single application will be reviewed for a student's eligibility for the federal Pell grant, ACG grant, FSEOG grant, Work-Study program, NYSID scholarships or fellowships, and New York State aid, if applicable.

Pratt Institute

School of Art & Design

200 Willoughby Ave., Brooklyn, NY 11205 | 718-636-3630 | www.pratt.edu/academics/art_design

UNIVERSITY PROFILE
Private
Urban
Residential
Semester Schedule
Co-ed

STUDENT DEMOGRAPHICS
Undergraduate: 2,498
Graduate: 1,709

Male: 34%
Female: 66%

Full-time: 90%
Part-time: 10%

EXPENSES
Tuition: $33,500
(undergraduate)
Room & Board: $9,756
(undergraduate)

ADMISSIONS
200 Willoughby Ave.
Brooklyn, NY 11205
718-636-3514
visir@pratt.edu

DEGREE INFORMATION

Major / Degree / Concentration	Enrollment	Requirements for entry	Graduation rate
Interior Design Bachelor of Fine Arts	171	Portfolio; High school transcripts SAT or ACT; Letters of recommendation Application	85%
Interior Design Master of Science	173	Portfolio required for 2 year, optional, but encouraged, for 3 year program; Letters of recommendation; Application	90%

TOTAL PROGRAM ENROLLMENT
Undergraduate: 216
Graduate: 176

Male: 16%
Female: 84%

Full-time: 95%
Part-time: 5%

International: 36%
Minority: 23%

Job Placement Rate: 85%

SCHOLARSHIPS / FINANCIAL AID
Pratt offers undergraduate students two main types of scholarships: a generous program of merit-based scholarships and restricted and endowed scholarships. In addition, need-based grants (gift) are added to the package to make the cost of attendance more affordable for more families.

TOTAL FACULTY: 55
Full-time: 5%
Part-time: 95%
Online: 0%

NCIDQ Certified: 5%
Licensed Interior Designers: 5%
LEED Certified: 20%

INTERIOR DESIGN ADMINISTRATION
Anita Cooney, Chair
Karin Tehve, Assistant Chair
Aston Gibson, Assistant to the Chair

PROFESSIONAL / ACADEMIC AFFILIATIONS
American Society of Interior Designers
International Interior Design Association
Interior Design Educators Council

CIDA ACCREDITATION
Bachelor of Fine Arts—Interior Design
(2009, 2015)

PROGRAM DESCRIPTION AND PHILOSOPHY

Undergraduate Interior Design at Pratt provides the ultimate learning environment in New York City, Interior Design capital of the United States, as well as a challenging course of study for students preparing themselves for a career in a field with enormous potential. It is widely acknowledged that Interior Design education, as it is taught across the United States, began at Pratt. That so many of our alumni are found in the *Who's Who of Interior Designers* is no surprise. The Interior Design program is consistently ranked among the top in the country in an annual independent professional survey. Students have the opportunity to study Interior Design as an integral element of the built environment: shaping space as well as planning and furnishing it. Light, color, form, and space are the classic elements of interior architecture with which students work in a series of design studies and related courses. At Pratt, students focus on a variety of Interior Design projects that grow more complex as the curriculum proceeds.

The Graduate Interior Design Program at Pratt, like its undergraduate counterpart, is an architecturally oriented program with emphasis on spatial design rather than surface embellishment. All aspects of space—scale, proportions, configuration, and light sources, as well as textures, materials, and colors—are studied in relation to their effect on the human spirit. Students are drawn from all parts of the world and, by way of the Qualifying Program, from a variety of disciplines, creating an intellectually and aesthetically stimulating ambience in the studios. Our students are a select group who understand that creativity is a serious business. They come to Pratt to work hard and prepare to enter a field in which the designer must be multifaceted and able to provide innovative design solutions. Our faculty members are also practicing professionals who bring the realities of real-world interactions with clients and contractors into the classroom.

FACILITIES

Wood shop, RP lab with laser cutter, materials library, library, computer labs

ONLINE / DISTANCE LEARNING

Not available

COURSES OF INSTRUCTION

Students are encouraged to take advantage of the many courses offered at Pratt that will enable them to fully develop their interests and talents. Electives may be chosen from any department in the Institute; an enormous menu of courses is available for the pursuit of individual interests.

- Design I, II, III, IV, V, VI
- Construction Systems
- Working Drawings
- Construction Documents
- Architectural Drawing
- Color And Materials
- Lighting Design
- Environmental Theory
- Directed Research
- Furniture Design
- Presentation Techniques
- CADD I, II, III

The program culminates with a thesis project; students may test their competence in all aspects of the profession, or pursue an academic research-oriented approach to study emerging issues and problems. The Exhibition Design Intensive is an alternative to the traditional thesis track and offers students a one-year immersion in exhibition design in the final year.

INTERNSHIPS

Not required. Most students have worked at one to two internships before graduating. Experiences range from work in large interiors or architecture office to small practitioners.

STUDY ABROAD

Junior year spring term in Copenhagen at DIS
summer study for graduates and undergraduates in Copenhagen at DIS

NOTABLE ALUMNI

Not reported

STUDENT ACTIVITIES AND ORGANIZATIONS

Tarp—student run sustainable design magazine, *CSDS*—sustainable design organization

FACULTY SPECIALIZATIONS AND RESEARCH

Not reported

Rochester Institute of Technology

School of Design, College of Imaging Arts and Sciences

73 Lomb Memorial Dr., Rochester, NY 14623 | http://cias.rit.edu/design

UNIVERSITY PROFILE
Private
Suburban
Residential
Commuter
Semester Schedule
Co-ed

STUDENT DEMOGRAPHICS
Undergraduate: 11,118
Graduate: 5,655

Male: 65%
Female: 35%

Full-time: 98%
Part-time: 2%

EXPENSES
Tuition: $28,866
Room & Board: $9,259

ADMISSIONS
Bausch & Lomb Center
60 Lomb Memorial Dr.
Rochester, NY 14623
585-475-6631
admissions@rit.edu

DEGREE INFORMATION

Major / Degree / Concentration	Enrollment	Requirements for entry	Graduation rate
Interior Design Bachelor of Fine Arts	80	Portfolio review	98%

TOTAL PROGRAM ENROLLMENT
Undergraduate: 80
Graduate: Not reported

Male: 5%
Female: 95%

Full-time: 100%
Part-time: 0%

International: 5%
Minority: 5%

Job Placement Rate: Not reported

SCHOLARSHIPS / FINANCIAL AID
Scholarships and Financial Aid are
administered by the Office of Financial
Aid in the Admissions Department

TOTAL FACULTY: 6
Full-time: 2.5
Part-time: 4
Online: 0

NCIDQ Certified: 50%
Licensed Interior Designers: 33%
LEED Certified: 40%

INTERIOR DESIGN ADMINISTRATION
Patti LaChance, Chair, School of Design
Charles Lewis, AIA, Professor and Chair,
  Department of Interior Design

PROFESSIONAL / ACADEMIC AFFILIATIONS
Interior Design Educators Council

CIDA ACCREDITATION
Bachelor of Fine Arts (2007, 2013)

PROGRAM DESCRIPTION AND PHILOSOPHY

This CIDA Accredited program acknowledges that interior design is the creative integration of form, materials, function, and aesthetics within interior space. To accomplish this the designer must develop an understanding of, and sensitivity to, past history, future technology, environment, economics, architecture and societal needs and aspirations. We aspire to educate students to be designers who contribute to their professions, communicate effectively within their discipline, have a life-long attitude of inquiry and make a positive impact on society. To this end, we promote an innovative educational community that balances expression, imaginative problem-solving, aesthetic understanding, professional responsibility and creativity.

FACILITIES

Wallace Center, numerous computer labs, Model Shop, Interior Studios, Interior Design Resource library, Vignelli Center

ONLINE / DISTANCE LEARNING

Not available

COURSES OF INSTRUCTION

- Architectural Drawing
- Model Building & Human Dimension
- Interior Perspective Rendering
- CAD
- Intro to Interior Design
- Hospitality Design
- Application of Color and Light
- Retail Design Interior Specifications
- Office Design & Planning
- Building Construction Systems
- History of Architecture
- Interiors and Furniture
- Multi-story/Multi-purpose Design
- Building Codes and Regulations
- Environmental Control Application
- Career Planning
- Working Drawings
- Health-care Design
- Business Practices and Special Projects
- In addition students are expected to take Foundation courses and Liberal Art courses

INTERNSHIPS

Not required of majors. Students are employed in architectural firms, Interior Design consulting firms, corporations, and institutions primarily in New York State, along the Eastern seaboard, and the west coast.

STUDY ABROAD

Study Abroad Office—Students may elect study abroad through numerous other university programs.

NOTABLE ALUMNI

Not reported

STUDENT ACTIVITIES AND ORGANIZATIONS

Student Interior Design Club

FACULTY SPECIALIZATIONS AND RESEARCH

- Architecture
- Preservation
- Sustainable Design
- Designing Spaces with Pets in Mind

School of Visual Arts

Interior Design Department

133 West 21st St., 11th floor, New York, NY 10011 | 212-592-2572 | www.sva.edu

DEGREE INFORMATION

Major / Degree / Concentration	Enrollment	Requirements for entry	Graduation rate
Interior Design Bachelor of Fine Arts	61	Portfolio review Essay	100%

TOTAL PROGRAM ENROLLMENT
Undergraduate: 61
Graduate: Not reported

Male: 5%
Female: 95%

Full-time: 98%
Part-time: 2%

International: Not reported
Minority: Not reported

Job Placement Rate: 90%

SCHOLARSHIPS / FINANCIAL AID
Financial aid consists of scholarships, grants, loans, and work-study. Scholarships and grants are considered gift aid, as these awards do not have to be paid back. Loans and work-study are considered self-help, as students must repay loans or work to earn the award. Students are considered for merit based awards because of their academic performance and achievement while a student's financial information is considered for need based awards.

TOTAL FACULTY: 26
Full-time: Not reported
Part-time: 100%
Online: Not reported

NCIDQ Certified: Not reported
Licensed Interior Designers: Not reported
LEED Certified: 20%

INTERIOR DESIGN ADMINISTRATION
Jane Smith, Chair
Simone Clemente, Assistant to the Chair
Damon Dixon, Systems Administrator

PROFESSIONAL / ACADEMIC AFFILIATIONS
American Society of Interior Designers
International Interior Design Association
Interior Design Educators Council

CIDA ACCREDITATION
Bachelor of Fine Arts in Interior Design (2004, 2010)

PROGRAM DESCRIPTION AND PHILOSOPHY

The Interior Design department specializes in educating students whose primary interest is entering the profession of Interior Design in areas that emphasize inventiveness over routine practice.

The chief mission of the Interior Design program centers on developing a sense of professionalism, with creativity, among its students to prepare them for the keenly competitive demands of the complex Interior Design world. Professionalism is equated not only with the development of personal standards and discipline that are integral to the realities of the work place but, seeks to instill a measure of responsibility to humanity.

The department strives to educate the Interior Design student as designer, practitioner and well-rounded individual. The intellectual, aesthetic, and ethical development of the student is essential. Theoretical, critical, and philosophical topics are explored in order to introduce new areas of rational and intuitive understanding to the students' abilities to evaluate their own work and that of others. Our graduates should be able to function not just as design professionals, but as thinking individuals who are aware of how we live and work in the world we build.

FACILITIES

We are extremely proud of the caliber of academic and professional faculty members and instructional personnel that are associated with the department. We are able to draw from industry leaders that provide the highest levels of expertise, experience and varying points of view and who are dedicated to providing the students with the most current information available in a constantly changing world

ONLINE / DISTANCE LEARNING

Not available

COURSES OF INSTRUCTION

Year 1 (Foundation Courses)
Drafting: Basic Building Systems
Drawing: Perspective
Principles of Interior Design
Introduction to Designing Interiors
Computer-Aided Drafting and Design/ CAD Lab
Introduction to Computer Design
Furniture and Finishings

Year 2
Design Studio I & II
Color Theory and Rendering
Building and Interior Systems I & II
World Architecture: Art and Interior Design
Western Architecture: Art and Interior Design
Current Issues in Interior Design by Visiting Professionals I & II
Interior Materials and Finishes
Interior Detailing

Year 3
Design Studio III & IV
Lighting and Specialty Design
Modern and Contemporary Interiors
Influences in Contemporary Interiors
Sustainable Design

Year 4
Design Studio V: Thesis & Design Studio VI: Thesis/Portfolio
Interior Design: Professional Practice
Practical Applications for the Interior Design Professional

INTERNSHIPS

Required of majors at 2nd Year. SVA Interior Design students work in a variety of firms, large and small, in all aspects of Interior Design and architecture, showroom, etc. Some notable firms that have employed and/or interned our students are Gensler, Perkins & Will, HB Design, HOK, Corgan Architects, INARCH, Spacesmith, Avena, to name a few.

STUDY ABROAD

SVA offers both summer abroad and semester abroad programs. Summer Arts Abroad programs are up to three weeks in length and are open to anyone who meets the course prerequisites.

Third year, matriculated students may apply to the International Exchange Program (IEP) to study abroad for one semester at an affiliated exchange partner institution. Countries currently represented in the IEP include France, Germany, Israel, Italy, the Netherlands, Norway, Spain, Sweden, Switzerland, Portugal and the United Kingdom.

NOTABLE ALUMNI

Not reported

STUDENT ACTIVITIES AND ORGANIZATIONS

Not reported

FACULTY SPECIALIZATIONS AND RESEARCH

We are extremely proud of the caliber of academic and professional faculty members and instructional personnel that are associated with the department. We are able to draw from industry leaders that provide the highest levels of expertise, experience and varying points of view and who are dedicated to providing the students with the most current information available in a constantly changing world.

Syracuse University

Department of Design, College of Visual & Performing Arts

The Warehouse, 350 W. Fayette St., Syracuse, NY 13202 | 315 443 2455 | http://vpa.syr.edu/art-design/design/

UNIVERSITY PROFILE
Private
Urban
Residential
Semester Schedule
Co-ed

STUDENT DEMOGRAPHICS
Undergraduate: 13,000
Graduate: 5,000

Male: 42%
Female: 58%

Full-time: 99%
Part-time: 1%

EXPENSES
Tuition: $34,970
Room & Board: $12,850

ADMISSIONS
202 Crouse Collge
College of Visual and
Performing Arts
Syracuse, NY 13244
315-443-2769
admissu@syr.edu

DEGREE INFORMATION

Major / Degree / Concentration	Enrollment	Requirements for entry	Graduation rate
Interior Design Bachelor of Fine Arts	100	Portfolio review	99%

TOTAL PROGRAM ENROLLMENT
Undergraduate: 100
Graduate: 0

Male: 5%
Female: 95%

Full-time: 99%
Part-time: 1%

International: 10%
Minority: 15%

Job Placement Rate: 80%

SCHOLARSHIPS / FINANCIAL AID
Not reported

TOTAL FACULTY: 8
Full-time: 65%
Part-time: 35%
Online: 0%

NCIDQ Certified: 12%
Licensed Interior Designers: 12%
LEED Certified: 12%

INTERIOR DESIGN ADMINISTRATION
Sarah Redmore, Program Coordinator
Lucinda Havenhand, Chair Department of Design
Tracey Myers, Administrative Assistant

PROFESSIONAL / ACADEMIC AFFILIATIONS
American Society of Interior Designers
Interior Design Educators Council
Environmental Design Research Association

CIDA ACCREDITATION
Bachelor of Fine Arts in Interior Design (2009, 2015)

PROGRAM DESCRIPTION AND PHILOSOPHY

We facilitate the development of curious and critical thinkers. Students thoughtfully consider, challenge, and engage existing perceptions within a broadly diverse educational setting to effect positive change in a constantly evolving global environment.

FACILITIES

PC Lab, Mac Lab, Technical Fabrication Shop, Wood and Metals Shop, Plastic Shop, Fabric Printing, Sewing Lab, SU Art Galleries, Design Gallery, Everson Museum of Art, SU Archives, SU Lubin House NYC

ONLINE / DISTANCE LEARNING

Not available

COURSES OF INSTRUCTION

- Environmental Design I, II, III, IV
- Environmental Factors
- Design
- Culture and Sustainability
- Design Issues
- Furniture and Light Workshop
- Communication and Presentation I and II
- Professional Practice
- Environmental Design Thesis

INTERNSHIPS

Not required for majors but available to students with Junior standing. Interns are typically placed at companies such as Perkins + Will, Design Continuum, King and King, Cook + Fox, Tom Filicia Designs, Swanke Hayden Connell.

STUDY ABROAD

London and Florence

NOTABLE ALUMNI

Tom Filicia *"Queer Eye for the Straight Guy"* and *"Dress My Nest"*

STUDENT ACTIVITIES AND ORGANIZATIONS

ASID, Student Compeitions, COLAB (Collaborative Laboratory S.U., Multidisciplinary Charettes, Office of Community Engagement projects, "Scholarship in Action." Students have direct engagement with the community, with real projects, in relation to other design disciplines and academic units around the campus as well as will corporate sponsors.

FACULTY SPECIALIZATIONS AND RESEARCH

- Design Research and Theory
- Sustainability
- Fabrication and Construction
- Materials
- Socially Conscious Design

Villa Maria College

Interior Design Program

240 Pine Ridge Rd., Buffalo, NY 14225 | 716-961-1843 | www.villa.edu/interior_design.html

UNIVERSITY PROFILE
Private
Urban
Commuter
Semester Schedule
Co-ed

STUDENT DEMOGRAPHICS
Undergraduate: 525
Graduate: n/a

Male: Not reported
Female: Not reported

Full-time: Not reported
Part-time: Not reported

EXPENSES
Tuition: $15,100
Room & Board: Not reported

ADMISSIONS
240 Pine Ridge Rd.
Buffalo, NY 14225
(716) 961-1805
admissions@villa.edu

DEGREE INFORMATION

Major / Degree / Concentration	Enrollment	Requirements for entry	Graduation rate
Interior Design Assistant Associate in Applied Science	Not reported	Not reported	Not reported
Interior Design Bachelor of Fine Arts	Not reported	Not reported	Not reported

TOTAL PROGRAM ENROLLMENT
Undergraduate: 80
Graduate: Not reported

Male: 30%
Female: 70%

Full-time: 75%
Part-time: 25%

International: Not reported
Minority: Not reported

Job Placement Rate: n/a

SCHOLARSHIPS / FINANCIAL AID
See opposite page for more info.

TOTAL FACULTY: 4
Full-time: Not reported
Part-time: Not reported
Online: Not reported

NCIDQ Certified: 2
Licensed Interior Designers: 4
LEED Certified: Not reported

INTERIOR DESIGN ADMINISTRATION
Sandra Reicis

PROFESSIONAL / ACADEMIC AFFILIATIONS
Not reported

PROGRAM DESCRIPTION AND PHILOSOPHY

Interior Design program mission
The Interior Design Program mission encompasses the following five broad-based goals:

- To provide concepts and skills necessary for students preparing for professional careers in Interior Design
- To maintain acceptable academic and professional standards of performance
- To prepare graduates for advanced or graduate study and/or entry into the design field
- To develop off campus experiences through community projects, field trips, seminars, internships and travel abroad opportunities toward preparing design students to meet the demands of contemporary business and industry
- To prepare students to think critically, write clearly, and speak persuasively

To achieve the goals outlined above, the Interior Design Program at Villa Maria College integrates specific Interior Design courses with art foundation and liberal art courses, providing students with a well-balanced, integrated program of study.

FACILITIES

Two fully-equipped CAD studios, rendering lab, art shop facility and Interior Design resource room

ONLINE / DISTANCE LEARNING

None are offered online.

COURSES OF INSTRUCTION

- Drawing I
- Design I
- Communications
- Color Theory
- History of Interior Architecture
- Materials and Surfaces
- Construction and Building Systems
- Kitchen and Bath
- Environment
- Behavior and Design
- Professional Practices
- Safety and Accessibility
- Six CAD studio course options

INTERNSHIPS

Required of majors.

STUDY ABROAD

Available

NOTABLE ALUMNI

Not reported

STUDENT ACTIVITIES AND ORGANIZATIONS

Interior Design club and several student, service-based clubs

FACULTY SPECIALIZATIONS AND RESEARCH

Not reported

SCHOLARSHIPS / FINANCIAL AID

Villa Maria College has a dedicated staff of financial aid professionals willing to help students and parents throughout the entire financial aid process. The financial aid staff provides support in submitting the FAFSA, TAP, loan applications and loan counseling. The goal of the Financial Aid Office is to discuss to the students and parents all the options that exist in financing a college education at Villa Maria College.

Of the students enrolled at Villa Maria College for 2009-2010, 94% received some sort of financial aid. Villa Maria College works with each student on a need by need basis in evaluating for institutional grants or endowed scholarships available that particular academic year. Students can also qualify for merit based scholarships.

Students and parents are encouraged at anytime during their time at Villa Maria College to make an appointment with the Financial aid Office to discuss their concerns and questions about the financial aid process.

Bowling Green State University

Interior Design Program, School of Family and Consumer Sciences

Johnston Hall, BGSU, Bowling Green, OH 43403 | 419-372-2505 | www.bgsu.edu/colleges/edhd/fcs/interior

UNIVERSITY PROFILE
Public
Suburban
Residential
Semester Schedule
Co-ed

STUDENT DEMOGRAPHICS
Undergraduate: 17,000
Graduate: 3,000

Male: Not reported
Female: Not reported

Full-time: Not reported
Part-time: Not reported

EXPENSES
Tuition: $9,060 (in-state);
$23,978 (out-of-state)
Room & Board: $7,610

ADMISSIONS
110 McFall Center
Bowling Green State
University
Bowling Green, OH 43403
419-372-BGSU

DEGREE INFORMATION

Major / Degree / Concentration	Enrollment	Requirements for entry	Graduation rate
Interior Design Bachelor of Science	110	Acceptance to BGSU College of Education and Human Development Portfolio Review at the end of 1st year design studies	90%

TOTAL PROGRAM ENROLLMENT
Undergraduate: 110
Graduate: 0

Male: Not reported
Female: Not reported

Full-time: 98
Part-time: Not reported

International: Not reported
Minority: Not reported

Job Placement Rate: Not reported

SCHOLARSHIPS / FINANCIAL AID
Approximately 60% of BGSU students receive financial aid. www.busu.edu/colleges/edhd/scholarships

TOTAL FACULTY: 5
Full-time: 90%
Part-time: 10%
Online: Not reported

NCIDQ Certified: 2
Licensed Interior Designers: 2
LEED Certified: 1

INTERIOR DESIGN ADMINISTRATION
Dr. Deborah Wooldridge Ph.D., Professor
Director, School of Family and Consumer Sciences

PROFESSIONAL / ACADEMIC AFFILIATIONS
American Society of Interior Designers
International Interior Design Association
Interior Design Educators Council
Council of Architecture
Indian Institute of Architects
World Society of Ekistics
Design Research Society (Fellow)
EDRA
IHPP
ASA
AACS
Institute for High-Performance Planners

PROGRAM DESCRIPTION AND PHILOSOPHY

The 4-year degree program is structured to provide students with the knowledge and eligibility to take the NCIDQ Exam. The program is a mix of art, technology, and design students engaged in real-world experiences through Interior Design work co-ops. The curriculum provides a unique experience for students to take courses in collaboration with the School of Art, College of Technology, and College of Education and Human Development.

FACILITIES

Computer lab
Interior Design lab with workstations for computer and model-making
Toledo Museum of Art

ONLINE / DISTANCE LEARNING

Not reported

COURSES OF INSTRUCTION

- Lighting design for the Interior Environment
- Specifications, Codes, and Special Needs
- Green, Sustainable, and Universal Design for the Built Environment
- Contemporary Interiors
- Residential Design Studios
- History of Interiors
- Commercial Design Studios

INTERNSHIPS

Required of majors at Junior and Senior levels. Interns are typically placed at architectural, Interior Design firms, hospitality, and health-care.

STUDY ABROAD

Internships abroad in London, England, and the Sacci Program through School of Art in Florence.

NOTABLE ALUMNI

Not reported

STUDENT ACTIVITIES AND ORGANIZATIONS

Student Chapter of ASID, IIDA chapter

FACULTY SPECIALIZATIONS AND RESEARCH

- Facility Programming/Planning
- Sociocultural Aspects of Built Environment
- Design Research Methods
- Environment Behavior
- Sustainability in Design
- Design Education and the Profession
- Cultural Diversity and Design Education
- Expansion of Global AE and C Firms in Emerging Markets

College of Mount St. Joseph

Department of Interior Architecture and Design

Dorothy Meyer Ziv Art & Design Building, 5701 Delhi Rd., Cincinnati, OH 45233 | 513-244-4200 | http://www.msj.edu/

UNIVERSITY PROFILE
Private
Suburban
Commuter
Semester Schedule
Co-ed

STUDENT DEMOGRAPHICS
Undergraduate: 1,732
Graduate: 381

Male: 45%
Female: 55%

Full-time: 79%
Part-time: 21%

EXPENSES
Tuition: $21,200
Room & Board: $6,900

ADMISSIONS
College of Mt St Joseph
Admission Office
Cincinnati, OH 45233
513-244-4531
peggy_minnich@mail.msj.edu

DEGREE INFORMATION

Major / Degree / Concentration	Enrollment	Requirements for entry	Graduation rate
Interior Architecture and Design Bachelor of Fine Arts plus Marketing Minor	8	Acceptance to 3.0 gpa; Portfolio not required for Freshmen; Portfolio review after Sophomore year	Not reported

TOTAL PROGRAM ENROLLMENT
Undergraduate: 65
Graduate: Not reported

Male: 10%
Female: 90%

Full-time: 80%
Part-time: 20%

International: 1%
Minority: 1%

Job Placement Rate: Not reported

SCHOLARSHIPS / FINANCIAL AID
80% of Mount St. Joseph students receive scholarships/financial aid; the average package is $14,882. There are 7 scholarships exclusive to Art and Design with an additional 3 scholarships for upperclassmen.

TOTAL FACULTY: 5
Full-time: 40%
Part-time: 60%
Online: Not reported

NCIDQ Certified: 50%
Licensed Interior Designers: n/a
LEED Certified: 20%

INTERIOR DESIGN ADMINISTRATION
Kimberly Burke, Program Chair

PROFESSIONAL / ACADEMIC AFFILIATIONS
American Society of Interior Designers
International Interior Design Association
Interior Design Educators Council

PROGRAM DESCRIPTION AND PHILOSOPHY

The IAD+M program is an integrated, interdisciplinary sequence of courses which builds upon the strengths of a Liberal Arts and Sciences foundation, the user-centered, problem-solving skills and insights of Design and the goal-oriented, globally aware responsiveness of Marketing. This 4-year program will give graduates the knowledge and skills to unlock new opportunities in today's fast-paced economy. This preprofessional program offers the foundation for multiple career tracks or graduate study, including Interior Architecture, Architecture, Landscape Architecture, Product Design, Environmental Graphic Design, Socially Responsible Design, Environmental/Behavior Science, Anthropology, Management, Business, Marketing, Advertising, and Communications.

FACILITIES

Students are active in both ASID and IIDSA, as well as in sports, student government, campus events, student clubs and organizations, and the many service-learning opportunities at the Mount.

ONLINE / DISTANCE LEARNING

Not reported

COURSES OF INSTRUCTION

- 2D Design
- 3D Design
- Drawing
- Design Foundation
- Human-Centered Design: How We Live, Work, Play
- 21st Century Work
- Systems and Scale
- Landscape, Architecture, Interiors, Exhibition and Wayfinding
- Branded Environments
- Senior Thesis
- Visual Communication I - IV
- Lighting, Materials; Construction/ Structures, Environmental Tech.
- History of Architecture and Design; Sociology/Anthropology
- Principles of Marketing, Persuasion in the Marketplace
- Consumer Behavior
- International Marketing
- Market Research, World Communication

INTERNSHIPS

Not required

STUDY ABROAD

Available at Huron University in London

NOTABLE ALUMNI

Not reported

STUDENT ACTIVITIES AND ORGANIZATIONS

Students are active in both ASID and IIDSA, as well as in sports, student government, campus events, student clubs and organizations, and the many service-learning opportunities at the Mount.

FACULTY SPECIALIZATIONS AND RESEARCH

- Branded Environments and Experience Design
- Workplace Design
- Exhibtion and Digital Exhibition
- Cultural Heritage—Museums and Parks
- Business Management and Marketing
- Design Research, Strategy and Design Process
- Interdisciplinary Design
- Anthropology and Material Culture

Miami University

Department of Architecture & Interior Design, School of Fine Arts

101 Alumni Hall, Oxford, OH 45046 | 513-529-7210 | www.muohio.edu/interiordesign

UNIVERSITY PROFILE
Public
Rural
Residential
Semester Schedule
Co-ed

STUDENT DEMOGRAPHICS
Undergraduate: 14,671
Graduate: 2,213

Male: 46.1%
Female: 53.9%

Full-time: Not reported
Part-time: Not reported

EXPENSES
Tuition: $11,442 (in-state):
$26,202 (out-of-state)
Room & Board: $9,458

ADMISSIONS
301 S. Campus Ave.
Oxford, OH 45056
513-529-2531
oxfadmission@muohio.edu

DEGREE INFORMATION

Major / Degree / Concentration	Enrollment	Requirements for entry	Graduation rate
Interior Design Bachelor of Fine Arts	72	Admission into the university first, and then portfolio-based admission to the department. Admission to the major is possible in Fall only.	95%
Architecture Bachelor of Arts	280	Admission into the university first, and then portfolio-based admission to the department. Admission to the major is possible in Fall only.	95%

TOTAL PROGRAM ENROLLMENT
Undergraduate: 72
Graduate: 0

Male: 5%
Female: 95%

Full-time: 100%
Part-time: 0%

International: 5%
Minority: 5%

Job Placement Rate: 85%

SCHOLARSHIPS / FINANCIAL AID
Not reported

TOTAL FACULTY: 33
Full-time: 70%
Part-time: 30%
Online: 0%

NCIDQ Certified: 33%
Licensed Interior Designers: 0%
LEED Certified: 33%

INTERIOR DESIGN ADMINISTRATION
John Weigand, Chair and Professor, Department of Architecture and Interior Design
Craig Hinrichs, Graduate Program Director (M-ARC) and Associate Professor
Gulen Cevik, Interior Design Program Director and Assistant Professor

PROFESSIONAL / ACADEMIC AFFILIATIONS
International Interior Design Association
Interior Design Educators Council

CIDA ACCREDITATION
Bachelor of Fine Arts in Interior Design (2009, 2015)

PROGRAM DESCRIPTION AND PHILOSOPHY

Miami's program in Interior Design is one of a small number of programs administratively aligned with the major in architecture. The partnership within the department reflects the association between Interior Designers and architects in current practice and reinforces the interdisciplinary nature of design education. The program also draws on the strength of Miami's liberal arts education tradition by requiring coursework from several related programs across campus. Our student/faculty ratio for studio classes rarely exceeds 15:1.

FACILITIES

Within our specific building, students are provided with an in-house computer lab and printing facilities, a full woodshop, CNC Router, Materials Library, and the Wertz Art and Architecture Library which boasts over 60,000 titles. Additional on-campus facilities include computer labs and large format print facilities available within walking distance. We also have access to additional shop facilities within the school of engineering.

ONLINE / DISTANCE LEARNING
Not available

COURSES OF INSTRUCTION

First Year - Foundation Studios in design principles and graphic communication. The first year studios are combined with the major in architecture. First year students will also begin working on The Miami Plan (well-rounded course of study designed to provide a strong liberal arts base educations with exposure to humanities, social sciences, natural sciences, fine arts, and formal reasoning).

Second and Third Year—Courses of study include history and theory, computer-aided design, human factors, materials, and furniture design. These are designed to support the studio courses. During the summers following these two years, students are encouraged to pursue for-credit internships to gain practical experience.

Fourth Year - Becomes more self directed. In the fall, students will take a comprehensive studio where they undertake a single, semester-long project where they handle all the phases of a job and bring the project to completion. In the spring semester, students will take a Senior thesis studio where they concentrate on a project of their own choosing. This may be a real life project in conjunction with a firm or community organization.

INTERNSHIPS

Not required, but strongly encouraged at 2nd & 3rd years. Most graduates work in commercial Interior Design firms, architecture firms, and furniture dealerships. Other graduates choose careers in facilities management, historic preservation, retail sales, lighting design, sustainable design, or teaching. Specific Companies inlcude: Gensler, Callison, HOK, Perkins+Will, FRCH, Banish, BHDP, Pottery Barn, and Anthropologie among others.

STUDY ABROAD

Opportunities include Luxembourg, Italy, Switzerland, Turkey, Munich, Ghana—West Africa, and China as summer workshops or semester long experiences.

NOTABLE ALUMNI
Not reported

STUDENT ACTIVITIES AND ORGANIZATIONS

Students can also choose to participate in AIAS, and Green Oxford in addition to those listed below.

FACULTY SPECIALIZATIONS AND RESEARCH
Not reported

Ohio University

School of Art

528 Seigfred Hall, Athens, OH 45701 | 800-766-8278 | www.finearts.ohio.edu/art/

UNIVERSITY PROFILE
Public
Rural
Residential
Quarter Schedule
Co-ed

STUDENT DEMOGRAPHICS
Undergraduate: 17,000
Graduate: 5,000

Male: Not reported
Female: Not reported

Full-time: Not reported
Part-time: Not reported

EXPENSES
Tuition: $8,000
Room & Board: $8,000

ADMISSIONS
120 Chubb Hall
Athens, OH 45701
740-593-4100

DEGREE INFORMATION

Major / Degree / Concentration	Enrollment	Requirements for entry	Graduation rate
Human & Consumer Sciences **Bachelor of Science** Interior Architecture	100	2.0 gpa Competitive Portfolio Review	95%

TOTAL PROGRAM ENROLLMENT
Undergraduate: 100
Graduate: Not reported

Male: 10%
Female: 90%

Full-time: 100%
Part-time: Not reported

International: 8%
Minority: 5%

Job Placement Rate: 85%

SCHOLARSHIPS / FINANCIAL AID
General university scholarship potential, limited interior-design-specific scholarships.

TOTAL FACULTY: 4
Full-time: 100%
Part-time: Not reported
Online: Not reported

NCIDQ Certified: 50%
Licensed Interior Designers: Not reported
LEED Certified: 50%

INTERIOR DESIGN ADMINISTRATION
Matthew Ziff, Associate Professor, Area Coordinator
Vincent Wojtas, Assistant Professor
Tommy Crane, Assistant Professor

PROFESSIONAL / ACADEMIC AFFILIATIONS
Interior Design Educators Council

CIDA ACCREDITATION
Bachelor of Science (2007, 2013)

PROGRAM DESCRIPTION AND PHILOSOPHY

The mission of the Interior Architecture faculty is to provide an educational foundation that prepares graduates for entry-level positions in the interior design profession as well as preparing them for leadership positions in management and design. The Interior Architecture program's goals fall in line with those listed for the School of Human and Consumer Sciences. Additionally other major goals of the program are to provide learning experiences that enable the individual to solve interior space problems through creative exploration, research, assessment, and understanding of the psychological, sociological, and economic needs of those individuals for whom the project is being designed. The program engages a knowledge base that includes: design fundamentals, design analysis, programming, space planning, materials applications, lighting design, technical information (e.g. building codes and written specifications), the integration of digital technology for both exploration and presentation of ideas, and an understanding of the role of aesthetics in design and related disciplines.

FACILITIES

Program dedicated studio spaces, college computer labs, art studios, wood shop, museum facility.

ONLINE / DISTANCE LEARNING

No online major option

COURSES OF INSTRUCTION

- Lighting Fundamentals
- Materials and Contruction
- Color Theory
- Professional Practices in Interior Design
- History of Interiors I, II, III, Sequential Studio Curriculum of 9 Design Studio Courses culminating with a Senior Thesis Studio Senior year

INTERNSHIPS

Required of majors at Junior/Senior level. Interns are typically placed at companies including Interior Design, Architecture & Interior Design, Furniture Showrooms, Coroprate Design Departments.

STUDY ABROAD

Program trip to Asia, and many university based international study options.

NOTABLE ALUMNI

Not reported

STUDENT ACTIVITIES AND ORGANIZATIONS

Student Design Group

FACULTY SPECIALIZATIONS AND RESEARCH

- Environmental Issues in Design
- Design Philosophy
- Materials in Design

The Ohio State University

Department of Design, College of the Arts

128 North Oval Mall, Columbus, OH 43210 | 614-292-6746 | http://design.osu.edu/

UNIVERSITY PROFILE
Public
Urban
Quarter Schedule
Co-ed

STUDENT DEMOGRAPHICS
Undergraduate: 300
Graduate: 50

Male: 40%
Female: 60%

Full-time: 90%
Part-time: 20%

EXPENSES
Tuition: $8,500
Room & Board: Not reported

ADMISSIONS
Department of Design
380 Hopkins Hall
Columbus, OH 43210
614-292-6746
design@osu.edu

DEGREE INFORMATION

Major / Degree / Concentration	Enrollment	Requirements for entry	Graduation rate
Interior Space Design Bachelor of Science	100	2.5 gpa Entrance exam	90%

TOTAL PROGRAM ENROLLMENT
Undergraduate: 100
Graduate: 15

Male: 15%
Female: 85%

Full-time: 100%
Part-time: Not reported

International: 20%
Minority: 20%

Job Placement Rate: 90%

SCHOLARSHIPS / FINANCIAL AID
Scholarships and financial aid is coordinated by the universities admissions office, please check Web site: www.osu.edu

TOTAL FACULTY: 12
Full-time: 3 within the major + 9 for support courses
Part-time: 3
Online: Not reported

NCIDQ Certified: Not reported
Licensed Interior Designers: 1
LEED Certified: Not reported

INTERIOR DESIGN ADMINISTRATION
Paul Nini, Chairperson
Heike Goeller, Head of Interior Design
Jeff Haase, Interior Design coordinator

PROFESSIONAL / ACADEMIC AFFILIATIONS
American Society of Interior Designers
International Interior Design Association
Interior Design Educators Council

CIDA ACCREDITATION
Bachelor of Science in Design (2009, 2015)

PROGRAM DESCRIPTION AND PHILOSOPHY

Interior Space Design is directed towards the study, planning, and development of interior environments for human activity. Emphasis is on the aesthetics, efficiency, comfort, safety, and quality of interiors for commerncial, recreational, and institutional applications. The philosophy of the interior space dsign program is to prepare graduates to enter the professional practice of interior design and to contribute to its ongoing development. Utilizing a systematic problem solving and user-oriented approach the student will develop the professional competencies, skills, understanding, knowledge, and creative ability to design innovative interior environments.

FACILITIES

The Ohio State University is one of the 10 large land-grant universities offering courses ranging from agriculture and aviation to zoology... facilities include large and small research libraries (20) and archives, inside and outside athletic and recreational facilities, art galleries (including the Wexner Center for Experimental Art) numerous computer labs (including the Art and Design Advanced Computing Center) to only name a few...the university's Web site www.osu.edu offers detailed lists

ONLINE / DISTANCE LEARNING

Not available

COURSES OF INSTRUCTION
- Design orientation
- Drawing
- Color theory
- Art
- Architecture and design history
- Basic design
- Computer rendering courses
- Presentation techniques
- Design methodology
- Materials and processes
- Statistics
- Communication
- Business administration
- Retail design
- Restaurant design
- Exhibition design
- Lighting design
- Space psychology
- Ergonomics and anthropomentrics
- Professional practices

INTERNSHIPS

Required of majors at Junior level. Interns are typically placed at architectural offices, Interior Design offices, and furniture dealers

STUDY ABROAD

Formal exchange agreements with European universities, and also with Mexico and Taiwan

NOTABLE ALUMNI

Elle Chute, Chute Gerdeman Design Group
Karen Stone, Design Director Knoll International New York
Linda Gable Interior Design Director at NBBJ
Bob Lhota, Design Director at the GAP, San Francisco
Anthony Guido, Chairman UArts Philadelphia

Kelly Mooney, President and Chief Experience Officer at Resource Interactive
Justine Carlton, Director of Interior Design Research Lextant
Dale Greenwald, Director of Interior Design at Callison, N.Y.
Gene McHugh, Principle at Design Collective
Brian Shafley, President at Chute Gerdeman
Ann Black, Associate Professor, University of Cincinnati
Ed Dorsa, Assistant Director, Associate Professor, Virginia Tech School of Architecture + Design
Tom Morbitzer, Owner/Partner TUG Studio
Muqeem Khan, Assistant Professor at VCU Qatar
Pam Marcotte, Pam Marcotte Design
Linda Gabel, Senior Associate NBBJ

STUDENT ACTIVITIES AND ORGANIZATIONS

Numerous student organizations offer a variety of activities for all OSU students throughout the year; the Department of Design's student organization focuses on student mentorships, professional organization contacts, organization of special topic lectures, and fieldtrips to design offices.

FACULTY SPECIALIZATIONS AND RESEARCH
- Representation techniques
- Human and Environmental Psychology
- Design oriented cultural differences
- Sustainablity and Community Outreach Design Collaboration

University of Akron

Department of Clothing, Textiles, and Interior Design

School of Family & Consumer Sciences, 215 Schrank Hall South, Akron, OH 44325 | 330-972-7721 | www.uakron.edu

DEGREE INFORMATION

Major / Degree / Concentration	Enrollment	Requirements for entry	Graduation rate
Interior Design Bachelor of Arts	90	2.3 gpa Portfolio review after Sophomore year	99.9%

TOTAL PROGRAM ENROLLMENT
Undergraduate: 90
Graduate: 0

Male: 1%
Female: 99%

Full-time: 99%
Part-time: 1%

International: 6%
Minority: 4%

Job Placement Rate: 95%

SCHOLARSHIPS / FINANCIAL AID
The Leona W. Farris Scholarship for black university students; the Dr. Virginia L. Gunn Scholarship in Family and Consumer Sciences given to a non-traditional student; the Fred A. Kronseder and Helen W. Kronseder Scholarship; The Mae C. O'Neil Scholarship; The Clarissa D. Rainey, M.D. and Clarence W. Rainey, M.D. Scholarship; Family and Consumer Science Scholarship for residents of Lorain County, Ohio; The Akron-Canton Chapter and The Cleveland Chapter of the Construction Specification Institute; and the Home Builders Association Serving Portage and Summit Counties, Ohio. Other scholarships are advertised and listed on the program Web sites as they become available.

TOTAL FACULTY: 4
Full-time: 2
Part-time: 2
Online: 0

NCIDQ Certified: 2
Licensed Interior Designers: 1
LEED Certified: 0

INTERIOR DESIGN ADMINISTRATION
Sue Rasor-Greenhalgh, Interim Director, School of Family and Consumer Sciences, Professor
John L. Vollmer, Director, Interior Design Program, Associate Professor
Julie Whitmore, Assistant Professor, Interior Design

PROFESSIONAL / ACADEMIC AFFILIATIONS
American Society of Interior Designers
International Interior Design Association
Interior Design Educators Council

CIDA ACCREDITATION
Bachelor of Arts in Interior Design (2009, 2015)

PROGRAM DESCRIPTION AND PHILOSOPHY

- To provide a broad-based general education by requiring a broad-based core of liberal arts and sciences course which develop the skills and knowledge essential for all graduates of four-year baccalaureate programs.
- To provide a common core in family and consumer sciences by requiring a broad-based core of family and consumer science courses which provide the common knowledge-base for understanding the role of serving individuals and families in the environments in which they live and work.
- To provide a common body of knowledge of Interior Design by requiring a core of courses which reflects the common body of knowledge required in professional level programs of Interior Design.
- To maintain high-quality standards for Interior Design education through professional accreditation.
- To promote an agenda for scholarly and creative activities.
- To promote advancement of the profession through NCIDQ certification.

FACILITIES

The University of Akron is in northeast Ohio, less than 50 minutes from Cleveland, two hours from Columbus, and two hours from Pittsburgh. The University is close to two airports, including Cleveland-Hopkins International Airport, and just a one-hour flight to major U.S. cities, including Washington, D.C., Chicago, and New York. The University's metropolitan location provides a wide and exciting laboratory for students where they can interact with the professional community, obtain internships, and secure entry-level placement in the field of Interior Design. With a population of 225,000, Akron is Ohio's fifth-largest city. For the second time in recent years, Akron has been named an All-American City by the National Civic League. The campus is within easy driving distance to many of the country's finest cultural resources. Dining, shopping, and entertainment opportunities abound. Also nearby are scenic parklands and the Cuyahoga Valley National Recreation Area. Program facilities include a Lighting Lab, a computer lab and production facilities as well as a large resource library.

ONLINE / DISTANCE LEARNING

The BA in Interior Design is not currently offered online. Some online coursework is in progress.

COURSES OF INSTRUCTION

- Architectural Drafting
- Survey of History of Art I
- Foundation 2D Design
- Visual Arts Awareness
- Architectural Presentations I & II
- Introduction to Interior Design
- Textiles
- AutoCAD for Interior Design
- Light in Man-Made Environments
- Family Housing
- Interior Design Theory
- Programming and Space Planning
- Specifications for Interiors I
- Specifications for Interiors II
- History of Interior Design I
- History of Interior Design II
- Textiles for Interiors
- Senior Design Studios I/II/III/IV
- Decorative Elements in Interior Design
- Senior Portfolio Review
- The NCIDQ Examination
- Interior Design Internship

INTERNSHIPS

Required of majors at Junior level. The Interior Design Internship course provides a real-world work opportunity for students at the conclusion of their third year in the program through the internship course. This field experience, involves residential and commercial Interior Design business, architectural offices, Interior Design product showrooms, furniture retailers, and/or the related industries, extends students' formal education and is further preparation for successful completion of their capstone Senior studio coursework as well as preparation for entry-level positions in Interior Design.

STUDY ABROAD

Plans in progress to implement such.

NOTABLE ALUMNI

Todd Huckabone, National Sales Manger of Donghia

STUDENT ACTIVITIES AND ORGANIZATIONS

The University of Akron has a student chapter of The American Society of Interior Designers. Student members benefit from a wide range of educational, social, and service events and activities. The organization promotes strong relations with the business community, provides opportunities for professional development and growth, brings together future employees with potential employers and provides a resource center for all students. Students also join The International Interior Design Association as student members. The professional chapters of ASID and IIDA hold regular meetings and events such as a Student Career Day and tradeshows to which students are invited and welcome. Students formed a student chapter of USGBC.

FACULTY SPECIALIZATIONS AND RESEARCH

The program is administered by qualified, motivated faculty who encourage faculty/student interaction and give students personal attention. A faculty advising system is provided to help with students' course selection and broader goals. Faculty have a wide range of expertise including Interior Design, architecture, lighting, fine arts, history, textiles, merchandising, and family life.

University of Cincinnati

School of Architecture & Interior Design

7210 DAAP, PO Box 210016, Cincinnati, OH 45221 | 513-556-6426 | www.daap.uc.edu/said/

UNIVERSITY PROFILE
Public
Urban
Residential
Commuter
Quarter Schedule
Co-ed

STUDENT DEMOGRAPHICS
Undergraduate: 480
Graduate: 120

Male: 50%
Female: 50%

Full-time: 100%
Part-time: 0%

EXPENSES
Tuition: $10,065
Room & Board: $9,702

ADMISSIONS
University Pavilion Building,
Room 340
2624 Clifton Ave.
Cincinnati, OH 45221
513-556-1100
www.admissions.uc.edu

DEGREE INFORMATION

Major / Degree / Concentration	Enrollment	Requirements for entry	Graduation rate
Interior Design Bachelor of Science	180	1160 SAT or 26 ACT	90%

TOTAL PROGRAM ENROLLMENT
Undergraduate: 180
Graduate: 3

Male: 5%
Female: 95%

Full-time: 100%
Part-time: 0%

International: 6%
Minority: 6%

Job Placement Rate: 95%

SCHOLARSHIPS / FINANCIAL AID
INTD specific scholarship funds at $18,000 per year from a variety of sources. In addition, there School and College scholarships are available.

Students Receiving Scholarships or Financial Aid: 6%

TOTAL FACULTY: 28
Full-time: 100%
Part-time: 0%
Online: Not reported

NCIDQ Certified: 1
Licensed Interior Designers: 1
LEED Certified: 12

INTERIOR DESIGN ADMINISTRATION
Jim Postell, Associate Professor and INTD coordinator
Jay Chatterjee, full Professor, Interim School Director

PROFESSIONAL / ACADEMIC AFFILIATIONS
International Interior Design Association
Interior Design Educators Council

CIDA ACCREDITATION
Bachelor of Science in Interior Design (2009, 2015)

PROGRAM DESCRIPTION AND PHILOSOPHY

The five-year Bachelor of Science in Interior Design curriculum is comprehensive from the beginning. Because Interior Designers must be able to integrate practical, technical, and aesthetic factors in designing building interiors, we introduce students immediately to that challenge. Each level of the student's education engages knowledge and skills in problem discovery and resolution, critical and imaginative thinking, verbal and visual communication, and appropriate technologies.

Following two foundation years, Interior Design content studios provide students with opportunities to develop further their creative abilities through design projects for a variety of human activity settings. Interior Design students complete a total of six quarters of co-op work experiences during years two through five. Culminating the curriculum is a capstone Senior project in which students exercise their acquired knowledge and skills in a two-quarter design project of their own choosing.

FACILITIES

Central Computer Graphics Lab, Rapid Prototype Center, Materials Library, Library, Gallery, Wood and metal DAAPshop, DAAPstore, DAAPcafe.

ONLINE / DISTANCE LEARNING

Not available

COURSES OF INSTRUCTION

- Design Studio
- Communication Skills
- Design Science
- History, Theory, and Criticism
- Environmental Technology
- Professional Practice
- Co-op

INTERNSHIPS

Required of majors years 2-5. Interns are typically placed at large, medium, and small architecture and Interior Design offices across the country and abroad.

STUDY ABROAD

Faculty-led foreign study travel

NOTABLE ALUMNI

Eva Maddox, Michael Graves,

STUDENT ACTIVITIES AND ORGANIZATIONS

IIDA, OSID

FACULTY SPECIALIZATIONS AND RESEARCH

- Design
- Communication Skills
- Digital Design and Fabrication
- History, Theory, and Criticism
- Design Science
- Material Studies
- Furniture
- Lighting
- Professional Practice

Virginia Marti College of Art & Design

Interior Design Program

11724 Detroit Ave., Lakewood, OH 44107 | 216-221-8584 | www.vmcad.edu

UNIVERSITY PROFILE
Private
Urban
Commuter
Quarter Schedule
Co-ed

STUDENT DEMOGRAPHICS
Undergraduate: 37
Graduate: 0

Male: 6%
Female: 94%

Full-time: 77%
Part-time: 23%

EXPENSES
Tuition: $19,800
Room & Board: n/a

ADMISSIONS
11724 Detroit Ave.
Lakewood, OH 44107
212-221-8584
qmarti@vmcad.edu

DEGREE INFORMATION

Major / Degree / Concentration	Enrollment	Requirements for entry	Graduation rate
Interior Design Associate of Applied Business	37	Must have an overall composite score of 75 or better on the admission evaluation report. Speak with the admissions department for details.	85%

TOTAL PROGRAM ENROLLMENT
Undergraduate: 37
Graduate: 0

Male: 6%
Female: 94%

Full-time: 76%
Part-time: 24%

International: 0%
Minority: 11%

Job Placement Rate: 85%

SCHOLARSHIPS / FINANCIAL AID
Prior to enrolling to VMCAD, all applicants are encouraged to explore the availability of financial aid funding through state and federal agencies. Financial aid information and application assistance is provided by the college Financial Aid Office to help each student and his or her family understand the financial situation. VMCAD encourages every student to apply for federal aid on the FAFSA Web site.

Students Receiving Scholarships or Financial Aid: 70%

TOTAL FACULTY: 10
Full-time: 10%
Part-time: 90%
Online: 0%

NCIDQ Certified: 11%
Licensed Interior Designers: 33%
LEED Certified: 11%

INTERIOR DESIGN ADMINISTRATION
Virginia Marti, Veith / President
Dennis Marti, Assistant Director
Tim Meisse, Director of Education

PROFESSIONAL / ACADEMIC AFFILIATIONS
American Society of Interior Designers

PROGRAM DESCRIPTION AND PHILOSOPHY

VMCAD's Interior Design Program is based on the method used at the renowned Ecole des Beaux Arts School in Paris, France. The program emphasizes the technical and aesthetic aspects of interior design. Students learn to how to manipulate three-dimensional spaces creating a pleasing residential or commercial environment. The curriculum, taught by industry professionals, emphasizes both research techniques and critical thinking skills. Students are also taught how to communicate ideas visually and verbally. A variety of studio classes provide students with the tools needed to overcome a variety of design problems. interior design is diverse in its practice and career opportunities. VMCAD graduates are thoroughly equipped to compete successfully in this professional discipline.

FACILITIES

Residential, Commercial, contract Administration; Architectural graphic representation

ONLINE / DISTANCE LEARNING

No classes are offered online at this time.

COURSES OF INSTRUCTION

- Introduction to Interior Design
- Design Fundamentals
- Textiles
- Space Planning
- Drafting
- Interior Design Studio Classes(5)
- AutoCAD

INTERNSHIPS

Required of majors at 8th quarter.

STUDY ABROAD

Not available

NOTABLE ALUMNI

Ann Lahiff, Keith Smith, Linda Fugitt, Andrea Sims, Jonathan Sin-Jin Satayathum

STUDENT ACTIVITIES AND ORGANIZATIONS

Many college sponsored field trips are taken throughout the year.

FACULTY SPECIALIZATIONS AND RESEARCH

- Residential
- Commercial
- Contract Administration
- Architectural graphic representation

Oklahoma State University

Department of Design, Housing & Merchandising

431 HES Building, Stillwater, OK 74078 | 405-744-5035 | http://ches.okstate.edu/dhm/

UNIVERSITY PROFILE
Public
Suburban
Residential
Semester Schedule
Co-ed

STUDENT DEMOGRAPHICS
Undergraduate: 17,849
Graduate: 4,996

Male: 51.47%
Female: 48.53%

Full-time: 67%
Part-time: 33%

EXPENSES
Tuition: $7,500
Room & Board: $6,000

ADMISSIONS
219 Student Union
Stillwater, OK 74078
405-744-5358
800-233-5019 ext. 1
admissions@okstate.edu

DEGREE INFORMATION

Major / Degree / Concentration	Enrollment	Requirements for entry	Graduation rate
Interior Design Bachelor of Science	114	2.5 gpa Pass Freshman review process (portfolio, writing sample, gpa)	90%

TOTAL PROGRAM ENROLLMENT
Undergraduate: 114
Graduate: 6

Male: 20%
Female: 80%

Full-time: 95%
Part-time: 5%

International: .15%
Minority: 10%

Job Placement Rate: Not reported

SCHOLARSHIPS / FINANCIAL AID
Various annual academic scholarships and intership scholarships

Students Receiving Scholarships or Financial Aid: 85%

TOTAL FACULTY: 7
Full-time: 86%
Part-time: 14%
Online: 0%

NCIDQ Certified: 75%
Licensed Interior Designers: 75%
LEED Certified: 25%

INTERIOR DESIGN ADMINISTRATION
Randall R. Russ, Ph.D., Interim Department Head
Mr. William J Beitz, M.A., Interior Design Program Coordinator

PROFESSIONAL / ACADEMIC AFFILIATIONS
American Society of Interior Designers
International Interior Design Association
Interior Design Educators Council
Environmental Design Research Association

CIDA ACCREDITATION
Bachelor of Science (2008, 2014)

PROGRAM DESCRIPTION AND PHILOSOPHY
Program philosophy based on quality of life and the human perspective with emphasis in user assessment, concept statements, and program writing.

FACILITIES
Open studios, CAD labs, Resource Materials Library, Exhibition Gallery

ONLINE / DISTANCE LEARNING
Not available

COURSES OF INSTRUCTION
- Design Theory
- Graphics
- CAD
- Interidor Components
- Environmental Systems
- Sustainability Issues

INTERNSHIPS
Required of majors at Junior level. Interns are typically placed at Commercial Design, Hospitality, or Arch/ID firms.

STUDY ABROAD
Europe and Mexico

NOTABLE ALUMNI
Not reported

STUDENT ACTIVITIES AND ORGANIZATIONS
ASID, IFMA, IIDA

FACULTY SPECIALIZATIONS AND RESEARCH
- Graphics
- Lighting
- Product development
- Sustainability
- Facility Management

COMMUNITY COLLEGE TRANSFERS
Students enrolled at Tulsa Community College, with proper Freshman level coursework, may participate in the Freshman Review process as sophomores.

University of Central Oklahoma

Department of Design, College of Fine Arts & Design

100 N. University, Box 195 , Edmond, OK 73034 | 405-974-5200 | www.uco.edu/cfad/academics/design

DEGREE INFORMATION

Major / Degree / Concentration	Enrollment	Requirements for entry	Graduation rate
Interior Design Bachelor of Fine Arts	134	2.0 gpa Portfolio review after Freshman year	95%

TOTAL PROGRAM ENROLLMENT
Undergraduate: 134
Graduate: 5

Male: 6%
Female: 94%

Full-time: 65%
Part-time: 35%

International: 3%
Minority: 15%

Job Placement Rate: 60%

SCHOLARSHIPS / FINANCIAL AID
There are five scholarships available for students in the Interior Design program, with two of those available only to students in the department of Design, and the remaining scholarships available to other students within the College of Fine Arts and Design. Financial aid is available through the University in the form of grants, student loans, or a tuition waiver program for those students whose parents have less than $50,000 annual income.

Students Receiving Scholarships or Financial Aid: 69%

TOTAL FACULTY: 8
Full-time: 38%
Part-time: 62%
Online: 0%

NCIDQ Certified: 1
Licensed Interior Designers: 0
LEED Certified: 0

INTERIOR DESIGN ADMINISTRATION
John Clinton, Dean
Ruki Ravikumar, Department Chair
Valerie Settles, Program Director

PROFESSIONAL / ACADEMIC AFFILIATIONS
American Society of Interior Designers
Interior Design Educators Council

CIDA ACCREDITATION
Bachelor of Fine Arts (2007, 2013)

PROGRAM DESCRIPTION AND PHILOSOPHY

The UCO Interior Design program will continue to maintain high academic standards; assess and improve course content, instructional delivery, and degree requirements; maintain networking connections with the professional design community; and prepare students to get good jobs. The Interior Design program is a student-centered and a learning-centered environment which:

- Increases the production of design knowledge in order to enhance design performance.
- Prepares students for change.
- Fosters innovative thinkers.
- Allows/encourages independent and interdisciplinary projects.
- Networks with design communities; local, national, and global.
- Makes positive contributions to society.
- Provides professional career preparation.

FACILITIES

For the study of Interior Design within the department, students have access to a drafting studio, lecture space, classroom with laptop cart to use during classes, departmental computer lab with adjacent print center, and sample library. The University maintains an art museum as well as gallery spaces in several buildings for the display of student and professional work. The University Library contains an area dedicated to archives of University history.

ONLINE / DISTANCE LEARNING
Not available

COURSES OF INSTRUCTION
- Design Foundations I
- Design Foundations II
- Design Foundations III
- Design Foundations IV
- Interior Design I
- Universal Design
- Commercial Design I
- History of Interior Design I
- History of Interior Design II
- Computer Drafting I
- Materials for Interiors
- Residential Design
- Rendering Techniques
- Custom Furniture
- History of Interior Design III
- Systems Furniture
- Lighting for Interior Design
- History of Interior Design IV
- Estimating for Interior Design
- Commercial Design II
- Interior Design Practice
- Internship (1 hour)

INTERNSHIPS
Required of majors at Senior level. Interns are typically placed at Architectural Firms, Home Builders, Design Showrooms, Systems Furniture Dealers, Residential Designers (The Benham Companies, The Small Group, Scott Rice, Kellie Clements Designs, Neely Design Associates, Workplace Resources, Mister Robert Furniture, Meyer Architecture, Studio Architecture)

STUDY ABROAD
There are opportunities available through the University Center for Global Competency to study abroad or find an internship in a foreign country.

NOTABLE ALUMNI
Not reported

STUDENT ACTIVITIES AND ORGANIZATIONS
Students have the opportunity to join a student chapter of the American Society of Interior Designers (ASID) and hear guest speakers and participate in overnight field trips through that organization. An adjunct instructor also takes students on study tours abroad every spring, and a faculty member takes students on biannual trips to Chicago to attend NeoCon and tour local sites.

FACULTY SPECIALIZATIONS AND RESEARCH
- Commercial Design
- Rendering
- Custom Furniture Design
- Computer-Aided Design
- Research—Industrial Design
- Historic Preservation Education
- Design History
- Design Safety Related to Tornado Damage

University of Oklahoma

Department of Interior Design, College of Architecture

830 Van Vleet Oval, Gould Hall, Norman, OK 73019 | 405-325-2444 | http://id.coa.ou.edu/

UNIVERSITY PROFILE
Public
Urban
Commuter
Semester Schedule
Co-ed

STUDENT DEMOGRAPHICS
Undergraduate: 22,938
Graduate: Not reported

Male: Not reported
Female: Not reported

Full-time: Not reported
Part-time: Not reported

EXPENSES
Tuition: $7,423
Room & Board: $3,799

ADMISSIONS
Office of Admissions
Buchanan Hall Rm. 127
Norman, OK 73019
405-325-2252
admrec@ou.edu

DEGREE INFORMATION

Major / Degree / Concentration	Enrollment	Requirements for entry	Graduation rate
Interior Design Bachelor of Interior Design	105	2.5 gpa Portfolio review after Sophomore year	95%

TOTAL PROGRAM ENROLLMENT
Undergraduate: 105
Graduate: Not reported

Male: 4.8%
Female: 95.2%

Full-time: 97%
Part-time: 3%

International: 1%
Minority: 1%

Job Placement Rate: 85%

SCHOLARSHIPS / FINANCIAL AID
Scholarships within the division and college ranging from $500 to $2,000

TOTAL FACULTY: 6
Full-time: 100%
Part-time: Not reported
Online: Not reported

NCIDQ Certified: 100%
Licensed Interior Designers: Not reported
LEED Certified: Not reported

INTERIOR DESIGN ADMINISTRATION
Abimbola O. Asojo, NCIDQ 21989, AIA, IDEC, LEED AP, Associate Professor, Director of Interior Design

PROFESSIONAL / ACADEMIC AFFILIATIONS
American Society of Interior Designers
International Interior Design Association
Interior Design Educators Council
Environmental Design Research Association

CIDA ACCREDITATION
Bachelor of Interior Design (2010, 2016)

PROGRAM DESCRIPTION AND PHILOSOPHY

The mission of the Interior Design division is to provide professional undergraduate education in Interior Design within a collaborative, multi-disciplinary learning environment. The disciplinary perspective shares a common pedagogy with the College of Architecture divisions engaging high tech knowledge with high-touch skills to prepare new graduates to solve problems related to the global challenges facing the profession of Interior Design in practice.

The program strives to:
- Prepare entry level interior designers to work effectively with professionals from other disciplines engaged in the planning, design, and management of the built environment.
- Engage Interior Design students in the exploration of design within broad cultural contexts, addressing both regional and international contributions to the design of the built environment while utilizing resources across and beyond the campus.
- Integrate the expressive qualities embodied in the practice of Interior Design within the context of a technological learning environment.
- Challenge students by addressing contemporary and critical issues facing the profession.
- Ensure adequate curricular flexibility to accommodate future change affecting interior design education throughout the duration of a four-year program of study.
- Preserve and enhance problem-solving growth within a sequential studio sequence, continually expanding to encompass increasingly more complex concepts, skills, knowledge, and application strategies.
- Actively seek and promote the involvement of external organizations in collaborative partnerships, providing opportunities for students and faculty to engage in real-life design, community service, and service learning experiences.

FACILITIES

The College of Architecture plans to move to a newly remodeled building in Summer 2011. The building will house the Divisions of Interior Design, Architecture, Construction Science, Regional and City Planning, Landscape Architecture, and the Institute for Quality Communities. Learn labs, computer labs, lighting labs, resource room, studios, and high-tech classrooms are some of the new technology that will be available to the Interior Design program.

ONLINE / DISTANCE LEARNING
Not available

COURSES OF INSTRUCTION
- Design and Graphics Studio I, II & III
- Design I: Architectural Design and Human Factors
- Computer Applications in Interior Design
- Interior Construction
- Interior Materials and Specifications
- Advanced Computer Applications
- Interior Design II: Lighting Design
- Interior Design III: Commercial Design
- Construction Drawing and Detailing for Interiors
- History of Interior Design, Early Civilization to 1800
- History of Interior Design, 19th and 20th Centuries
- Furniture Design
- Interior Design Office Professional Practice
- Interior Design IV: Institutional and Corporate Design
- Interior Design V: Capstone
- Field Work
- Directed Readings
- Independent Study
- Special Studies
- Topics in Computer Application
- Design, Construction and Society
- Architecture and the Environment
- Modern and Contemporary Architecture
- Fundamental Financial Accounting
- Principles of Marketing

INTERNSHIPS
Not required, but available to 2nd-, 3rd- and 4th- year students. Interns are typically placed at Interior Design firms, Lighting Design firms, and Architecture firms.

STUDY ABROAD
Available

NOTABLE ALUMNI
In Fall 2009, the Interior Design program was ranked number 6 nationally by DesignIntelligence in its publication, *America's Best Architecture and Design Schools. The* division was also ranked second in the nation in the computer applications skills assessment area.

STUDENT ACTIVITIES AND ORGANIZATIONS
Active umbrella student orgranization Interior Design Student Association (IDSA) which combines both IIDA and ASID student chapters.

FACULTY SPECIALIZATIONS AND RESEARCH
The Interior Design division has three full-time faculty and three renewable term faculty who bring very strong credentials and many years of practice from Interior Design, architecture, construction, computing, art, and education. Faculty bring expertise in a variety of areas and these have significant influence on the program. Some of these areas include global design, diversity and multicultural issues, computer modeling and visualization, lighting design, furniture design, collaborative learning, and interactive learning environments.

The Art Institute of York, Pennsylvania

Interior Design Department

1409 Williams Rd., York, PA   17402 | 717-757-5552 | www.artinstitutes.edu/york

UNIVERSITY PROFILE
Private
Suburban
Commuter
Quarter Schedule
Co-ed

STUDENT DEMOGRAPHICS
Undergraduate: 670
Graduate: Not reported

Male: Not reported
Female: Not reported

Full-time: 80%
Part-time: 20%

EXPENSES
Tuition: Not reported
Room & Board: Not reported

ADMISSIONS
1409 Williams Rd.
York, PA 17402
717-757-5552
www.artinstitutes.edu/york

DEGREE INFORMATION

Major / Degree / Concentration	Enrollment	Requirements for entry	Graduation rate
Interior Design **Bachelor of Science**	Not reported	Not reported	Not reported
Kitchen & Bath Design **Associate of Science**	Not reported	Not reported	Not reported

TOTAL PROGRAM ENROLLMENT
Undergraduate: 648
Graduate: Not reported

Male: 65%
Female: 35%

Full-time: 65%
Part-time: 35%

International: 5%
Minority: 30%

Job Placement Rate: Not reported

SCHOLARSHIPS / FINANCIAL AID
Students Receiving Scholarships or
Financial Aid: 80%

TOTAL FACULTY: 35
Full-time: 23%
Part-time: 12%
Online: n/a

NCIDQ Certified: 3
Licensed Interior Designers: 3
LEED Certified: Not reported

INTERIOR DESIGN ADMINISTRATION
Tim Howard, President
Marla Price, Dean of Academic Affairs

PROFESSIONAL / ACADEMIC AFFILIATIONS
American Society of Interior Designers
International Interior Design Association
Interior Design Educators Council

PROGRAM DESCRIPTION AND PHILOSOPHY
Not reported

FACILITIES
All labs are available to students when not being used for classes until 10:00 PM daily

ONLINE / DISTANCE LEARNING
Not available

COURSES OF INSTRUCTION
- Survey of Modern Art
- Architecture
- Drawing
- Color Theory
- Fundamentals
- Perspective
- Visual Indication
- Theory & Development of Form
- Speech Adv. Comm.
- Computer Literracy
- Composition & Language
- Drafting
- Basics of Interior Design
- Space Planning
- History of Furniture
- Lighting
- Human Factors
- AutoCAD
- Office Deign
- Residential Design
- Codes/Barrier Free Design
- Environmental Design
- Mixed Medium Rendering
- Construction Documents
- Internship
- Materials & Specifications
- Photography
- Residential Kitchen & Bath Design
- Furniture Design
- Jewelry
- Ceramics
- Brand Marketing
- Financial Management
- Fund of Design
- Fund of Internet
- Sales and Persuasive Tech.
- Consumer Behavior
- Marketing
- Accounting
- Intellectual Property & Law
- E-Commerce
- HR Resource Mgmt.
- Speech
- Economics
- Composition & Language, I & II
- Intro to Retailing
- Fashion History
- Retail Math, Apparel Evaluation, & Construction
- Event & Fashion Show Production
- Visual Merchandising
- Store Planning
- Intro to Manufacturing
- Trends & Concepts in Apparel
- Product Development
- International Marketing and Buying
- Business Ownership
- Internship
- Textiles
- College Math
- Fashion Drawing
- Basic Drafting
- Digital Imaging for Multimedia and Web
- Etiquette for Today's Professional

INTERNSHIPS
Required of majors at Junior Quarter just before completing the program.

STUDY ABROAD
Not available

NOTABLE ALUMNI
Not reported

STUDENT ACTIVITIES AND ORGANIZATIONS
ASID Student Chapter, NKBA Student Chapter, AIGA Chapter, Seigraph Organization

FACULTY SPECIALIZATIONS AND RESEARCH
Lighting Effects on Autism

Chatham University

Interior Architecture Program, Art & Design Division

Chatham Eastside - 120 Woodland Rd. , Pittsburgh, PA 15232 | 412-365-1100 | www.chatham.edu/

UNIVERSITY PROFILE
Private
Urban
Residential
Semester Schedule
Women Only (undergraduate)
Co-ed (graduate)

STUDENT DEMOGRAPHICS
Undergraduate: 721
Graduate: 1143

Male: 0% undergraduate; 20% graduate
Female: 100% undergraduate; 80% graduate

Full-time: 78%
Part-time: 22%

EXPENSES
Tuition: $28,088 (undergraduate); $720 per credit (graduate)
Room & Board: $8,700 (undergraduate)

ADMISSIONS
Admission Office
Berry Hall
Woodland Rd.
Pittsburgh, PA 15232
admissions@chatham.edu (undergraduate)
gradadmissions@chatham.edu (MIA Program)
dvey@chatham.edu (MSIA Program)
800-837-1290 (undergraduate and MIA program)
412-365-1720 (MSIA Program)

DEGREE INFORMATION

Major / Degree / Concentration	Enrollment	Requirements for entry	Graduation rate
Interior Architecture Bachelor of Interior Architecture	20	Not reported	Not reported
Interior Architecture Master of Interior Architecture	22	3.0 gpa; Students with a gpa of below 3.0 may gain admittance to the program with approval from the program director.	Not reported
Interior Architecture Master of Science in Interior Architecture	8	3.0 gpa; Personal statement of intent	Not reported

TOTAL PROGRAM ENROLLMENT
Undergraduate: 20
Graduate: 30

Male: 0% (undergraduate); 13% (graduate)
Female: 100% (undergraduate); 87% (graduate)

Full-time: 80%
Part-time: 20%

International: 4%
Minority: 5%

Job Placement Rate: Not reported

SCHOLARSHIPS / FINANCIAL AID
Chatham University offers both need-based financial aid and merit-based scholarships.

TOTAL FACULTY: 12
Full-time: 25%
Part-time: 75%
Online: n/a

NCIDQ Certified: 25%
Licensed Interior Designers: N/A
LEED Certified: 25%

INTERIOR DESIGN ADMINISTRATION
Lori A. Anthony, Director, Interior Architecture Programs

PROFESSIONAL / ACADEMIC AFFILIATIONS
American Society of Interior Designers
Interior Design Educators Council
Environmental Design Research Association

CIDA ACCREDITATION
Master of Interior Architecture (2010, 2016)

PROGRAM DESCRIPTION AND PHILOSOPHY

The philosophy of the Interior Architecture program at Chatham University is fundamentally founded in responsibility for the outcome of design and global public service. The Interior Architecture program believes in evidence-based design and ethnography, an approach to analyzing user needs by studying the user, their practices, and artifacts in the context of their existing interior environment.

With a curriculum that balances spontaneity and creativity with the critical-thinking and problem-solving skills necessary to meet practical concerns, our graduates are prepared to excel in the profession of Interior Design. Our students must be able to solve design challenges, communicate, and present their solutions with authority, a strong design vocabulary, and professional communication skills.

We believe it is our responsibility to train engaged stewards of the environment, globally-conscious Interior Design professionals with consideration for the responsibility and outcomes of design and the needs of all user groups.

FACILITIES

Chatham Eastside is the University's newest academic facility and represents a significant investment in our expanding graduate programs as well as the future development of East Liberty, one of Pittsburgh's fastest-growing and historic neighborhoods. This LEED-Silver renovation project was completed by Rothschild Doyno Collaborative in July 2009. Our architects utilize sustainable design practices, recycled materials, and energy-efficienct lighting to create an academic and social space within a green environment.

The Interior Architecture programs enjoys state of the art facilities including a dedicated CAD lab for interior and landscape students, four design studios, a resource room housing sustainable materials and plenty of open pin-up space for informal class meetings and critiques.

ONLINE / DISTANCE LEARNING

The MSIA degree is an online degree

COURSES OF INSTRUCTION

(BIA and MIA Programs):
- Theory of Interior Architecture
- Drawing and Model Making
- Drafting & Graphics
- Green and Sustainable Design
- Environment and Behavior
- Interior Architecture I, II and III
- Interior Materials
- Building Codes
- Building Systems
- Visual Communication
- Construction Documents
- Professional Practice
- Tutorial/Capstone Studio
- Lighting and Acoustics
- Internship
- Community Service

(MSIA):
- Graduate Research Methods
- Interior Architecture Inquiry
- Current Issues in Interior Architecture
- Supervised Teaching
- Statistics
- Writing
- Thesis

INTERNSHIPS

Required of majors in their Senior year. Companies that interns are typically placed include Architecture/Design Firms, Showrooms, Dealerships, Foundations.

STUDY ABROAD

Through Chatham Abroad. The Chatham Abroad program offers eligible Chatham sophomores the experience of international study and travel as an integral part of their Chatham degree program. Chatham Abroad includes a series of academic courses focused on interdisciplinary topics, taught by Chatham faculty during the Maymester term. The courses, topics, and foreign sites vary from year to year, depending on faculty interests and experiences, the global economy, and current international political conditions. The primary goal of Chatham's internationalization experience is to provide an array of opportunities for every student regardless of major or discipline and to provide a campus environment conducive to training 'world ready women'. Chatham students and alumnae often describe their Chatham experience has one of transformation and, inevitably, this metamorphosis includes some element of an international experience that touches everyone.

NOTABLE ALUMNI

Not reported

STUDENT ACTIVITIES AND ORGANIZATIONS

Student chapter of ASID.

FACULTY SPECIALIZATIONS AND RESEARCH

- Historical Kitchen Design
- International Design
- Placemaking
- Environment and Behavior
- Healthcare

Drexel University

Department of Architecture & Interiors

33rd & Market St., Philadelphia, PA 19104 | 215-895-2071 | www.drexel.edu/westphal/

UNIVERSITY PROFILE
Private
Urban
Residential
Quarter Schedule
Co-ed

STUDENT DEMOGRAPHICS
Undergraduate: 13,500
Graduate: 9,000

Male: 55%
Female: 45%

Full-time: Not reported
Part-time: Not reported

EXPENSES
Tuition: $40,000
Room & Board: $12,000

ADMISSIONS
Admissions Office
32nd and Chestnut St.
Philadelphia, PA 19104
215-895-2071

DEGREE INFORMATION

Major / Degree / Concentration	Enrollment	Requirements for entry	Graduation rate
Interior Design Bachelor of Science	120	2.75 gpa	Not reported
Interior Architecture & Design Master of Science	80	3.0 gpa	90%
Interior Design & Interior Architecture Bachelor & Master degree	7	3.3 gpa	New program

TOTAL PROGRAM ENROLLMENT
Undergraduate: 120
Graduate: 80

Male: 5%
Female: 95%

Full-time: 100%
Part-time: 0%

International: 10%
Minority: Not reported

Job Placement Rate: 80%

SCHOLARSHIPS / FINANCIAL AID
Not reported

TOTAL FACULTY: 12
Full-time: 40%
Part-time: 60%
Online: 0%

NCIDQ Certified: 60%
Licensed Interior Designers: 60%
LEED Certified: 25%

INTERIOR DESIGN ADMINISTRATION
Jon Coddington, Department Head of Architecture and Interiors
Rena Cumby, Associate Department Head of Architecture and Interiors and Director of Interior Design Programs

PROFESSIONAL / ACADEMIC AFFILIATIONS
American Society of Interior Designers
International Interior Design Association
Interior Design Educators Council
Environmental Design Research
  Association

CIDA ACCREDITATION
Bachelor of Science in Interior Design
(2006, 2012)

PROGRAM DESCRIPTION AND PHILOSOPHY

Both the undergraduate and graduate programs prepare students for professional practice and achieve this through development of critical thinking, creative process, theory, and a critical component of liberal arts education. The program continually challenges conventional thinking, emphasizing the role Interior Designers play in the quality of life for the human and built environment. There is also an emphasis of the designer's social responsibility to the world they live in and to be productive citizens.

FACILITIES

Students have 24/7 studios—at this point they do not have dedicated desks but in the new building they will, drafting tables & parallel rules, open computer labs, 3D printer, laser cutter, wood shop, resource library, instructional computer lab, minimal exhibition space

ONLINE / DISTANCE LEARNING

Not available

COURSES OF INSTRUCTION

- Design I, II, III
- Intro Drawing
- Structure
- Interior Studio I, II
- Environment Theory
- History of Modern Architecture
- History of Furniture
- Residential
- Hospitality
- Commercial Studios
- Senior Thesis I, II, III
- Professional Practice,
- Construction Documents
- CAD I, II
- Orthographic Drawing
- Rendering
- Detailing
- Lighting
- Interior Materials
- Interior Systems
- History of Art I, II, III
- Multi-Media
- Painting
- Sculpture
- Textiles
- A number of general education requirements

INTERNSHIPS

Required of majors at Junior year. We have a Co-Op program. Our Co-Op students are placed in many of the major architectural/Interior Design firms in Philadelphia, New York, and Washington, as well as some across the country. There are also many Furniture Manufacturer's Rep firms in the surrounding Philadelphia areas as well as Fabric houses, and home furnishing establishments.

STUDY ABROAD

Two sketching tours—Paris and Rome, London Study Abroad program, DIS, Copenhagen Study Abroad, Prague Study Abroad—most of these but not all are offered through the University's Study Abroad Office.

NOTABLE ALUMNI

Not reported

STUDENT ACTIVITIES AND ORGANIZATIONS

Because we are a large university in an urban environment students have the benefit of a large and wide range of activities and organizations within the university as well as within the city environment.

FACULTY SPECIALIZATIONS AND RESEARCH

We have a wide variety of research interests—some include sustainability, school design and behavior, history, design teaching, etc.

COMMUNITY COLLEGE TRANSFERS

The undergraduate program does accept transfer students. Those students come from within the university, from other colleges and universities and from community colleges. Their academics and their portfolio work are evaluated to determine what their plan of study will entail.

La Roche College

Department of Interior Design

9000 Babcock Blvd., Pittsburgh, PA 15237 | 412-536-1024 | www.laroche.edu/majors/interior-design/interior-design.htm

UNIVERSITY PROFILE
Private
Suburban
Residential
Commuter
Semester Schedule
Co-ed

STUDENT DEMOGRAPHICS
Undergraduate: 1,230
Graduate: 126

Male: 38%
Female: 62%

Full-time: 80%
Part-time: 20%

EXPENSES
Tuition: Not reported
Room & Board: Not reported

ADMISSIONS
9000 Babcock Blvd.
Pittsburgh, PA 15237
412-536-1272

DEGREE INFORMATION

Major / Degree / Concentration	Enrollment	Requirements for entry	Graduation rate
Interior Design Bachelor of Science	Not reported	Portfolio review at two points within curriculum	Not reported

DEGREE INFORMATION
Not reported

TOTAL PROGRAM ENROLLMENT
Undergraduate: 80
Graduate: 0

Male: Not reported
Female: Not reported

Full-time: Not reported
Part-time: Not reported

International: Not reported
Minority: Not reported

Job Placement Rate: Not reported

SCHOLARSHIPS / FINANCIAL AID
Not reported

TOTAL FACULTY: 4
Full-time: 4
Part-time: Not reported
Online: Not reported

NCIDQ Certified: Not reported
Licensed Interior Designers: Not reported
LEED Certified: Not reported

INTERIOR DESIGN ADMINISTRATION
Maria Ripepi, Assistant Professor, Design Division Chair
Nicole Bieak Kreidler, Assistant Professor, Interior Design Department Chair

PROFESSIONAL / ACADEMIC AFFILIATIONS
American Society of Interior Designers
Interior Design Educators Council

CIDA ACCREDITATION
Bachelor of Science in Interior Design (2005, 2011)

PROGRAM DESCRIPTION AND PHILOSOPHY

The La Roche College Interior Design program believes that a successful Interior Design education enhances a student's innate creativity and interest in the built environment. An Interior Design education also effectively teaches the knowledge and skills needed to evolve holistic, thoughtfully conceived design solutions in response to humanity's aesthetic, emotional, and utilitarian design needs. The program's mission is to prepare students to perform as design professionals with a life-long desire to remain current in the profession and be advocates for design excellence, thereby promoting the importance of Interior Design to society.

This major prepares students for careers in commercial and residential Interior Design in large and small Interior Design and architecture firms, as well as industrial, commercial, and institutional organizations. It also provides a solid foundation for students who wish to own a design firm or pursue a graduate degree in design. The Interior Design program fosters the transition to the professional world by requiring all majors to complete an internship experience in the field prior to graduation.

FACILITIES

Studio classrooms and Open Studio, CAD Lab, resource library, messy assembly room

ONLINE / DISTANCE LEARNING

Not reported

COURSES OF INSTRUCTION

- Interior Design Graphics
- Interior Design I
- Interior Design Graphics II
- Drawing I
- Foundation Design I
- Foundation Design II
- Computer Graphics for Interior Design
- History of Interior Design and Architecture I
- Textiles for Interiors
- Interior Design II (A and B)
- History of Interior Design and Architecture II
- Building Technology I: Construction Systems
- Architectural Rendering
- Building Technology II: Finish Materials
- Interior Design III (A and B)
- History of Interior Design and Architecture III
- Building Technology III: Lighting and Electrical Systems
- Building Technology IV: Control Systems
- Business Practices for Interior Design
- Contract Documents
- Interior Design Internship I
- Senior Design Seminar I
- Senior Design Seminar II

INTERNSHIPS

Required of majors

STUDY ABROAD

Available

NOTABLE ALUMNI

Not reported

STUDENT ACTIVITIES AND ORGANIZATIONS

ASID Student Chapter

FACULTY SPECIALIZATIONS AND RESEARCH

Not reported

Mercyhurst College

Department of Interior Design

501 E. 38th St., Erie, PA 16546 | 814-824-2368 | http://interiordesign.mercyhurst.edu/

UNIVERSITY PROFILE
Private
Suburban
Residential
Trimester Schedule
Co-ed

STUDENT DEMOGRAPHICS
Undergraduate: 4,022
Graduate: 352

Male: 41%
Female: 59%

Full-time: 84%
Part-time: 16%

EXPENSES
Tuition: $26,648
Room & Board: $9,915

ADMISSIONS
501 E. 38th St.
Erie, PA 16546
800-825-1926 Ext. 2202
admissions@mercyhurst.edu

DEGREE INFORMATION

Major / Degree / Concentration	Enrollment	Requirements for entry	Graduation rate
Interior Design Bachelor of Arts	52	2.75 gpa in major; 2.5 gpa overall Portfolio review after Sophomore year	90%

TOTAL PROGRAM ENROLLMENT
Undergraduate: 52
Graduate: n/a

Male: 14%
Female: 86%

Full-time: %
Part-time: %

International: 1%
Minority: 0%

Job Placement Rate: 90%

SCHOLARSHIPS / FINANCIAL AID
We provide merit-based scholarships for students which are renewable with appropriate minimum gpas. All students are encouraged to submit the Free Application for Federal Student Aid (FAFSA) as there are additional need-based scholarship and grant options available.

Students Receiving Scholarships or Financial Aid: 100%

TOTAL FACULTY: 4
Full-time: 75%
Part-time: 25%
Online: Not reported

NCIDQ Certified: 75%
Licensed Interior Designers: NA
LEED Certified: 25%

INTERIOR DESIGN ADMINISTRATION
Kathy Weidenboerner, Chairperson, Department of Interior Design

PROFESSIONAL / ACADEMIC AFFILIATIONS
American Society of Interior Designers
International Interior Design Association
Interior Design Educators Council

PROGRAM DESCRIPTION AND PHILOSOPHY

The faculty believes that education is a lifelong process of guided and purposeful activity, directed toward the development of the individual according to his/her needs, abilities, interests, and potential; that education is not merely a passive acquisition of knowledge but the meaningful interpretation of that knowledge, and an understanding capable of producing intelligent decisions and actions; that learning is a change in behavior brought about through experience; that the identification of learning outcomes is done cooperatively by the student and teacher; that self-discovery, self-growth, and self-expression are best achieved in a relaxed and open environment which remains sensitive and adaptive to the student's needs and abilities; and that the teacher is a facilitator of that self-discovery and self-growth. They further believe that learning in the professional environment, where students interact with clients and professionals and can apply theoretical principles, is very effective in developing professional proficiency as well as classroom/studio oriented education.

The meaning of this philosophy for Interior Design education is that the curriculum should provide a judicious balance of learning experience with essential knowledge and understanding to be gained in the physical, behavioral and social sciences, humanities, professional sciences, and communicative sciences. As potential translators of architectural and interior science, the students need the science (knowledge) and the art (skill) inherent in the Interior Design profession. Only when they have cultivated moral values can they translate this science and art into action, in a wide variety of settings, with sensitivity, self-reliance, social concern, and genuine compassion for others.

FACILITIES

Design studios and laboratory facilities are available for use exclusively by Interior Design students. Mercyhurst's on-campus drafting studio, materials lab, resource library, and computer lab with the latest computer aided drafting and design software provide students the technical expertise needed to enter the design industry. Studio spaces and laboratories are available to students 24 hours a day, seven days a week when the college is in session.

ONLINE / DISTANCE LEARNING

Not available

COURSES OF INSTRUCTION

- Interior Design Studios I-V
- Technical Graphics I-IV
- Environmental Design
- Color and Light
- History of Interior Design and Architecture I, II
- Interior Design Graphics
- Materials, Systems, and Assemblies, I, II
- Building Technology
- Programming and Research
- Senior Seminar I, II

INTERNSHIPS

Required of majors at Junior level. Interns are typically placed at companies such as the Design Alliance Architects, VA Medical Center, National Cancer Institute, Weber, Murphy, Fox Architects, Caruso Design Group, Burt Hill Kosar Rittelman Associates, Gunther J. Kaier Architects, Inc., Kim Barnes Studio, InScale Architects, Harris Office Furniture, AJ Grack Interiors, Andrea's Kitchens Plus Interior Design, Sanner Office Supply, Period, Environments for Life, ASI Signage Innovations, Cogdell & Mendralla Architects, Candace Sveda Interior Design, Inc., Iskalo Development Corporation, Millington Lockwood Business Interiors.

STUDY ABROAD

Available

NOTABLE ALUMNI

Not reported

STUDENT ACTIVITIES AND ORGANIZATIONS

The Interior Design Club representing an ASID Student Chapter and IIDA Student Memberships, Habitat for Humanity, plus over 90 other organizations and honors societies including The Green Team and featuring academics, recreation, service, leadership, and special interests.

FACULTY SPECIALIZATIONS AND RESEARCH

Commercial and Residential Design including Healthcare, Corporate, Hospitality, and Retail, Human-Environment Interaction, Green Design and Sustainability, Color and Light, and Interior Design and Architectural History.

Philadelphia University

Interior Design Program, School of Architecture

School House La. & Henry Ave., Philadelphia, PA 19144 | 215-951-2828 | www.philau.edu/architecture/

UNIVERSITY PROFILE
Private
Suburban
Urban
Residential
Semester Schedule
Co-ed

STUDENT DEMOGRAPHICS
Undergraduate: 2,884
Graduate: 602

Male: 33%
Female: 67%

Full-time: 87%
Part-time: 13%

EXPENSES
Tuition: $27,428
Room & Board: $9,182

ADMISSIONS
4201 Henry Ave.
Philadelphia, PA 19144
1-800-951-7287
Admissions@PhilaU.edu

DEGREE INFORMATION

Major / Degree / Concentration	Enrollment	Requirements for entry	Graduation rate
Interior Design Bachelor of Science	195	Not reported	Not reported
Interior Architecture Master of Science First Professional degree	Pending 2011	Not reported	Not reported

TOTAL PROGRAM ENROLLMENT
Undergraduate: 195
Graduate: pending

Male: 6%
Female: 94%

Full-time: 98%
Part-time: 2%

International: 4%
Minority: 13%

Job Placement Rate: 79%

SCHOLARSHIPS / FINANCIAL AID
See Admissions on our Web site for more info.

TOTAL FACULTY: 22
Full-time: 23%
Part-time: 77%
Online: 0%

NCIDQ Certified: 50%
Licensed Interior Designers: Not reported
LEED Certified: 50%

INTERIOR DESIGN ADMINISTRATION
Vini Nathan, Dean, School of Architecture
Lauren Baumbach, Director, Interior Design
Terry Ryan, Administrative Assistant

PROFESSIONAL / ACADEMIC AFFILIATIONS
American Society of Interior Designers
International Interior Design Association
Interior Design Educators Council

CIDA ACCREDITATION
Bachelor of Science in Interior Design (2007, 2013)

PROGRAM DESCRIPTION AND PHILOSOPHY

Philadelphia University's Interior Design program offers a comprehensive education in Interior Design. The program covers small scale to large scale projects including residential, commercial, hospitality, retail, health care, and corporate design. We emphasize history/theory, conceptual design, tectonics, making and craft, and the exploration of materiality.

FACILITIES

23,000sf Architecture and Design Center, Ravenhill Design Studios, Smith House Studios, Computer Labs, Weber Model & Fabrication Shop, Laser Lab, Gutman Library, Interior Design Materials & Resource Library, Kanbar Campus Center, Gallagher Athletic Facilites, and The Learning & Advising Center

ONLINE / DISTANCE LEARNING

Not available

COURSES OF INSTRUCTION

- Design I to VII
- Capstone Research & Programming
- Senior Capstone Project
- Visualization I & CAD II
- History of Architecture & Interiors I to IV
- Building Technology
- Interior Building Technology
- Building Systems
- Materials & Textiles
- Professional Practice
- Presentation Techniques
- Furniture Design

INTERNSHIPS

Not required, but available after second year of study

STUDY ABROAD

Four established programs in Italy, Denmark, England, and Australia

NOTABLE ALUMNI

Kim Wannop - Set Designer and 2009 Emmy Nominee for *"Bones"*

STUDENT ACTIVITIES AND ORGANIZATIONS

IIDA (International Interior Design Association), Campus Chapter, ASID (American Society of Interior Designers) Student Chapter and numerous other student organizations... Field trips to building sites, and firms in the mid-Atlantic region, School of Architecture Lecture Series, and multiple regional and national design competitions.

FACULTY SPECIALIZATIONS AND RESEARCH

Our faculty are comprised of designers who are practitioners, researchers, and educators. Virtually all of our faculty practice or have practiced in the field of Interior Design and some engage in research. Their concentrations in practice and research include: corporate design, hospitality design, health care design, residential design, sustainable design, indoor air quality, furniture design, exhibit design, historic preservation, and design pedagogy.

Winthrop University

Department of Design, College of Visual & Performing Arts

343 McLaurin Hall, Rock Hill, SC 29733 | 803-323-3686 | www2.winthrop.edu/vpa/design/

UNIVERSITY PROFILE
Public
Urban
Residential
Semester Schedule
Co-ed

STUDENT DEMOGRAPHICS
Undergraduate: 5,100
Graduate: 1,150

Male: 31%
Female: 69%

Full-time: Not reported
Part-time: Not reported

EXPENSES
Tuition: $11,606 in-state
Room & Board: varies

ADMISSIONS
Winthrop University
Rock Hill, SC 29733
800-WINTHROP (946-8476)
admissions@winthrop.edu

DEGREE INFORMATION

Major / Degree / Concentration	Enrollment	Requirements for entry	Graduation rate
Interior Design Bachelor of Fine Arts	88	2.5 gpa Portfolio review after Freshman year	85%

TOTAL PROGRAM ENROLLMENT
Undergraduate: 88
Graduate: 50

Male: 5%
Female: 95%

Full-time: 85%
Part-time: 15%

International: 1%
Minority: 16%

Job Placement Rate: 90%

SCHOLARSHIPS / FINANCIAL AID
Not reported

TOTAL FACULTY: 6
Full-time: 50%
Part-time: 50%
Online: Not reported

NCIDQ Certified: 50%
Licensed Interior Designers: 50%
LEED Certified: 33%

INTERIOR DESIGN ADMINISTRATION
Chad Dresbach, Chair
David Beatty, Coordinator, Interior Design

PROFESSIONAL / ACADEMIC AFFILIATIONS
American Society of Interior Designers
International Interior Design Association
Interior Design Educators Council

CIDA ACCREDITATION
BFA in Art with a concentration in Interior Design (2006, 2012)

PROGRAM DESCRIPTION AND PHILOSOPHY

The mission of the Interior Design program at Winthrop University is to strive for a high standard of design education in order to provide a learning environment that encourages the development of highly competent Interior Design professionals at the baccalaureate level. The program focuses on the ability to design quality interior environments that contribute to the well-being and safety of individuals and groups along with incorporating a concern for the environment and society at large.

The philosophy and purpose of the Interior Design program is based on the following areas that are valued for an Interior Design program and education.

- Broad liberal arts, basic creative arts, design fundamentals, and design theory—The program is built on the concept of professional education within a framework of liberal arts education.
- Strong understanding of the design process- The program places the focus of Interior Design education on process. The sequence of courses builds on developing skills in the complex process of Interior Design. Design problems are solved by students using a thorough and systematic approach.
- Holistic approach to solving design problems across disciplines—The program considers a multitude of factors that influence a design, including client/user needs, human welfare and safety, functional, economical, and utilitarian solutions, as well as physical, psychological, and contextual fit. Design concepts look at the total environment, and also raise awareness for the world environment and issues of sustainability.

- Team approach to the design process—the program recognizes that the design process involves the interaction of professionals from a variety of disciplines.

FACILITIES

Two primary studio spaces in Rutledge Hall which are multifunctioning studios with the capability of working in either a computer or non-computer design environment. Additionally, lecture and computer lab space are available for the program's use in the new Owens Hall facility. Students have 24/7 access to INDS studios, computers, and drafting tables. The Resource Room (which INDS never had before) is now a discrete and secured facility.

ONLINE / DISTANCE LEARNING
Not available

COURSES OF INSTRUCTION
- Design Drawing
- Intro. Art History I
- Intro. Art History II
- Intro. Comp. Sci. (modules A, B, F)
- Interior Design Fundamentals
- Interior Design Studio: Fundamentals
- INDS Portfolio Review
- Spatial Analysis and Theory I
- Presentation Techniques I
- Textiles and Materials
- Int. Des. and Architecture History I
- Int. Des. and Architecture History II
- Spatial Analysis and Theory II
- Presentation Techniques II
- CAD for Interior Design
- Intro. to Building Systems
- Int. Des. Contract Documents
- Lighting Design
- Codes and Standards
- Cooperative Education Experience
- Interior Design Studio I
- Interior Design Studio II
- Adv. Comp. Apps. for Int. Design

- Professional Practices for Interior Design
- Interior Design Studio III
- Interior Design Studio IV
- Portfolio Preparation
- Senior Thesis Preparation
- Senior Thesis
- Prep. of Oral and Written Reports

INTERNSHIPS
Required of majors at Junior level. Strong job market in the Charlotte, NC metro region at architecture and Interior Design firms

STUDY ABROAD
Available

NOTABLE ALUMNI
Not reported

STUDENT ACTIVITIES AND ORGANIZATIONS
Departmental and IDO (Interior Design Organization) Activities:
- Interaction with the local IIDA and ASID chapters at industry volunteer, employment, enrichment and social events
- Volunteer opportunities such as Habitat for Humanity
- Trips to local, regional and international market venues and conferences
- Guest speakers from the professional world and industry related field trips
- Enrichment sessions regarding Portfolio Development, Resume Preparation, Interviewing, Networking, and Advanced Computer Programs
- Departmental activities such as the annual Arts Ball and gallery shows
- Social activities and fellowship

FACULTY SPECIALIZATIONS AND RESEARCH
Not reported

South Dakota State University

Consumer Sciences Department

SNF Building, Rotunda Lane, Box 2275A, Brookings, SD 57007 | 605-688-5196 | www.sdstate.edu/ehs/programs/

UNIVERSITY PROFILE
Public
Rural
Residential
Semester Schedule
Co-ed

STUDENT DEMOGRAPHICS
Undergraduate: 11,200
Graduate: 1,200

Male: 47.2%
Female: 52.8%

Full-time: Not reported
Part-time: Not reported

EXPENSES
Tuition: $6,500 (resident
tuition and fees)
Room & Board: $5,000

ADMISSIONS
Box 2201
Brookings, SD 57007
605-688-6891
admission@sdstate.edu

DEGREE INFORMATION

Major / Degree / Concentration	Enrollment	Requirements for entry	Graduation rate
Education & Human Sciences Bachelor of Science Interior Design	65	Not reported	Not reported

TOTAL PROGRAM ENROLLMENT
Undergraduate: 65
Graduate: Not reported

Male: 5%
Female: 95%

Full-time: 100%
Part-time: 0%

International: 0%
Minority: 0%

Job Placement Rate: 80%

SCHOLARSHIPS / FINANCIAL AID
Many scholarships are available within the college. Scholarships may be specific for an Interior Design students, an international travel scholarship, internship scholarship, an individual with higher gpa or above, a student from a specific county within South Dakota, and many others. The Design & Visual Arts Group, Inc. (DVAGI) includes all design programs across campus; this group sponsors a fundraising event that provides travel scholarships for SDSU students within the design programs. Financial aid is available to students who complete the appropriate paperwork and qualify.

TOTAL FACULTY: 4
Full-time: 3
Part-time: 1
Online: 1

NCIDQ Certified: 2
Licensed Interior Designers: 1
LEED Certified: 2

INTERIOR DESIGN ADMINISTRATION
Jane Hegland, Department Head and
Assistant Dean
Linda Nussbaumer, Interior Design
Program Coordinator

PROFESSIONAL / ACADEMIC AFFILIATIONS
American Society of Interior Designers
Interior Design Educators Council

CIDA ACCREDITATION
Bachelor of Science in Education and
Human Sciences (2007, 2013)

PROGRAM DESCRIPTION AND PHILOSOPHY

The Interior Design program at SDSU is an accredited program through the Council of Interior Design Accreditation, which focuses on designs that promote the health, safety, and well being of people in the built environment with an emphasis on sustainability. The program prepares graduates to succeed in the profession throughout the region, nationally and internationally. The overarching goal of the Interior Design program prepares graduates for practice in the Interior Design profession and educates them by enriching their personal and professional lives.

FACILITIES

Students are required to purchase their own laptop computers and software. However, three computers are available within the studios for student use as needed. Students have 24/7 access to the building and studio where they enjoy wireless access, onine printer, plotter, model building tools, paper cutter and mat cutter, and a resource library. Each studio has drafting tables, pin-up space, storage lockers, and shelving for in-prcess work. The program also utilizes the department gallery space to display student work. Additionally, The South Dakota Art Museum on campus provides students with access to art work by local and/or famous artists.

ONLINE / DISTANCE LEARNING

Not available

COURSES OF INSTRUCTION

- Introduction to Interior Design I
- Introduction to Interior Design II
- Design II (Color Theory)
- Textiles
- Materials
- History of Interiors
- Art Appreciation
- Seminar: Sustainable Issues in Design
- Interior Design Studio I (Sophomore)
- Interior Design Studio II (Sophomore)
- Lighting and Acoustics
- Building Systems I
- Building Systems II (Codes)
- Professional Practices
- A Business course
- Interior Design Studio III (Junior)
- Interior Design Studio IV (Junior)
- Practicum
- Portfolio
- Interior Design Studio V (Senior)
- Interior Design Studio VI (Senior)

INTERNSHIPS

Required of majors between Junior and Senior year. Students locate internships in a variety of firms. The most common are within architectural firms, Interior Design firms, retail establishments, and kitchen manufacturers.

STUDY ABROAD

SDSU's International Affairs Department provides

NOTABLE ALUMNI

Not reported

STUDENT ACTIVITIES AND ORGANIZATIONS

Approximately 50% of the Interior Design students join the ASID-Student Chapter. This organization holds monthly meeting, enjoys getting-to-know-you activities, and conducts fundraisers to support travel to the career expo in Minneapolis, MN.

FACULTY SPECIALIZATIONS AND RESEARCH

Faculty are engaged in research related to indoor air qualtiy, nursing home design, designing for the baby boomers, teaching methods in Interior Design history courses, strawbale construction, and more.

The Art Institute of Tennessee–Nashville

Interior Design Department

100 Centerview Dr., Suite 250, Nashville, TN 37214 | 615-874-1067 | www.artinstitutes.edu/nashville

UNIVERSITY PROFILE
Private
Suburban
Commuter
Quarter Schedule
Co-ed

STUDENT DEMOGRAPHICS
Undergraduate: 650
Graduate: 0

Male: 45%
Female: 55%

Full-time: 60%
Part-time: 40%

EXPENSES
Tuition: $30,208
Room & Board: n/a

ADMISSIONS
100 Centerview Dr., Suite 250
Nashville, TN 37214
615-874-1067
www.artinstitutes.edu/
nashville

DEGREE INFORMATION

Major / Degree / Concentration	Enrollment	Requirements for entry	Graduation rate
Interior Design Bachelor of Fine Arts	33	3.0 gpa	Not reported

TOTAL PROGRAM ENROLLMENT
Undergraduate: 33
Graduate: 0

Male: 9%
Female: 91%

Full-time: 60%
Part-time: 40%

International: 0%
Minority: 12%

Job Placement Rate: Not reported

SCHOLARSHIPS / FINANCIAL AID
Federal and State financial aid available.

Students Receiving Scholarships or
Financial Aid: 94%

TOTAL FACULTY: 6
Full-time: 2
Part-time: 4
Online: 0

NCIDQ Certified: 3
Licensed Interior Designers: 2
LEED Certified: 1

INTERIOR DESIGN ADMINISTRATION
Robert W. Brown, Director, Interior
Design Department

PROFESSIONAL / ACADEMIC AFFILIATIONS
American Society of Interior Designers
International Interior Design Association

304

PROGRAM DESCRIPTION AND PHILOSOPHY
Comprehensive Interior Design program. Learning centered.

FACILITIES
Computer lab, resource center, library

ONLINE / DISTANCE LEARNING
Not available

COURSES OF INSTRUCTION
- Introduction to Interior Design
- Architectural Drafting
- Space Planning
- Residential Design
- Corporate Design
- Hospitality Design

INTERNSHIPS
Not required

STUDY ABROAD
Provided through the Pittsburgh campus of Art Institutes.

NOTABLE ALUMNI
Not reported

STUDENT ACTIVITIES AND ORGANIZATIONS
Student chapter ASID

FACULTY SPECIALIZATIONS AND RESEARCH
Lighting, medical facilities

East Tennessee State University

Department of Engineering Technology, Surveying & Digital Media

213 Wilson Walls Hall, Johnson City, TN 37614 | 423-439-7822 | www.etsu.edu/scitech/entc/

DEGREE INFORMATION

Major / Degree / Concentration	Enrollment	Requirements for entry	Graduation rate
Interior Design Bachelor of Science	400	C or better	85%

TOTAL PROGRAM ENROLLMENT
Undergraduate: 75
Graduate: 0

Male: 0%
Female: 100%

Full-time: 50%
Part-time: 50%

International: 0%
Minority: 0%

Job Placement Rate: Not reported

SCHOLARSHIPS / FINANCIAL AID
Not reported

TOTAL FACULTY: 3
Full-time: 2
Part-time: 1
Online: 0

NCIDQ Certified: 3
Licensed Interior Designers: 0
LEED Certified: 0

INTERIOR DESIGN ADMINISTRATION
Dr. Keith Johnson, Chair, Department of Engineering Technology, Surveying and Digital Media
Sharon Becker, Assistant Professor and Interior Design Program Coordinator
Rae Dutro, Adjunct

PROFESSIONAL / ACADEMIC AFFILIATIONS
Not reported

PROGRAM DESCRIPTION AND PHILOSOPHY

The Interior Design concentration offers preparation for entry-level positions in residential and commercial design firms, sales, design consulting, computer-aided design, and other related design areas.

FACILITIES

Not reported

ONLINE / DISTANCE LEARNING

Not reported

COURSES OF INSTRUCTION

- Critical Reading
- 2D Design
- Visual Thinking
- Interior Design Fundamentals
- Architectural Drafting: Studio I
- Critical Thinking/Argument
- Using Information Technology
- Color Theory
- Sustainable Design
- Visual Communication: Studio II
- Construction Fundamentals
- Historical Interiors I
- Design for Human Behavior
- Interior Design Presentation: Studio III
- Historical Interiors II
- Materials & Finishes
- Residential Design: Studio IV
- Interior Building Systems & Components
- AutoCAD for Interior Design: Studio V
- Project Scheduling
- Lighting
- Commercial Design: Studio V
- Professional Practices in Interior Design
- Mixed-Use Design: Studio VII
- Interior Design Internship
- Senior Design Studio: Studio VII

INTERNSHIPS

Required of majors at Senior level.

STUDY ABROAD

Not reported

NOTABLE ALUMNI

Not reported

STUDENT ACTIVITIES AND ORGANIZATIONS

Not reported

FACULTY SPECIALIZATIONS AND RESEARCH

Not reported

Middle Tennessee State University

Human Sciences Department

P.O. Box 86, Murfreesboro, TN 37132 | 615-898-2884 | **www.mtsu.edu/humansciences/**

UNIVERSITY PROFILE
Public
Suburban
Residential
Semester Schedule
Co-ed

STUDENT DEMOGRAPHICS
Undergraduate: 22,299
Graduate: 2,889

Male: 47%
Female: 53%

Full-time: 76%
Part-time: 24%

EXPENSES
Tuition: $6,048
Room & Board: $5,322
housing only. Meal plans
optional.

ADMISSIONS
Cope Administration
Building 208
Murfreesboro, TN 37132
615-898-2111
admissions@mtsu.edu

DEGREE INFORMATION

Major / Degree / Concentration	Enrollment	Requirements for entry	Graduation rate
Interior Design Bachelor of Science	Not reported	2.5 gpa and application process after 30 hours of required coursework	Not reported

TOTAL PROGRAM ENROLLMENT
Undergraduate: 125
Graduate: 0

Male: Less than 1%
Female: More than 99%

Full-time: 84%
Part-time: 16%

International: Less than 1%
Minority: 16%

Job Placement Rate: 85% (prior to 2009)

SCHOLARSHIPS / FINANCIAL AID
The Human Sciences Department has
six scholarships open to Interior Design
majors with annual award amounts
ranging up to $3000. The Office of
Financial Aid has grants, scholarships,
work study, and loans which are also
available to Interior Design majors.

TOTAL FACULTY: 4
Full-time: 100%
Part-time: 0%
Online: 0%

NCIDQ Certified: 25%
Licensed Interior Designers: 75%
LEED Certified: 0%

INTERIOR DESIGN ADMINISTRATION
Dr. Dellmar Walker, Human Sciences
  Department Chair
Sharon S. Coleman, Interior Design
  Program Coordinator

PROFESSIONAL / ACADEMIC AFFILIATIONS
American Society of Interior Designers
International Interior Design Association
Interior Design Educators Council
Environmental Design Research
  Association

CIDA ACCREDITATION
Bachelor of Science (2010, 2016)

PROGRAM DESCRIPTION AND PHILOSOPHY

The practice of Interior Design requires synthesis of knowledge from a broad range of areas to successfully solve problems related to the physical environment. From the technical field, the knowledge of building systems, codes, environment, construction, materials, and finishes must be meshed with aesthetic needs. Added to this are the economics of cost, selling, productivity and manufacturing, and the changing social, psychological, and physical needs of people interacting with others and the environment. Underlying the application of this knowledge is the responsibility to protect the safety and support the well-being of the public. The result is a full circle of factors drawn together by the Interior Designer to provide environments that enhance work, play, learning, and living. The education of Interior Designers should include courses that exposes students to technology, art, business, and social sciences in addition to Interior Design and a sound base of liberal arts courses, preparing students for a successful career and for success in other aspects of their life. The mission of the Interior Design program at MTSU is to provide educational preparation for entry level positions in the field. The curriculum prepares students for discipline related employment or admission to graduate school. The program also provides public service to the community and profession, utilizing existing research in student/ faculty related projects as well as participation in professional organizations.

FACILITIES

Dedicated computer lab, program specific studios, university library with integrated technology, on-campus bookstore, university recreation center, new student center under construction

ONLINE / DISTANCE LEARNING

Not available

COURSES OF INSTRUCTION

- Principles of Interior Design
- History of Interiors
- Art Survey
- Drawing
- Residential Design
- Introduction to Commercial Design
- Contract Design
- Lighting Design
- Contract Documents
- Interior Design Visual Presentations
- Does not include required general education courses

INTERNSHIPS

Not required

STUDY ABROAD

Available

NOTABLE ALUMNI

Not reported

STUDENT ACTIVITIES AND ORGANIZATIONS

ASID/IIDA student chapter, annual showcase of student work, annual Lecture Series, intramural sports, college athletics, fraternities and sororities

FACULTY SPECIALIZATIONS AND RESEARCH

- Legislation and registration
- Lighting
- Healthcare
- Learning styles
- Project management
- Textiles

O'More College of Design

Department of Interior Design

423 S. Margin St., Franklin, TN 37064 | 615-794-4254 | www.omorecollege.edu/content/interioroverview.html

UNIVERSITY PROFILE
Private
Suburban
Commuter
Semester Schedule
Co-ed

STUDENT DEMOGRAPHICS
Undergraduate: 182
Graduate: 0

Male: 15%
Female: 85%

Full-time: 95%
Part-time: 5%

EXPENSES
Tuition: $21,944
Room & Board: n/a

ADMISSIONS
423 S. Margin St.
Franklin, TN 37064
615-794-4254 / 1-888-662-OMC
clee@omorecollege.edu
mdabbs@omorecollege.edu
jseitz@omorecollege.edu
thurt@omorecollege.edu

DEGREE INFORMATION

Major / Degree / Concentration	Enrollment	Requirements for entry	Graduation rate
Interior Design Bachelor of Fine Arts	60	2.35 gpa and 19 ACT minimum Home Exam may be required	80%

TOTAL PROGRAM ENROLLMENT
Undergraduate: 60
Graduate: 0

Male: 15%
Female: 85%

Full-time: 80%
Part-time: 20%

International: 5%
Minority: 10%

Job Placement Rate: 80%

SCHOLARSHIPS / FINANCIAL AID
Academic Scholarship, Portfolio Scholarship, Work-Study, Payment Plan, Tennessee Hope Lottery Scholarship, Tennessee Student Assistance Award, Federal Assistance, State Assistance, Robert C. Byrd Honors Scholarship Program, Ned McWherter Scholars Program, Dependent Children Scholarship Program

Students Receiving Scholarships or Financial Aid: 85%

TOTAL FACULTY: 33
Full-time: 23%
Part-time: 77%
Online: 0%

NCIDQ Certified: 3
Licensed Interior Designers: 3
LEED Certified: 0

INTERIOR DESIGN ADMINISTRATION
Lance Westbrooks - Executive Vice President and Provost
Shari Fox - Academic Dean
David Koellein - Chair, Interior Design

PROFESSIONAL / ACADEMIC AFFILIATIONS
American Society of Interior Designers
International Interior Design Association
Interior Design Educators Council

CIDA ACCREDITATION
Bachelor of Fine Arts Majoring in Interior Design (2010, 2016)

PROGRAM DESCRIPTION AND PHILOSOPHY

The Interior Design program at O'More College of Design is guided by the idea that spaces, once shaped, shape their occupants in turn. To design a space well is to set a suitable stage for the activities that compose the human experience. Interior designers are trained to command the relationship of interior space to all other spaces, to social and environmental health in local and global contexts, and to the lives of individuals and cultures. Our graduates must be uniquely equipped with not only the knowledge to create interior spaces that meet physical and social needs, but also the capacity to inspire others through creative and critical thought.

FACILITIES

CAD, Revit, Google Sketchup, Photoshop, Twilight, Piranesi

ONLINE / DISTANCE LEARNING

Not available

COURSES OF INSTRUCTION

- Basic Drafting
- CAD Lab
- Design Drawing
- Detailing
- Codes and Regulations
- Architectural Studio
- Business Practices
- Interior Design Studios 1-5
- Senior Major Studio
- Research and Documentation
- Sustainable Design
- Urban Design
- Materials and Textiles
- History of Furniture
- Illumination
- Interior Design Internship
- Design Fundamentals 1 & 2
- Design Theory and the Built Environment
- History of Art, Architecture, and Design 1 & 2
- Structures, Materials and Systems
- Color Theory and Application
- Basic Drawing

INTERNSHIPS

Required of majors at Junior/Senior level. Interns are typically placed at a variety of Firms; Interior Design and Architecture.

STUDY ABROAD

O'More-Ireland: A summer semester in Abbey-Leix Ireland, the ancestral home of the O'Mores; Ireland internships; and educational and artistic exchanges. O'More-Grand Tour: International travel courses which provide research, training, and travel to various international communities each year—Paris, Germany-Austria, Rome, Greece-Turkey, Italy, Prague-Budapest, Scandinavia.

NOTABLE ALUMNI

Not reported

STUDENT ACTIVITIES AND ORGANIZATIONS

ASID, IIDA, USGBC, SGA

FACULTY SPECIALIZATIONS AND RESEARCH

- Urban Design
- Furniture Craftmanship
- Illumination

University of Memphis

Department of Architecture

404 Jones Hall, Memphis, TN 38152 | 901-678-2724 | http://architecture.memphis.edu

UNIVERSITY PROFILE
Public
Urban
Commuter
Semester Schedule
Co-ed

STUDENT DEMOGRAPHICS
Undergraduate: 16,719
Graduate: 4,288

Male: 38%
Female: 62%

Full-time: 69%
Part-time: 31%

EXPENSES
Tuition: Not reported
Room & Board: Not reported

ADMISSIONS
101 Wilder Tower
Memphis, TN 38152
800-669-2678
recruitment@memphis.edu

DEGREE INFORMATION

Major / Degree / Concentration	Enrollment	Requirements for entry	Graduation rate
Interior Design Bachelor of Fine Arts	40	Entry portfolio Candidacy portfolio review after three semesters	Not reported
Architecture Bachelor of Fine Arts	95	Entry portfolio Candidacy portfolio review after three semesters	Not reported
Architecture Master of Architecture	15	3.0 gpa Preprofessional degree in architecture of related field Portfolio review	Not reported

TOTAL PROGRAM ENROLLMENT
Undergraduate: 40
Graduate: n/a

Male: 0%
Female: 100%

Full-time: 100%
Part-time: 0%

International: 1%
Minority: 1%

Job Placement Rate: 90%

SCHOLARSHIPS / FINANCIAL AID
Not reported

TOTAL FACULTY: 6
Full-time: 67%
Part-time: 33%
Online: n/a

NCIDQ Certified: 33%
Licensed Interior Designers: 33%
LEED Certified: 16%

INTERIOR DESIGN ADMINISTRATION
Michael Hagge, Chair, Department of Architecture
Sherry Bryan, Director, Architecture Program
Michael Chisamore, Director of the Interior Design Program

PROFESSIONAL / ACADEMIC AFFILIATIONS
International Interior Design Association
Interior Design Educators Council
Environmental Design Research Association

CIDA ACCREDITATION
Bachelor of Fine Arts in Interior Design (2008, 2014)

PROGRAM DESCRIPTION AND PHILOSOPHY

The mission of the Department of Architecture is to prepare graduates to enter the professional practice of architecture or Interior Design and to serve the Memphis and Mid-South region through research, engaged scholarship, interdisciplinary collaboration, and creative expression that contributes to sustainable, stable communities and enhances the quality of life for all citizens.

The goals of the department are: to provide the highest quality professional education through a well-rounded discovery-based curriculum in both the art and science of design with emphasis on processes, professional standards, and the practical application of design and technology; to provide research opportunities for faculty and students with emphasis on "hands on" multi-disciplinary projects through which students gain valuable professional experience while providing services to the citizens of the region; and to expand opportunities for Architecture and Interior Design students by bringing them together with faculty and students in the City Planning and Real Estate Development programs to address public issues, support stable and sustainable neighborhoods, and develop community visions throughout the region.

FACILITIES

Instructional space dedicated to architecture and Interior Design includes design studios for all six academic years, classrooms, two CAD and Visualization labs, special purpose rooms, seminar rooms, and a wood and metal shop. All students enrolled in a design studio course have 24-hour access to their dedicated space within the appropriate studio. A resource library and small faculty library are available for students to use in their research. The department also has two apartment-style residences located on campus and equipped with studio space as well as computer facilities.

ONLINE / DISTANCE LEARNING
Not available

COURSES OF INSTRUCTION
- Foundations Sequence
- Professional and Technical Sequence
- History and Theory Sequence
- Computer Sequence
- Design Studio Sequence
- Thesis
- Electives
- University General Education Courses

INTERNSHIPS
Required of majors at 4th year. Interns are typically placed at architecture and design firms

STUDY ABROAD
The Department of Architecture and the University of Memphis offer study abroad programs.

NOTABLE ALUMNI
Not reported

STUDENT ACTIVITIES AND ORGANIZATIONS
American Institute of Architecture Students (AIAS), Alpha Rho Chi (APX), the Construction Specifications Institute Student Affiliate (CSI-S), the International Interior Design Association Campus Center (IIDA), and the National Organization of Minority Architecture Students (NOMAS). The Department of Architecture is in the process of establishing a chapter of the American Society of Interior Designers (ASID).

FACULTY SPECIALIZATIONS AND RESEARCH
- Architecture
- Urban Design
- Interior Design
- Historic Preservation
- Architectural Illustration
- City Planning
- Sustainable Design
- Architectural Education
- City Building

Watkins College of Art, Design & Film

Department of Interior Design

2298 Rosa L. Parks Blvd., Nashville, TN 37228 | 615-277-7447 | www.watkins.edu/

UNIVERSITY PROFILE
Private
Urban
Commuter
Semester Schedule
Co-ed

STUDENT DEMOGRAPHICS
Undergraduate: 398
Graduate: n/a

Male: 58%
Female: 42%

Full-time: 59%
Part-time: 41%

EXPENSES
Tuition: $17,940
Room & Board: $6,000

ADMISSIONS
2298 Rosa L. Parks Blvd
Nashville, TN 37228
615-383-4848
admissions@watkins.edu

DEGREE INFORMATION

Major / Degree / Concentration	Enrollment	Requirements for entry	Graduation rate
Interior Design Bachelor of Fine Arts	64	2.0 gpa Portfolio review after Freshman year	92%

TOTAL PROGRAM ENROLLMENT
Undergraduate: 64
Graduate: n/a

Male: 3%
Female: 97%

Full-time: 57%
Part-time: 43%

International: 4%
Minority: 6%

Job Placement Rate: 90%

SCHOLARSHIPS / FINANCIAL AID
Watkins offers federal and non-federal aid, grants, federal and non-federal workstudy opportunities and many scholarships including scholarships based on merit.

Students Receiving Scholarships or Financial Aid: 92%

TOTAL FACULTY: 9
Full-time: 33%
Part-time: 66%
Online: 0%

NCIDQ Certified: 66%
Licensed Interior Designers: 33%
LEED Certified: 22%

INTERIOR DESIGN ADMINISTRATION
Jennifer Overstreet, Department Chair

PROFESSIONAL / ACADEMIC AFFILIATIONS
American Society of Interior Designers
International Interior Design Association
Interior Design Educators Council
Environmental Design Research
   Association

CIDA ACCREDITATION
Bachelor of Fine Arts, Interior Design
(2010, 2016)

PROGRAM DESCRIPTION AND PHILOSOPHY

Watkins Interior Design program offers a studio-based curriculum intended to educate the student who is intent on a professional career as a registered Interior Designer with strong links to the communities that are impacting the twenty-first century. The program allows students to pursue service-learning projects that provide many valuable real-world learning experiences. The program assists students in the development of professional presentation techniques and technical skills, abilities to create innovative designs, analyze and solve problems and apply appropriate material use while meeting codes.

FACILITIES

The Watkins campus was and still is being designed with interaction in mind. Laptops are required by the beginning of the Sophomore year and Internet access is wireless throughout the campus providing ease of independent working and collaboration. Because laptops are required for all Interior Design majors, the most up-to-date software is provided for each student while in the Interior Design program including AutoCAD, Revit, 3D Studio Max, SketchUp, Photoshop and Microsoft Office. Pin-up and Digital critique spaces are provided throughout the department and campus as well. The Interior Design department is dedicated to providing adequate working spaces for students to engage their mind, train their eye, and cultivate talent.

ONLINE / DISTANCE LEARNING

As of now, classes are not offered online, but will be soon.

COURSES OF INSTRUCTION

- Design Fundamentals
- Architectural Drawing
- Space Planning and Human Factors
- Building Construction and Detailing
- Interior Materials and Specifications
- History of Architecture & Interiors I & II
- Presentation Techniques
- Lighting I & II
- CAD I & II
- 3D Digital Modeling
- Residential Studio
- Commercial & Advanced Commercial Studios
- Advanced Materials
- Portfolio Design
- Internship
- Professional Practices, Sustainability
- Codes & Regulations
- Seminar in Design Theory
- Senior Thesis Research and Project

INTERNSHIPS

Required of majors at Junior level and up. Interns are free to choose an internship of their liking as long as it is approved by the internship coordinator. Most internships are placed within residential or commercial Interior Design and architecture firms, but are not limited to those options.

STUDY ABROAD

Every year the students have the opportunity to study abroad. This opportunity is offered through the Fine Arts Department and available to all BFA majors. I different country is chosen every year.

NOTABLE ALUMNI

Beth Haley, Beth Haley Designs
Shonna Sexton, Sexton Studios

STUDENT ACTIVITIES AND ORGANIZATIONS

The Watkins Interior Design Program has two Interior Design student organizations American Society of Interior Designers (ASID) and International Interior Design Association (IIDA). Both are organized collaboratively by the students. Such activites include monthly meetings introducing new productlines and their local representatives, a bi-annual YART Sale, and fund rasing opportunities for local organizatoins including Habitat for Humanity.

FACULTY SPECIALIZATIONS AND RESEARCH

One of the strengths of the faculty in the Interior Design department is our diversity. All of the Interior Designers and architects that teach in the Interior Design department have different areas of study and research interest. Some of those areas include sustainability, theory-based design, 3D digital modeling, health-care, and hospitality design.

Abilene Christian University

Art & Design Department, College of Arts & Sciences

Don H. Morris Center, Rm 142, Abilene, TX 79699 | 325-674-2000 | www.acu.edu/academics/cas/art

UNIVERSITY PROFILE
Private
Urban
Residential
Semester Schedule
Co-ed

STUDENT DEMOGRAPHICS
Undergraduate: 3,841
Graduate: 997

Male: 47%
Female: 53%

Full-time: 82%
Part-time: 18%

EXPENSES
Annual Tuition: $22,000
Room & Board: $7,500

ADMISSIONS
http://www.acu.edu/
admissions/freshmen/info/
index.html
325-674-2650
tnb99a@acu.edu

DEGREE INFORMATION

Major / Degree / Concentration	Enrollment	Requirements for entry	Graduation rate
Interior Design Bachelor of Science	75	Portfolio review after 1st year	75%

TOTAL PROGRAM ENROLLMENT
Undergraduate: 75
Graduate: Not reported

Male: 3%
Female: 91%

Full-time: 97%
Part-time: 3%

International: 3%
Minority: 5%

Job Placement Rate: 80% in 6 months

SCHOLARSHIPS / FINANCIAL AID
Each year around $7,000 is awarded
competitively to Interior Design majors.
Selection is based upon in-class
performance and submission of an
essay. Awards are possible following the
Freshman year.

Students Receiving Scholarships or
Financial Aid: 96%

TOTAL FACULTY: 4
Full-time: 3%
Part-time: 1%

NCIDQ Certified: 2%
Licensed Interior Designers: 2%
LEED Certified: 1%

INTERIOR DESIGN ADMINISTRATION
Dr. Royce Money, President
Dr. Jeanine Varner, Provost
Kitty Wasemiller, INTD Program
 Director

PROFESSIONAL / ACADEMIC AFFILIATIONS
American Society of Interior Designers
Interior Design Educators Council

CIDA ACCREDITATION
Bachelor of Science in Interior Design
(2005, 2011)

PROGRAM DESCRIPTION AND PHILOSOPHY

The Bachelor of Science in Interior Design curriculum utilizes a progressive aesthetic applied to interiors and architectural contexts. The students explore design solutions using classical as well as an innovative variety of approaches. Students develop far reaching technological skills on a campus that capitalizes on cutting edge twenty-first Century technology and learning techniques. Students produce solutions for environments within various economic, social, and cultural settings. As many as 50% of the department's Interior Design students study abroad. The rigorous coursework leads students to implement solutions after experimentation of both theoretical and real-world contexts. The student's artistic sensibiities as well as business acumen are developed in the major specific curriculum. The liberal arts and faith-based approach to learning and designing is central to the educational environment at ACU. Above all, the goal of the curriculum is to develop professionals who have integrity and are critical thinkers, producing solutions for the benefit of the masses. Oftentimes when asked why a prospective student is interviewing with the ACU Interior Design program, the prospect relates they have searched for a Christian university offering a CIDA accredited Interior Design degree.

FACILITIES

Dedicated classrooms, drafting lab, and computer lab. Wood shop and sculpture studio are also available. Presentation gallery spaces.

COURSES OF INSTRUCTION

- Interior Components
- Design Studio I, II, III
- Building Systems
- Architectural Design I & II
- Advance Design

INTERNSHIPS

Required of majors at Senior level

STUDY ABROAD

Available

NOTABLE ALUMNI

Jennifer McGregor, IIDA, LEED AP - Jennifer McGregor, LLC

STUDENT ACTIVITIES AND ORGANIZATIONS

Student Chapter of ASID

FACULTY SPECIALIZATIONS AND RESEARCH

The faculty hold specializations in Design Process, Creativity in Design, Sustainable Design, History of Architecture and Furnishings, and Professional Practice

Baylor University

Department of Family & Consumer Sciences

One Bear Place #97346, Waco, TX 76798-7346 | 254-710-3626 | www.baylor.edu/fcs

UNIVERSITY PROFILE
Private
Urban
Residential
Semester Schedule
Co-ed

STUDENT DEMOGRAPHICS
Undergraduate: 12,149
Graduate: 2,465

Male: 44%
Female: 56%

Full-time: 96%
Part-time: 4%

EXPENSES
Tuition: $26,966
Room & Board: $8,331

ADMISSIONS
One Bear Pl. #97056
Waco, TX 76798-7056
254-710-3435 / 800-229-5678

DEGREE INFORMATION

Major / Degree / Concentration	Enrollment	Requirements for entry	Graduation rate
Interior Design **Bachelor of Arts**	14	Portfolio review process after Sophomore and Senior years	Not reported
Family & Consumer Sciences **Bachelor of Science** **Interior Design**	79	Portfolio review process after Sophomore and Senior years	Not reported

TOTAL PROGRAM ENROLLMENT
Undergraduate: 93
Graduate: N/A

Male: %
Female: 97%

Full-time: 94%
Part-time: 6%

International: 2%
Minority: 15%

Job Placement Rate: Not reported

SCHOLARSHIPS / FINANCIAL AID
Not reported

TOTAL FACULTY: 4
Full-time: 2
Part-time: 2
Online: 0

NCIDQ Certified: 2
Licensed Interior Designers: Not
  reported
LEED Certified: Not reported

INTERIOR DESIGN ADMINISTRATION
Suzy Weems, Department Chair
Adair Bowen, ID Program Coordinator

PROFESSIONAL / ACADEMIC AFFILIATIONS
American Society of Interior Designers
Interior Design Educators Council

CIDA ACCREDITATION
BA and BS in Family and Consumer
Sciences (2005, 2011)

PROGRAM DESCRIPTION AND PHILOSOPHY

Interior Design faculty and faculty of supporting disciplines aspire to foster in the student a commitment to designing and improving the built environment with respect and regard for the health, safety, and well-being of all users. Emphasis is placed on: building a sound foundation at the Freshman and Sophomore level through both a strong knowledge base and hands-on experiences to allow for critical problem-solving and creative expression at the Junior and Senior level; the design process, placing special emphasis on research as critical to effective problem-solving; a commitment to ethical, responsible design solutions which support the sustainability of the environment from a global perspective; embracing technology in classroom delivery and student production techniques with flexibility and acceptance of change as necessary for the quality and advancement of the educational experience.

FACILITIES

Drafting Lab (24 hr), Computer Lab; upper level students only (24 hr)

ONLINE / DISTANCE LEARNING

Not available

COURSES OF INSTRUCTION

- Interior Design Graphics I & II
- Fundamentals of Interior Desgin
- Textiles Science
- Building Systems and Codes
- Computer Aided Drafting and Design
- History of Interiors I & II
- Lighting for Interiors
- Interior Design Studio I, II, III, and IV
- Materials and Finishes for Interiors
- Interior Design Presentation Studio
- 3-D AutoCAD and Design Graphics
- Interior Design Field Experience

INTERNSHIPS

Required of majors at Junior level. Placed at HOK, Catherine Dolen & Associates, HDR, HKS Inc., Vision 360, Alliance Architects, Wilson and Associates, Concepts 4.

STUDY ABROAD

Europe Trip every 2 years

NOTABLE ALUMNI

Christi Proctor, Catherine Dolan

STUDENT ACTIVITIES AND ORGANIZATIONS

Student ASID

FACULTY SPECIALIZATIONS AND RESEARCH

Not reported

COMMUNITY COLLEGE TRANSFERS

Consistent with Baylor's equivalency and general education requirements

Sam Houston State University

Department of Family & Consumer Sciences

P.O. Box 2177, Huntsville, TX 77341 | 936-294-1242 | www.shsu.edu/~hec_www/

UNIVERSITY PROFILE
Public
Rural
Commuter
Semester Schedule
Co-ed

STUDENT DEMOGRAPHICS
Undergraduate: 16,550
Graduate: 250

Male: 50%
Female: 50%

Full-time: 75%
Part-time: 25%

EXPENSES
Tuition: Not reported
Room & Board: Not reported

ADMISSIONS
1903 University Ave.
Estill Bldg, Ste 112
Huntsville, TX 77341
936-294-1828
admissions@shsu.edu

DEGREE INFORMATION

Major / Degree / Concentration	Enrollment	Requirements for entry	Graduation rate
Interior Design Bachelor of Arts	20	2.0 gpa	80%
Interior Design Bachelor of Science	50	2.0 gpa	80%

TOTAL PROGRAM ENROLLMENT
Undergraduate: 300
Graduate: 12

Male: 5%
Female: 95%

Full-time: 75%
Part-time: 25%

International: 1%
Minority: 3%

Job Placement Rate: 80%

SCHOLARSHIPS / FINANCIAL AID
Generally open to full-time Junior and Senior students with a gpa of 3.0 or above.

TOTAL FACULTY: 10
Full-time: 7
Part-time: 3
Online: Not reported

NCIDQ Certified: 2
Licensed Interior Designers: 1
LEED Certified: Not reported

INTERIOR DESIGN ADMINISTRATION
Dr. Janis H. White, FCS Department Chair
Dr. Laura K. Burleson, IND Program Director

PROFESSIONAL / ACADEMIC AFFILIATIONS
American Society of Interior Designers
Interior Design Educators Council

PROGRAM DESCRIPTION AND PHILOSOPHY

The program's objective is to produce graduates that have the knowledge and skills in keeping with the expectations of the Interior Design industry for entry-level employment.

FACILITIES

Computerized drafting lab, resource lab

ONLINE / DISTANCE LEARNING

Not available

COURSES OF INSTRUCTION

- Architectural Graphics for Interior Design
- Development in History of Furniture
- Design Theory and Materials
- Design Process
- Residential Design Commercial Design I
- Commercial Design II

INTERNSHIPS

Required of majors. Interns are typically placed with Residential Designers, Design/Build Firms, Architectural Firms, Commercial Design Firms

STUDY ABROAD

Advanced elective in textile/chemistry

NOTABLE ALUMNI

Not reported

STUDENT ACTIVITIES AND ORGANIZATIONS

ASID Student Chapter

FACULTY SPECIALIZATIONS AND RESEARCH

- Design for Aging individuals
- Design Writing
- Studio Teaching

Stephen F. Austin State University

School of Human Sciences

P.O. Box 13014, Nacogdoches, TX 75962 | 936-468-4502 | www.sfasu.edu/hms

UNIVERSITY PROFILE
Public
Rural
Residential
Semester Schedule
Co-ed

STUDENT DEMOGRAPHICS
Undergraduate: Not reported
Graduate: Not reported

Male: Not reported
Female: Not reported

Full-time: Not reported
Part-time: Not reported

EXPENSES
Tuition: Not reported
Room & Board: Not reported

ADMISSIONS
Office of Admissions
P.O. Box 3051 SFA
Nacogdoches, TX 75962
936-469-2504

DEGREE INFORMATION

Major / Degree / Concentration	Enrollment	Requirements for entry	Graduation rate
Interior Design **Bachelor of Science**	120	2.0 gpa Portfolio review after Sophomore year	95%

TOTAL PROGRAM ENROLLMENT
Undergraduate: Not reported
Graduate: Not reported

Male: Not reported
Female: Not reported

Full-time: 95%
Part-time: 5%

International: 3%
Minority: 6%

Job Placement Rate: 95%

SCHOLARSHIPS / FINANCIAL AID
Numerous Department and School
scholarships are available.

Students Receiving Scholarships or
Financial Aid: 40%

TOTAL FACULTY: 4
Full-time: 4
Part-time: 2
Online: Not reported

NCIDQ Certified: 3
Licensed Interior Designers: 4
LEED Certified: Not reported

INTERIOR DESIGN ADMINISTRATION
Not reported

PROFESSIONAL / ACADEMIC AFFILIATIONS
Interior Design Educators Council

CIDA ACCREDITATION
Bachelor of Science in Interior Design
(2008, 2014)

PROGRAM DESCRIPTION AND PHILOSOPHY

Rated one of the best in Texas by employers. Students' strengths are space planning, codes, and knowledge of ADA.

FACILITIES

Design Center, Computer Lab

ONLINE / DISTANCE LEARNING

Graduate programs

COURSES OF INSTRUCTION

- Codes
- Residential Design
- Commercial Design 1 & 2
- Lighting, Cabinetry
- Creative Solutions
- Materials

INTERNSHIPS

Required of majors at Junior/ Senior levels. Interns are typically placed at companies such as Disney, Corrigan Architectural firm, HRT, Goodwin and Lasister Engineering and Architectural firm, Hesters and Sanders Architecture, Leo A. Daly Architectural, and The Kitchen Source.

STUDY ABROAD

Available

NOTABLE ALUMNI

Sandy Hale, Lori Foux, LaLa Dickerson, Barba Eielteman

STUDENT ACTIVITIES AND ORGANIZATIONS

Student group—Student Chapter of ASID

FACULTY SPECIALIZATIONS AND RESEARCH

Sally Ann Swearingen - Design Center/ FAcilities/ Codes; Mitzi Perritt—Healthcare and lighting; Leisha Bridwell—Rendeering; Donna Pharris—Environmental

COMMUNITY COLLEGE TRANSFERS

Montogomery College, San Jacintio, Angelina College

Texas Christian University

Department of Design, Merchandising & Textiles

2722 West Berry St., Fort Worth, TX 76109 | 817-275-7499 | www.demt.tcu.edu

UNIVERSITY PROFILE
Private
Suburban
Residential
Semester Schedule
Co-ed

STUDENT DEMOGRAPHICS
Undergraduate: 7,640
Graduate: 1,213

Male: 41%
Female: 59%

Full-time: 88%
Part-time: 12%

EXPENSES
Tuition: $28,250
Room & Board: $6,200

ADMISSIONS
2800 S. University Dr. # 112
Fort Worth, TX 76129
817-257-7490
frogmail@tcu.edu

DEGREE INFORMATION

Major / Degree / Concentration	Enrollment	Requirements for entry	Graduation rate
Interior Design Bachelor of Science	120	2.5 gpa Portfolio review during first semester of Sophomore year— program is cut to 15 students	95%

TOTAL PROGRAM ENROLLMENT
Undergraduate: 113
Graduate: 0

Male: 4.4%
Female: 95.6%

Full-time: 100%
Part-time: 0%

International: 3.5%
Minority: 7.1%

Job Placement Rate: 52.7%

SCHOLARSHIPS / FINANCIAL AID
One need-based scholarship is offered for Interior Design majors, specific to the semester Study Abroad program in Italy.

TOTAL FACULTY: 6
Full-time: 100%
Part-time: 0%
Online: 0%

NCIDQ Certified: 30%
Licensed Interior Designers: 20%
LEED Certified: 0%

INTERIOR DESIGN ADMINISTRATION
Dr. Janace Bubonia. Department Chair
Dr. Laura Prestwood. Interior Design
 Coordinator

PROFESSIONAL / ACADEMIC AFFILIATIONS
American Society of Interior Designers
International Interior Design Association
Interior Design Educators Council
Illuminating Engineering Society
International Association of Lighting
 Designers
National Council for Interior Design
 Qualification

CIDA ACCREDITATION
Bachelor of Science (2004, 2010)

PROGRAM DESCRIPTION AND PHILOSOPHY

Interior Design is a four- year-lock step program at TCU. A formal portfolio review is initiated during the fall of the Sophomore year. Acceptance by the Interior Design faculty is necessary for continuation in the program. The Interior Design curriculum is a highly intensive studio experience. Interior Design majors develop fundamental skills in a curriculum that provides study in computer aided design, lighting, building construction, business and professional practice, color, materials and finishes. The major offers Study Abroad programs in France and Italy. All majors are required to complete a professional internship. The Council for Interior Design Accreditation (CIDA) has continuously accredited the curriculum since 1978. The Center for Lighting Education, established in 1998 and unique to this area of the country and the program offers students hands-on lessons in lighting application and the use of color, angles and intensities to create different moods and atmospheres for retail purposes. An interdisciplinary Lighting Minor integrates the disciplines of fashion merchandising, Interior Design, and theatre to explore lighting for visual presentation.

FACILITIES

On campus: Dedicated Computer Lab, Materials Resource Area. In Fort Worth: Kimbell Art Museum, Modern Art Museum, Amon Carter Museum.

ONLINE / DISTANCE LEARNING

Not available

COURSES OF INSTRUCTION

- Design Fundamentals
- Lighting Fundamentals
- Architectural Components;
- CAD for Interiors
- History of Interiors
- Special Purpose Design
- Professional Practices.

INTERNSHIPS

Required of majors at the end of Junior Year. Interns are typically placed at companies such as Bouyea & Associates Inc., Callison, Corgan Associates Inc., Duncan Miller Ullman, HKS Inc., Jan Showers & Associates, Johnson Light Studio, Joseph Minton, Knoll, Looney & Associates, Mandarin Oriental Hotel Group, Morrison Seifert Murphy, Paul Duesing Partners, Staffelbach Design Associates, Wilson &Associates

STUDY ABROAD

Available

NOTABLE ALUMNI

Not reported

STUDENT ACTIVITIES AND ORGANIZATIONS

The TCU Interior Design Association (TIDA) is a student organization designed to foster interaction between Interior Design majors and the industry. Any Interior Design major can become a member of TIDA as a part of their program of study. TIDA sponsors monthly meetings where guest speakers provide insightful information on Interior Design. Topics have included portfolio development, programming, latest trends in color and design and product information. Phi Upsilon Omicron, Beta Zeta Chapter at TCU, is a national honor society recognizing and encouraging achieved excellence in scholarship, leadership and service.

FACULTY SPECIALIZATIONS AND RESEARCH

Laura Prestwood, PhD, Associate Professor, Interior Design Coordinator, Director of TCU Center for Lighting Education, Director of Women's Studies, Lighting Design, Healthcare, and Women's Studies; Jane Kucko, PhD, Associate Professor, Director for the Center for International Studies: TCU Abroad, International Education, Design Process; Sarajane Eisen, PhD, Assistant Professor, Healing Environments in Healthcare; Amy Roehl, MFA, Assistant Professor, Residential and Commercial Design, Integration of Professional and Educational Design Communities; Gayla Jett Shannon, MArch, Assistant Professor of Professional Practice, Professional Practice, Technology, Design Process, Color; Julie Ballantyne, MFA, Instructor, Illustration, Design Fundamentals

Texas State University

Department of Family & Consumer Sciences
Interior Design Program, 601 University Dr., San Marcos, TX 78666 | 512-245-2155 | **www.fcs.txstate.edu**

UNIVERSITY PROFILE
Public
Suburban
Residential
Commuter
Semester Schedule
Co-ed

STUDENT DEMOGRAPHICS
Undergraduate: 24,525
Graduate: 4,757

Male: 44.2%
Female: 55.8%

Full-time: 73%
Part-time: 27%

EXPENSES
Tuition: $7,500
Room & Board: Varies, avg.
$7,000

ADMISSIONS
601 University Dr.
San Marcos, TX 78666
512-245-2364
ck10@txstate.edu

DEGREE INFORMATION

Major / Degree / Concentration	Enrollment	Requirements for entry	Graduation rate
Family & Consumer Sciences Bachelor of Science Interior Design	Not reported	2.5 gpa Completion of three pre-ID courses with C or better	Not reported

TOTAL PROGRAM ENROLLMENT
Undergraduate: 250
Graduate: 0

Male: 6.8%
Female: 93.2%

Full-time: 67.6%
Part-time: 32.4%

International: unknown
Minority: 26%

Job Placement Rate: Not reported

SCHOLARSHIPS / FINANCIAL AID
University student loans and many scholarships, six department/ program scholarships

TOTAL FACULTY: 8
Full-time: 87.5%
Part-time: 12.5%
Online: 0%

NCIDQ Certified: 38%
Licensed Interior Designers: 50%
LEED Certified: 13%

INTERIOR DESIGN ADMINISTRATION
Dr. Denise Trauth, President
Dr. Maria Canabal, Department Chair
Mrs. Nancy O. Granato, ID Program
  Coordinator

PROFESSIONAL / ACADEMIC AFFILIATIONS
American Society of Interior Designers
International Interior Design Association
Interior Design Educators Council

CIDA ACCREDITATION
Bachelor of Science in Family & Consumer Science - Major in Interior Design (2009, 2015)

PROGRAM DESCRIPTION AND PHILOSOPHY

Philosophy: The program exists to provide an educational experience that develops the ability to think critically, creatively, and ethically. It fosters an atmosphere of respect for the environment and all individuals towards bringing them to their fullest potential. It is dedicated to instilling character, integrity, compassion, diligence, and a lifelong pursuit of learning and professional excellence.

Mission: To prepare students to be responsible and competent entry-level Interior Design professionals.

- To provide students maximum opportunity for intellectual growth and creative expression.
- To instill in students an enduring respect for humanity and the environment.
- To imbue students with a sense of service and social obligation.
- To serve as a socially responsive educational resource for the larger community.

FACILITIES

Two on-site computer labs/ classrooms with tech support and others around campus, wireless Internet and projection equipment in most classrooms, a large extensive university library with access to others statewide. Museums abound in Austin, San Antonio, Dallas, and Houston.

ONLINE / DISTANCE LEARNING

Not available

COURSES OF INSTRUCTION

- Design Graphics I (manual)
- Design Graphics II (digital)
- CAD/Revit
- History of Interiors
- Housing and Environment
- Visual Presentation Techniques
- Materials and Sources
- Interior Lighting Design
- Comprehensive Interior Design (Codes)
- Professional Practices
- Residential and Commercial Interior Design Studios
- Research/Environmental Design Studio
- Internship
- Portfolio Development

INTERNSHIPS

Required of majors at Senior level. Interns are typically placed at companies such as small and large Interior Design or architectural firms, lighting design firms, office design/ furniture firms, residential furniture/ design studios, institutional and government design departments, to name a few. Locations can be state, national or international.

STUDY ABROAD

Through Art Dept. and other programs or schools.

NOTABLE ALUMNI

Not reported

STUDENT ACTIVITIES AND ORGANIZATIONS

Phi Upslon Omicron is the FCS Honor Society. ASID and IIDA Student Chapters, a new EGB chapter (Emerging Green Builders), Bobcat Build and Habitat for Humanity, Annual Juried Interior Design Student Show on campus.

FACULTY SPECIALIZATIONS AND RESEARCH

- Lighting and Vision
- Housing and Elderly
- Urban Design
- Fiber Art
- Environmental Psychology
- Architecture
- Historic Preservation
- Theory
- Methodology
- Criticism

Texas Tech University

Department of Design, College of Human Sciences

Box 41220, Lubbock, TX 79409-1220 | 806-742-3050 | www.depts.ttu.edu/hs/dod/

DEGREE INFORMATION

Major / Degree / Concentration	Enrollment	Requirements for entry	Graduation rate
Interior Design Bachelor of Interior Design	176	3.0 gpa transfer Portfolio review after Freshman year	49%
Environmental Design Master of Science	17	gpa, transcripts, letters of recommendation, portfolio, resume, TOEFL scores for international students	Not reported
Interior & Environmental Design Doctor of Philosophy	4	gpa, transcripts, letters of recommendation, portfolio, resume, TOEFL scores for international students	Not reported

TOTAL PROGRAM ENROLLMENT
Undergraduate: 176
Graduate: 13

Male: 10%
Female: 90%

Full-time: 90.3%
Part-time: 9.7%

International: 2.3%
Minority: 16.5%

Job Placement Rate: Specific data not available.

SCHOLARSHIPS / FINANCIAL AID
The Department of Design awards/ distributes scholarship funds totaling $38,242. Not all departmental scholarships have criteria for ID/ENVD students. Of the scholarships that can be awarded to ID/ENVD students, a total of $12,000 was awarded to our students for the 2010-2011 award year.

TOTAL FACULTY: 7
Full-time: 6
Part-time: 1
Online: 0

NCIDQ Certified: 3
Licensed Interior Designers: 3
LEED Certified: 1

INTERIOR DESIGN ADMINISTRATION
Dr. Cherif Amor, Interim Department Chair
Dr. Zane D. Curry, Associate Department Chair, Interior Design Program Director
Dr. JoAnn Shroyer, Director Graduate Programs

PROFESSIONAL / ACADEMIC AFFILIATIONS
American Society of Interior Designers
International Interior Design Association
Interior Design Educators Council
Environmental Design Research Association

CIDA ACCREDITATION
Bachelor of Interior Design (2009, 2015)

PROGRAM DESCRIPTION AND PHILOSOPHY

Accredited by the Council for Interior Design Accreditation, the Bachelor of Interior Design program provides a sound curriculum that prepares individuals as entry-level Interior Designers. The curriculum also may serve as preparation for continued study in graduate schools offering advanced degrees in Interior Design or related areas.

FACILITIES

College of Human Sciences/ Department of Design: 3 Computer labs and 4 Interior Design studios. University: 3D Graphics lab, multiple museums, archives, libraries, etc.

ONLINE / DISTANCE LEARNING

Not available

COURSES OF INSTRUCTION

- Interiors I, II, & III
- Lighting Systems
- Period Furnishings I& II
- Advanced Design Processes
- Computer Aided Drafting for ID I & II
- Studio Procedures and Professional Practices
- Internship
- Advanced Interiors
- Collaboration Studio

INTERNSHIPS

Required of majors at Junior level.

STUDY ABROAD

Danish Institute for Study Abroad, American Intercontinental University Study Abroad and Internship Programs Etc.

NOTABLE ALUMNI

Asem Obeidat (Ph.D. 2008 and is currently Assistant Dean at Yarmouk University in Jordan)Jan Parker, Director of Art Institu, te program in Dallas, Texas Victor Castillo, RID, Associate Principal, Alamo Architects, San Antonio John Dubard, Parkhill Smith and Cooper, Lubbock

STUDENT ACTIVITIES AND ORGANIZATIONS

Student Organizations: International Interior Design Association, American Society of Interior Designers

FACULTY SPECIALIZATIONS AND RESEARCH

Home environments with special emphasis on social, psychological, cultural and economic contexts: Learning environments for individuals with Autism Spectrum Disorders: Adaptive Re-use: Humanistic issues impacting citizens of the elder population: Interior Design Education and Retention: Building component technology and development.

COMMUNITY COLLEGE TRANSFERS

Texas Tech University System is implementing a "2+2" formula-- two years community college then students are transferred to TTU for the completion of the degree plan.

University of North Texas

Department of Design, College of Visual Arts & Design

1155 Union Circle #305100, Denton, TX 75080 | 940-565-3621 | www.art.unt.edu/design

UNIVERSITY PROFILE
Public
Suburban
Commuter
Semester Schedule
Co-ed

STUDENT DEMOGRAPHICS
Undergraduate: 28,474
Graduate: 7,648

Male: 44%
Female: 56%

Full-time: 70%
Part-time: 30%

EXPENSES
Tuition: $5,360
Room & Board: $6,534

ADMISSIONS
1155 Union Circle #311277
Denton, TX 76203
940-565-2681
undergrad@unt.edu

DEGREE INFORMATION

Major / Degree / Concentration	Enrollment	Requirements for entry	Graduation rate
Interior Design Bachelor of Fine Arts	225	2.5 gpa Portfolio review after Freshman & Sophomore years	Not reported

TOTAL PROGRAM ENROLLMENT
Undergraduate: 225
Graduate: 1

Male: 2%
Female: 98%

Full-time: Not reported
Part-time: Not reported

International: Not reported
Minority: Not reported

Job Placement Rate: 100%

SCHOLARSHIPS / FINANCIAL AID
Not reported

TOTAL FACULTY: 5
Full-time: 100%
Part-time: Not reported
Online: Not reported

NCIDQ Certified: 60%
Licensed Interior Designers: 40%
LEED Certified: 20%

INTERIOR DESIGN ADMINISTRATION
Dr. Robert Milnes – Dean
Cynthia Mohr- Chair-Department of
  Design

PROFESSIONAL / ACADEMIC AFFILIATIONS
American Society of Interior Designers
International Interior Design Association
Interior Design Educators Council
Environmental Design Research
  Association

CIDA ACCREDITATION
Bachelor of Fine Arts (2009, 2015)

PROGRAM DESCRIPTION AND PHILOSOPHY

The Interior Design curriculum at the University of North Texas is based on the belief that Interior Designers have design responsibilities for all spaces built for human occupancy. The curriculum prepares the student for challenges found in accepting and analyzing a problem, assessing existing conditions, researching and synthesizing a solution, visually and orally presenting a solution, and reviewing the process for insights for future improvements, all with the goal of creating Interior Design solutions for the improvement of the physical environment and the protection of the safety of the inhabitants.

FACILITIES

Computer Labs with Adobe Creative Suite, AutoCAD, Revit, College of Visual Arts & Design Visual Recource Collection, Interior Design Sample Room

ONLINE / DISTANCE LEARNING

Not available

COURSES OF INSTRUCTION

- Drawing I & II
- Design I & II
- Art Appreciation
- Intro to Interior Design
- Art History Survey I & II
- Drawing for Interior Design
- AutoCAD
- Presentation Techniques
- Building Systems
- Millwork & Detailing
- 20th Century Architecture & Interiors
- Textiles
- Special Topics in Interior Design
- Space Planning I, II, III, IV, V
- Professional Practices
- Internship

INTERNSHIPS

Required of majors at Senior level. Interns are typically placed at companies such as Gensler, HOK, HKS, Corgan & Associates, Leo A Daly, Forrest Perkins, Duncan Miller & Ullman, Interprise Design, WaterMark Design Studio, Hayslip Design Associates, M Group, Vision 360, Inventure Design, LLC, Nelson + Morgan Architects,

STUDY ABROAD

Through the University of Dundee, Scotland—Duncan of Jordanstone College of Art and Design

NOTABLE ALUMNI

Not reported

STUDENT ACTIVITIES AND ORGANIZATIONS

Student chapters of ASID and IIDA

FACULTY SPECIALIZATIONS AND RESEARCH

- Lighting
- Evidence Based-Design
- Green Design/Sustainability & Life Cycle Issues
- Culture & Pedagogy

University of Texas at Austin

Interior Design Program, School of Architecture

1 University Station; MC B7500, Austin, TX 78712 | 512-471-6249 | http://soa.utexas.edu/interiordesign

DEGREE INFORMATION

Major / Degree / Concentration	Enrollment	Requirements for entry	Graduation rate
Interior Design Bachelor of Science	50	SAT score Two essays	100%
Interior Design Master of Interior Design	5	Portfolio review recommendations Prior Degree in Interior Design Transcript	New in Fall 2010

TOTAL PROGRAM ENROLLMENT
Undergraduate: 55
Graduate: begins Fall 2010

Male: 7%
Female: 92%

Full-time: 100%
Part-time: Not reported

International: 7%
Minority: 9%

Job Placement Rate: 95%

SCHOLARSHIPS / FINANCIAL AID
Many students are eligible for financial aid through our financial aid office on campus. For scholarships in Interior Design we have the: 1) Deborah Ann Rock Scholarship in Interior Design; 2) the Edward Perrault Presidential Scholarship in Interior Design; and, 3) numerous scholarships students may apply for through our School of Architecture, based primarily on merit.

Students Receiving Scholarships or Financial Aid: 50%

TOTAL FACULTY: 5
Full-time: 100%
Part-time: Not reported
Online: Not reported

NCIDQ Certified: 40%
Licensed Interior Designers: 60%
LEED Certified: 0%

INTERIOR DESIGN ADMINISTRATION
Dr. Nancy Kwallek, Director of Interior Design
Gene Edward Mikeska, Endowed Chair for Interior Design

PROFESSIONAL / ACADEMIC AFFILIATIONS
American Society of Interior Designers
International Interior Design Association
Interior Design Educators Council
Environmental Design Research Association

CIDA ACCREDITATION
Bachelor of Science in Iterior Design (2008, 2014)

PROGRAM DESCRIPTION AND PHILOSOPHY

Upon successful completion of the degree, graduates will have strengths in the areas of: Methodology, History and Theory, Technical Knowledge, Communication, and Professional Practice. The faculty encourages the creative of interiors that promote quality of life for the occupants as well as the function and meaning of interiors as related to the client's and user's performance and satisfaction.

FACILITIES

Full computer lab faculties with state-of-the-art software; Anderson Archives in the school; Blanton Museum on campus; Harry Ransom Research Center; one of the top 10 library systems in the country.

ONLINE / DISTANCE LEARNING

Not available

COURSES OF INSTRUCTION

- Interiors and Society
- Design I, II, III, IV, V, VI
- Visual Communication I,II
- History of Interiors I
- Construction I
- Environmental Controls I, II
- Advanced Design (1), [2]

INTERNSHIPS

Required of majors between the 3rd and 4th years. 45% work in corporate Interior Design first; 10% in residential; 10% in architecture firms; 35% unknown.

STUDY ABROAD

Fourth year students may opt to study in Europe or Italy during the fall semester.

NOTABLE ALUMNI

Trisha Wilson, Dallas.

STUDENT ACTIVITIES AND ORGANIZATIONS

AMPERSAND Student Organization (combination of IIDA & ASID)

FACULTY SPECIALIZATIONS AND RESEARCH

Director's research is in effects of the ambience of the office interior on office workers, specifically studying color's affect and sustainabilty versus off-gassing.

COMMUNITY COLLEGE TRANSFERS

Our 60 slots for incoming students into the BS degree are primarily devoted to incoming Freshman. Although a number of students are admitted as change of major students (some people call these transfer students). Change of major students probably make out about 1/3rd of our undergraduate students in Interior Design. Because our entrance requirements are so high (highest SAT score requirement on campus) there is generally not enough space left for a traditional transfer student from another university.

University of Texas at San Antonio

Interior Design Program, College of Architecture

501 West Durango Blvd., San Antonio, TX 78207 | 210-458-3010 | www.utsa.edu/architecture

UNIVERSITY PROFILE
Public
Urban
Commuter
Semester Schedule
Co-ed

STUDENT DEMOGRAPHICS
Undergraduate: 25,006
Graduate: 3,678

Male: 43.88%
Female: 56.11%

Full-time: 40.16%
Part-time: 59.84%

EXPENSES
Tuition: $5,452.50
Room & Board: $9,141.00

ADMISSIONS
One UTSA Circle
San Antonio, TX 78249
(210) 458-4599
prospects@utsa.edu

DEGREE INFORMATION

Major / Degree / Concentration	Enrollment	Requirements for entry	Graduation rate
Interior Design Bachelor of Science	149	Entry is determined by the gpa of the 28 semester credit hours required in the Foundation Year of the College of Architecture.	Not reported

TOTAL PROGRAM ENROLLMENT
Undergraduate: 180
Graduate: n/a

Male: 8.7%
Female: 91.3%

Full-time: 73.2%
Part-time: 26.8%

International: 4.7%
Minority: 52%

Job Placement Rate: 90%

SCHOLARSHIPS / FINANCIAL AID
Fourty-seven of 149 students (32%) receive financial aid for the spring 2010 semester.

Students Receiving Scholarships or Financial Aid: 32%

TOTAL FACULTY: 48 (COLLEGE OF ARCHITECTURE)
Full-time: 75%
Part-time: 25%
Online: 0%

NCIDQ Certified: 2
Licensed Interior Designers: 3
LEED Certified: 3

INTERIOR DESIGN ADMINISTRATION
Dr. John Murphy, Dean, College of Architecture
Dr. Gayle Nicoll, Chair, Department of Architecture
Susan Lanford - Interior Design Program Coordinator

PROFESSIONAL / ACADEMIC AFFILIATIONS
International Interior Design Association

CIDA ACCREDITATION
Bachelor of Science in Iterior Design (2010, 2016)

PROGRAM DESCRIPTION AND PHILOSOPHY

The Interior Design (IDE) program supports a commitment to excellence in education with a humanistic focus by providing students with a challenging academic program emphasizing resourceful, flexible, adaptable, innovative, creative thinking and problem solving, applied research, and hands-on experience of design theory applied to educational activities. The Interior Design (IDE) program is a professional program leading to the practice of design through a set of core values grounded in design fundamentals. The IDE program believes these values not only inform, guide, and define the professional practice but respond to the ongoing global development of the profession. Through collaboration with the community and design professionals we foster education and research in sustainable practice, creativity, design theories, and workmanship, resulting in graduates prepared for culturally innovative leadership who have a commitment to professional ethics and a lifelong passion for learning.

FACILITIES

Students have convenient access to a comprehensive and current range of information (bound, electronic, or online) about Interior Design and relevant disciplines as well as product information and samples. The library at 1604 and downtown library have over 3,637 volumes, videos, and periodicals for Interior Design and decorative arts. The UTSA library participates in a variety of cooperative library aggreements at the local, regional, national, and international level. All IDE students have access to a WEBCT/Blackboard bulletin board which contains articles, job postings, product links, software tips and more. A product library is located adjacent to the Junior and Senior studios, containing a range of product samples and literature, both from textbooks and from manufacturers.

ONLINE / DISTANCE LEARNING

Not available

COURSES OF INSTRUCTION

- History of Interior Furnishings
- Building Technology
- Interior Materials and Assemblies
- Details & Construction Graphics
- Interior Design Studios
- Color and Light

INTERNSHIPS

Not required of majors. Our alumni are working at Gensler, P.D.R., and other noteworthy firms.

STUDY ABROAD

Barcelona, Spain, Italy, Mexico City, Norogachi

NOTABLE ALUMNI

Charlie Kane, Kristy Ferguson, Radiance Ham

STUDENT ACTIVITIES AND ORGANIZATIONS

Leadership is promoted through our active student organization, IIDA Campus Center. Students participate routinely with the Professional Chapter on programs, events, CEU's, Project Tours, workshops, trade shows.

FACULTY SPECIALIZATIONS AND RESEARCH

Areas of specialization within the Interior Design core faculty include Interior Design, Architectural Design, Architectural and Interior Design History, Product Design and Manufacturing, Professional Practice, Urban Planning. Interior Design faculty (through education, teaching experience, professional practice, creative research, continuing education, and LEED certification) remain current in their chosen areas of interest and expertise. This range of educational and professional experience provides for a well-balanced team.

Salt Lake Community College

Interior Design Program, School of Arts & Communication

231 E. 400 S., Salt Lake City, UT 84111 | 801-957-3929 | www.slcc.edu/interior

UNIVERSITY PROFILE
Public
Urban
Commuter
Semester Schedule
Co-ed

STUDENT DEMOGRAPHICS
Undergraduate: 60,000
Graduate: n/a

Male: 45%
Female: 55%

Full-time: 40%
Part-time: 60%

EXPENSES
Tuition: $6,000
Room & Board: n/a

ADMISSIONS
PO BOX 30808
Salt Lake City, UT 84130-0808
801-957-4298

DEGREE INFORMATION

Major / Degree / Concentration	Enrollment	Requirements for entry	Graduation rate
Interior Design Associate of Applied Science	120	Assessment test	99%

TOTAL PROGRAM ENROLLMENT
Undergraduate: 120
Graduate: NA

Male: 20%
Female: 80%

Full-time: 40%
Part-time: 60%

International: 10%
Minority: 15%

Job Placement Rate: 80%

SCHOLARSHIPS / FINANCIAL AID
Not reported

TOTAL FACULTY: 11
Full-time: 0
Part-time: 11
Online: Not reported

NCIDQ Certified: 3
Licensed Interior Designers: 8
LEED Certified: 3

INTERIOR DESIGN ADMINISTRATION
Mojdeh Saklaki, Director

PROFESSIONAL / ACADEMIC AFFILIATIONS
American Society of Interior Designers
International Interior Design Association

PROGRAM DESCRIPTION AND PHILOSOPHY

We offer a selection of classes that introduces the students to almost every facet on interior design; we also have small classes and lots of community work & internship.

FACILITIES

Computer labs, textile labs, libray

ONLINE / DISTANCE LEARNING

Not yet

COURSES OF INSTRUCTION

- Introduction to Interior Design
- Theory & Psychology of Color
- Drafting for Interior Designers
- Historic Furnishings
- Contemporary Furnishings
- Material & Components of Design
- Perspective Drawing/Rendering
- Kitchen & Bath Design
- Lighting
- Commercial Space Planning
- Interior Design AutoCAD I
- Construction Principles
- Portfolio Preparation
- Internship
- Professional Practice

INTERNSHIPS

Required of majors. Interns are placed at every company that needs Interior Designers

STUDY ABROAD

Not available

NOTABLE ALUMNI

Not reported

STUDENT ACTIVITIES AND ORGANIZATIONS

Interior Design club, IIDA & ASID chapters

FACULTY SPECIALIZATIONS AND RESEARCH

LEED, Sustainable design

COMMUNITY COLLEGE TRANSFERS

Majority of our students start working right after the graduation; the ones who decide to move to a four-year degree have been very successful in transferring all their classes.

Weber State University

College of Applied Science & Tecnology

1503 University Circle, Ogden, UT 84408 | 801-626-6913 | www.weber.edu/interiordesign

UNIVERSITY PROFILE
Public
Urban
Commuter
Semester Schedule
Co-ed

STUDENT DEMOGRAPHICS
Undergraduate: Not reported
Graduate: Not reported

Male: Not reported
Female: Not reported

Full-time: Not reported
Part-time: Not reported

EXPENSES
Tuition: Not reported
Room & Board: Not reported

ADMISSIONS
Not reported

DEGREE INFORMATION

Major / Degree / Concentration	Enrollment	Requirements for entry	Graduation rate
Interior Design Bachelor of Science	80	2.5 gpa	75%

TOTAL PROGRAM ENROLLMENT
Undergraduate: Not reported
Graduate: Not reported

Male: 2%
Female: 98%

Full-time: Not reported
Part-time: Not reported

International: Not reported
Minority: Not reported

Job Placement Rate: 90-100%

SCHOLARSHIPS / FINANCIAL AID
Not reported

TOTAL FACULTY: 5
Full-time: 1
Part-time: 1
Online: Not reported

NCIDQ Certified: 50%
Licensed Interior Designers: 0%
LEED Certified: 0%

INTERIOR DESIGN ADMINISTRATION
Jan Slabaugh, Program Coordinator

PROFESSIONAL / ACADEMIC AFFILIATIONS
American Society of Interior Designers
International Interior Design Association
Interior Design Educators Council

CIDA ACCREDITATION
Bachelor of Science or Bachelor of Art in Interior Design—Technical Sales (2009, 2015)

PROGRAM DESCRIPTION AND PHILOSOPHY
Not reported

FACILITIES
Not reported

ONLINE / DISTANCE LEARNING
Not reported

COURSES OF INSTRUCTION
- Architectural Drafting
- CAD
- Intro. to ID. Presentation
- Textiles
- Materials
- Lighting
- Business Practice
- Residential
- Commercial
- Senior Project
- Space Planning
- Architectural Detailing
- Practicum
- Seminar
- Historical and American
- Modern Architecture
- Interiors & Furnishings
- Prespective Rendering
- Kitchen/Bath
- Protfolio
- Internship

INTERNSHIPS
Required of majors

STUDY ABROAD
Not available

NOTABLE ALUMNI
Not reported

STUDENT ACTIVITIES AND ORGANIZATIONS
Not reported

FACULTY SPECIALIZATIONS AND RESEARCH
Not reported

James Madison University

School of Art & Art History

800 South Main St., MSC 7101, Harrisonburg, VA 22807 | 540.568-6661/540-568-6216 | www.jmu.edu/art

UNIVERSITY PROFILE
Public
Rural
Residential
Semester Schedule
Co-ed

STUDENT DEMOGRAPHICS
Undergraduate: 16,896
Graduate: 1,504

Male: 40%
Female: 60%

Full-time: 94%
Part-time: 6%

EXPENSES
Tuition: $3,930 (in-state)
$10,312 (out-of-state)
Room & Board: $3,850

ADMISSIONS
JMU Office of Admissions.
MSC 1010
Harrisonburg, VA 22807
540-568-5681
admissions@jmu.edu

DEGREE INFORMATION

Major / Degree / Concentration	Enrollment	Requirements for entry	Graduation rate
Interior Design Bachelor of Fine Arts	60	Portfolio review after Sophomore year	95-100%

TOTAL PROGRAM ENROLLMENT
Undergraduate: 60
Graduate: 0

Male: 5-10%
Female: 90-95%

Full-time: 95-100%
Part-time: 0-5%

International: 0%
Minority: 11%

Job Placement Rate: 90-100%

SCHOLARSHIPS / FINANCIAL AID
Art scholarships and Achievement
Awards
- Marlene & Peter Coe Visual Arts Scholarship
- New Market Arts & Crafts Scholarship
- P. Buckley Moss Endowed Scholarship
- J. Binford Walford Scholarship
- Kathleen G. Arthur Scholarship For Study In Florence, Italy
- Dr. Jay D. Kain Art Education Scholarship
- Suzanne Luck Scholarship
- Rob Miller Graphic Design Scholarship
- Art History Forum Award
- Crystal Theodore Service With Scholarship Award
- Frances Grove Scholarship Award
- Alan Tschudi Outstanding Senior Studio Art Award
- Martha B. Caldwell Outstanding Senior Art History Award

TOTAL FACULTY: 5
Full-time: 60%
Part-time: 40%
Online: 0%

NCIDQ Certified: 20%
Licensed Interior Designers: 20% (CID)
LEED Certified: 40%

INTERIOR DESIGN ADMINISTRATION
Leslie Bellavance, Professor and Director of the School of Art & Art History
Ronn Daniel, Associate Professor and Interior Design Area Coordinator

PROFESSIONAL / ACADEMIC AFFILIATIONS
American Society of Interior Designers
International Interior Design Association
Interior Design Educators Council

CIDA ACCREDITATION
Bachelor of Fine Arts (2008, 2014)

PROGRAM DESCRIPTION AND PHILOSOPHY

JMU's Interior Design program educates leaders in the profession of Interior Design. The program offers an intensive education in the design process. The curriculum instills purpose, craft, technological competence, and versatile thinking. The graduates are passionately dedicated to the creation of meaningful interiors.

The Interior Design program is fully accredited by the Council for Interior Design Accreditation. Graduates of the program are encouraged to take the National Council for Interior Design Qualification exam after two years of work experience.

The Interior Design curriculum is centered around a 6-studio sequence. The teaching of design process and a design ethos is at the heart of the program.

Additional required coursework in interior & architectural history, materials & methods, computer drawing & modeling, mechanical drawing, and professional practices supplement the studio sequence and support design projects of increasing sophistication and complexity.

Students are required to complete a professional internship and faculty encourage students to pursue opportunities for study abroad.

FACILITIES

Every Interior Design student is provided a dedicated desk in the Interior Design studio. All students have 24-hour access to the studio as well as the Interior Design Computer Lab, which contains 20 workstations and associated scanners, printers, and plotter. Interior Design students also have access to the extensive facilities of the School of Art and Art History, including a professionally managed woodshop, the professionally managed Sawhill Art Gallery, the student-managed art Works Gallery, the Madison Art Collection archive, and through elective course-work, professional-quality art facilities in fibers, ceramics, metals, photography, animation, sculpture, printmaking, graphic design, and painting.

ONLINE / DISTANCE LEARNING

Not available

COURSES OF INSTRUCTION

- Interior Design Studio I
- Interior Design Studio II
- Portfolio Review
- Interior Design Studio III
- Interior Design Studio IV
- Interior Design Studio V
- Interior Design Studio VI—Thesis
- Architectural Graphics
- CAD I: Digital Design
- CAD II: Digital Design
- Materials and Methods I
- Materials and Methods II
- Professional Practice
- Internship
- History of Interior Design
- Modern Architecture

INTERNSHIPS

Required of majors, typically completed during the summer after Junior year. JMU Interior Design students typically find internships at architectural offices, design firms, construction firms, and showrooms located throughout the mid-Atlantic region.

STUDY ABROAD

Extensive study-abroard programs are available at James Madison University; including notable programs in Florence, Berlin, Salamanca, London, and over 50 other international destinations.

NOTABLE ALUMNI

Lisa Layman

STUDENT ACTIVITIES AND ORGANIZATIONS

Student chapters of ASID and IIDA

FACULTY SPECIALIZATIONS AND RESEARCH

- Sustainable Design
- Phenomenology
- History and Theory of Modern Architecture
- Contemporary Design Theory
- Digital representation
- 19th-century Architectural and Design History

Lord Fairfax Community College

Division of Business, Technology, Science & Health Professions

BTSHP, 173 Skirmisher Lane, Middletown, VA 22645 | 540-868-7280 | www.lfcc.edu

UNIVERSITY PROFILE
Public
Rural
Commuter
Semester Schedule
Co-ed

STUDENT DEMOGRAPHICS
Undergraduate: 7,900
Graduate: 0

Male: 38%
Female: 62%

Full-time: 22%
Part-time: 78%

EXPENSES
Tuition: $2,456
Room & Board: n/a

ADMISSIONS
173 Skirmisher Lane
Middletown, VA 22645
540-868-7107
admissions@lfcc.edu

DEGREE INFORMATION

Major / Degree / Concentration	Enrollment	Requirements for entry	Graduation rate
Interior Design Certificate	8	Not reported	Not reported

TOTAL PROGRAM ENROLLMENT
Undergraduate: 2,300
Graduate: 0

Male: 40%
Female: 60%

Full-time: 25%
Part-time: 75%

International: 2%
Minority: 2%

Job Placement Rate: Not reported

SCHOLARSHIPS / FINANCIAL AID
Students may apply for financial aid using the FAFSA and scholarship applications.

Students Receiving Scholarships or Financial Aid: 65%

TOTAL FACULTY: 85
Full-time: 10%
Part-time: 75%
Online: 25%

NCIDQ Certified: Not reported
Licensed Interior Designers: 1%
LEED Certified: Not reported

INTERIOR DESIGN ADMINISTRATION
Richard Elam, Interim Dean
Chris Coutts, Vice President of Learning

PROFESSIONAL / ACADEMIC AFFILIATIONS
Not reported

PROGRAM DESCRIPTION AND PHILOSOPHY

To expose students to basic Interior Design principles. To prepare students for entry-level positions in an Interior Design environment such as furniture stores and other retail stores.

FACILITIES

Computer labs

ONLINE / DISTANCE LEARNING

Not available

COURSES OF INSTRUCTION

- Interior Design
- Period Residential Design
- Styles of Furniture and Interiors

INTERNSHIPS

Not available

STUDY ABROAD

Not available

NOTABLE ALUMNI

Not reported

STUDENT ACTIVITIES AND ORGANIZATIONS

Not reported

FACULTY SPECIALIZATIONS AND RESEARCH

Not reported

Marymount University

Interior Design Department

2807 North Glebe Rd., Arlington, VA 22207 | 703-284-1560 | www.marymount.edu/academics/programs/interior

UNIVERSITY PROFILE
Private
Suburban
Residential
Semester Schedule
Co-ed

STUDENT DEMOGRAPHICS
Undergraduate: 2,224
Graduate: 1,256

Male: 28% undergraduate;
23% graduate
Female: 72% undergraduate;
77% graduate

Full-time: 85%
undergraduate; 40% graduate
Part-time: 15%
undergraduate; 60% graduate

EXPENSES
Tuition: $22,370
Room & Board: $9,745

ADMISSIONS
2807 North Glebe Rd.
Arlington, VA 22207
703-284-1500
admissions@marymount.edu

DEGREE INFORMATION

Major / Degree / Concentration	Enrollment	Requirements for entry	Graduation rate
Interior Design Bachelor of Arts First Professional Degree	126	gpa, SAT, ACT	61%
Interior Design Master of Arts First Professional Degree	50	3.0 gpa, GRE Portfolio review after seven prerequisite courses	Not reported
Interior Design Master of Arts Post Professional Degree	6	3.0 gpa, GRE Undergraduate in design	Not reported

TOTAL PROGRAM ENROLLMENT
Undergraduate: 126
Graduate: 56

Male: 7%
Female: 93%

Full-time: 70%
Part-time: 30%

International: 6%
Minority: 25%

Job Placement Rate: 100%

SCHOLARSHIPS / FINANCIAL AID
Marymount offers scholarships for academic and/or need-based situations. 85% of the undergraduate students across campus receive some sort of financial assistance.

Students Receiving Scholarships or Financial Aid: 69%

TOTAL FACULTY: 18
Full-time: 39%
Part-time: 61%
Online: 0%

NCIDQ Certified: 50%
Licensed Interior Designers: 50%
LEED Certified: 33%

INTERIOR DESIGN ADMINISTRATION
Dr Robert Paul Meden, Chair
Ms Robin Wagner, Assistant Chair & Director, Graduate Program

PROFESSIONAL / ACADEMIC AFFILIATIONS
American Society of Interior Designers
International Interior Design Association
Interior Design Educators Council

CIDA ACCREDITATION
Bachelor of Arts (2005, 2011)
Master of Arts in Interior Design (2005, 2011)

PROGRAM DESCRIPTION AND PHILOSOPHY

Marymount's Bachelor of Arts in Interior Design program will prepare you for a career as a creative, ethically responsible, proficient Interior Designer. The curriculum of the program combines general education classes, known as the University's Liberal Arts Core, with professionally directed coursework to develop practitioners with a commitment to critical thinking, lifelong learning, and concern for the well-being of people and the environment. The combined coursework provides a broad understanding of human needs within the built environment as required for practice, and also foster an interdisciplinary approach to design. Your coursework in the major integrates aesthetic theory, architectural principles, human-behavior concepts, technology, business practices, and sustainable design. In the classroom, your focus will be on design knowledge and skills, as well as a comprehensive design process with emphasis upon the development of programming skills. This includes proficiencies that address client goals and needs, graphic and written communication, problem solving, critical thinking, ethics, and social responsibility. Although industry-standard computer software is taught, drafting and freehand sketching skills are emphasized for effective design communication.

FACILITIES

Aside from a full compliment of facilities on the main campus, upper level Interior Design courses are also offered at our Reston Center. Needless to say, being near the Nation's Capital, a wealth of resources are available for the students, field trips, guest lectures, and available adjuncts.

ONLINE / DISTANCE LEARNING
Not available

COURSES OF INSTRUCTION
- Introduction to Interior Design
- Architectural Graphics I, II, III
- CADD
- Interior Design Studios I, II, III, IV, V, and VI
- Textiles
- History of Interiors I, II
- Building Technology
- Lighting Design
- Business Procedures
- Assorted Interior Design electives
- Fine Arts foundation course
- History of Art I, II
- University Liberal Arts Core

INTERNSHIPS

Required of majors, usually seniors, some juniors. Interns are typically placed at companies such as AI, Architectural Interiors; Brennan, Beer, Egorman, Architects; Burt Hill Kosar Rittleman; Davis, Carter, Scott, Ltd.; Einhorn, Yaffee, Prescott, Architects; ForestPerkins Associates; Freddie Mac; Gensler & Associates; Hillier Group; HNTB, Howard, Needles, Tannebaum & Bergdorf; Leo A Daly; Page Southerland Page; Peck, Peck & Associates; Perkins Will Associates; RTKL International; Smithsonian-Air and Space Museum; Studios Architecture; Ward-Hale Design Associates

STUDY ABROAD
Various locations, for full semester, or shorter summer study trips

NOTABLE ALUMNI
Not reported

STUDENT ACTIVITIES AND ORGANIZATIONS
Marymount University's student organization for Interior Design majors is the Interior Design Alliance (IDA). As a member, you can join either American Society of Interior Designers (ASID) or the International Interior Design Association (IIDA) or both. The Interior Design Alliance sponsors and organizes special events and trips for students. Membership in student organizations is a proven way to meet design professionals and jump-start the networking process. ID undergraduate and graduate students are encouraged to join the IDA.

FACULTY SPECIALIZATIONS AND RESEARCH
Each faculty member has specific areas of interest, posted on the Web site; students are encouraged to become involved in research as freshmen entering the University through required Discover courses.

COMMUNITY COLLEGE TRANSFERS
Based upon seating availabilty, very competitive

Radford University

Department of Interior Design & Fashion

211 McGuffey Hall, PO Box 6967, Radford, VA 24142 | 540-831-5386 | http://id-f.asp.radford.edu/

UNIVERSITY PROFILE
Public
Suburban
Residential
Semester Schedule
Co-ed

STUDENT DEMOGRAPHICS
Undergraduate: 8,000
Graduate: 700

Male: Not reported
Female: Not reported

Full-time: Not reported
Part-time: Not reported

EXPENSES
Tuition: $8,640
Room & Board: $3,485

ADMISSIONS
Radford University
Martin Hall 115
PO Box 6903
Radford, VA 24142
540-831-5371
admissions@radford.edu

DEGREE INFORMATION

Major / Degree / Concentration	Enrollment	Requirements for entry	Graduation rate
Interior Design **Bachelor of Fine Arts**	185	2.0 gpa for university and 2.5 in major Portfolio review at end of Sophomore year	75%
Design Culture **Bachelor of Science**	New Program	2.0 gpa for university and 2.5 in major Portfolio review at end of Sophomore year	Not reported
Design Management **Bachelor of Science**	New Program	2.0 gpa for university and 2.5 in major Portfolio review at end of Sophomore year	Not reported

TOTAL PROGRAM ENROLLMENT
Undergraduate: 325
Graduate: 0

Male: 5%
Female: 95%

Full-time: Not reported
Part-time: Not reported

International: Not reported
Minority: Not reported

Job Placement Rate: 80%

SCHOLARSHIPS / FINANCIAL AID
The university, college, and department have scholarships available for students. Specific to the department are the: Dr. Susan Barnard [Interior Design], Dr. Fernand Gard and Dr. Roslyn Lester [Fashion Design].

TOTAL FACULTY: 10
Full-time: 95%
Part-time: 5%
Online: 0%

NCIDQ Certified: 50%
Licensed Interior Designers: 2
LEED Certified: 1

Interior Design ADMINISTRATION
Dr. Lennie Scott-Webber, Chair
Mrs. Debbie Hairston, Administrative Assistant

PROFESSIONAL / ACADEMIC AFFILIATIONS
American Society of Interior Designers
International Interior Design Association
Interior Design Educators Council

CIDA ACCREDITATION
BFA in Design with a concentration in Interior Design (2006, 2012)

PROGRAM DESCRIPTION AND PHILOSOPHY

The Department of Interior Design & Fashion prepares students for professional careers in the design industries. The department seeks to provide a supportive physical, academic, and creative environment in which each student can develop his/her own ability to pursue knowledge and employ a wide variety of innovative and analytical processes. At our essence is design. A strength is the balance of business, creative and technical knowledge the students receive; close one-on-one studios; Interior Design has, we believe, the first education design studio in the country.

FACILITIES

computer labs/wireless campus, state-of-art softward for these majors, IT support, laptop requirement, museum, concert and performance halls, art galleries; historic costume collection

ONLINE / DISTANCE LEARNING

Not available

COURSES OF INSTRUCTION

- Design Fundamentals
- Intro to Design
- Design Psychology
- Business of Design
- Textiles
- Media Presentation
- Presentation Techniques
- Studios I:IV
- General Education courses
- Global Design
- Apparel Production
- Economics
- Marketing
- Senior Show & Portfolio
- Pre-internship and Internship
- History of Interiors or Fashion

INTERNSHIPS

Required of majors at 3rd year. Interns are typically placed at architectural and Interior Design firms, retail merchandising firms, fashion design firms

STUDY ABROAD

Multiple opportunities from across campus

NOTABLE ALUMNI

Not reported

STUDENT ACTIVITIES AND ORGANIZATIONS

At RU there is always plenty to do and then some. You will find a plethora of educational and fun-filled activities, approximately 160 student clubs or organizations to join, sporting events to cheer on the Highlanders and so much more.

FACULTY SPECIALIZATIONS AND RESEARCH

Creative and academic scholarship; fashion design, healthcare, education design, professional practice

COMMUNITY COLLEGE TRANSFERS

Looked at on an individual basis

The Art Institute of Seattle

Interior Design Department
2323 S. Elliot Ave., Seattle, WA 98121 | 206-448-0900 | www.artinstitutes.edu/Seattle

UNIVERSITY PROFILE
Private
Urban
Commuter
Quarter Schedule
Co-ed

STUDENT DEMOGRAPHICS
Undergraduate: 1,500
Graduate: 0

Male: Not reported
Female: Not reported

Full-time: Not reported
Part-time: Not reported

EXPENSES
Tuition: Not reported
Room & Board: Not reported

ADMISSIONS
2323 S. Elliot Ave.
Seattle, WA 98121

DEGREE INFORMATION

Major / Degree / Concentration	Enrollment	Requirements for entry	Graduation rate
Interior Design Associate of Applied Arts	Not reported	Not reported	Not reported
Interior Design Bachelor of Science	Not reported	Not reported	Not reported
Residential Design Diploma	Not reported	Not reported	Not reported

TOTAL PROGRAM ENROLLMENT
Undergraduate: 170
Graduate: 0

Male: Not reported
Female: Not reported

Full-time: Not reported
Part-time: Not reported

International: Not reported
Minority: Not reported

Job Placement Rate: Not reported

SCHOLARSHIPS / FINANCIAL AID
Students Receiving Scholarships or Financial Aid: 90%

TOTAL FACULTY: 5
Full-time: 67%
Part-time: 33%
Online: 0%

NCIDQ Certified: 3
Licensed Interior Designers: 2
LEED Certified: 1

INTERIOR DESIGN ADMINISTRATION
Joan Bouillon - Dean
Scott Carnz - Assistant Deat
William Edgar - Director of Interior
  Department

PROFESSIONAL / ACADEMIC AFFILIATIONS
American Society of Interior Designers
International Interior Design Association

CIDA ACCREDITATION
Bachelor of Fine Arts (2010, 2016)

PROGRAM DESCRIPTION AND PHILOSOPHY
CIDA approved Interior Design college

FACILITIES
computer labs with technology, library and online library.

ONLINE / DISTANCE LEARNING
Not reported

COURSES OF INSTRUCTION
- 2D & 3D design
- Drafting 1, 2, & 3
- Textiles
- Space Planning
- Career Development
- Materials & Sources
- Residential
- Commercial
- Global
- Adaptive Reuse
- Specialty Design

INTERNSHIPS
Required at Senior level. Interns are typically placed at a wide variety of architectural and design firms.

STUDY ABROAD
Available

NOTABLE ALUMNI
Not reported

STUDENT ACTIVITIES AND ORGANIZATIONS
IDNG—Interior Design networking group

FACULTY SPECIALIZATIONS AND RESEARCH
Architecture & design.

Bellevue College

Interior Design Department

3000 Landerholm Circle SE, Bellevue, WA 98007 | 425-564-1000 | http://bellevuecollege.edu

STUDENT DEMOGRAPHICS
Undergraduate: 34,000
Graduate: 0

Male: 41%
Female: 59%

Full-time: 53%
Part-time: 47%

EXPENSES
Tuition: $87/credit hour (residents)
$250/credit hour (non-residents)
$196/credit hour (upper-division credits for BAA ID)
Room & Board:

ADMISSIONS
Student Services: Admission
3000 Landerholm Circle, SE
Bellevue, WA 98007

DEGREE INFORMATION

Major / Degree / Concentration	Enrollment	Requirements for entry	Graduation rate
Interior Design Bachelor of Applied Arts	91	Interior Design-related associate's degree or equivalent from an accredited college or university totaling 90 credits which include the following: Art History (5), Science (5), English Composition (5), Quantitative & Symbolic Reasoning (5), Social Science (5); Cumulative gpa of 2.0 or better	New program in 2010
Interior Studies Associate of Arts	250+	Admission to Bellevue College	Not reported

TOTAL PROGRAM ENROLLMENT
Undergraduate: 361
Graduate: 0

Male: 8%
Female: 92%

Full-time: 172
Part-time: 189

International: 2%
Minority: 23%

Job Placement Rate: Not reported

SCHOLARSHIPS / FINANCIAL AID
Not reported

TOTAL FACULTY: 20
Full-time: 4
Part-time: 16
Online: 4

NCIDQ Certified: 3
Licensed Interior Designers: Not reported
LEED Certified: 4

INTERIOR DESIGN ADMINISTRATION
Star Rush, Dean, Arts & Humanities Division
Dan Beert, Chair, Interior Design
Amy Masgai, Program Manager, Interior Design

PROFESSIONAL / ACADEMIC AFFILIATIONS
American Society of Interior Designers
International Interior Design Association
Interior Design Educators Council

CIDA ACCREDITATION
Bachelor of Applied Arts in Interior Design (2006, 2012)

PROGRAM DESCRIPTION AND PHILOSOPHY

The Bachelor of Applied Arts in Interior Design is an upper-division, 97-credit course of study for students who have completed a two year foundation in Interior Design-related studies. Accredited by the Council for Interior Design Accreditation (CIDA), the BAA offers a professionally relevant curriculum based on a foundation of holistic, creative problem-solving. Students gain insight into the various forms of spatial configuration; learn from historic and modern precedent; and employ strategies that lead to practical, innovative, sustainable, and socially relevant solutions for interior environments. Multi-disciplinary studios help students focus their interests while learning from experts in the professional field. This creates opportunities for highly collaborative student-faculty-industry relationships throughout the program.

In-depth practicum experience and a required capstone project encourage students to engage in self-directed investigation of Interior Design-related issues, and to customize their education to meet their interests and career goals. The program helps students expand their knowledge and skills to prepare for Interior Design jobs that require advanced qualifications.

FACILITIES

- Two dedicated studios for fourth-year capstone students
- Two CAD labs of 24 stations each.
- Two drafting studios
- Critique space
- Resource-Materials Library

ONLINE / DISTANCE LEARNING

Not reported

COURSES OF INSTRUCTION

- Associate in Arts Courses
- Foundation Studios: 2D Design, Color Theory, Drawing, 3D Design
- Art History
- Introduction to Interior Design
- Digital Design Tools
- Interior Design Studio I
- Interior Design Studio II
- Interior Materials & Sources
- Introduction to Computer-Aided Design
- Design Illustration
- Digital Design Presentation
- Interior Design Studio III
- Contract Documents
- Interior Design Theory
- History of Interiors & Furniture
- Modern Interiors & Furniture
- Design & Fabrication
- Interior Building Systems
- Lighting for Interiors
- Interior Design Studio (choice of three): Residential, Hospitality, Workplace, Learning Environments, Healthcare, Retail, Sustainability, Special Topics
- Design Research
- Capstone Design Studio I
- Capstone Design Studio II
- Professional Practices & Principles
- Practicum in Interior Design

INTERNSHIPS

Required of Bachelor of Applied Arts majors.

STUDY ABROAD

Not available

NOTABLE ALUMNI

Not reported

STUDENT ACTIVITIES AND ORGANIZATIONS

Interior Design Student Association; participation in Seattle-area professional organization activities: IIDA, ASID, NKBA

FACULTY SPECIALIZATIONS AND RESEARCH

Not reported

COMMUNITY COLLEGE TRANSFERS

Articulation to Washington State University—Interior Design, Spokane, WA

Washington State University, Pullman

Department of Interior Design

PO Box 642435, Pullman, WA 99164-2435 | 509-335-4118 | http://id.wsu.edu

UNIVERSITY PROFILE
Public
Suburban
Commuter
Semester Schedule
Co-ed

STUDENT DEMOGRAPHICS
Undergraduate: 21,726
Graduate: 4,375

Male: 47%
Female: 53%

Full-time: 83.3%
Part-time: 16.7%

EXPENSES
Tuition: $7,088
Room & Board: $8,886

ADMISSIONS
PO Box 641067
Pullman, WA 99164-1067
888-468-6978
admiss2@wsu.edu

DEGREE INFORMATION

Major / Degree / Concentration	Enrollment	Requirements for entry	Graduation rate
Interior Design Bachelor of Arts	135	2.5 gpa	90%
Interior Design Master of Arts	21	3.0 gpa	90%

TOTAL PROGRAM ENROLLMENT
Undergraduate: 80
Graduate: 21

Male: 13%
Female: 87%

Full-time: 93%
Part-time: 7%

International: 13%
Minority: 9%

Job Placement Rate: Not reported

SCHOLARSHIPS / FINANCIAL AID
Most students—incoming Freshman, transfer students, continuing undergraduates, and graduate students—need to fill out just one application in order to be considered for more than 700 scholarship awards. Complete the WSU scholarship application by January 31. You do not have to repay any funds that are awarded. Department Scholarships awarded by the College of Agriculture, Human and Natural Resource Sciences are:

- Interior Design Scholarship
- Elshe Marie Fulfs Hinrichs Scholarship

Students Receiving Scholarships or Financial Aid: 65%

TOTAL FACULTY: 9
Full-time: 100%
Part-time: 0%
Online: 0%

NCIDQ Certified: Not reported
Licensed Interior Designers: Not reported
LEED Certified: Not reported

INTERIOR DESIGN ADMINISTRATION
Dr. John Turpin, Dept. Chair
Linda N. Johnson, Assistant Director
Nancy Blossom, Director
  Interdisciplinary Design Institute

PROFESSIONAL / ACADEMIC AFFILIATIONS
American Society of Interior Designers
International Interior Design Association
Interior Design Educators Council
Environmental Design Research
  Association

CIDA ACCREDITATION
Bachelor of Arts in Interior Design (2010, 2016)

PROGRAM DESCRIPTION AND PHILOSOPHY

Through the integration of design, research, and theory, Interior Design contributes to the betterment of human condition from the individual to the global community. As such, we recognize and respect the interdependence of natural, social, and economic systems in framing design problems.

FACILITIES

Product and Resource Rooms, computer labs, laser cutter, model shop.

ONLINE / DISTANCE LEARNING

Not available

COURSES OF INSTRUCTION

Interior Design Studio (I, II, III, IV, V, VI, VII), Design Issues; Basic Environmental Design Studio; Design Communication I & II; Perception and Communication I & II; The Built Environment; Visual Communication; Materials & Components; History of Design I & II; Interior Design Theory; Fundamentals of Planning & Design I & II; Interior Building Systems; Professional Procedures; Beginning Computer Applications (CAD); Construction Communication/ Codes; Advanced Interior Construction & Detailing; Advanced Planning & Design I & II; Portfolio and Representation; Field Trips

INTERNSHIPS

Interships are offered but not required for degree. Students have had interships at Integrus Architecure, OMS Architecture, Madse, Mitchell, Evenson and Conrad, NAC Architecture.

STUDY ABROAD

Yes, Paris Study Abroad, AIU London, Florence (2013)

NOTABLE ALUMNI

Sari Graven, Marian Evenson, Nicole Cecil, Luke Van Dyun

STUDENT ACTIVITIES AND ORGANIZATIONS

ASWSUS, Interior Design Student Club, NW IIDA Student Chapter

FACULTY SPECIALIZATIONS AND RESEARCH

Nancy Blossom, MA, FIDEC, IIDA
Professor and Director, Interdisciplinary Design Institute
Research: History theory and criticism, environment-behavior relationships, curriculum and pedagogy.

Robert Krikac, MS
Associate Professor
Research: The integration of history, theory and research with the practice of Interior Design; sketching as thinking; interdisciplinary design and issues related to the design of commercialoffices.

Janetta McCoy, MS, PhD
Associate Professor, Graduate Coordinator
Research: The impact of the physical work environment on the intellectual and physical performance of people within organizations; leadership in design and creative teamwork; stress as an outcome of the work environment; gender bias in teaching evaluations; design for children with autism and development disabilities.

Matt Melcher, M.Arch
Associate Professor
Research: Poetics of assembly, detail and materiality, graphic communication, and representative; urban space as Interior Design; light and phenomenology; process as product in the design discipline.

Linda Nelson Johnson, MA
Associate Professor, Assistant Director
Research: Gender issues and diversity in design; historic preservation of structures, interiors and ornamentation; design foundation pedagogy.

Kathleen Ryan, MA
Assistant Professor
Research: Sketching and creativity of Interior Design students; wayfinding and interpretive exhibit issues in museum and zoo settings.

Jo Ann Asher Thompson, MA, PhD, FIDEC, FIIDA
Professor
Research: Environment-behavior relationships; distance learning education; cognitive perceptions of interior space; linking education and practice; criticism and theory.

Judy Theodorson, M.Arch
Assistant Professor
Research: High performance buildings and interiors; sustainable design and theory; daylighting design; conceptualization and communication of light; field studies of built environments.

John Turpin, PhD
Associate Professor & Department Chair
Research: Interior Design history; women's studies in Interior Design; design criticism and theory.

COMMUNITY COLLEGE TRANSFERS

Not reported

Washington State University, Spokane

Department of Interior Design

PO Box 1495, 412 E. Spokane Falls Blvd., Spokane WA 99210 | 509-358-7920 | http://id.wsu.edu

UNIVERSITY PROFILE
Public
Suburban
Commuter
Semester Schedule
Co-ed

STUDENT DEMOGRAPHICS
Undergraduate: 53.6%
Graduate: 46.4%

Male: 25.6%
Female: 74.4%

Full-time: 70.5%
Part-time: 29.5%

EXPENSES
Tuition: $7,088
Room & Board: n/a

ADMISSIONS
PO Box 641067
Pullman, WA 99164-1067
509-358-7978
enroll@wsu.edu

DEGREE INFORMATION

Major / Degree / Concentration	Enrollment	Requirements for entry	Graduation rate
Interior Design Bachelor of Arts	135	2.5 gpa	90%
Interior Design Master of Arts	21	3.0 gpa	90%
Interior Design Articulation Program Bachelor & Master of Arts	Not reported	4th year of the WSU BA Interior Design program with a cumulative gpa of 3.0 or above; statement of intent; oral presentation of a design project.	Not reported

TOTAL PROGRAM ENROLLMENT
Undergraduate: Not reported
Graduate: Not reported

Male: Not reported
Female: Not reported

Full-time: Not reported
Part-time: Not reported

International: 14%
Minority: 3.1%

Job Placement Rate: Not reported

SCHOLARSHIPS / FINANCIAL AID
Most students-incoming Freshman, transfer students, continuing undergraduates, and graduate students need to fill out just one application in order to be considered for more than 700. Department Scholarships awarded by the College of Agriculture, Human and Natural Resource Sciences are:
- Interior Design Scholarship
- Elshe Marie Fulfs Hinrichs Scholarship

Students Receiving Scholarships or Financial Aid: 65%

TOTAL FACULTY: 9
Full-time: 100%
Part-time: 0%
Online: 0%

NCIDQ Certified: Not reported
Licensed Interior Designers: Not reported
LEED Certified: Not reported

INTERIOR DESIGN ADMINISTRATION
Dr. John Turpin, Dept. Chair
Linda N. Johnson, Assistant Director
Nancy Blossom, Director
  Interdisciplinary Design Institute

PROFESSIONAL / ACADEMIC AFFILIATIONS
American Society of Interior Designers
International Interior Design Association
Interior Design Educators Council
Environmental Design Research Association

CIDA ACCREDITATION
Bachelor of Arts in Interior Design (2010, 2016)

354

PROGRAM DESCRIPTION AND PHILOSOPHY

Our program offers a balanced approach in Interior Design with exposure to art, architecture, and humanities. Both community college and WSU, Pullman students have the opportunity to complete their bachelors degree in the Design Institute's collaborative studio environment.

WSU, Pullman students spend their third and fourth years at the Design Institute. Students from Spokane Falls Community College spend their fourth year at the Design Institute.

Washington State University, Spokane offers an exciting (4+1) BA/MA Interior Design Articulation program that enables students to complete both a professional undergraduate degree and a graduate degree in Interior Design in five years. One of the few cutting edge Interior Design programs in the nation, it prepares students to acquire advanced specialization and creative design skills, while enhancing critical thinking and problem solving abilities.

Qualified students may apply for entry into an articulated (4+1) BA/MA degree program the last year of undergraduate study at WSU that leads to a master's degree completed in one year of graduate study. The (4+1) BA/MA degree culminates in a non-thesis design research project.

The goals of the program are:
- To provide students with opportunities to explore advanced design theories, problem solving techniques, methodologies, and individual research and design applications;
- To provide students with opportunities for interdisciplinary exchange through the core curriculum at the Interdisciplinary Design Institute;
- To contribute to and advance the body of knowledge pertaining to Interior Design and the built and natural environments;
- To prepare graduates to pursue careers as Interior Design educators, directors of Interior Design research, and/or practitioners of Interior Design.

FACILITIES
Product and Resource Rooms, computer labs, laser cutter, model shop.

ONLINE / DISTANCE LEARNING
Not available

COURSES OF INSTRUCTION
Interior Design Studio (I, II, III, IV, V, VI, VII), Design Issues; Basic Environmental Design Studio; Design Communication I & II; Perception and Communication I & II; The Built Environment; Visual Communication; Materials & Components; History of Design I & II; Interior Design Theory; Fundamentals of Planning & Design I & II; Interior Building Systems; Professional Procedures; Beginning Computer Applications (CAD); Construction Communication/Codes; Advanced Interior Construction & Detailing; Advanced Planning & Design I & II; Portfolio and Representation; Field Trips

INTERNSHIPS
Interships are offered but not required for degree. Students have had interships at Integrus Architecure, OMS Architecture, Madse, Mitchell, Evenson and Conrad, NAC Architecture.

STUDY ABROAD
Paris Study Abroad, AIU London, Florence (2013)

NOTABLE ALUMNI
Sari Graven, Marian Evenson, Nicole Cecil, Luke Van Dyun

STUDENT ACTIVITIES AND ORGANIZATIONS
ASWSUS, Interior Design Student Club, NW IIDA Student Chapter

FACULTY SPECIALIZATIONS AND RESEARCH
Faculty specializations and research include the following:
- History theory and criticism
- Environment-behavior relationships
- Curriculum and pedagogy
- Integration of history
- Theory and research with the practice of Interior Design
- Sketching as thinking
- Interdisciplinary design and issues related to the design of commercial offices
- Impact of the physical work environment on the intellectual and physical performance of people within organizations
- Leadership in design and creative teamwork
- Stress as an outcome of the work environment
- Gender bias in teaching evaluations
- Design for children with autism and development disabilities
- Poetics of assembly, detail and materiality, graphic communication, and representative
- Urban space as Interior Design; light and phenomenology; process as product in the design discipline
- Gender issues and diversity in design
- Historic preservation of structures, interiors and ornamentation
- Design foundation pedagogy
- Sketching and creativity of Interior Design students
- Wayfinding and interpretive exhibit issues in museum and zoo settings
- Environment-behavior relationships
- Distance learning education; cognitive perceptions of interior space
- Linking education and practice; criticism and theory
- High performance buildings and interiors
- Sustainable design and theory
- Daylighting design
- Conceptualization and communication of light
- Field studies of built environments
- Interior Design history; women's studies in Interior Design; design criticism and theory.

Mount Mary College

Interior Design Department, Art & Design Division

2900 N. Menomonee River Pkwy., Milwaukee, WI 53222 | 414-256-1213 | www.mtmary.edu/dept_interiordesign.htm

UNIVERSITY PROFILE
Private
Urban
Commuter
Semester Schedule
Women Only

STUDENT DEMOGRAPHICS
Undergraduate: 1,925 total undergrads and grads

Male: 0%
Female: 100%

Full-time: Not reported
Part-time: Not reported

EXPENSES
Tuition: $21,668
Room & Board: Not reported

ADMISSIONS
2900 N. Menonomee River Pkwy
Milwaukee, WI 53222
800-321-6265
admiss@mtmary.edu

DEGREE INFORMATION

Major / Degree / Concentration	Enrollment	Requirements for entry	Graduation rate
Interior Design Bachelor of Arts	50	College admission requirements	90%

TOTAL PROGRAM ENROLLMENT
Undergraduate: 50
Graduate: 0

Male: 0%
Female: 100%

Full-time: 80%
Part-time: 20%

International: 0%
Minority: 18%

Job Placement Rate: Not reported

SCHOLARSHIPS / FINANCIAL AID
Students Receiving Scholarships or Financial Aid: 100%

See opposite page for more info.

TOTAL FACULTY: 7
Full-time: 3
Part-time: 4
Online: 0

NCIDQ Certified: 29%
Licensed Interior Designers: 58%
LEED Certified: 29%

INTERIOR DESIGN ADMINISTRATION
Pamm Steffen, Chairperson of Art & Design Division
Leona Knobloch-Nelson, Chairperson of Interior Design Department
Judy Heun, Administrative Assistant

PROFESSIONAL / ACADEMIC AFFILIATIONS
American Society of Interior Designers
International Interior Design Association

CIDA ACCREDITATION
Bachelor of Arts/Interior Design (2009, 2015)

PROGRAM DESCRIPTION AND PHILOSOPHY
The Interior Design department, in support of the College mission to create an environment for the development of the whole person with an emphasis on leadership, integrity, and social justice, offers a comprehensive, current, and accredited education. The program prepares students for present and future demands in the Interior Design profession; to solve problems with creativity, integrity, and critical thinking; and to recognize their responsibility to the profession, environment, and global community.

THE PHILOSOPHY OF THE INTERIOR DESIGN DEPARTMENT
The Interior Design department faculty recognizes and responds to the continual changes in technology, skills, specializations, and the industry as they impact Interior Design and related fields. The faculty provides academic and experiential course work augmented by community outreach professional involvement, and on-on-one student contact in and out of the classroom.

FACILITIES
Marion Art Gallery
Interior Design CAD Lab
Interior Design Resource Library

ONLINE / DISTANCE LEARNING
No online major

COURSES OF INSTRUCTION
- Sustainable Design
- Lighting Design
- Residential Studio
- Commercial Studio
- History of Architecture and Interiors
- Building Construction

INTERNSHIPS
Required of majors at the Junior/Senior level. Interns are typically placed at commercial and residential firms (architectural and interiors), dealerships, and sales companies.

STUDY ABROAD
Some of the Mount Mary trips have included the following locations Rome, Ireland, Denmark, Sweden, Germany, Peru, Spain, and China.

NOTABLE ALUMNI
Not reported

STUDENT ACTIVITIES AND ORGANIZATIONS
Mount Mary College ASID/IIDA Student Chapter

FACULTY SPECIALIZATIONS AND RESEARCH
Many of the faculty are practicing professionals

SCHOLARSHIPS / FINANCIAL AID
Caroline Scholars Program—This prestigious scholarship covering tuition, room, and board is renewable for up to three years. Full-time, financial eligible first year students with a strong interest in social justice are encouraged to apply. Download the informational brochure. Please note, the application deadline for the Fall 2010 cohort has passed.

Midtown Scholarship Program—This unique program offers young women of Milwaukee academic, personal, and financial support as they pursue their degree at Mount Mary. The Midtown Scholarship award guarantees that an eligible student's federal, state, and Mount Mary gift assistance cover between 70 and 80 percent of tuition costs. This scholarship is awarded to up to 50 full-time students annually through an application and interview process.

Frederick R. Layton Art Scholarship—This prestigious scholarship of $100 to $500 per year is given to students interested in pursuing a career full time in the art field. Please note, the application deadline has passed.

Friends of Mount Mary College Funded Scholarships—Additional scholarships are available through the generosity of college friends and donors. These donor-funded scholarships are based on major, interest, and other criteria. By completing a single application, students will be reviewed for eligibility for all of the Friends of Mount Mary College Funded Scholarships. Please note, the application deadline has passed.

University of Wisconsin, Madison

Design Studies Department, School of Human Ecology

475 N. Charter St., Rm. 2318 Sterling Hall, Madison, WI 53706 | 608-262-2651 | www.sohe.wisc.edu/ds

UNIVERSITY PROFILE
Public
Urban
Residential
Semester Schedule
Co-ed

STUDENT DEMOGRAPHICS
Undergraduate: 26,979
Graduate: 8,817

Male: 48%
Female: 52%

Full-time: 95%
Part-time: 5%

EXPENSES
Tuition: $4,156.88
(undergraduate, resident)
Room & Board: $8,040.00

ADMISSIONS
Armory & Gymnasium
716 Langdon St.
Madison, WI 53706
608-262-3961
onwisconsin@admissions
.wisc.edu

DEGREE INFORMATION

Major / Degree / Concentration	Enrollment	Requirements for entry	Graduation rate
Interior Design Bachelor of Science	Not reported	2.75 gpa Pre-major course work (see Program Description and Philosophy)	Not reported

TOTAL PROGRAM ENROLLMENT
Undergraduate: 140
Graduate: 16

Male: Not reported
Female: Not reported

Full-time: Not reported
Part-time: Not reported

International: Not reported
Minority: Not reported

Job Placement Rate: Not reported

SCHOLARSHIPS / FINANCIAL AID
Not reported

TOTAL FACULTY: NOT REPORTED
Full-time: Not reported
Part-time: Not reported
Online: Not reported

NCIDQ Certified: Not reported
Licensed Interior Designers: Not reported
LEED Certified: Not reported

INTERIOR DESIGN ADMINISTRATION
Not reported

PROFESSIONAL / ACADEMIC AFFILIATIONS
American Society of Interior Designers
Interior Design Educators Council

CIDA ACCREDITATION
B.S.- Environment Textiles & Design- Interior Design (2004, 2010)

PROGRAM DESCRIPTION AND PHILOSOPHY

The Interior Design major is a four-year professional program accredited by the Council for Interior Design Accreditation (CIDA). The program develops student creativity in the design and planning of interior spaces by emphasizing the process and communication of design as well as the product of design. Students learn to integrate the art of design with the social sciences concerning the interaction of people and their environment, the history of design, and the physical sciences relating to the effects of materials on the physical health and comfort of inhabitants. Insight into professional practice is enhanced through internship experiences.

Course content includes developing design communication skills such as sketching, rendering, computer-aided drafting and design, and three-dimensional modeling with exposure to both residential and commercial interiors. In addition, courses in art history, history of interiors, business, engineering, and art are required. A final portfolio is required before graduation.

Students who wish to pursue the Interior Design major begin in Pre-Professional Course Sequence segment of the program. Continuation into the ID professional courses sequence involves an application process at the end of each fall semester. Admission is based upon evaluation of a student's performance in the Pre-Professional phase of the curriculum. This includes a minimum of 18 credits from selected university general studies courses (i.e., arts and humanities, science, and social studies), and 15 credits of designated design-related courses.

After completion of the first phase of the program, and upon acceptance into the professional course sequence of the ID major, all Interior Design students must purchase a laptop computer with a minimum hardware specification and software licenses. Financial aid packages are adjusted for the purchase. Mininum specifications for the laptop computers can be found below.

Students interested in Interior Design may enroll in the School of Human Ecology during their Freshman year. Transfer students may take longer to complete their degree than students entering the program, as they must complete the Pre-Professional Course requirements and the four sequential Interior Design studios. Transfer students will need to have their records reviewed to determine if transferred courses work fulfill program requirements.

FACILITIES

Computer Lab, Design Gallery, Interior Design Resource Room, Helen Louise Allen Textile Collection, Ruther Ketterer Harris Library

ONLINE / DISTANCE LEARNING

Not reported

COURSES OF INSTRUCTION

- Design Fundamentals I and II
- Interior Design I
- Person and Environment Interactions
- Design: Sketching and Rendering
- CAD: Architecture and Interiors
- Twentieth Century Design
- Textile Science

INTERNSHIPS

Not reported

STUDY ABROAD

Feng Shui/China

NOTABLE ALUMNI

Not reproted

STUDENT ACTIVITIES AND ORGANIZATIONS

American Society of Interior Designers (ASID), Phi Upsilon Omicron, American Society of Textile Chemists and Colorists (AATCC)

FACULTY SPECIALIZATIONS AND RESEARCH

- Architectural Space
- Design Process,
- Workplace Design
- Environment and Behavior Studies
- Design Visualization
- Asian Design & Feng Shui
- Naturally Occuring Retirement Communities
- Ethnic Culture and Residential Environment in context of globalization
- Twentieth Century Design
- History Interiors and History of European Interiors

University of Wisconsin, Stout

Department of Art & Design

235A Applied Arts Bldg., Menomonie, WI 54751 | 715-232-1097 | www.uwstout.edu/cas/artdes/index.shtml

DEGREE INFORMATION

Major / Degree / Concentration	Enrollment	Requirements for entry	Graduation rate
Interior Design Bachelor of Fine Arts	170	Portfolio Review	87%

TOTAL PROGRAM ENROLLMENT
Undergraduate: 802
Graduate: 0

Male: 37%
Female: 63%

Full-time: 91%
Part-time: 9%

International: Not reported
Minority: Not reported

Job Placement Rate: 100%

SCHOLARSHIPS / FINANCIAL AID
Range of financial aid scholarships

TOTAL FACULTY: 4 Interior Design / 40 in whole department
Full-time: 100%
Part-time: Not reported
Online: Not reported

NCIDQ Certified: 50%
Licensed Interior Designers: 50%
LEED Certified: Not reported

INTERIOR DESIGN ADMINISTRATION
Ron Verdon, Department Chair
Tamara Brantmeier, Program Director
John Murphy, Dean of the College of Arts, Humanities & Social Sciences

PROFESSIONAL / ACADEMIC AFFILIATIONS
American Society of Interior Designers
International Interior Design Association
Interior Design Educators Council

CIDA ACCREDITATION
Bachelor of Fine Arts – Art/Interior Design (2006, 2012)

PROGRAM DESCRIPTION AND PHILOSOPHY

The program prepares students to produce functional, aesthetic, and meaningful interior environments (residential, commercial, and public spaces) by integrating human factors, art and design concepts, space planning, and knowledge of architecture, building construction, codes, specifications, materials, and furnishings.

FACILITIES

Laptop program provides individual laptop computers and extensive design-related software, additional advanced computer labs, wood shop, metal shop, two galleries, and senior level studio space for each student.

ONLINE / DISTANCE LEARNING

Not available

COURSES OF INSTRUCTION

- Foundation courses in Art
- Design and Architecture
- Interior Design Studios
- Specifications
- Construction Documentation
- Lighting Design
- Furniture/Human Body and Form
- Senior Thesis Project
- Fine Art

INTERNSHIPS

Not required of majors. Interns are typically placed at architecture firms, Interior Design studios, or corporations.

STUDY ABROAD

Available

NOTABLE ALUMNI

Not reported

STUDENT ACTIVITIES AND ORGANIZATIONS

ASID, IIDA

FACULTY SPECIALIZATIONS AND RESEARCH

Design Communication, Universal Design, Construction Documentation, Sustainablity, Lighting/Lighting Design, Interior Design Education, Ethics in Design

Waukesha County Technical College

Education, Interior Design and Human Services

800 Main St., Pewaukee, WI 53072 | 262-691-5258 | www.wctc.edu

UNIVERSITY PROFILE
Public
Suburban
Commuter
Semester Schedule
Co-ed

STUDENT DEMOGRAPHICS
Undergraduate: 32,000
Graduate: n/a

Male: 40%
Female: 60%

Full-time: 62%
Part-time: 38%

EXPENSES
Tuition: $110 per credit
Room & Board: n/a

ADMISSIONS
800 Main St.
Pewaukee, WI 53072
262-691-5400
www.wctc.edu

DEGREE INFORMATION

Major / Degree / Concentration	Enrollment	Requirements for entry	Graduation rate
Interior Design Associate of Applied Science	Not reported	Not reported	Not reported

DEGREE INFORMATION
Not reported

TOTAL PROGRAM ENROLLMENT
Undergraduate: 176
Graduate: n/a

Male: 5%
Female: 95%

Full-time: Not reported
Part-time: Not reported

International: Not reported
Minority: Not reported

Job Placement Rate: 80%

SCHOLARSHIPS / FINANCIAL AID
Available to students: Federal Direct Loans and Scholarships/Grants

Students Receiving Scholarships or Financial Aid: 25%

TOTAL FACULTY: 10
Full-time: 30%
Part-time: 70%
Online: Not reported

NCIDQ Certified: 30%
Licensed Interior Designers: Not reported
LEED Certified: Not reported

INTERIOR DESIGN ADMINISTRATION
Mary Iverson, Associate Dean

PROFESSIONAL / ACADEMIC AFFILIATIONS
American Society of Interior Designers
International Interior Design Association
Interior Design Educators Council

PROGRAM DESCRIPTION AND PHILOSOPHY

Interior Design students will learn to create, design, draft, and combine colors and textures to provide commercial or residential clients with aesthetically pleasing and environmentally correct interiors. Students will also develop a strong foundation in computer-assisted design, furnishings, lighting, textiles and sales.

FACILITIES

Classrooms, Computer Labs, Interior Design Studio

ONLINE / DISTANCE LEARNING

Not at this time

COURSES OF INSTRUCTION

- Principles of Interior Design
- History of Furniture
- Space Planning
- Textiles' Intro to Commercial Design
- Kitchen and Bath
- Interior Finishes
- Illustration

INTERNSHIPS

Required of majors at 2nd year. Interns are typically placed at Interior Design consulting firms, industry-related sales and architectural design firms.

STUDY ABROAD

Not available

NOTABLE ALUMNI

Not reported

STUDENT ACTIVITIES AND ORGANIZATIONS

ASID Club; Interior Design Associate Degree Club

FACULTY SPECIALIZATIONS AND RESEARCH

- Sales
- AutoCad
- Commercial and Residential Interior Design

COMMUNITY COLLEGE TRANSFERS

Transfer possibilities to the University of Wisconsin System and private area colleges

West Virginia University

Division of Design & Merchandising
Davis College of Agriculture, Natural Resources & Design 702 Allen Hall, Morgantown, WV 26508 | www.design.wvu.ed

UNIVERSITY PROFILE
Public
Rural
Residential
Semester Schedule
Co-ed

STUDENT DEMOGRAPHICS
Undergraduate: 22,000
Graduate: 7,000

Male: Not reported
Female: Not reported

Full-time: Not reported
Part-time: Not reported

EXPENSES
Tuition: $5,500
Room & Board: $7,500

ADMISSIONS
P.O. Box 6009
Morgantown, WV 26506-6009
304-293-2121
go2wvu@mail.wvu.edu

DEGREE INFORMATION

Major / Degree / Concentration	Enrollment	Requirements for entry	Graduation rate
Interior Design Bachelor of Science	130	2.5 gpa Performance review after first year	90%

TOTAL PROGRAM ENROLLMENT
Undergraduate: 130
Graduate: Not reported

Male: 4%
Female: 96%

Full-time: 99%
Part-time: 1%

International: 6%
Minority: 5%

Job Placement Rate: 75%

SCHOLARSHIPS / FINANCIAL AID
Not reported

TOTAL FACULTY: 9
Full-time: 60%
Part-time: 40%
Online: Not reported

NCIDQ Certified: 12%
Licensed Interior Designers: Not reported
LEED Certified: 25%

INTERIOR DESIGN ADMINISTRATION
Dr. Barbara McFall, Division Director
Dr. Cindy Beacham, Program Chair

PROFESSIONAL / ACADEMIC AFFILIATIONS
American Society of Interior Designers
Interior Design Educators Council
Environmental Design Research Association

CIDA ACCREDITATION
Bachelor of Science in Design & Merchandising/Interior Design (2010, 2016)

PROGRAM DESCRIPTION AND PHILOSOPHY
The mission to this program is to make quality of living better through the application of design.

FACILITIES
Computer labs, studio spaces, Faro scanning technology

ONLINE / DISTANCE LEARNING
Not reported

COURSES OF INSTRUCTION
- Introduction to Design
- Space Planning
- Design Thinking
- Lighting
- Codes & Construction
- Green Built Environment
- Residential Design Studio
- Contract Design Studios

INTERNSHIPS
Not required

STUDY ABROAD
All students are required to study abroad the second semester of their 3rd year in the program.

NOTABLE ALUMNI
Vivien Woofter—US GSA Office (Foreign Embassy & Restoration)
Alexis Behrens—Ruby Memorial Hospital
Jen Sale—Disney

STUDENT ACTIVITIES AND ORGANIZATIONS
ASID, Community Design Team, Habitat for Humanity

FACULTY SPECIALIZATIONS AND RESEARCH
Design Thinking, Sustainable Design, Energy Efficiency, Preservation, Technology Applications, Art/Craft, Fabrication, Aesthetics of Sacred Spaces, GeoDesign, Design Economics

Algonquin College

Interior Design Program, School of Media and Design

1385 Woodroffe Ave., Ottawa, ON K2G 1V8 | 613-727-4723 | www.algonquincollege.com/

UNIVERSITY PROFILE
Public
Suburban
Commuter
Semester Schedule
Co-ed

STUDENT DEMOGRAPHICS
Undergraduate: 53,180
Graduate: n/a

Male: 50%
Female: 50%

Full-time: 33%
Part-time: 67%

EXPENSES
Tuition: $5,500 cdn + Fees &
Expenses
Room & Board: $7,250 cdn

ADMISSIONS
1385 Woodroffe Ave.
Ottawa, ON K2G 1V8
613-727-0002 or 1-800-565-
4723
AskAlgonquin@
algonquincollege.com

DEGREE INFORMATION

Major / Degree / Concentration	Enrollment	Requirements for entry	Graduation rate
Interior Design Bachelor of Applied Arts	190	12U Math, 12U English, plus four more 12U courses; 70% gpa; portfolio with home test and essay	90%

TOTAL PROGRAM ENROLLMENT
Undergraduate: 180
Graduate: n/a

Male: 2%
Female: 98%

Full-time: 75%
Part-time: 20%

International: 15%
Minority: n/a

Job Placement Rate: 90%

SCHOLARSHIPS / FINANCIAL AID
We offer $175,000 in scholarships.
We administer federal and provincial
student loan programs, scholarships and
bursaries; general and program-related
bursary funding from money donated
by the College, individuals, companies
and other organizations. Refer to the
Web site: hwww.algonquincollege.
com/financialaid/index.html for further
information and details.

TOTAL FACULTY: 30
Full-time: 20%
Part-time: 80%

NCIDQ Certified: 25%
Licensed Interior Designers: 50%
LEED Certified: 25%

INTERIOR DESIGN ADMINISTRATION
Russell Mills, Dean, School of Media and
Design
Margaret Pegie-Stark, Chair
Michele Zanetti, Program Coordinator

PROFESSIONAL / ACADEMIC AFFILIATIONS
American Society of Interior Designers
Interior Design Educators Council
Interior Designers of Canada

CIDA ACCREDITATION
Bachelor of Applied Arts in Interior
Design (2008, 2014)

PROGRAM DESCRIPTION AND PHILOSOPHY

Our program philosophy is to provide students with the most comprehensive, responsible, and enriched education possible, in terms of both a professional and liberal arts education. It is our earnest belief that Interior Designers of the future must not only be competent within the realm of current and future professional standards, but be able to seek out and critically question the role of Interior Design. We strive to encourage students to engage in a broad approach to problem-solving, to draw and reflect on diverse fields of knowledge in the creative pursuit of appropriate human-centered solutions for the built-environment. Not only to solve problems, but to seek new opportunities within the ever-expanding boundaries of the design disciplines. Our program goal is to facilitate students to adopt a broad worldview, considering cultural diversity and sustainability as the foundations for socially responsible design.

Our program is housed within the new Algonquin Centre for Construction Excellence. This unique LEED—platinum facility is designed to promote an inter-disciplinary learning/teaching environment through real-life sustainable practices, and encourages collaboration between architecture and design professionals as well as other construction related disciplines.

ONLINE / DISTANCE LEARNING

Not yet available, on-line credit-courses and 'bridging' courses for transfer from diploma to degree programs will be offered in 2011 for both students and professionals.

FACILITIES

World-class LEED Platinum sustainable building (Fall 2011), featuring a 'living-lab' where the building itself will be part of the curriculum and learning experience (for example, the latest sustainable strategies will be exposed and accessible for study including multiple building sensors that will monitor such things as energy use, air quality, water consumption, etc.). An entire building floor dedicated to student spaces such as locker rooms, internet café, resource library, commons hub, work rooms, collaborative pods, and multimedia computer labs in addition to woodworking and carpentry workshop, modelling room, open-discipline critique space, inter-disciplinary studio and work spaces, sample/product test areas, applied research space, video-conferencing, exhibit hall, mobile classrooms, and living/teaching green spaces such as a 4-story living wall and green roof.

COURSES OF INSTRUCTION

Project-based studios with increasing complexity for various space types such as: residential, corporate (public & private), healthcare & institutional, retail & hospitality. Pre-requisite technical courses such as design drawing, construction detailing, hand and computer aided drafting, 3D modelling and animation, graphic design, lighting, building codes and product specifications.

Note: Manditory lap-top program for 3rd and 4th year levels.

INTERNSHIPS

Required of majors at end of 3rd year.

Students are typical placed at interior design and architectural firms, lighting design firms, corporate and government design and facilities departments, locally and abroad.

Students select a preferred interest, such as residential, healthcare, hospitality and then they are matched as best as possible to an employer with these specialties. Some of the firms have included:

HOK ,Toronto, Ottawa; Clodagh, New York; Yabu Pushelerg; Stantec, Calgary; Judy Newcombe, Toronto Cannon, Toronto; JOI Design, Germany; Ndos Arquitectura L'Hospitalet de Llobregat, Barcelona; Shang hai, China; Revenue Canada, Ottawa; RCMP, Ottawa; Cooper Gardner Architects, Bermuda

STUDY ABROAD

Not available

NOTABLE ALUMNI

Not reported

STUDENT ACTIVITIES AND ORGANIZATIONS

Professional association student membership, volunteer oppurtunities at industry related events, educational field trips, and participation in industry trade shows.

FACULTY SPECIALIZATIONS AND RESEARCH

Housing and gender studies; architectural history and theory; universal design with an emphasis on the aging population; hospitality and retail design; designing for mental health, pediatrics and homes for the aged and long-term care; sustainability building practices for residential and commercial; project management and contract documentation; graphic art and design; design thinking and design process

The Art Institute of Vancouver

Interior Design Department

2665 Renfrew St., Vancouver, BC V5M 0A7 | 604-298-5400 | www.artinstitutes.edu/vancouver/

DEGREE INFORMATION

Major / Degree / Concentration	Enrollment	Requirements for entry	Graduation rate
Interior Design Diploma	120	High school graduation; Application and essay; English requirements	90%

STUDENT DEMOGRAPHICS
Undergraduate: Not reported
Graduate: Not reported

Male: Not reported
Female: Not reported

Full-time: Not reported
Part-time: Not reported

TOTAL PROGRAM ENROLLMENT
Undergraduate: 120
Graduate: Not reported

Male: 20%
Female: 80%

Full-time: 80%
Part-time: 20%

International: Not reported
Minority: Not reported

Job Placement Rate: 90%

TOTAL FACULTY: 13
Full-time: 25%
Part-time: 75%
Online: Not reported

NCIDQ Certified: 25%
Licensed Interior Designers: 50%
LEED Certified: 25%

INTERIOR DESIGN ADMINISTRATION
Seng Sengsavanh, Academic Director of Interior Design

EXPENSES
Tuition: Not reported
Room & Board: Not reported

SCHOLARSHIPS / FINANCIAL AID
We offer $175,000 in scholarships for high school students each year.

PROFESSIONAL / ACADEMIC AFFILIATIONS
Not reported

ADMISSIONS
2665 Renfrew St.
Vancouver, BC
V5M 0A7
604-298-5400
www.artinstitutes.edu/vancouver/

PROGRAM DESCRIPTION AND PHILOSOPHY

The mission of our Interior Design diploma program is to graduate students prepared for their profession, able to conceive and execute viable, creative design solutions in diverse occupations within our current market realities. The Interior Design Diploma program is a program rich in theory and practice. The focus on theory at the beginning of the program articulates the guiding principles which provide the foundation for the hands-on application of design concepts. Students will develop abilities in all aspects of the design of three-dimensional space, both residential and commercial and rooted in a historical and cultural context. They will learn how to communicate design solutions through a variety of visual media. They will also learn how the profession interfaces with others and how to manage the business of their profession. Our students will develop aesthetic and ethical sensitivities over the course of the program. They will graduate prepared to enter the fields of commercial and residential Interior Design. Graduates of the AIV Interior Design diploma program will be eligible to write the NCIDQ exam upon completion of the required work experience.

FACILITIES
- Computer Labs
- Drafting Labs
- Material Resource Room
- Resource Library
- Plotting Room

ONLINE / DISTANCE LEARNING
We offer a few courses through our Pittsburch Online Campus.

COURSES OF INSTRUCTION
- Basics of Interior Design
- Space Planning
- Programming
- Human Factors
- Lighting
- Environmental Design
- Thesis
- Portfolio Development

INTERNSHIPS
We provide internship opportunities to Senior students.

Placement: Residential Interior Design firms, Commercial Interior Design firms, Architectural Design firms, Real Estate Development firms, Industry Suppliers, etc.

STUDY ABROAD
Students may study at another Art Insitute Campus for a quarter or two.

NOTABLE ALUMNI
Aleem Kassam
Miho Naria
Jade Kwok
Kate Cannatta

STUDENT ACTIVITIES AND ORGANIZATIONS
Annual Interior Design Trip to New York. Our students can become members with IDIBC—Interior Designers Institute of British Columbia.

FACULTY SPECIALIZATIONS AND RESEARCH
Residential Design, Commercial Design (Hospitality, Retail, Corporate), Environmental Design

COMMUNITY COLLEGE TRANSFERS
Students may transfer their credits to any other AI systems campuses or other local colleges/universities.

Humber College

Design Cluster School of Applied Technology

205 Humber College Blvd., Toronto, ON M9W 5L7 | 416-675-6622 | http://humber.ca/appliedtechnology/

UNIVERSITY PROFILE
Public
Suburban
Commuter
Semester Schedule
Co-ed

STUDENT DEMOGRAPHICS
Undergraduate: 17,000
Graduate: Not reported

Male: Not reported
Female: Not reported

Full-time: Not reported
Part-time: Not reported

EXPENSES
Tuition: $6,108.9 (domestic);
$11,730 (international)
Room & Board: varies

ADMISSIONS
205 Humber College Blvd.
Toronto, ON M9W 5L7
415-675-6622

DEGREE INFORMATION

Major / Degree / Concentration	Enrollment	Requirements for entry	Graduation rate
Interior Design Bachelor of Applied Arts	150	Ontario Secondary School Diploma (OSSD); Grade 12U English (ENG4U) with a minimum grade of 65 percent. If English is not your first language, refer to the English Language proficiency Policy; any Grade 11 or Grade 12 U or M Mathematics with a minimum of 60 percent; Four Grade 12 U or M courses in addition to those listed above with a minimum of 65 percent overall average; Digital portfolio and writing sample.	Not reported

TOTAL PROGRAM ENROLLMENT
Undergraduate: Not reported
Graduate: Not reported

Male: Not reported
Female: Not reported

Full-time: Not reported
Part-time: Not reported

International: Not reported
Minority: Not reported

Job Placement Rate: 85%

SCHOLARSHIPS / FINANCIAL AID
Entrance Scholarships funded by the provincial government are available to students of applied degree programs. They are renewable based on maintenance of gpa. Small awards and bursaries are awarded to students in the program annually. These range from $100-$500 each.

TOTAL FACULTY
Full-time: 30%
Part-time: 70%
Online: 0%

NCIDQ Certified: 50%
Licensed Interior Designers: 75% (registered in Ontario not licensed)
LEED Certified: 25%

INTERIOR DESIGN ADMINISTRATION
Kelly Gluck, Program Coordinator, BAA Interior Design
Susan Krausz, Associate Dean, School of Applied Technology
Denise Devlin-Li, Dean, School of Applied Technology

PROFESSIONAL / ACADEMIC AFFILIATIONS
Interior Design Educators Council
Interior Designers of Canada

CIDA ACCREDITATION
Bachelor of Applied Arts: Interior Design (2007, 2013)

PROGRAM DESCRIPTION AND PHILOSOPHY
We are committed to facilitating a holistic learning experience for our students which exemplifies professionalism and accountability, nurturing the knowledge and skills necessary to meet the increasingly complex and changing practice of Interior Design.

FACILITIES
The heart of our curriculum is reflected by the organization of our facilities. We have shared studio spaces, computer labs, lecture/discussion rooms and a student resource center which is interdisciplinary—shared by students in Design Foundation, Interior Decorating, and Interior Design.

ONLINE / DISTANCE LEARNING
Not available

COURSES OF INSTRUCTION
- Interior Design Studio
- Design Communications (including digital media, manual drafting, drawing, perspective and rendering)
- Interior Detailing
- Design Theory

INTERNSHIPS
Required of majors between 3rd and 4th year for a period of 14 weeks, paid. The greater Toronto Area is the design capital of Canada and we are blessed with a broad range of design and architecture firms at which our students find meaningful placements. In the past two years students have interned at HOK Toronto Office, Straticam, Gluckstein & Associates, Crayon Design.

STUDY ABROAD
All students take a course entitled Site Studies, 50% of which is a major off-site tutorial researched, planned and led by third year Interior Design students.

NOTABLE ALUMNI
Not reported

STUDENT ACTIVITIES AND ORGANIZATIONS
Student Empowerment teams bring the four years of program together for common goals such as the Public Relations and Social Committee, Design Citizenship and Environmental Committee and targeted fundraising groups for student initiatives such as graduation shows.

FACULTY SPECIALIZATIONS AND RESEARCH
We are a student-centered facility with a focus on learning rather than published research.

Kwantlen Polytechnic University

Interior Design Department

8771 Lansdowne Rd., Richmond, BC V6X 3V8 | 604-599-2755 | www.kwantlen.ca/design/interior_design

UNIVERSITY PROFILE
Public
Suburban
Commuter
Semester Schedule
Co-ed

STUDENT DEMOGRAPHICS
Undergraduate: 17,000
Graduate: n/a

Male: Not reported
Female: Not reported

Full-time: Not reported
Part-time: Not reported

EXPENSES
Tuition: Varies depending
upon citizenship
Room & Board: n/a

ADMISSIONS
Shahnaz Rauf
Richmond Admissions
Surrey BC V3W 2M8
604-599-2585
shahnaz.rauf@kwantlen.ca

DEGREE INFORMATION

Major / Degree / Concentration	Enrollment	Requirements for entry	Graduation rate
Interior Design Bachelor of Interior Design	80	Please refer to General University Admission Requirements at: www.kwantlen.ca/	80%

TOTAL PROGRAM ENROLLMENT
Undergraduate: 100%
Graduate: Not reported

Male: 20%
Female: 80%

Full-time: 100%
Part-time: Not reported

International: Varies
Minority: Varies

Job Placement Rate: 90%

SCHOLARSHIPS / FINANCIAL AID
Please refer to this Web address
www.kwantlen.ca/awards.html

TOTAL FACULTY: 9–12
Full-time: 33%
Part-time: 66%
Online: 0%

NCIDQ Certified: 80%
Licensed Interior Designers: registered
LEED Certified: 20

INTERIOR DESIGN ADMINISTRATION
Barbara Duggan, Dean
Lucie Gagne, Interior Design
  co-coordinator
Broenda Snaith, Interior Design
  co-coordinator

PROFESSIONAL / ACADEMIC AFFILIATIONS
Interior Design Educators Council
Environmental Design Research
  Association
Interior Designers of Canada

CIDA ACCREDITATION
Bachelor of Interior Design (2006, 2012)

PROGRAM DESCRIPTION AND PHILOSOPHY

The program works closely with the professional design community and responds to the needs and advice of that community through the following aims:

- Provide an education that includes all facets of Interior Design with emphasis on experience and skills in theory, research, critical analysis, problem-solving, design concepts, working drawings and specifications, technology, presentation media techniques, professional business practices and procedures, and awareness of human needs in built environments
- Prepare students for work in Interior Design and/or architectural offices
- Provide a practical and theoretical knowledge base that conforms to the definition and practice of Interior Design as described by the National Council for Interior Design Qualification (NCIDQ) and as endorsed in the North American definition of an Interior Designer
- Provide design education, using specific reference to Interior Design, which will allow students to develop career readiness for an interdisciplinary design environment

The mission of the program is "educating leaders for the profession of Interior Design." For more information you may view our department Web site at: www .kwantlen.ca/design/interior_design.

FACILITIES

We are a laptop program, there are computer labs, plotters, printers, library, collaborative activity room/ sample library.

ONLINE / DISTANCE LEARNING

Not available

COURSES OF INSTRUCTION

- Studio I
- Materials
- Design Awareness I
- Drawing for Interior Design
- Design Communication I
- Studio II
- Components
- Design Awareness II
- Design Communication II
- Studio III
- Building Systems I
- Design Theories I
- Drawing and Rendering I
- Environmental Human Factors
- Studio IV
- Building Systems II
- Design Theories II
- Drawing & Rendering II
- Studio V
- Building Systems III
- Design Theories III
- Site Tutorial
- Major Site Tutorial
- Studio VI
- Contract Documentation
- Deisgn Theories IV
- Representation
- Senior Studio
- Advanced Design Studies
- Professional Practice I
- Professional Practice II
- Computer Drawing I
- Computer Drawing II
- Interior Design Practice Experience

INTERNSHIPS

Required of majors between years 3 and 4. Interns are placed mainly within the Vancouver, BC, professional design community, with some exceptions.

STUDY ABROAD

Some existing student exchange opportunities are avaiable.

NOTABLE ALUMNI

Many leaders of the local Interior Design community

STUDENT ACTIVITIES AND ORGANIZATIONS

Kwantlen Emerging Green Builders

FACULTY SPECIALIZATIONS AND RESEARCH

Diverse faculty, many practice Interior Design locally, many interested in sustainable approaches, all are concept driven.

RCC Institute of Technology

Interior Design Department, Academy of Design

2000 Steeles Ave. West, Concord, ON L4K 4N1 | 905-669-0544 | **www.rccit.ca/academy-of-design/interior-design/**

UNIVERSITY PROFILE
Private
Urban
Commuter
Quarter Schedule
Co-ed

STUDENT DEMOGRAPHICS
Undergraduate: Not reported
Graduate: Not reported

Male: Not reported
Female: Not reported

Full-time: Not reported
Part-time: Not reported

EXPENSES
Tuition: Not reported
Room & Board: Not reported

ADMISSIONS
2000 Steeles Ave. West
Concord, ON L4K 4N1
1-866-467-0661/ 1-866-838-6542
aodt.ca - request information

DEGREE INFORMATION

Major / Degree / Concentration	Enrollment	Requirements for entry	Graduation rate
Interior Design 3-year Diploma	80	Portfolio review	Not reported

TOTAL PROGRAM ENROLLMENT
Undergraduate: 80
Graduate: n/a

Male: Not reported
Female: Not reported

Full-time: Not reported
Part-time: Not reported

International: Not reported
Minority: Not reported

Job Placement Rate: 90%

SCHOLARSHIPS / FINANCIAL AID
Not Reported

TOTAL FACULTY: 20
Part-time: 99%

NCIDQ Certified: Not reported
Licensed Interior Designers: Not reported
LEED Certified: Not reported

INTERIOR DESIGN ADMINISTRATION
Rick Davey, President and Chief Executive Officer
Rhonda Geraghty, Chair, Interior Design Program
Annie John, Director, Academic and Student Services

PROFESSIONAL / ACADEMIC AFFILIATIONS
Interior Design Educators Council
Interior Designers of Canada

PROGRAM DESCRIPTION AND PHILOSOPHY
The Interior Design 2-year and 3-year diploma programs provide academic preparation that is recognized by the Interior Design profession as meeting the highest educational requirements for entry into the profession. Students are prepared with a strong skill-base in theoretical, analytical, and applied design. Taught by a diverse faculty of industry-related professionals, students produce functional and innovative design solutions within the built environment to meet the needs of a dynamic and ever-changing global society. The program is registered with the Private Career College Unit of the Ministry of Training, Colleges and Universities and recognized by the Association of Registered Interior Designers of Ontario. Small class size and quarterly intake make it possible for students to move through the program at an accelerated pace.

FACILITIES
Not reported

COURSES OF INSTRUCTION
Not reported

INTERNSHIPS
Required of majors

STUDY ABROAD
Not reported

NOTABLE ALUMNI
Kate Zeidler, Kimberly Seldon, Karen Sealy

STUDENT ACTIVITIES AND ORGANIZATIONS
Not reported

FACULTY SPECIALIZATIONS AND RESEARCH
Not reported

Ryerson University

School of Interior Design

350 Victoria St., Toronto, ON M5B 2K3 | 416-979-5188 | **www.ryerson.ca/interior/**

UNIVERSITY PROFILE
Private
Urban
Commuter
Semester Schedule
Co-ed

STUDENT DEMOGRAPHICS
Undergraduate: 25,000
Graduate: 1,950

Male: 45%
Female: 55%

Full-time: Not reported
Part-time: Not reported

EXPENSES
Tuition: $6,048 cdn
Room & Board: $1,100

ADMISSIONS
350 Victoria St.
Toronto ON M3B 2K3
https://choose.ryerson.ca/
myuniversity/login.html?

DEGREE INFORMATION

Major / Degree / Concentration	Enrollment	Requirements for entry	Graduation rate
Interior Design Bachelor of Interior Design	320	Portfolio Interview, drawing text and other criteria required. Some mail-in portfolios permissible depending on distance of applicant from school. Academic requirements at www.ryerson.ca/ undergraduate/ admission/ overview/#minimum	80%

TOTAL PROGRAM ENROLLMENT
Undergraduate: 320
Graduate: n/a

Male: 20%
Female: 80%

Full-time: 100%
Part-time: Not reported

International: 2.6%
Minority: Not reported

Job Placement Rate: 96%

SCHOLARSHIPS / FINANCIAL AID
The Government Assistance Programs and Bank Student Loans are available for eligible students. In addition, there are Ryerson University entrance scholarships that are competitive in nature. Canadian secondary school provincial applicants with final averages of 90% and higher who meet the terms and conditions for scholarship are guaranteed an entrance scholarship of $2500-4000. For fuller information prospective student should visit the following site: http://www.ryerson.ca/ currentstudents/awards/entrance.

TOTAL FACULTY: 21
Full-time: 48%
Part-time: 52%
Online: 9%

NCIDQ Certified: 40%
Licensed Interior Designers: 30%
LEED Certified: 10%

INTERIOR DESIGN ADMINISTRATION
Annick Mitchell, Chair
Barbara Vogel, Associate Chair
Stephanie Fibiger, Academic Student Coordinator

PROFESSIONAL / ACADEMIC AFFILIATIONS
Interior Design Educators Council

CIDA ACCREDITATION
Bachelor of Interior Design (2010, 2016)

PROGRAM DESCRIPTION AND PHILOSOPHY

The School takes a humanistic view of design to place the user at the center of our interest in placemaking; the creation of meaningful spaces that fully support human activity. Also shaping our approach to Interior Design are concerns with ecological sustainability, global relevance, economic exigencies, and emerging technologies. By means of a careful understanding of context, cultural practices, and research into human values and needs, projects engage students with broad issues at all levels of the program.

FACILITIES

As a downtown university campus in one of the world's most multicultural cities, our School reflects both the intense cultural diversity and the draw of being right in one of North America's important design centers. Interaction with the professional world of design as guest speakers and project critics as well as the opportunity for numerous field trips to see design offices, showrooms, and built work make for for a rich and varied educational experience. Our location in Toronto also gives students exposure to a wide range of design events. Opportunities to participate in the annual Interior Design Show as well as IIDEX/NeoCon have ranged from attending the show to designing an annual booth for not only the school, but for other exhibitors. At Ryerson itself, students are privileged to be housed in their own building on campus, a recently renovated nineteenth-century warehouse. This unique building contains classrooms, a studio, a gallery, large workshops and a significant design resource center. The building is available for student use 24/7. Computer laboratories are shared with other Faculty of Communication and Design students although there are computers for student use in the design studio.

ONLINE / DISTANCE LEARNING

Not available

COURSES OF INSTRUCTION

- Design Dynamics
- Interior Design Studios
- Art and Design History courses (all 4 years)
- Design Communications (3 years including drawing, rendering and computer applications)
- Design Technology (all 4 years)
- Environmental Psychology
- Professional Practice

INTERNSHIPS

Required of majors after 3rd year. While most students find employment in the Toronto area, many students choose to find placements in the rest of Canada or abroad, typically in the Far East or the United States. With the help of our internship coordinator, students find work in Interior Design offices although some students work in related industries. Students are required to fill out log books, have them signed by their supervisors, and write a placement report.

STUDY ABROAD

International exchanges and studios

NOTABLE ALUMNI

Glen Puschelberg, George Yabu, Brian Gluckstein, Fenwick Bonnell, Joe Pettipas, Diego Burdi, Paul Filek, Keith Rushbrook, Marion Marshall

STUDENT ACTIVITIES AND ORGANIZATIONS

Student activities include numerous charrettes with other members of the university community as well as participation in design competitions. An annual 3 or 4 day field trip with all first and second year students takes place in the fall term in such cities as Montreal, New York, Pittsburg, Chicago, and Boston. 4th-year students often undertake field trips (abroad or locally) as part of their project work. The student council participates in local charitable activities during the course of the school year.

FACULTY SPECIALIZATIONS AND RESEARCH

Faculty research interests speak to the rich variety of faculty professional backgrounds. They include such fields as museum and exhibit design, hospitality design, studies in cultural identity, gender and diversity studies, design history, material studies, transmutable and transportable environments, urban/interior interfaces, and the scholarship of design education. Faculty are also well represented in creative endeavors participating in a wide variety of exhibitions.

University of Manitoba

Department of Interior Design

201 Russell Building, Winnipeg, MB R3T 2N2 | 204-474-6948 | http://umanitoba.ca/interiordesign/

DEGREE INFORMATION

Major / Degree / Concentration	Enrollment	Requirements for entry	Graduation rate
Master of Interior Design First Professional	35	3.0 gpa Portfolio Statement of interest Letters of reference Transcripts	90%
Master of Interior Design Post Professional	8	3.0 gpa Portfolio Statement of research interest Letters of reference Transcripts	90%

TOTAL PROGRAM ENROLLMENT
Undergraduate: n/a
Graduate: 52

Male: 6%
Female: 94%

Full-time: 98%
Part-time: 2%

International: 2%
Minority: 21%

Job Placement Rate: 100%

SCHOLARSHIPS / FINANCIAL AID
Several scholarships and bursary funds are available to Canadian and international students. Eligibility for most, but not all, is determined by incoming or achieved gpa. Selected scholarships are available for students with special interests in career specialties such as sustainable design or design education.

Students Receiving Scholarships or Financial Aid: 10%

TOTAL FACULTY: 16
Full-time: 50%
Part-time: 50%
Online: Not reported

NCIDQ Certified: 20%
Licensed Interior Designers: Not reported
LEED Certified: 25%

INTERIOR DESIGN ADMINISTRATION
Dr. Mary Anne Beecher, Department Head
Yvonne Halden, Graduate Student Advisor

PROFESSIONAL / ACADEMIC AFFILIATIONS
Interior Design Educators Council
Interior Designers of Canada

CIDA ACCREDITATION
Master of Interior Design (2005, 2011)

378

PROGRAM DESCRIPTION AND PHILOSOPHY

The MID post-professional degree is a research-oriented degree for persons with a first professional degree in Interior Design. Students in this stream wish to pursue a highly customized program of study that provides an opportunity to do in-depth research based on a foundation of Research Methods. Four core courses and three elective courses related to a student's research topic/interest are required. The program culminates in an original independent research project that is directed by an advisor and a committee.

The MID-professional degree focuses on innovative design, research and critical thinking. Students in this stream integrate diverse technical and theoretical knowledge through studio-based investigations. Professionalism and an understanding of contemporary practice form the core of the curriculum. This program challenges students to link cultural issues and theories to design-based inquiry as a means of exploring the potential of Interior Design to foster health, comfort and beauty to the built environment. Students take a combination of topical design studios and seminar-style courses. The program culminates in an independent comprehensive theoretically-based Interior Design project that is directed by an advisor and a committee.

FACILITIES

Special facilities include a computer lab and print facility, video production suite, electronics experimentation suite, workshop, art and architecture branch of university library, product catalog collection and sample library, photodocumentation space, dedicated design studios.

ONLINE / DISTANCE LEARNING

The 21-credit Masters of Interior Design-post-professional degree can be completed at a distance. Four required courses are delivered as a combination of one week block courses on campus and online courses. Additional elective courses may be taken in residence, online, or from another institution (preapproval required). Thesis research is completed independently under the direction of an advisor and a committee.

COURSES OF INSTRUCTION

- Design Research Methods
- Theory Seminar 1 and 2
- Sensory Technology sequence
- Professionalism and Practice

INTERNSHIPS

Not required

STUDY ABROAD

A service-learning studio is offered in a developing country every other year during the months of May and June. This course is developed in conjunction with Architects Without Borders Canada. Students may also elect to participate in an exchange program for one semester with Fachhoschsuchule Dusseldorf, Germany.

NOTABLE ALUMNI

Not reported

STUDENT ACTIVITIES AND ORGANIZATIONS

Students may belong to any of several student-led organizations with our faculty, including an Interior Design student organization.

FACULTY SPECIALIZATIONS AND RESEARCH

Our faculty is interdisciplinary with broad-ranging interests that include investigations of sustainable Interior Design practices, workplace culture and environment, gendered space, vernacular interiors, cross-cultural service learning, creative practice, post-occupancy evaluation, design processes, and design pedagogy. The majority of our faculty members have a Ph.D. and most have degrees in both Interior Design and a second discipline.

Interior Design Schools Indexes

Interior Design Schools by Degrees Offered

Southwest Florida College, *34*

University of New Haven, *33*

West Valley College, *32*

Bachelor of Applied Arts (B.A.A.)

Algonquin College, *53, 366–67*

Bellevue College, *52, 350–51*

Central Michigan University, *39, 194–95*

Humber College, *53, 370–71*

Sheridan Institute of Technology & Advanced Learning, *54*

Bachelor of Applied Interior Design

Mount Royal University, *53*

Bachelor of Applied Science (B.A.S.)

International Academy of Design & Technology–
Nashville, *48*

Seminole State College, *34*

Bachelor of Arts (B.A.)

Anderson University, *48*

Art Center Design College, Albuquerque, *43, 62–63*

Art Center Design College, Tucson, *28, 62–63*

Art Institute of Charlotte, The, *44*

Art Institute of Colorado, The, *32, 108–9*

Art Institute of Kansas City, The, *37*

Art Institute of Las Vegas, The, *42*

Art Institute of Salt Lake City, *51*

Art Institute of Tucson, The, *28*

Ball State University, *36, 158–59*

Baylor University, *49, 318–19*

Becker College, *39*

California State University, Fresno, *30*

Central Michigan University, *39, 194–95*

Chaminade University, *35*

Colorado State University, *32, 110–11*

Ferris State University, *40*

Freed-Hardeman University, *48*

Illinois State University, *35, 152–53*

Interior Designers Institute, *30, 94–95*

Kent State University, *45*

Lambuth University, *49*

Lonestar College System, *50*

Marymount University, *51, 344–45*

Mercyhurst College, *47, 296–97*

Michigan State University, *40*

Mississippi College, *41*

Mount Mary College, *53, 356–57*

New Jersey Institute of Technology, *42, 240–41*

New York School of Interior Design, *43, 254–55*

North Dakota State University, *45, 234–35*

Park University, *41*

Purdue University, *37*

Salem College, *45*

Samford University, *28*

Sam Houston State University, *50, 320–21*

San Diego State University, *31*

Seattle Pacific University, *52*

Sullivan College of Technology & Design, *38, 172–73*

University of Akron, *46, 276–77*

University of Central Arkansas, *29*

University of Charleston, *52*

University of Kentucky, *38, 174–75*

University of New Haven, *33*

University of Northern Iowa, *37*

University of the Incarnate Word, *50*

Ursuline College, *46*

Utah State University, *51*

Washington State University, Pullman, *52, 352–53*

Washington State University, Spokane, *52, 354–55*

Wentworth Institute of Technology, *39, 188–89*

Bachelor of Design

University of Florida, *34, 124–25*

Bachelor of Fine Arts (B.F.A.)

Academy of Art University, *29, 70–71*

American InterContinental University, Atlanta, *34*

American InterContinental University, Los Angeles, *29*

American InterContinental University, South Florida, *33*

Arcadia University, *47*

Art Institute of Atlanta, *34, 126–27*

Art Institute of Austin, *49*

Art Institute of Charleston, The, *48*

Art Institute of Dallas, The, *49*

Art Institute of Houston, The, *49*

Art Institute of Jacksonville, *33*

Art Institute of Michigan, The, *39*

Interior Design Schools by Degrees Offered

Certificate Programs

Interior Design Schools by Degrees Offered

Monroe Community College, *43*
Monterey Peninsula College, *31, 96–97*
Montgomery College, *38*
New Hampshire Institute of Art, *42*
New York School of Interior Design, *43, 254–55*
Ohlone College, *31*
Orange Coast College, *31*
Owens Community College, *46*
Palomar College, *31*
Phoenix College, *28*
Portland Community College, *47*
Red Rocks Community College, *32*
Saddleback College, *31*
San Diego Mesa College, *31*
San Jacinto College, *50*
San Joaquin Delta College, *31*
Santa Fe Community College, *43*
Santa Monica College, *32*
Santa Rosa Junior College, *32*
Seminole State College, *34*
Solano Community College, *32*
St. Louis Community College, *41*
St. Mary's University, *50*
Tidewater Community College, *51*
Triton College, *36*
University of California, Berkeley Extension, *32, 104–5*
Ursuline College, *46*
Ventura College, *32*
West Valley College, *32*

Diploma Programs

Art Institute of Vancouver, *53, 368–69*
British Columbia Institute of Technology, *53*
Central Piedmont Community College, *44, 222–23*
Centre for Arts & Technology, *53*
Dakota County Technical College, *41*
Dawson College, *53*
Delgado Community College, *38, 178–79*
Fanshaw College, *53*
Northern Alberta Institute of Technology, *53*
RCC Institute of Technology, *54, 374–75*
St. Claire College, *54*
Sullivan College of Technology & Design, *38, 172–73*

Master of Arts (M.A.)

Corcoran College of Arts + Design, *52*
Cornell University, *43, 248–49*
Harrington College of Design, *35, 150–51*
Interior Designers Institute, *30, 94–95*
Marymount University, *51, 344–45*
Marywood University, *47*
Michigan State University, *40*
New England School of Art & Design at Suffolk University, *39, 186–87*
Oregon State University, *46*
San Diego State University, *31*
Savannah College of Art & Design, Atlanta, *34, 136–37*
Savannah College of Art & Design, Savannah, *35, 136–37*
University of Akron, *46, 276–77*
University of Kentucky, *38, 174–75*
University of Massachusetts, Amherst, *39*
University of Minnesota, *41, 204–5*
University of Missouri, *41, 212–13*
Washington State University, Pullman, *52, 352–53*
Washington State University, Spokane, *52, 354–55*
Wayne State University, *40*

Master of Fine Arts (M.F.A.)

Academy of Art University, *29, 70–71*
Brenau University - Evening Weekend College, *34, 130–31*
Brenau University - Women's College, *34, 132–33*
Columbia College, Chicago, *35, 146–47*
Endicott College, *39, 184–85*
George Washington University, *52*
Iowa State University, *37, 142–43*
Miami International University of Art & Design, *34, 122–23*
Moore College of Art & Design, *47*
New York School of Interior Design, *43, 254–55*

Ohio State University, *46, 274–75*
Parsons The New School for Design, *43*
San Diego State University, *31*
Savannah College of Art & Design, Atlanta, *34, 136–37*
Savannah College of Art & Design, Savannah, *35, 136–37*
University of Central Oklahoma, *46, 284–85*
University of Georgia, *35, 138–39*
University of North Texas, *50, 330–31*
University of Wisconsin, Madison, *53, 358–59*
Virginia Commonwealth University, *51*

Interior Design Schools by Majors, Concentrations, and/or Areas of Emphasis

Architectural/Landscape/Interiors

Otis College of Art & Design, *31, 100–101*

Design Culture

New York School of Interior Design, *43, 252–53*

Design Management

Radford University, *51, 346–47*

Facilities Management

Michigan State University, *40*

History of Decorative Arts

New York School of Interior Design, *43, 252–53*

Interior Architecture

Academy of Art University, *29, 70–71*

California State Polytechnic University, *30*

California State University, Sacramento, *30, 82–83*

Chatham University, *47, 290–91*

City College of San Francisco, *30, 88–89*

College of Mount St. Joseph, *45, 268–69*

Columbia College, Chicago, *35, 146–47*

Drexel University, *47, 292–93*

Lawrence Technological University, *40, 200–201*

Marywood University, *47*

Ohio University, *45, 272–73*

Philadelphia University, *48, 298–99*

Rhode Island School of Design, *48*

Santa Monica College, *32*

School of the Art Institute of Chicago, *36*

University of California, Berkeley Extension, *32, 104–5*

University of California, UCLA Extension, *32, 102–3*

University of Houston, *50*

University of Louisville, *38*

University of Nevada, Las Vegas, *42*

University of North Carolina at Greensboro, *45, 230–31*

University of Oregon, *47*

University of Wisconsin, Stevens Point, *53*

Woodbury University, *32, 106–7*

Interior Design

Abilene Christian University, *49, 316–17*

Adrian College, *39*

Alexandria Technical Institute, *40*

Alfred State College, *43, 246–47*

Algonquin College, *53, 366–67*

Amarillo College, *49*

American InterContinental University, Atlanta, *34*

American InterContinental University, Los Angeles, *29*

American InterContinental University, South Florida, *33*

American River College, *29, 72–73*

Anderson University, *48*

Anne Arundel Community College, *38, 190–91*

Antelope Valley College, *29*

Antonelli College, *41*

Appalachian State University, *44, 218–19*

Arapahoe Community College, *32*

Arcadia University, *47*

Arizona State University, *28, 60–61*

Art Center Design College, Albuquerque, *43, 62–63*

Art Center Design College, Tucson, *28, 62–63*

Art Institute of Atlanta, The, *34, 126–27*

Art Institute of Austin, The, *49*

Art Institute of California (The)–Hollywood, *29*

Art Institute of California (The)–Inland Empire, *29, 74–75*

Art Institute of California (The)–Los Angeles, *29*

Art Institute of California (The)–Orange County, *29, 76–77*

Art Institute of California (The)–San Diego, *29, 78–79*

Art Institute of California (The)–San Francisco, *29, 80–81*

Art Institute of Charleston, The, *48*

Art Institute of Charlotte, The, *44*

Art Institute of Colorado, The, *32, 108–9*

Art Institute of Dallas, The, *49*

Art Institute of Ft. Lauderdale, The, *33*

Art Institute of Houston, The, *49*

Art Institute of Indianapolis, The, *36*

Art Institute of Jacksonville, The, *33*

Art Institute of Kansas City, The, *37*

Art Institute of Las Vegas, The, *42*

Art Institute of Michigan, The, *39*

Art Institute of New York City, The, *43*

Art Institute of Ohio (The)–Cincinnati, *45*

Art Institute of Philadelphia, The, *47*

Art Institute of Phoenix, The, *28, 64–65*

Art Institute of Pittsburgh, The, *47*

Art Institute of Portland, The, *46*

Art Institute of Salt Lake City, *51*

Kitchen & Bath Design

Lighting Design